Downers Grove Public Library
1050 Curtiss St.
Downers Grove, IL 60515
(630) 960-1200
www.downersgrovelibrary.org

GAYLORD

IN *BROWN*'S WAKE

LAW AND CURRENT EVENTS MASTERS

David Kairys, Series Editor

Also in this series

In *Brown*'s Wake

*Legacies of America's
Educational Landmark*

MARTHA MINOW

UNIVERSITY PRESS

2010

OXFORD
UNIVERSITY PRESS

Oxford University Press, Inc., publishes works that further
Oxford University's objective of excellence
in research, scholarship, and education.

Oxford   New York
Auckland   Cape Town   Dar es Salaam   Hong Kong   Karachi
Kuala Lumpur   Madrid   Melbourne   Mexico City   Nairobi
New Delhi   Shanghai   Taipei   Toronto

With offices in
Argentina   Austria   Brazil   Chile   Czech Republic   France   Greece
Guatemala   Hungary   Italy   Japan   Poland   Portugal   Singapore
South Korea   Switzerland   Thailand   Turkey   Ukraine   Vietnam

Published by Oxford University Press, Inc.
198 Madison Avenue, New York, New York 10016

www.oup.com

Oxford is a registered trademark of Oxford University Press

Library of Congress Cataloging-in-Publication Data
Minow, Martha, 1954–
In Brown's wake: legacies of America's educational landmark / Martha Minow.
p. cm.—(Law and current events masters)
Includes bibliographical references and index.
ISBN 978-0-19-517152-5
1. Discrimination in education—Law and legislation—United States—History.
2. Segregation in education—Law and legislation—United States.   I. Title.
KF4155.M56 2010
344.73'0798—dc22   2009050141

9 8 7 6 5 4 3 2 1

Printed in the United States of America
on acid-free paper

To Josephine and Newton Minow

Preface and Acknowledgments

This book has been in the works for some time. Decades ago, Joseph Featherstone and Walter McCann at the Harvard Graduate School of Education and John Simon, Robert Cover, and Owen Fiss at the Yale Law School offered encouragement and tough questions; so did Judge David Bazelon and Justice Thurgood Marshall who also gave me the chance to help them work on judicial decisions directly and indirectly flowing from *Brown v. Board of Education*.

The book as it stands reflects enormous contributions of students and colleagues at the Harvard Law School. I hope it also manifests at least some of the crucial support and advice offered by Lani Guinier. Elena Kagan's encouragement of this work—and her challenges to elements of its analysis—proved invaluable; as dean, she insisted that I take the research leave that allowed me to write the lion share of the chapters. I am grateful for the inspiration and engagement of Mort Horwitz, Frank Michelman, and Larry Tribe. When Randy Kennedy and Ken Mack offered their expertise and close readings of several chapters, they sharpened my focus and improved the analysis. The parallel and complementary efforts of Susan Cole, Charles Ogletree, and David Wilkins make their generous assistance to mine all the more special. When I was first conceiving of the book's themes, research by Shelli Calland, Alexandra O'Rourke, Ben Apatoff, Laura Blum-Smith, Natalie Wagner, and Rachel Singer made a huge difference. Talia Milgrim-Elcott and Deborah Gordon Klehr, once my students, are now my teachers and guides on the terrain of thoughtful school reform. I am also grateful for the creative assistance of Janet Katz of the Harvard Law School Library.

I became a dean in the midst of completing this book. Kerri Burridge, Veronica Ortega, and Catherine Claypoole made it possible for me to manage my new duties while finding me time to write and edit. I know I could never have reached the end without the comments and research help of Mario Apreotesi, Lena Konanova, Toby Merrill, Jennifer Siegel, Jenna Statfield, and the incomparable Jude Volek. Kristin Flower's extraordinary management of the entire editorial process leaves me in awe; that she did all this while taking on new administrative duties confirms my long-standing suspicion: she is a magician. Kristin, along with Toby and Mario, coordinated the superb work of a team of dedicated and terrific students who worked around the clock to check the citations and develop feedback on the manuscript. I thank the marvelous team of Danielle Tenner, James Bickford, Marianna Jackson, Christopher Kulawik, Marissa McKeever, Allison Ray, Sunny Lee, Michelle Wu, Jeremy Haber, Mark Stanisz, Amanda Klemas, and Adriana Zimova. As for the specific comments and research by students and former students over many years—Ishan Bhabha, James Bickford, Zoila Hinson, Colleen Roh, Mark Stanisz, Amanda Klemas, Sridhar Prasad, Previn Warren, Brian Alexander, Zachary Elsea, Julia Choe, Emily Matthews, Catherine Fischl, Danielle Purifoy, Mike Addis, Benjamin Saltzman, Janelle Weinstock, Jeff Howard, and Adriana Zimova, I hope the finished book is worthy of the gift of your insights and expertise.

Communities outside Harvard Law School nurtured this project. Adam and Miriam Szubin and Vicky Spelman offered memorable and useful questions at pivotal times. The members of the Pentimento lunch group, Larry Blum, Mary Casey, and Rick Weissbourd, offered close readings, psychological and philosophical insights, and their own invigorating passions for equal educational opportunities and moral engagement.

The connections and tensions between equal opportunity for individuals and equal treatment of groups crystallized for me in crucial conversations with Richard Shweder and Hazel Markus as we worked together on the book, *Just Schools: Pursuing Equality in Societies of Difference* (2008). Participants in our Law and Culture working group, supported by the Social Science Research Council and the Russell Sage Foundation, and especially Claude Steele, John Bowen, Austin Sarat, and James Banks challenged and deepened my understanding of the pursuit of justice through schooling in societies with diverse populations and histories of social division and hierarchy. I give deep thanks to my coeditors and fellow working group members for the chance to try out my ideas in my chapter "We're All for Equality, in U.S. School Reforms: But What Does It Mean?" and to Margot Strom, Adam Strom, and other friends at Facing History and Ourselves for the superb New York University conference on *Just Schools* and for many conversations about schooling and justice. Audiences at Boston College's Boise Center for Religion and American Public Life and at Brandeis University also helped as I developed this work.

Dean Avi Soifer's invitation to the University of Hawai'i's William S. Richardson School of Law and the warm welcome of faculty, students, and community members—especially Avi, Marlene Booth, and Eric Yamamoto—showed me a model of inclusion while teaching me a great deal about education for Native Hawai'ians. I thank Dean Bob Klonoff at Lewis and Clark Law School and the firm of Stoel Rives for hosting me in a rich and productive series of discussions about *Brown* and Dr. Martin Luther King, Jr., and I also thank Liz Schneider and Stephanie Wildman for inviting me to write about the Vorchheimer case. Kate Bartlett, Judge Sandra Lynch, Emily Martin, Mike Klarman, Jim Ryan, Kimberly Jenkins Robinson and Zanita Fenton kindly shared their knowledge and wisdom about civil rights and education reform. Thanks, too, to Nancy Cott and Barbara Grosz for thoughtful exchanges on single-sex schools.

I am grateful for Nomi Stolzenberg's insights into the Satmar Hasidic community, Joe Singer's thoughts about education and American Indians, and discussions about pluralism in education with Rabbi Danny Lehman and Rabbi Marc Baker. Collaboration with David Rose, Anne Meyer, Chuck Hitchcock, and the whole team at the Center for Applied Special Technology taught me about universal design and inclusive education, motivated initially to reach students with disabilities but revitalizing learning for all. And thanks to the many people who allowed me and my students to interview them and to reference what we learned in footnotes.

David Kairys, thank you for your example of engaged work and scholarship in civil rights and for inviting me to propose a book for your series at Oxford University Press. There my project found the wise and encouraging guidance first of Dedi Felman, then Niko Pfund and David McBride, and the careful work of Megan Kennedy and Angela Chnapko. I am so grateful to this team.

I tried out portions of the book's argument and analysis over the past several years. I thank the publishers listed below for allowing me to draw here on published versions of those initial efforts.

The following material was taken from previously published works.

Informing chapter 1: Introductory Essay: "Surprising Legacies of *Brown v. Board*," 16 WASHINGTON UNIVERSITY JOURNAL OF LAW AND POLICY 11 (2004).

"After *Brown*: What Would Martin Luther King Say?," 12 LEWIS & CLARK LAW REVIEW 599 (2008).

Informing chapter 2: "Single-sex Public Schools before and after *Vorchheimer v. School District of Philadelphia*," in *Gender Stories* (Elizabeth Schneider and Stephanie Waldman, eds.) (Foundation Press, forthcoming).

Informing chapters 2 and 6: "Reading the World: Law and Social Science," in *Transformations in American Legal History: Essays in Honor of Morton J. Horwitz*, vol. 2 (Daniel Hamilton and Alfred Brophy, eds.) (Harvard University Press, forthcoming).

Informing chapter 3: "The Government Can't, May, or Must Fund Religious Schools: Three Riddles of Constitutional Change for Laurence Tribe," 42 TULSA LAW REVIEW 911 (2007) and "Just Education: An Essay for Frank Michelman," 39 TULSA LAW REVIEW 547 (2004).

Informing chapter 5: "Reforming School Reform," 68 *Fordham Law Review* 257–288 (November 1999).

Finally, I give deepest thanks to my family. Mira Singer and Joe Singer gave me the gift of fun as well as the assignment to find fun every day. They also provided material support of all kinds ranging from invaluable advice on the book cover to insights about the promise and limits of pluralism. My extended family has been a source of unceasing support. The efforts of Josephine and Newton Minow to engage our entire family in the pursuit of equality, justice, tolerance, and pluralism shaped me and my own education. The dedication of this book to my parents is a small token of my thanks for this foundation, for their support of my studies in education and in law, and for continuing to be my most challenging and best teachers.

Contents

IN *BROWN*'S WAKE

Introduction

[T]hose fifty years since Brown *have seen the fortunes of black America advance and retreat, but the decision is always cause for sober celebration, not impotent dismay.... In 1954, the Federal government's brief in* Brown *argued that school desegregation was a Cold War imperative, a necessary weapon to win America's battles overseas. Current events give us the same imperative—to prove to enemy and ally alike that our commitment to justice is sincere.*

—Julian Bond

Making sense of *Brown v. Board of Education,* decided the same year I was born, and understanding what it did and did not achieve have occupied me since I can remember.[1] When the fiftieth anniversary of the ruling arrived, scholars and media pundits debated whether the case deserved its landmark status and whether it had delivered in any meaningful way on the promise of racial equality for African Americans—or if it instead was ineffectual or counterproductive.[2] Those are important questions, and this book grapples with them. Yet largely missing from the public discussions was the enormous influence of *Brown* in schools beyond race. The Supreme Court's embrace of the ideal of equal opportunity and its critique of the separate-but-equal approach to education transformed the treatment of immigrants, students learning English, girls, students with disabilities, and poor students in American schools; religion in schools; school choice; and social science evidence about schooling—and the story of these changes deserves telling. That is what this book aims to do, even as it tells of a mixed legacy of *Brown* in these other contexts while also tracing reverberations of *Brown* outside the United States. To tell these stories is to engage with public policy debates over separate versus mixed instruction in meeting the needs of varied kinds of students. Nested within larger disputes over the viability of the racial integration ideal, this effort also explores the emergence of *Brown* as a resource for enterprising and visionary reformers concerned with gender, disability, religion, and other topics. The legacies of *Brown* invite a look at the capacity of individuals to push and achieve change using law and social science; the histories are interconnected with social movements as well as unexpected consequences of resulting reforms.

Chapter 1 offers an analysis of what this landmark U.S. Supreme Court case did and did not accomplish when it banned official racial segregation in public schools. I consider whether the lawyers' goal ever was integration, defined to mean both the side-by-side instruction of students of different races and the creation of school communities with a sense of common purpose and membership bridging different identities, histories, and past opportunities. The unanimous Supreme Court in *Brown* declared that "[s]eparate educational facilities are inherently unequal," but how much did that quell a rejection of actual separation or instead simply ban the use of racial classification by government actors? Was it a rejection of the experience of schooling with homogeneous classrooms or the exclusion of blacks from educational resources given to white children? Looking at what motivated lawyers and other activists offers an avenue into *Brown*'s history. Taking advantage of the many efforts to reconsider the case during and since its fiftieth anniversary, the chapter reviews the legal content of the decision, its partial implementation, and judicial retreat ultimately marked by the Supreme Court's rejection of voluntary racial desegregation as part of school choice plans.[3] The chapter also explores the significant contributions of remarkable individuals who developed strategies, the role of social movements, and the emerging use of social science research in the search for racial equality.

Chapter 2 traces the direct and indirect uses of *Brown* by advocates and policy-makers turning to the education of immigrants, students learning English, and girls—and also boys—disadvantaged by conventional schools and classrooms. It asks how schools best enhance educational opportunity: by mixing different kinds of students or by separating students for specialized instruction? A genuine assessment of this question in these contexts complicates *Brown*'s declaration that "[s]eparate educational facilities are inherently unequal." The chapter examines strategies pursued by innovative reformers, shifting political alignments, and practices through time as Americans have grappled with the ideal of equal educational opportunity regardless of the student's immigrant status, home language, or gender.

Chapter 3 pursues repercussions of *Brown* in the advocacy for students with disabilities and students identifying as gay, lesbian, bisexual, or transgendered, and for fights over the treatment of religion and socioeconomic class in American education. Advocates drew explicit analogies to *Brown* and pursued broader initiatives for educational opportunity in these contexts. Lawyers and other advocates undertook litigation and legislation and new social movements. Notable innovators won victories and hit obstacles as they at times pushed for integration and at other times favored separate instruction, and when they sought to define equality in terms of neutrality or in terms of reallocated resources.

The educational treatments of American Indians and Native Hawai'ians have their own complex histories; these are examined in chapter 4. The uses and limitations of *Brown* for these students reflect distinctive legal and political contexts while raising questions of group rights in courts, legislatures, and politics. A complex case involving education for children with special needs in a village founded by and composed largely of Satmar Hasidic Jews prompted the Supreme Court to consider competing consequences of *Brown v. Board of Education*. The chapter thus considers how education organized around group-based identities rallies supporters in pursuit of better outcomes, whether measured by standard educational measures or other criteria. And the chapter examines how individual advocates and social movements have continued to use law and social science in struggles over integrated and separate education.

Chapter 5 explores how school choice evolved from a euphemism for dodging court-ordered racial segregation into a strategy for school reform endorsed by civil rights advocates, business leaders, and school reformers. Proposals for school vouchers, tax credits, magnet schools, and charter schools initially may have attracted people seeking to avoid *Brown* but over time these options attracted people seeking to implement *Brown* and its vision of integration. As the chapter charts, advocates of school choice have explicitly copied the strategies used in *Brown*, showing how the case's influence can run in several directions. Geographic and economic factors work to determine who genuinely has educational choices. People with sufficient resources to live in suburbs or to pay for private school tuition can select desirable schools while those who are poor or unable to leave urban areas of concentrated poverty so often face inadequate public schools and few alternatives. The chapter considers ways school choice invites new forms of self-segregation into special-identity schools yet holds potential to promote integration across lines such as race, class, gender, immigrant status, language, and disability.

The lawyers, judges, and justices involved in *Brown* introduced a distinctive use of social science as an advocacy tool. They triggered heated controversies over particular studies and over social science as a predicate for legal decision-making. Chapter 6 tracks the uses of social science in the *Brown* litigation as well as the growth, after the decision, of the particular field within social psychology that asks whether and when contact between people from different backgrounds alters preexisting prejudices and relationships. While acknowledging continuing disputes over the reliability and limitations of social science research itself, the chapter delves into several bodies of research addressing why social integration (across lines of race, culture, gender, class, disability, and other categories) in schools and workplaces benefits society. Benefits of social integration can include preventing stereotyping and dehumanization; promoting mutual engagement and the ability of individuals to take the perspective of others unlike themselves; assisting individuals in working together in mixed groups to solve problems and perform other tasks; enlarging the resource of social capital and networking across different groups; and promoting a sense of solidarity and civic membership. With a look at workplaces, military service, and national service as avenues for social integration beyond schools, the chapter also revisits the potential for schools to seek social integration. The chapter considers the particular success of schools run by the U.S. military.

Chapter 7 follows *Brown*'s influence beyond the United States and traces work of advocates for equality in schools in Northern Ireland, South Africa, and eastern Europe. It is not an accident that advocates have found the case meaningful in these settings of historic social division. Here, too, surface issues of school choice, treatment of language differences among students and students identified as having disabilities, and debates over mixing or separating students recur. International perspective sheds light on *Brown's* mixed legacy in actually promoting equal opportunity, as well as its power as a resource for change agents. In both the United States and in other countries, unexpected results and complex political shifts illuminate legacies of *Brown* while sharpening lingering questions, such as these: How much can schools alter societal patterns of social hierarchy? When does the separation of a group of students (by disability, immigration status, language, or other trait) signal hurtful exclusion, and when does it signal respect for group distinctions or traditions or tailored accommodations? Is learning side by side important or irrelevant to reducing prejudices and power differentials across differences of race, gender, language, religious affiliation, sexual orientation, and the like? As individuals, groups, and nations define themselves in struggles over schooling, how do school systems pursue individual equality and equal treatment of groups? What are the prospects for social integration and for reducing achievement gaps in schools, whether measured in terms of individuals' race, ethnicity, gender, disability, or other traits? The stories behind *Brown v. Board of Education* and the people inspired by it offer resources for each new generation of change agents, as the ripples in *Brown*'s wake continue to spread.

What *Brown* Awakened

The only way to get the white folks to give us decent schools was to make it be their schools too.

—Thurgood Marshall

Brown v. Board of Education established equality as a central commitment of American schools but launched more than a half century of debate over whether students from different racial, religious, gender, and ethnic backgrounds, and other lines of difference must be taught in the same classrooms.[1] *Brown* explicitly rejected state-ordered racial segregation, yet neither law nor practice has produced a norm of racially integrated classrooms. Courts restrict modest voluntary efforts to achieve racially mixed schools.[2] Schools in fact are now more racially segregated than they were at the height of the desegregation effort.[3]

Talk of this disappointing development dominated the events commemorating the fiftieth anniversary of the *Brown* decision.[4] Instead of looking at the composition of schools and classrooms, policy-makers measure racial equality in American schooling by efforts to reduce racial differentials in student performance on achievement tests, and those efforts have yielded minimal success. Historians question whether the lawyers litigating *Brown* undermined social changes already in the works or so narrowed reforms to the focus on schools that they turned away from the pursuit of economic justice. Commentators have even questioned whether the Court's decision itself ever produced real civil rights reform.[5] Although *Brown* focused on racial equality, it also inspired social movements to pursue equal schooling beyond racial differences, and it yielded successful legal and policy changes addressing the treatment of students' language, gender, disability, immigration status, socioeconomic

status, religion, and sexual orientation. These developments are themselves still news, inadequately acknowledged and appreciated as another
key legacy of *Brown*. Yet here, too, judges, legislators, school officials,
experts, and parents disagree over whether and when equality calls for
teaching together, in the same classrooms, students who are or who are
perceived to be different from one another. Parents and educators have at
times pushed for separate instruction and at times for instructing different students side by side. As the twenty-first century proceeds, equality in
law and policy in the United States increasingly calls for mixing English-
language learners with English-speaking students and disabled with nondisabled students, but students' residential segregation and school assignments often produce schools and classrooms divided along lines of race,
ethnicity, and socio-economic class.

Meanwhile, as state and federal governments assess equality in terms
of student performance on achievement tests, schools and communities
promote instructional programs that drill material for tests. Some deploy
a variety of specialized programs designed around features of the students' identity, such as gender or immigrant status. Other programs offer
a focus on a culture or language or personal trait that may attract and
sort students by identity characteristics.[6] Understanding *Brown*'s accomplishments and facing its limitations in addressing how schools pursue
equality requires locating what the Court's decision did and did not do,
what the plaintiffs and their lawyers did and did not seek, and how the
case has played out in law and educational practice. This chapter concentrates on these issues in terms of race. It examines how the legal ideal of
equal educational opportunity and status in common schools changed
over time to focus on pursuing parity in test score results and guarding
individuals against any use of racial classifications. The following chapters will look at the repercussions of *Brown* for education based on other
dimensions of student identity.

What *Brown* Did and Did Not Do

The most famous decision of the U.S. Supreme Court, *Brown v. Board
of Education,* stands both as the landmark of social justice embraced by
law and the symbol of limits on social reform led by courts.[7] It ruled that
public schooling is subject to review under the equal protection clause
of the U.S. Constitution and that official racial segregation inherently
violates that equality requirement. What is less clear is whether that same
equal protection analysis calls for racial mixing—side-by-side instruction
of students of different races in the same school and classrooms—or the
even more ambitious goal of integration, creating a shared community
of mutual respect, common goals, and joint ownership of education
within a multiracial student body.[8] The Court's own words eliminated
racial segregation as an acceptable practice in schools governed by the

Constitution's equal protection clause, but the Court-supervised remedial process produced protracted and sometimes violent conflicts over the
succeeding decades and decreasing success in advancing either the ideal
or the reality of the integration or even simply racially mixed schools.
Since the 1980s, judicial withdrawal from school desegregation suits and
patterns of residential segregation have contributed to what some call
increasing racial "resegregation" in public schools in the United States
and have cast doubt on whether mixing students of different races is
feasible, much less required by the commitment to equality. Calling it
"resegregation" or "segregation," though, elides the difference between
officially mandated and informally or indirectly produced patterns, a distinction that U.S. courts have made central to the determination of a constitutional violation and court-ordered remedy. Even if the resurgence
of racially identified schools is understood to stem from complex patterns of private choices and biases of whites, racialized housing patterns,
economic disadvantages disproportionately affecting students of color,
and the residues of past official segregation, it dramatically decreases the
likelihood that students from different races will spend much school time
with students from other backgrounds.

The Harvard Civil Rights Project concluded a recent study by noting:

> Although American public schools are now only 60 percent white nation-
> wide and nearly one fourth of U.S. students are in states with a majority
> of nonwhite students, most white students have little contact with minority
> students except in the South and Southwest. The vast majority of intensely
> segregated minority schools face conditions of concentrated poverty, which
> are powerfully related to unequal educational opportunity. Students in seg-
> regated minority schools can expect to face conditions that students in the
> very large number of segregated white schools seldom experience. Latinos
> confront very serious levels of segregation by race.[9]

White families with options avoid racially mixed schools.[10] Of the fifty-
three hundred communities with fewer than one hundred thousand people in this country, at least 90 percent of the residents are white.[11] Large
urban districts, in which 70 percent of the students are nonwhite and
over half are poor or near poor, face higher levels of violence, disruption,
and dropping out and lower test scores than suburban schools.[12] The gap
in achievement when students are compared by race persists across all
age groups, even when controlled for economic class. These results raise
questions about the ability of teachers and classrooms to overcome educational disadvantage. Thus *Brown* in retrospect is an emblem both of
social change and obdurate racialized divisions, occasioning both celebration and critique.[13]

The Court in *Brown* discussed the crucial importance of racial integration of students—but did not mandate mixing students of different races
in the same school and same classrooms, nor did it address governance
and control of schools. Courts can overturn explicit racially segregative
laws without producing racial mixing in schools; *desegregation* could

mean simply the elimination of segregative laws and practices, leaving schools racially separate due to the private choices of families and residential patterns of racial separation.[14] And courts can eliminate historically black schools without demanding that black parents and teachers share in governing the desegregated schools and without attacking practices that replicate racial prejudice and distrust.

A vivid example of the difference between racial mixing and integration at a public school system appeared in Charleston, Mississippi. Subject to court-ordered desegregation in 1970, the school system mixed students, but racial separation persisted in many aspects of the students' social lives. Notably, the school did not sponsor a racially integrated prom. Instead, private funds paid for racially separate proms—even though actor Morgan Freeman, a native of the region, offered in 1997 to pay for a racially mixed event. Not until 2008 did an integrated prom take place.[15] Integration takes more than ending segregation and more than putting students of different identities in the same school. It requires effective efforts to dismantle prejudices, to build common experiences around shared goals, and to assess success in terms of social ties across groups—not merely numbers of students attending the same school or even convergence in individual academic tests scores.

Courts since *Brown* declare that enough time has passed since the elimination of intentional and explicit segregation to stop using judicial measures to remedy patterns of racial separation within public schools.[16] Because of *Brown,* schools stopped explicitly assigning students to schools that separate them by race, but parents and communities can produce similar results indirectly through housing patterns, district lines, and even some forms of school choice. Students of different races can enroll in the same school but attend different classes, sit at different lunch tables, and have separate and incomparable educational experiences. Racially mixed enrollments do not by themselves reach the further step that Dr. Martin Luther King, Jr., defined as "integration: constructive equality of oneness"[17] into a community of love, justice, and brotherhood, recognizing the human dignity, individual rights, and interdependence of each person.[18]

Slices of Dr. King's vision of integration do appear in the rise of African Americans as leaders in institutions and practices that once were entirely white and in the proud support of multiracial constituencies for these leaders. Kenneth Chennault of American Express, Cathy Hughes of TV One, Alwyn Lewis of Sears, and Richard Parson of Time Warner are simply the most visible African American heads of major corporations;[19] Oprah Winfrey's popular daytime show led the pack for twenty-five years, and no one had more influence in book publishing, film and television production, and philanthropy even before the launch of her cable television channel.[20] Many other talented African Americans command large and racially diverse audiences in media, sports, and other entertainment industries. Blacks coach as well as play for major sports teams.[21] By 2007, 11 percent of federal judges were African Americans.[22] The Broadway hit and movie *Hairspray* makes "feel-good" entertainment out of condemning segregation and celebrating integration in its full sense of communities among people mutually committed to the dignity and rights of each, and relishing the freedom and creativity diverse groups of people can express together. And in 2008, the United States elected a black candidate as president of the United States from a field of serious candidates that included a Hispanic governor and a white female senator as well as several white men.[23] Yet the racial gap in American educational achievement and the increasingly racially separate schools raise unavoidable questions about *Brown's* effects.

Was Integration Ever the Goal?

The "resegregation" of American public schools makes it tempting to argue that integration was never the goal but merely a means toward the still viable end of equal opportunity. The racial and ethnic enrollment patterns emerging in the United States are striking, especially from the vantage points of black and Hispanic students. In 2000, 72 percent of African-American students nationwide attended predominantly minority schools, compared with 63 percent in 1980; 37 percent of African-American and 38 percent of Hispanic students in 2000 attended schools with 90 percent or more minority enrollment.[24] It is white students who are most isolated from other students: the average white student attends schools where more than three-quarters of his or her peer group in the school are also white.[25] With integration across the color line remote, it is convenient to conclude that it was never the point.

There is some historical support for this view. Recent scholarship makes clear that the civil rights movement initially pursued economic equality through jobs and equal treatment in commercial and criminal law.[26] The extreme exclusion of African Americans from economic, social, and political opportunities in the United States—and the daily risk of terrorizing violence sanctioned by the states in the Deep South—fueled the campaigns of the National Association for the Advancement of Colored People (NAACP) under the equal protection clause from the 1930s on. Given the Supreme Court's approval of "separate but equal" in *Plessy v. Ferguson*,[27] the early NAACP strategy was to press for equal expenditures for racially separate schools. In the case of graduate and professional schools, that meant exposing the states' failures to provide *any* program for black students—and in this arena, combining black and white students seemed far more feasible and cost-effective than building entirely separate campuses.

The pursuit of equal resources continued as the NAACP's lawyers turned to public elementary and high schools; the strategy for equal opportunity pursued integration at least in part on the theory that "green follows white." The dollars spent on white students would have to benefit black students if the students sat side by side in the same school. Looking back on the strategy, lawyer (later judge) Robert Carter has recalled: "we believed that the surest way for minority children to obtain their constitutional right to equal educational opportunity was to require removal of all racial barriers in the public school system, with black and white children attending the same schools. . . . Integration was viewed as the means to our ultimate objective, not the objective itself."[28]

This was a retrospective statement made long after the deep troubles with integration emerged, but it no doubt reflects something real. From the vantage point of fifty and more years after *Brown*, the elusiveness of full integration accompanies many reassessments, with commentators emphasizing that integration (perhaps meaning racial mixing?) was a means, not the goal. Harvard Law Professor Charles Ogletree stresses that many African Americans would have rather kept their jobs and positions of influence as teachers, school principals, and janitors "than see their charges bused to white schools run by white principals where white educators often made the children all too grimly aware of their distaste for the new state of affairs."[29] Roy Brooks, law professor at the University of San Diego, argues that integration has failed as a school reform program and urges a focus on achievement of black students in their practically speaking racially separate schools.[30] Derrick Bell, visiting law professor at New York University, and Mary Dudziak, legal historian at the University of Southern California, emphasize that the victory in *Brown* had more to do with the efforts by the United States to improve its international image during the Cold War than with any real commitment to improve educational lives for disadvantaged and minority students.[31] Leading education policy expert, and a professor at Stanford University, Linda Darling reviewed the resegregation patterns in an essay that simply ends with a crisp and cogent summary of the school reforms needed to achieve equality.[32] Most striking is the omission of integration as a strategy toward that goal.

Many people on the front lines of scholarship and advocacy addressing equal educational opportunities do not now see racial integration (in the sense of either racial mixing or creation of a common multiracial community) as necessary or feasible. Sheryll Cashin, professor of law at Georgetown University, puts it succinctly in observing that black people "have become integration weary."[33] So have education officials. The superintendent of the Boston public schools said a few years ago: "My issue is focusing on how to improve education for all children in this city . . . and not [to] be distracted or have a lot of energy and resources going into debates around students assignment."[34]

Yet it would be wrong to deny the long-standing importance of integration as a goal in the civil rights struggles for advocates of racial equality. In the 1840s, before the Civil War and the end of slavery, abolitionist publisher Benjamin Roberts tried to enroll his daughter in a white school in Boston. He pursued integration in order both to obtain the best educational opportunity for his daughter and to make schools the place for preparing for a society of equals.[35] His lawyers, including a leading white antislavery advocate, framed a challenge to the legislated segregation and made this radical argument for full equality to the Massachusetts Supreme Court: "The school is the little world where the child is trained for the larger world of life...and therefore it must cherish and develop the virtues and the sympathies needed in the larger world."[36] They argued further that the inculcation of caste distinction among citizens precluded "those relations of Equality which the constitution and Laws promise to all."[37] This court challenge to officially mandated segregation failed in 1849 but helped to trigger the Massachusetts legislature's abolition of segregated schools in 1855.[38] Similar efforts by blacks in California pursued both legislative and judicial objections to state-mandated school segregation,[39] but failed at the state level.[40]

After the Civil War, and the Reconstruction amendments, political backlash formalized segregation by law through the passage of Jim Crow laws, while vigilante violence arrived as a tool of white supremacy.[41] In real respects, legal and economic restrictions continued for African Americans long after the legal end of slavery.[42] In this context, neither racial mixing nor the fuller ideal of integration could be separated from the search for economic opportunity, political participation, physical safety, and social respect. Given the background of slavery, government policies and private threats of lynching enforced forms of white supremacy predicated on segregation. Eliminating segregation would require eliminating the racial hierarchy that enforced and depended upon it. Jim Crow laws excluded blacks from commercial and public spaces through white control of economic and political resources. Official segregation arose in the South alongside strategies to obstruct blacks from voting—and the separate facilities created for blacks, from railroad cars to schools, never approximated the white facilities in quality.[43] Undoing racial hierarchy and race-based exclusion would entail the creation of a shared community of equals and an end to both the segregation and the race-based domination it reflected.[44] Ending lynching and ensuring opportunities for education and work stood at the top of the agenda for advocates in the years following the Civil War, with some African-American leaders, exemplified by Booker T. Washington, seeking conciliation and accommodation and others more militantly pressing for an end to racialized treatment, including an end to segregation.[45]

The NAACP owes its roots to the more insistent Niagara Movement, a group led by W. E. B. Du Bois and William Monroe Trotter and launched in 1905 to pursue equal education, complete enfranchisement, enforcement of the Fourteenth and Fifteenth Amendments, and the end of forced segregation.[46] The Declaration of the Niagara Movement spoke more of ending oppression, violence, condescension, and abuse than seeking integration in its demanding of equal treatment.[47] Yet the Niagara group also opposed distinctions drawn solely on race or color and expressly targeted instances of legally mandated segregation for change; they protested the Jim Crow cars on trains as making blacks "pay first-class fare for third-class accommodations" where they faced "insults and discomfort," and sought "equal treatment in places of public entertainment."[48] Attacking the degradation and dishonor of segregation, the activists also emphasized instances when the refusal of integration spelled complete denial of opportunity. The most explicit call for integration in the Niagara Movement's 1905 statement was its blasting of military and naval training schools for excluding blacks, despite the service of African-Americans in five wars.[49]

Thus, the Niagara Declaration did not insist on mixing black and white students in public schools. Instead, it demanded access to schooling with high aspirations, a familiar plea in African-American struggles for freedom.[50] Demanding rights, the document also embraced correlative duties, including the duty "to send our children to school"; the document advanced a very clear and comprehensive conception of education, crucial to self-respect and self-development, yet again without reference to racial mixing or integration.

> We want our children educated. The school system in the country districts of the South is a disgrace and in few towns and cities are the Negro schools what they ought to be. We want the national government to step in and wipe out illiteracy in the South. Either the United States will destroy ignorance or ignorance will destroy the United States.

> And when we call for education we mean real education. We believe in work. We ourselves are workers, but work is not necessarily education. Education is the development of power and ideal. We want our children trained as intelligent human beings should be, and we will fight for all time against any proposal to educate black boys and girls simply as servants and underlings, or simply for the use of other people. They have a right to know, to think, to aspire.[51]

With its declaration, the Niagara Movement challenged the appeasing and accommodationist stance taken by other black leaders. Over time, the Niagara Movement gave rise to the NAACP, which protested second-class treatment, bigotry, and injustice experienced by African Americans.[52] Civil rights advocates at both the NAACP and the Department of Justice wanted to tackle the Jim Crow system of segregation and discrimination throughout public and private institutions, including the private labor markets in agriculture and factories.[53] The lawyers attacked economic coercion as well as racial stigma. They pursued injustices that included barriers to entering professions, salary differentials, and exclusion from government, restaurants, public entertainment, and accommodations.[54] Facing inferior treatment even in the relief offered during the Great Depression, African Americans objected and in some instances obtained protections from these injustices.[55] Meanwhile, a new movement dedicated to literary and artistic creativity encouraged political realignment, with many leaving the Republican Party after the depression and manifesting the potential political power of the community.[56]

Nonetheless, at the same time as these advances, separate and inferior schools for African Americans became entrenched during the 1920s and 1930s. Southern states could not afford to support the dual school systems mandated by their segregation laws, and the contrast between schools for white and for black students manifested white supremacy and concretely subordinated blacks and their chances for any advancement. This situation gave rise to tactical debates over the relative priority of desegregation and equalization of resources. The Margold Report of 1931 sketched a strategy for the NAACP to attack unequal, separate schools and also to attack separate schools as habitually unequal.[57] Charles Hamilton Houston, dean of Howard Law School, pondered the strategy and explored the conditions of southern public schools before joining the NAACP staff in 1935, just after the organization erupted in a disagreement over whether to challenge the segregation of public schools.[58]

The challenge came, ironically, from W. E. B. Du Bois, who shared the ultimate goal of integration but opposed the implicit critique of black institutions that would come with a challenge to segregation. Du Bois grew increasingly pessimistic that the dream of integration could be achieved. In 1933, dubious that the workers would soon unite across the racial divide, as socialist theorists imagined,[59] Du Bois described persistent social ostracism of blacks and described racial segregation as "at present inevitable,"[60] even as he joined a planning conference for the NAACP to define the fight against racial segregation and color discrimination.[61] The poor treatment of African Americans during the New Deal solidified Du Bois's pessimism. The vision of integration—sharing common spaces and common goals—must have seemed remote, given the presumption held even by liberal white political leaders that blacks and whites would continue to live and work in separate worlds. Franklin Delano Roosevelt's New Deal recruited African-American leaders to roles as political advisors but confined them to problems affecting the black community, essentially excluding them from policy-making for the nation's recovery and relief.[62] The New Deal programs also largely excluded blacks as beneficiaries, so as not to offend southern whites.[63] Du Bois wrote about these developments while documenting the dire prospects for even the most educated African Americans as the nation dealt with the consequences of the economic Depression.[64]

Then, in the midst of organizational and leadership struggles at the NAACP and its magazine, *Crisis*, Du Bois published a controversial defense of racial separation in January 1934.[65] He stressed that "[t]heoretically the Negro needs neither segregated schools nor mixed schools. What he needs is Education."[66] He further explained that segregated schools would be better than mixed schools where Negroes were harassed or degraded.[67] Yet, in language that could not be more relevant today, Du Bois wrote:

> I know that this article will forthwith be interpreted by certain illiterate nitwits as a plea for segregated Negro schools. It is not. It is saying in plain English that a separate Negro school where children are treated like human beings, trained by teachers of their own race, who know what it means to be black, is infinitely better than making our boys and girls doormats to be spit and trampled upon and lied to by ignorant social climbers whose sole claim to superiority is the ability to kick niggers when they are down.[68]

Two decades later, Martin Luther King, Jr., expressed a similar view.[69] He stressed that if the choice is solely between racial mixing in a school where teachers and fellow students disparage students of color, separate instruction with qualified teachers who believe in the students of color would be a better option. The social context of schooling—including parents, teachers, and broader community—can offer role models, reinforce values, and build in social supports for student aspirations and achievement or it can instead produce alienation, cultural collision, self-doubt, or hostility. Hence, even racially separate schooling would be better than schools that undermine the aspirations, confidence, and achievement of students of color. Yet truly integrated education, with access to students from different backgrounds and walks of life, and an atmosphere of mutual respect and commitment to advancing the dignity and rights of each, would be better still.

In 1934, these issues were explosive. Du Bois pushed unsuccessfully for a vote on his ambivalent defense of racial separation and ultimately resigned from the NAACP. His proposal accelerated debates within the organization and prompted the board not only to reject his view but also to issue a resolution barring salaried NAACP employees from criticizing the organization's policy, initiatives, or leadership.[70] Pressed to articulate its position, the NAACP unambiguously castigated segregation and embraced a vision of equality inconsistent with racially separate (but equal) institutions and worlds. The organization's explicit condemnation of "enforced segregation" left unclear the status of black institutions and separation embraced by blacks, even if not entirely voluntary.[71]

Assessments of feasibility—in terms of politics and law—no doubt framed different views about whether equal respect and opportunity would be better secured by desegregated schools or by directing more resources to segregated schools in the 1930s, as in the present. Scholars writing for the *Journal of Negro Education* in 1935 cast doubt on legal challenges to segregated schooling by documenting the failure of forty-four such cases.[72] Their depiction of the racialized disparity in educational opportunity simultaneously cried out for improvements simply at the level of resources. Private philanthropy could offer resources to improve separate schools for blacks more than legal and political efforts could challenge segregated schooling.[73]

Even though full-scale racial integration seemed distant, separate instruction simply could not work for graduate and professional training, which grew much in demand among blacks after World War I. Only racial mixing would open access to the education, credentials, and job opportunities that these programs represented. Acknowledging that separate institutions would be both exorbitant and less effective, several states appropriated money for out-of-state graduate training for Negroes in order to preserve in-state, white-only public institutions. The NAACP convinced both a state trial judge and a state appellate court that a program of this sort in Maryland denied equal treatment.[74] In 1938, the U.S. Supreme Court also rejected this out-of-state strategy, ruling in *Missouri ex rel Gaines v. Canada* that each state must provide education within the state in order to satisfy its duty to all of its citizens.[75] The goal of integration became bound up with the recognition that separate institutions would not only be too expensive but also would never offer access to the same social networks and resources that a shared and integrated institution would.[76] Houston led the NAACP effort to challenge separate graduate and professional programs as either shams or woefully and—indeed—inherently inadequate. Here, integration emerged as a goal precisely because diverse people do and should become resources for each other.

It was easier to show inequality where the separate black institutions were nonexistent or patent fabrications—and it was also easier to find plaintiffs willing to proceed with cases at the professional and graduate school level than at the elementary and secondary school level.[77] Winning one case did not immediately resolve the issue, however. More states proceeded to offer out-of-state tuition or stall on applications to professional schools at state universities.[78] But the principle that equal protection of the law required access to the same state institution emerged clearly from the NAACP's litigation efforts.

Attacking segregated universities and unequal salaries for schoolteachers, NAACP litigation proceeded between 1935 and 1950, alongside growing community-based activism and protests against Jim Crow and racial discrimination.[79] Beyond the litigation strategy of the NAACP, A. Philip Randolph planned a mass mobilization through a march on Washington to protest continuing segregation and Jim Crow in education.[80] Randolph put off the march after President Roosevelt set up the Fair Employment Practices Committee to address discrimination in federal jobs, but the organizing initiative continued.[81]

Working on varied fronts, activists fought racial oppression throughout the 1940s. Initially founded in the North and dominated by whites, the NAACP over time developed chapters across the South and affiliated strongly with black churches.[82] A network of advocates bridging the NAACP, the Communist Party, New Deal programs, progressive civic alliances, and historically black colleges enabled increasingly active local and national political assaults on racial inequality.[83] Membership in the NAACP soared as World War II stimulated domestic as well as international movements against colonialism and racialized empires.[84] In the 1940s, Bayard Rustin and Pauli Murray both risked their liberty in objecting to Jim Crow practices.[85] Vocal and courageous, they took direct actions to protest racist treatment. Rustin published a narrative about how his nonviolent refusal to sit as prescribed in the back of a bus led to a court hearing—and to surprising gestures of respect.[86] Pauli Murray also resisted directives to sit in a segregated location and pushed for equal treatment.[87]

Racial riots erupted in 1943.[88] Rumors percolated in crowded communities of impoverished people that African Americans migrating from the South would take jobs from whites, sparking tensions and violence. African Americans serving in the armed services encountered Jim Crow–style humiliations and identified segregation as a burning postwar issue, emphasizing the contrast between their public service and the refusal of service to them on buses and in restaurants back home.[89] Partial racial integration emerged in the armed services over time out of necessity, and racially separate troops were combined as military commanders deemed necessary, but it halted at the point of integrating platoons and barracks.[90] Walter White of the NAACP convinced President Harry Truman to create a President's Committee on Civil Rights. The committee's 1947 report condemned official segregation of schools in the South and unofficial segregation of schools in the North for failing to provide the *equal* part of "separate but equal" educational opportunities for Negroes.[91]

Other minority groups also took up the fight for equality. Advised in part by Thurgood Marshall at the NAACP, Mexican Americans in California brought a court challenge to school segregation practices, which officials justified in part to provide explicit instruction in American values, work habits, and sanitation. The plaintiffs convinced the federal district court in 1946 that the segregationist practices violated the Fourteenth Amendment's guarantee of equal protection of the laws; the appeals court affirmed in 1947.[92] Governor Earl Warren repealed the last of California's segregationist statutes the same year,[93] seven years before he presided as chief justice over the Supreme Court's rejection of the "separate but equal" doctrine in schooling.

As an attorney in the solicitor general's office for the U.S. Department of Justice, Philip Elman convinced the attorney general that the lawyers for the United States should write amicus briefs as civil rights cases worked their way through the courts. For the prior case of *Shelly v. Kramer*,[94] Elman helped author an amicus brief condemning governmental support of all forms of racial discrimination in support of the plaintiff challenging racially restrictive covenants in residential housing.[95] Elman recalled how a black lawyer (Charles Vaughn) in another racially restrictive covenant case emphasized: "In this Court, this house of the law, the Negro today stands outside, and he knocks on the door, over and over again. He knocks on the door and cries out, 'Let me in, let me in, for I too have helped build this house.'"[96] The image of entrance and inclusion in the spaces of the polity dominated the legal attack on racial discrimination, and presumed that at least some kind of integration would result.[97]

The lawyers and leaders of the NAACP began to talk explicitly about targeting segregation not only in terms of unequal resources but also in challenging legally segregated public elementary and high schools. They pursued what was then considered cutting-edge social science research suggesting psychological injuries resulted from segregated education.[98] This represented a direct rejoinder to the assertion by the Court's majority in *Plessy v. Ferguson* that blacks themselves were to blame for any negative association with the regime of "separate but equal."[99] The NAACP's use of social science also spurred a field of social psychological research, and larger uses of social science in social reform litigation.[100]

In terms of a larger strategy, the NAACP lawyers struggled to find a way that could succeed and not set back the progress under way in efforts to remedy unequal resources for schools and other public facilities by demanding equal expenditures in the legally-mandated racially separate institutions.[101] Marshall understood each suit as its own educational and organizing effort; he also had great confidence in law and in the American people's respect for decisions of the courts.[102] In 1950 the NAACP resolved simply to pursue education on a nonsegregated basis in all of its future education litigation.[103] Scholars can and do debate the depths of naïveté or sophistication of the lawyers. There are disputes over the extent to which these lawyers realized the difficulties ahead and the degree of faith they vested in law to produce changes in social attitudes and behaviors.[104] But there is no dispute that by the time of *Brown*, civil rights lawyers sought to end segregated schooling and advance equal opportunities and treatment for nonwhite and white students. The watching community understood that, and both supporters and opponents understood that the struggle for equal treatment was now aimed at assuring that black and white students would attend school together.[105]

Revisiting What *Brown* Decided

Ending official segregation was the explicit goal, then, of the cases that became known as *Brown v. Board of Education*. The plaintiffs' lawyers who pursued desegregation faced real risks of undermining efforts to equalize resources—and still failing to secure the supposed end of racially separate schools. Five separate suits proceeded with the dual strategy of exposing the material inadequacy of the schools allotted to blacks and attacking separate facilities as inevitably unequal.[106] The litigation documented disparities between black and white schools in terms of transportation, books, and teachers. Some of the schools had no desks. Parents named in the suits lost their jobs and faced harassment.[107] The suit arising in South Carolina initially sought buses and more resources for the black schools, but the plaintiffs' lawyers reframed the suit to include the claim that separate schools could never be fully equal.[108] Losing in the district court, the plaintiffs ultimately pursued the case to the Supreme Court, where the Court combined it with suits coming from Kansas, Virginia, Delaware, and the District of Columbia. Just as lawyers had hoped, this consolidation of suits showed that a widespread practice of segregation was at issue and built on evidence of the injuries caused to blacks from segregation across many communities.

As in some of the prior NAACP cases, an amicus brief from the Department of Justice supported the plaintiffs in *Brown* at the Supreme Court. That brief maintained that the plaintiffs deserved a remedy to fix the demonstrably unequal conditions in the schools for blacks and the inequalities that existed beyond the physical facilities.[109] It also argued that ending Jim Crow laws should be understood in light of the global struggle between freedom and tyranny.[110] Because Soviet propaganda pointed to racial discrimination in the United States, ending Jim Crow would boost America's apparent devotion to democracy and position in the global struggle between democracy and communism.

At the Supreme Court in 1952, NAACP lawyer Robert Carter argued that segregation tended to assign blacks to an inferior class and lower their aspirations and educational development. The NAACP lawyers contended that even adhering to the separate-but-equal formula, equality was obstructed when segregation in the Kansas schools curbed the motivation of black students to learn and segregation in the Virginia schools produced long-term education deprivations for black students.[111] Marshall asserted that even if expenditures increased and improved black schools, "the significant point was that segregation took African Americans out of the mainstream of American life."[112]

But when Marshall stressed that "[t]he only thing that we ask for is that the state-imposed racial segregation be taken off, and to leave the county school board, the county people, the district people," Justice Felix Frankfurter raised a serious caution: "I think that nothing would be worse than for this Court—I am expressing my own opinion—nothing would be worse, from my point of view, than for this Court to make an abstract declaration that segregation is bad and then have it evaded by tricks."[113] This prescient concern anticipated dangers that occurred in early efforts to implement *Brown*. Indeed, it is worth considering whether the current patterns of racial separation, or "resegregation," in schools reflect not some natural result of private preferences but instead the confirmation of Justice Frankfurter's warning that the Court's abstract declaration could be evaded.

Justice Frankfurter's worries reflected concern that the Court's own legitimacy would be impaired if it issued an order that no one respected. Initial division among the justices both reflected and increased such worries. Disagreeing about how to rule, the Supreme Court justices postponed deciding in 1953 by setting the case for reargument and directing the lawyers to address whether those who had drafted and enacted the Fourteenth Amendment requirement of equal protection of the law expected it to terminate segregated schools, whether the courts had the power to abolish segregation, and whether gradual desegregation would fall within the judicial remedial authority.[114] In its brief prepared for the reargument, the NAACP team reviewed the history of segregation as a policy undermining the Fourteenth Amendment: "Segregation was designed to insure inequality.... Separate but equal is a legal fiction. There never was and never will be any separate equality."[115] With the leadership of a new chief justice—Earl Warren, who had served as governor of California and helped end segregation in that state—the Supreme Court accepted the claim that official segregation communicated an unacceptable message of "separate is inherently unequal" in the context of public schooling.[116]

Among the memorable ideas in the Supreme Court's landmark opinion in *Brown*, three stand out:

1. In these days, it is doubtful that any child may reasonably be expected to succeed in life if he is denied the opportunity of an education. Such an opportunity, where the state has undertaken to provide it, is a right that must be made available to all on equal terms.[117]
2. To separate [black children] from others of similar age and qualifications solely because of their race generates a feeling of inferiority as to their status in the community.[118]

And:

3. We conclude that, in the field of public education, the doctrine of "separate but equal" has no place. Separate educational facilities are inherently unequal.[119]

In the context of intentional and invidious governmentally imposed racial segregation, these three ideas point to the same result. The way to produce equal opportunity in education is to end racial segregation; if separation is inherently unequal, then equality requires its ending. Yet over time, to a degree that would have surprised the NAACP lawyers and observers at the time of the *Brown* decision,[120] the three ideas no longer seem to point in the same direction. Once residential patterns begin to give rise to racially separate schools, equal opportunity to gain an education and succeed in life no longer seems to require mixing students of different backgrounds, or so courts conclude. Equal opportunity demands ending the official assignment of students to different schools on the basis of their race, but there is no longer a corollary of bringing students with different racial and ethnic identities together in the same school and in the same classrooms. The late Denise Morgan, professor of law at New York Law School, made the point sharply: "Attending predominantly Black schools can be harmful to Black children because those schools tend to be educationally inferior, not because Black children are inferior, or because access to white children is inherently positive."[121] This view admirably rejects the remnants of white racial prejudice that suggest that a school with a predominantly black student body cannot be excellent— but also rejects an understanding of diverse social networks as an important feature of open opportunities. Nor does this view treat racial mixing as a critical step toward building an integrated world of diverse people involved with and caring about one another's lives.

Did the Court in *Brown* find racially separate education inherently unequal because it tended to be educationally inferior or because segregated education communicated and reinforced racial hierarchy? The Court did not sort out these two options; nor did it clarify how racially separate instruction could avoid the stamp of hierarchy, eliminate the disparities in educational resources, or overcome the deprivation of vital social interactions across group identities. In 1954, the justices seemed to assume that terminating official segregation would simply produce racially mixed schools. In southern districts, where black students often had to pass neighborhood white schools to get to the colored school, the end of racialized school assignments was supposed to produce racially mixed schools, if people complied with such changes. Yet the risk of resistance preoccupied many of the justices.

Clearly worried about political turmoil,[122] the Court put off its decision about how to remedy segregated schools for another year, as the justices and others debated whether gradual or swift desegregation would give rise to more social resistance.[123] President Dwight D. Eisenhower failed to signal support or authorize prompt aggressive enforcement and instead urged moderation and local decision-making.[124] So the Court waited until 1955 to announce what its rejection of official segregation would mean in practice. Then, in its remedial decision, the court delegated to local district courts the task of designing the remedy for officially segregated schools. This decision itself opened up new avenues for avoidance, delay, and resistance to actual mixing of students. The Court directed that the defendant school districts make a "prompt and reasonable start" toward compliance. It instructed the district courts to solicit actual desegregation plans from the school board defendants in the five cases and required delivery of the plans within ninety days. Yet at the same time, the Court introduced the incongruous notion of "all deliberate speed" as the guide for the timing of desegregation plans.[125]

"All deliberate speed" was the compromise offered by a Court preoccupied with white resistance to racial equality.[126] The dramatic moment of resistance in Little Rock—when Governor Faubus brought out the Arkansas National Guard to prevent nine black students from enrolling in the Central High School—led a reluctant President Eisenhower to send in national troops.[127] The Supreme Court affirmed this federal power to implement *Brown*, but southern resistance persisted in almost every school district and, on some accounts *Brown* itself produced backlash, halting progress otherwise underway.[128]

"Desegregation" easily could be equated, then, with simply dissolving officially segregated schools. For communities actually to produce racially mixed schools would take years of further litigation and law enforcement against violent resistance. The dream of real integration, in which students from different backgrounds and colors would find common goals in communities committed to mutual success and well-being, remained remote even from discussion, much less reality.

Only fifteen months after *Brown*, a group of white men brutally lynched fourteen-year-old Emmett Till in Mississippi after he reportedly whistled at a white woman.[129] An all-white jury acquitted the men prosecuted for the murder, and Emmett Till's mother insisted on an open casket, attracting international media exposure of his mutilated body. The incident exposed the strict code of racial caste enforced by vigilante violence and a corrupted legal system and is widely credited with sparking grassroots movements for (still unrealized) universal civil rights.[130]

Against the backdrop of this and other violent incidents, school desegregation stalled in the South. White resistance took the forms of delays, segregative school assignment plans using proxies for race, and overt refusals to comply.[131] Organizations involving influential whites cropped up across the South to fight implementation of *Brown* and effectively mobilized commercial and vigilante threats and retaliations against anyone who urged integration.[132] After the remand of the five cases consolidated in *Brown,* the district court in South Carolina forbade racial segregation but explicitly distinguished that from requiring integration.[133] In Virginia, the legislature cut off public funds for any racially integrated school, and the governor decided to close schools rather than integrate them.[134] The NAACP filed successful challenges to these laws until both the Virginia Supreme Court of Appeals and the federal Court of Appeals rejected the school-closing statute.[135] The state legislature responded by repealing the compulsory school law,[136] and local authorities closed the public schools in Prince Edward County in 1959. Private schools, supported by state tuition grants and county tax credits, opened their doors to educate the county's white children.[137] This marked only one of many times when private schools became associated with resistance to desegregation. In this extreme instance, most of the county's seventeen hundred black children had no educational opportunities for five years, although neighboring Norfolk Catholic High School integrated voluntarily soon after the *Brown* decision of 1954. In Prince Edward County, the local NAACP organization tried to organize alternatives for black students while also challenging the resistance to desegregation.[138] A full ten years after *Brown*, the Supreme Court rejected the white community's evasions of the desegregation mandate and declared that the time for " 'deliberate speed' ha[d] run out."[139]

Although this was the most extreme instance, other federal courts delayed serious enforcement in the face of resistance to desegregation.[140] The Supreme Court left enforcement to the federal district courts, which had discretion to slow desegregation to a standstill.[141] Although some counties voluntarily desegregated, segregation persisted in most southern school districts,[142] with the vocal defense of ninety-six U.S. senators and representatives, governors, and mayors.[143] The Court turned a corner when in 1958 it unanimously rejected state resistance to a school board plan to desegregate the high school in Little Rock, Arkansas,[144] and this time President Eisenhower backed the Court fully.[145] Yet still, until 1960, 1.4 million black schoolchildren in the Deep South remained in fully segregated schools,[146] and by 1964, integrated schooling reached only one in eighty-five black students in the eleven southern states that had joined the Confederacy during the Civil War.[147]

Desegregation and Integration: Glimpsed and Lost

One reporter noted the irony that southern white legislators who opposed integration could declare "You can't legislate human relations" at the same time that they extended Jim Crow restrictions to sports, music, school, eating, and talking.[148] White resistance to equality for blacks also contributed to creating the conception of "whiteness" as a single group, erasing previously significant distinctions among Irish, Italian, Anglo-Saxon, German, and other national and ethnic groups.[149] In response to white resistance, the civil rights movement grew through networks of black churches, the organizational and mobilization gifts of ministers, and the courage and strength of the many ordinary people of many races who forged this mass movement.[150] Grassroots politics, boycotts of bus transportation and commercial businesses, sit-ins, and marches generated local and national attention and ultimately federal political action. Martin Luther King, Jr., led a movement of civil disobedience that drew three hundred thousand people to join in the 1963 March on Washington and ultimately impelled the adoption of the 1964 Civil Rights Act. The Act was also propelled, in part, by sympathy for the slain president John F. Kennedy and shepherded to success by the commitment and political skills of the new president, Lyndon Johnson.[151]

Aided with the tools given to the federal government by the 1964 Civil Rights Act and energized by the civil rights movement that pushed for it, the federal Department of Justice, federal judges, and public officials began actually to dismantle officially dual school districts and to desegregate parks, buses, courthouses, and hotels. The Act authorized the federal Department of Justice not only to enforce *Brown* through litigation but also to withhold federal funds from school systems that discriminated against African Americans. For the first time, the nation experienced serious federal enforcement of *Brown*. The enactment of the Voting Rights Act of 1965 also altered the larger political landscape and political calculus, enabling enforcement.

Reinforced with justices appointed by Democratic presidents,[152] the Supreme Court itself joined in enforcing school desegregation and rejecting the delaying tactics of resisting school districts. The Court in 1968 rejected a "freedom of choice" plan under which students could select which school to attend, independent of race. While 15 percent of black students in the New Kent County, Virginia, system opted to attend white schools, no white students elected to join those who remained in the historically black schools.[153]

In 1970, Republican president Richard Nixon demonstrated bipartisan consensus and expressed commitment to enforce the law. His staff organized biracial groups of leaders in the seven key southern states to plan for peaceful and orderly implementation of desegregation.[154] In 1971, the Supreme Court, with the participation of justices appointed by Nixon, authorized district courts to order comprehensive desegregation plans, including assignments of all students of a given grade to the same school, alteration of attendance zones, and busing students to schools on the basis of race (in a school system where fourteen thousand of the twenty-four thousand African-American students still attended schools that were all black).[155] By 1972, the previously segregated southern schools became the least segregated in the country.[156] School desegregation then moved North with the affirmation of the Court.[157] Between 1964 and the early 1980s, high school graduation rates for black students escalated, and their performance on standardized tests moved closer to the performance of white students.[158] Notable, but inadequately publicized, was the fact that the high school graduation rate and test performance of white students also increased during the same period.[159] Although this period combined serious enforcement of desegregation and increased federal funding of schooling, the major study of equal educational opportunities commissioned by Congress in 1964 reported that the "[a]ttributes of other students account for far more variation in the achievement of minority group children than do any attributes of school facilities and slightly more than do attributes of staff."[160]

This was the high-water mark. It lasted only briefly. A majority of whites told opinion pollsters that the Johnson administration was pursuing civil rights too aggressively.[161] Opponents renamed desegregation "forced busing" and protested it in many regions. In Boston, the protests turned violent, further inflaming an antibusing movement launched even before the court-ordered desegregation plan started.[162] White families with sufficient resources fled to the suburbs or private schools.[163] The conservative appointees to the Supreme Court rejected a challenge to interdistrict disparities in school expenditures in Texas.[164] They then enabled and perhaps fostered white flight from desegregating districts and set back the cause of integration. In *Milliken v. Bradley* in 1974, the Court confined desegregation orders to district lines and forbade the inclusion of suburbs to rectify urban segregation despite the evidence that decisions at the level of the entire state contributed to the racial segregation in the city.[165] The Court treated differences in the racial composition between neighboring school districts as beyond its remedial power. Characterizing this decision as a limit of the remedy to the geographic reach of the culpable official segregation, the Court failed to acknowledge the long-standing roles of local, state, and federal government in promoting and enforcing racial segregation in housing and real estate.[166] City borders would henceforth confine both desegregation plans and the enclaves of impoverished and despairing neighborhoods increasingly victimized by violence and drugs. Usually treated as "de facto" rather than official segregation, the racial patterns dividing residential areas and district school lines even now reflect decades of practices affected, if not directed, by law.

One scholar, writing in 1976, captured familiar perceptions of the time, describing persistent racial segregation in California this way: "The fact remains that most California white parents do not want their children transported to schools with predominantly poor minority student bodies located in black or brown neighborhoods. The parents fear that such schools will be educationally inferior and that their children will be victims of violence and reverse discrimination. Certainly none of these fears are without foundation, but it is possible that they are exaggerated by underlying racist feelings."[167] White families with financial means voted with their feet; they preferred predominantly white communities and white schools, which they associated with better opportunities for their children.[168]

However described or understood, the confluence of public actions and private decisions increasingly jeopardized the goal of making schools places where students from different races and backgrounds learned together—and the courts attributed the results to private choices beyond the reach of public policy. Justice Louis Powell treated residential segregation as a product of economic and social forces beyond both school board action and legitimate judicial remedy when he dissented from the Court's approval of a desegregation plan in 1979.[169] Others on the Court joined his view of residential segregation as beyond state action and beyond constitutional purview. Recasting *Brown* as a rejection of legally mandated segregation, the Supreme Court began to draw sharp lines between official and intentional governmental segregation, warranting a desegregation remedy, and "de facto" segregation resulting from individual choices or social practices and exempt from judicial remedy. Most white parents repeatedly demonstrated a preference for majority white schools,[170] and these choices became understood as protected and private. Given historic residential patterns, legacies of racially restrictive covenants, the convergence of race and economic class, and government policies producing marginalized ghetto neighborhoods, whites from the 1970s onward could choose largely white schools by moving to the suburbs, selecting private schools, or arranging placement of their children in high academic tracks.[171] In urban districts, desegregation plans had to redistribute dwindling numbers of white students, and courts overtly worried that further desegregation efforts would simply spur more "white flight."[172] Forms of reaction challenged the use of racial categories even to promote racial integration. Classification by race rather than racial hierarchy became the target; resistance to affirmative action in higher education and employment mounted during the 1990s. By 1999, the Boston

School Committee voted to end mandatory busing in the face of a lawsuit claiming that white children were discriminated against in the district's desegregation plan.[173] Echoing a strategy used in *Brown,* lawyers recruited social scientists in the disputes over desegregation remedies; some lawyers and others even tried to reexamine and dispute social science findings used in the *Brown* litigation itself.[174]

The Supreme Court replaced its 1968 call to remove segregation "root and branch" with a 1991 declaration that discrimination need only be "eliminated to the extent practicable."[175] Since that time, school districts under desegregation orders have successfully petitioned to end judicial supervision, and racial segregation has increased as districts have returned to assigning students to neighborhood schools.[176] The Supreme Court has allowed the termination of judicially supervised desegregation plans when the vestiges of official racial segregation seem remote, even when presented with increasingly racially separated schools. This is a major reason why the percentage of black students attending schools where the majority of other students are children of color has increased across the country over the past decade,[177] reversing the trend from the prior decade, when courts monitored school assignments.[178] The political factors affecting Court membership surely influenced these developments as much as shifting demographic patterns. The country's conservative political shift and election of Republicans who appointed conservative justices reflected, at least in part, resentments of working- and middle-class whites.[179] No new justice after Thurgood Marshall would reach the Supreme Court through a Democratic president's nomination for twenty-six more years.[180] In the meantime, the Court not only turned away from desegregation, racial mixing, and integration but also curbed the ability of agencies, private parties, and school systems to pursue them.[181] And it has allowed local districts to use new student assignments, rezoning, and redistricting to undo racial mixing and increase segregation.[182]

As the population has become even more diverse, with increasing numbers of Hispanics and immigrants from many regions, the goal and practice of integration has grown more complicated over recent decades.[183] Public schools in the United States thus are growing more separated by race and ethnicity at the same time that the school population grows more diverse.[184] Families of color face not only economic hurdles in moving to prosperous communities with good schools but also direct discrimination in the mortgage and housing markets.[185] School-aged children in America can claim every possible racial, ethnic, and religious background. The number of U.S. residents who speak a language other than English at home increased by 47 percent during the 1990s[186] reaching 17 percent of households in Portland, Oregon, 47.6 percent of households in New York City, 57.8 percent in Los Angeles by the year 2000.[187] In New York City, school-aged children speak 190 languages;[188] in Los Angeles, 90 languages. Immigrant children and the children of immigrants attend schools now in every county in the United States. Immigration and birthrates combined

make Asians and Latinos an increasing presence, with the Hispanic population doubling between 1970 and 1990, and the Asian population tripling
during that time frame.[189] As of 1990, the percentage of school-aged children in the United States who were Hispanic exceeded the percentage who
were African American.[190]

Reflecting this shifting demography, "diversity" is embraced and
defended by the U.S. military and Fortune 500 companies as crucial to their
own missions.[191] The United Colours of Benetton proved to be an arresting
and durable marketing campaign for a clothing line,[192] and a conservative
Republican President, George W. Bush, appointed an African-American
man and then an African-American woman to be secretary of state, a
Mexican-American man first as his White House counsel and then as
attorney general of the United States, and two Asian Americans to other
cabinet posts.[193] Growing rates of intermarriage and romances produce
enough multiracial individuals who want to be so identified to modify
how the census keeps track of individuals's racial identities.[194]

This is the context for school "resegregation" and for the decline of the
integrationist ideal. Scholars agree that desegregation did not fail. Desegregation worked to produce interracial contact and raise the educational
opportunities for both blacks and whites until courts and school districts
allowed it to end.[195] The courts lost their nerve. Many whites took advantage of reduced judicial enforcement to opt for mainly white schools—
and the courts obliged by confining remedies within the borders of those
districts with judicially determined illicit governmental racial segregation.
Hispanics and new immigrants face increasingly diminishing chances to
attend school with middle-class whites. And many African Americans
have started to give up on the hard work that the effort to achieve integration has required of them.[196]

What Failed and What Endures after *Brown*

Efforts to end racial segregation in schools could fail in two quite different
ways. They could fail, in fact, to bring about racial mixing. Or they could
bring about racial mixing that turns out to replicate the racial hierarchy and
subordination expressed in the segregated system. Evasion is the first problem; perpetuation is the second. The racial desegregation effort following
Brown has suffered both fates. Decades of resistance preceded new patterns
of public and private actions, producing racially identifiable schools that in
turn mirror the economic and social disparities between whites and members of other races, even as the nation grows more diverse. Courts and communities have failed to sustain desegregation efforts that worked. Strikingly,
the racial achievement gap persists in racially mixed middle-class schools—
even among African Americans and Hispanics who are themselves middle-
class, and among academically motivated and focused students of color.[197]
Whether in the same school or in substantially separate schools, students

across the country, with notable exceptions, continue to register a racial gap in school achievement (measured by test scores) that mirrors the gap between whites and African Americans and Latinos in home ownership, occupation, education, and wealth.[198] Disparities in access to educational resources also persist when the experiences of white students are compared with those of black and Hispanic students.

Meanwhile the ideal of integration no longer motivates many people of any race. In 2000, Richard Kahlenberg surveyed national attitudes and asserted that there is a consensus that integrated schools seem like a good idea but "we shouldn't do anything to promote them."[199] Equal opportunity remains the established goal of American schooling, at least since *Brown*, but racial mixing and the aspiration to build an inclusive and collaborative multiracial community prompts resistance from many quarters. This resistance is not confined to whites. When in 1934 W. E. B. Du Bois raised concerns that the desegregation focus could leave black children worse off than they would be in segregated schools, he had to resign from his post as editor of the NAACP's magazine, *Crisis*. Since that time, a series of advocates and scholars devoted to redressing racial oppression have followed Du Bois in defending separate educational institutions for students of color; they are more likely to emphasize the importance of high expectations and achievement than experiments in racial mixing.[200] Like the NAACP lawyers who argued in the 1940s over whether attacking segregated schools would undermine progress toward equalizing educational resources available to black students, advocates in this new century have explored whether financial and programmatic solutions will work better than the disappointing desegregation initiatives.[201]

Justice Clarence Thomas's resistance to desegregation efforts resonates with many African Americans who are insulted by the suggestion that educational excellence cannot occur in an entirely or predominantly black or black and Hispanic school.[202] For them, the betrayal of *Brown*'s promise lies not in finding students of color in schools largely with other students of color but instead in the low expectations and low achievement levels widely found among these students.[203] This line of concern could proceed one step further to question the aspiration of integration as a tool not only of condescension but of cultural oppression. In the context of education for Native Americans, contemporary critics blame segregated boarding schools for stripping children of their familial and cultural ties—but critics also attack early attempts to educate Indian children in California alongside white children for destroying family bonds and producing alienation, frustration, and high dropout rates among the Indian children.[204] Some people express nostalgia for all-black schools which often served as centers of community.[205] Culturally oriented claims similarly appear among some advocates of "Afro-centric" education, elevating a focus on African and African-American history and culture to root African-American students, enhance their self-esteem, and preserve their distinctiveness.

One does not have to embrace such cultural claims (and Justice Thomas probably does not) to conclude that mixing students of different backgrounds by itself does not produce equality if the adults and students replicate stereotypes and stratification based on race. The overrepresentation of minority students in special education classes for students with learning or emotional disabilities raises questions about the reliability of these assignments and the possibility that negative racial attitudes resurface in the form of disability labels long after they are legally ruled out of bounds.[206]

Increased uses of "alternative education" for students who have been disciplined present real questions about new and still-hidden modes of racial segregation.[207] Minority students face disproportionately high disciplinary actions, resulting in high rates of exclusion from mainstream classes.[208] Sometimes called the "pushout" process, or the "school-to-prison pipeline," school systems, police, and juvenile justice programs combine in a process that removes students from mainstream schools and puts them in separate programs that often involve lockup, searches, and little educational value.[209] In Mississippi, African-American students are referred to alternative schools at a rate two to three times greater than white students.[210]

Doubts about the commitment and capacity of racially mixed schools to ensure that minority students are treasured, well taught, and prepared for a still-prejudiced society are underscored by research findings about contemporary school practices.[211] Renewed interest in the accomplishments of all-black schools during segregation and the commitment that teachers and communities had to these schools and their students underscores historic paths to individual success outside the integrationist ideal.[212] Ironically, perhaps, as *Brown* spurred an emphasis on individual academic success rather than remedying group-based oppression, it also in some communities dismantled the segregated all-black institutions that offered role models and a sense of communal commitment to the success of their members. After waves of backlash to court-ordered desegregation and shifting membership of the federal courts, legal doctrine generated by *Brown* focuses on freedom from racial classification rather than racial integration or actual equal educational opportunity.

All of these developments, though, suggest that what failed after *Brown* was societal commitment to alter the assumptions and practices of racial hierarchy that produced segregation. Those assumptions often persist even in schools with racial mixing. It is African-American and Hispanic students living in areas of concentrated poverty who are most hurt by the decline of desegregation efforts. They are consigned to disproportionately inadequate and poorly performing public schools. They lose access to other social networks. White students in predominantly white schools have generally better educational opportunities and higher performing schools. Yet students of all backgrounds lose the benefits offered by the integrationist project: the benefits of working with diverse groups and building a sense of "we" through common goals and experiences. Given the importance to employers of the ability to work with diverse teams and the relevance of a sense of "we" to democratic governance, the entire nation loses as well.

Faced with limited time and capacity to push any school initiative, educators and parents increasingly confront a choice between renewed efforts for integration and redoubled initiatives in predominantly minority schools for quality instruction with high expectations. Race consciousness is an indispensable dimension of either avenue, as is underscored by the focus on student race in the performance measures mandated by the federal No Child Left Behind Act.[213] That race consciousness was strenuously advocated by conservatives and Republicans, led by President George W. Bush. Yet political and legal backlash to desegregation initiatives has contributed to the highly abstract debate, occupying courts and commentators, about eliminating any consideration of race or ethnicity in student school assignment in order to create a color-blind society.[214] The Supreme Court's preoccupation with color-blindness in schools is especially odd, given the persistent racial gap in achievement, the risks of misidentification of students of color in the context of special education, and the Court's own veneration of *Brown*.[215] Attention to race remains indispensable whether used in assessment of children's educational and life chances, progress toward the integration ideal, or defenses of separate instruction.[216]

Nonetheless, the Supreme Court shows increasing hostility toward the use of racial classifications, even when school systems pursue voluntary school integration. This preoccupation reflects the Court's conflation of college and university affirmative action debates with challenges in achieving education opportunity for students from kindergarten through high school. Chief Justice Roberts's opinion for the Court's plurality in *Parents Involved in Community Schools v. Seattle School District No. 1* focused on race-conscious school assignments in explaining why four members of the Court rejected voluntary integration plans in Seattle and in Jefferson County, Kentucky, in 2007.[217] The opinion concludes:

> Before *Brown*, schoolchildren were told where they could and could not go to school based on the color of their skin. The school districts in these cases have not carried the heavy burden of demonstrating that we should allow this once again—even for very different reasons.... The way to stop discrimination on the basis of race is to stop discriminating on the basis of race.[218]

As an aspiration, the closing sentence in this passage echoes statements of Thurgood Marshall as attorney for the plaintiffs in *Brown* as well as the soaring rhetoric of Martin Luther King, Jr.[219] Yet as a guide for current conduct in a nation marked by persistent and increasing racial gaps in opportunity and achievement, a ban on race consciousness can seem frustrating to communities willing to tackle the problem. The ring of an aphorism cannot hide the distortion of the past implied by this analysis. The burden before *Brown* was not merely racial classification, borne somehow equally by white and black children, but white supremacy, inscribed in Jim Crow laws, social customs, and the attitudes of private individuals. Those burdens remain so profound that communities in Seattle and Jefferson County, Kentucky, have repeatedly pursued through their elected school boards the projects of ensuring equal educational opportunities and ending segregation established in *Brown* in 1954.

The five members of the Supreme Court who did not join the plurality opinion in *Parents Involved* reject the aphoristic reduction of *Brown* to color-blind school assignments. Justice Anthony Kennedy's separate opinion does so explicitly.[220] Justice Stephen Breyer's opinion for the four remaining justices does so repeatedly.[221] And Justice John Paul Stevens describes Chief Justice Roberts's reinterpretation of *Brown* as a "cruel irony" because it treats the rejection of racial exclusion in *Brown* as if it bans the racial inclusion represented by the voluntary plans at issue in Seattle and Jefferson County.[222] Underscoring the departure represented by Chief Justice Roberts's interpretation of *Brown*, Justice Stevens concluded his opinion by observing: "It is my firm conviction that no Member of the Court that I joined in 1975 would have agreed with today's decision."[223]

The turn away from *Brown*, rejecting even voluntary integration plans, is all the more notable given the Court's retrenchment since 1974 from court-ordered desegregation. The Court retreated from emphatic enforcement of desegregation when lower courts tried to include suburbs in remedying urban segregation, and when diminishing numbers of white students remained in districts that had been subject to court orders for decades.[224] This judicial retreat from school integration did not occur because of recent public opposition to court action. It reflects the election of President George W. Bush–itself rendered by a Supreme Court judgment—and his appointments of Chief Justice John Roberts and of Justice Samuel Alito. It may reflect understandable worries about judicial efficacy. Yet it was the Court's own confinement of remedies to individual school districts that invited white families to move out of affected districts and defeat integration efforts.

Neither legitimacy nor efficacy concerns explain the Court's rejection of voluntary desegregation plans, enacted by school boards fully subject to the approval and disapproval of their electorates. Instead, the rejection of these voluntary plans seems part of an abstract political project to equate equal protection with colorblindness and to terminate affirmative action. The result favors white anxieties in an increasingly multiracial nation. Suppressing the distinctive history of slavery and the post–Civil War amendments in response to it, the national retrenchment in the civil rights struggle required converting the equal protection clause into a rejection of racial classifications rather than of racial subordination.[225]

Critics question how the Court's insistence on color blindness advances any plausible route for remedying legacies of racial injustice.[226]

Preoccupation with affirmative action—called by its opponents "reverse discrimination"—offers a partial explanation for the recent judicial focus on colorblindness as the measure for equal protection of the laws, particularly where scarce resources like places in elite universities, public contracts, or employment are at issue. White resistance to change in these contexts takes the form of righteous opposition to preferences of any sort, although allocating those scarce resources bears little resemblance to the assignment of children to supposedly equivalent schools in the same public districts in Seattle and Jefferson County. Even without Justices Roberts and Alito, the Court had enacted its ambivalence about affirmative action by tethering its approval for diversity rationales for racially conscious university and college admissions to an expectation that attention to race and ethnicity would no longer be necessary—and no longer acceptable—twenty-five years after the 2003 decision.[227] The ticking of that clock accelerated with the Court's rejection of the modest voluntary use of race to balance student assignments within public school districts. As a result, poor children of color remain far less likely to find teachers and schools able to launch them into lives of economic success or social and political equality with middle-class white peers.

Yet *Brown* and the struggles to implement its vision over the subsequent half century did end Jim Crow laws mandating racial separation. Equal opportunity has become the settled touchstone for American schooling. It is impossible to imagine the inclusion of race-based categories in the reporting requirements for the federal, bipartisan No Child Left Behind Act without *Brown* and its elevation of equal educational opportunity for students of all races, even though the Act and the federal government in general have made no new commitments to integrating schools. The Act on paper offers transfers to students in low-performing schools, yet education secretary Margaret Spellings, appointed by President George W. Bush, told the states that their actual use of this feature is "unacceptably low."[228] The election of President Barack Obama crosses a landmark in the nation's racial experience, but his administration focuses on school improvement, not racial integration. Access to equal educational opportunities remains remote for countless children in America, and the experiences of true integration across the color line is the exception, not the rule. And too many poor children, disproportionately of color, have no access to the kind of educational opportunities available in most suburban high schools, in many parochial schools, and in schools run by the U.S. military where teachers, parents, and larger community values converge in matching high expectations, emotional and pedagogical support, and role models devoted to children's educational success.

These disappointments with *Brown* are by now well known and well discussed. Seldom, though, in assessments of *Brown* do critics consider how the lawyers' effort producing the landmark racial desegregation case and the mass movements following it inspired movements pursuing equal schooling along lines of gender, disability, language, immigration,

class, and even religion and sexual orientation. If examined, those repercussions of *Brown* expand the vision of equal opportunity across other
dimensions of diversity and give rise to further debates over integration.

Just as courts delayed, then pressed, then backed off from requirements to educate students of different races in the same classrooms,
some of these difficulties recur in debates over education for girls and
boys; students with and without disabilities; students learning English
and students who already speak it; recent immigrants and their neighbors; poor children and those who are not poor; and Muslims and
Christians, Jews, atheists, and students of other religions; as well as gay-
lesbian-transgendered youth and their straight or unidentified peers.
Again following on the experiences with *Brown*, social science research
has emerged as a critical element in the arguments over how to achieve
equality in these contexts.[229] Although public and private school choice
offered escape routes for whites avoiding desegregation orders, renewed
choice initiatives open new avenues for mixing students while also stimu-
lating special mission schools, including identity-based programs that are
Afrocentric, or centered around interests such as the Arabic language or
girls' leadership. The repercussions of *Brown* beyond race, the impact of
new school choice options, the growth of social science assessments of
intergroup contact, and the symbolism of the case and its use as touchstone in struggles around the globe, all topics pursued in this book, are
as much the legacy of this landmark case as the disappointing status of
racial integration in American schooling.

Expanding Promise, Debating Means

*Separate and Integrated Schooling for Immigrants,
English-language Learners, Girls, and Boys*

> *May it please the Court, I think if appellants' construction of the
> Fourteenth Amendment should prevail here, there is no doubt in my mind
> that it would catch the Indian within its grasp just as much as the Negro.
> Should it prevail, I am unable to see why a state would have any further
> right to segregate its pupils on the ground of sex or on the ground of age
> or on the ground of mental capacity.*
> —John Davis, representing South Carolina,
> *Brown v. Board of Education*

Spurred by the social and legal struggles surrounding *Brown*, parents and advocates during the twentieth century and into the present have pursued equal schooling along other dimensions of exclusion and inequality by working through court challenges, legislation, and other initiatives.[1] *Brown* enshrined equality as the entitlement for all students, even as the work leading to and following *Brown* identified avenues for advocates concerned for students learning English, immigrants, girls, boys, and others left out or mistreated by public schooling. American public schools have grown preoccupied with the aspiration of equality and the language of inclusion.[2] Yet no less pervasive is the struggle over whether equality is to be realized through integrated or separate settings. The debates involve politics, prejudices, and social science studies. Shifting political tides and cultural attitudes, as well as legal debates, reflect and also aggravate uncertainties about what kinds of instruction actually promote equal opportunities for all children.

Immigrants, Noncitizens, and English-language Learners

Often called "a nation of immigrants" (with the elision, then, of Native Americans[3] and slaves), the United States has offered opportunities but also presided over mistreatment of newcomers on the basis of language, accent, derogatory ideas about their country of origin, or general negative attitudes toward foreigners.[4] Such attitudes include the conflation of "foreign" with "illegal,"[5] the confusion of immigrant with noncitizen,[6] and the equation of being a speaker of Spanish (and other native tongues) with being "non-American."[7] The tradition of forced assimilation starts first not with immigrants but with the Native Americans, beginning with the Civilization Act of 1819, under which the government removed Indian children from their family cultures and placed them in federally funded missionary schools, not to further integrate them with other students but to "civilize" them.[8] In addition, as the United States displaced Mexico in parts of the Southwest, families who never moved gradually found themselves dealing with a contest over language, race, and culture. Even before *Brown*, Mexican American families successfully challenged the separate-but-equal doctrine and prompted the repeal of California's official school segregation—in a law signed by Earl Warren, California's then governor, before he became chief justice of the U.S. Supreme Court and the author of *Brown*.[9]

Immigrants, children of immigrants, and students learning English risk discriminatory treatment for overlapping reasons: (1) if they are immigrants or the children of immigrants; (2) if they are not citizens; (3) if they are not English speakers; and (4) if they or their parents want them to keep or learn the language and culture of their ancestral country. Protesting wholesale exclusion and inferior opportunities no longer provokes controversy, but educators, parents, politicians, and pundits fight over assimilation versus cultural preservation. These intense disagreements marshall warring social science information and infuse struggles over litigation and legislation as much now as a century ago.

Panic over immigration is a long-standing thread of American history.[10] At the turn of the twentieth century, public schools focused on Americanizing immigrants and children of immigrants who came in large waves to this country between 1880 and 1920.[11] Periodic nativist movements against immigrants have generated initiatives to deny education to noncitizen children or to put them and their parents in jeopardy of deportation, but such initiatives have failed politically and constitutionally.[12] Critics of harsh nationalism, both then and now, endorsed pluralism, renamed and revamped as multiculturalism, over rigid Americanizing tactics. Analogies to racial equality help, as do normative claims of dignity and equality. Moreover, exclusion of noncitizen children from public education founders on the practical point that many, if not most, of these children will stay in this country and will contribute more economically, socially, and politically if they have received an education.[13]

Also, immigrant parents give birth to citizen children, complicating any effort to exclude along the lines of citizenship.

Nonetheless, the options for schooling can be starkly limited and at times unwelcoming for children who are immigrants or the children of immigrants. The language of instruction, the treatment of holidays, and the content of the social science curriculum push students into a single shared national identity, when many would prefer recognition of multiple communities within the nation.[14] *Brown* underscored the importance of schooling as the key entry point for jobs and civic participation. Education has the same practical importance for immigrants, their children, and English-language learners. But shifting population patterns and contrasting desires among immigrants, as well as long-standing residents, lead some to seek mixed, integrated schools exclusively using English, while others endorse separate programs or schools for immigrants as a kind of crash course in English and in learning to learn, and still others seek distinctive instruction in the language and culture of their parents or ancestors.

Educational challenges for immigrant children and children of immigrants circle around the language issue, as school systems struggle to accommodate growing numbers of immigrant students. In some parts of the United States, there are enclaves where Spanish has long been the dominant language (particularly in the areas where the United States spread into what had been Mexico). Ensuring English proficiency and excellence is more difficult when students live in homes and neighborhoods where English is not pervasive. This is only one sliver of the problem. Latinos, more than any other group, fare worse on measures of educational disadvantage, including separation from students of other backgrounds, concentration in schools with high rates of poverty, dropout rates, and educational attainment.[15] The influx of immigrants increased dramatically across the country between 1930 and 2000, while estimates currently indicate that more new immigrants will arrive without documentation than legally each year for the foreseeable future.[16] Given these patterns and different birthrates in the immigrant and nonimmigrant populations, an estimated 20 percent of school-aged children across the country have at least one immigrant parent and more than six in ten babies born in the New York City area since 2000 have at least one foreign-born parent.[17] Rapid and large increases in the immigrant populations in states such as Georgia, Nevada, and North Carolina are without precedents.[18]

Historically, children who are immigrants, children of immigrants, or children learning English have faced complete exclusion from school, assignment to segregated schools, punishment for speaking their native language, bans against instruction in their family's language, and formal and informal pressures to abandon family language and culture.[19] Still, even before *Brown*, isolated but successful lawsuits ended segregation of Mexican American students.[20] Political and legal movements and broader advocacy initiatives for immigrant children and children learning English emerged in the wake of *Brown* and its legislative and judicial repercussions.

In 1973, the Supreme Court acknowledged evidence that public school discrimination against Hispanics resembled discrimination against African Americans and asserted that each group deserved opportunities to be integrated with Caucasian students.[21] Turning to legislative solutions chiefly at the state level, Mexican-American parents in California mobilized in the early 1960s to challenge the failure of public schools to meet their children's needs due to school cultures, teacher attitudes, and language barriers.[22] When the Brownfield, California, school system responded with plans to use federal and state funds for a bilingual-bicultural school, some white parents objected, but the project proceeded.[23] Advocates across the country successfully pushed for the Bilingual Education Act of 1968, introduced by Senator Ralph Yarborough of Texas, as a response to the high dropout rate of Spanish-surnamed students.[24] As enacted, the law turned to focus on children of limited English-speaking ability (later called limited English proficient or English-language learners) and simultaneously shifted from a notion of enrichment to a conception of remedial or compensatory education.[25] The Act offered funds for educational programs, training for teachers and teacher aides, development and dissemination of materials, and parent involvement projects for students with limited knowledge of English.

The same year Congress enacted this law, advocates founded the Mexican American Legal Defense Fund (MALDEF) and self-consciously emulated the NAACP as an advocacy organization pursuing civil rights through litigation and legislation.[26] MALDEF emerged four years after Congress enacted the 1964 Civil Rights Act, following the 1963 March on Washington and President Johnson's vow to fulfill slain President Kennedy's promise of civil rights legislation. The language of that Act included protection against discrimination on the basis of national origin.

The actual source and conception of this provision is not well documented, coming as it did before the founding of a visible national advocacy group for immigrants. The phrase "national origin" was used to define quotas in the Immigration Act of 1924, establishing a regime that lasted until 1952 and limited immigrants by country of origin.[27] The phrase codified protections previously contained in executive orders that protected people seeking employment with the federal government from discrimination on the basis of ancestry or country of origin.[28] Working out the meaning of this commitment in schools to guard against national origin discrimination—and to secure equal protection for immigrants and students learning English—remains an ongoing struggle.[29]

Bilingual Education or English Language Acquisition?

Over the course of the 1970s and 1980s, local and national groups worked to interpret the emerging civil rights commitments for the education of immigrants and their children. Would equal opportunity for these students require changes in schools? If so, should accommodations focus solely on English acquisition, or on supporting the students' learning of other subjects while gaining knowledge of English? Is sustaining the students' home language independently valuable? Contests over these choices at each level of government engaged not only educators and parents but also social scientists in clashing assessments of teaching methods. Initial victories in some states and federal administrative actions established a public duty to do something to assist students learning English. Further contests generated strong commitments to bilingual education and then a backlash against it, ultimately yielding bans in some states and a federal shift to English language acquisition assistance, even as questions of accommodation and respect for language differences persist.

The Civil Rights Act's national origin protection became the vehicle for national policy governing education for children whose primary language is not English. Interpreted to guard against discrimination on the basis of birthplace, ancestry, culture, or linguistic characteristics, including surname, the Act supplied authorization to the Department of Health, Education, and Welfare to issue guidelines governing bilingual education and students learning English. In a 1970 memo, the Department offered support for bilingual instruction when it directed school districts enrolling more than 5 percent national-origin-minority group children to take "affirmative steps to rectify the language deficiency in order to open its instructional program to these students."[30]

The same year, Edward Steinman, a San Francisco poverty lawyer (and later a law professor), filed a class action suit on behalf of many students of Chinese origin to press enforcement of the federal regulations requiring accommodation for students without English proficiency.[31] According to one account, the suit arose after a University of California graduate student, Ling-Chi Wang, consulted with Steinman about unsuccessful requests that school officials alter the "sink-or-swim" approach to instructing immigrant children from many backgrounds.[32] The school system was already undergoing litigation for racial segregation, and school officials reportedly acknowledged but did nothing to respond to the problems experienced by non-English-speaking students, despite meetings with concerned parents. Steinman later recounted that he thought there would be less prejudice against Chinese immigrants than against Mexican immigrants.[33] Steinman selected Kinney Kinmon Lau, the son of one of his other clients, as named plaintiff.[34] Lau was born in Hong Kong and a decade after the suit recalled feeling lonely and isolated in school when he knew little English.[35] Yet he reported that he later resisted the school's offer of English as a Second Language (ESL) classes, because other students "laughed at you" if you were labeled as an ESL student.[36] The suit on behalf of Lau and others alleged violations of the Fourteenth Amendment and Section 601 of the Civil Rights Act of 1964, which denies federal financial assistance to recipients of federal aid that engage in discrimination against racial groups. None of the plaintiffs spoke or read English; none of their teachers spoke Chinese. About

1,066 of the students attended special classes to learn English at least part of the day, but the remaining 1,800 students received no direct English instruction.[37] The plaintiffs lost in both the district court and the court of appeals, which reasoned that the schools provided the same opportunities to all children and that the law afforded the plaintiffs no remedy. The majority for the appellate court concluded that law afforded no remedy because "[e]very student brings to the starting line of his educational career different advantages and disadvantages caused in part by social, economic and cultural background, created and continued completely apart from any contribution by the school system."[38]

As the case moved to the Supreme Court, the plaintiffs gained assistance through friend-of-the-court briefs from the U.S. Department of Justice, MALDEF, and other groups. The Supreme Court in 1974 reversed the lower court decisions.[39] Justice William O. Douglas noted for the unanimous Court that California law denied high school diplomas to students lacking proficiency in English yet offered no English instruction to the 1,800 immigrant children. "Under these state-imposed standards there is no equality of treatment merely by providing students with the same facilities, textbooks, teachers, and curriculum; for students who do not understand English are effectively foreclosed from any meaningful education," reasoned the Court, resting on the statutory authority and not reaching the constitutional claim.[40] Upholding the regulations issued by the federal Department of Health, Education, and Welfare, the Court found the San Francisco school district in violation because it received federal funds yet the "Chinese-speaking minority receive[d] fewer benefits than the English-speaking majority from respondents' school system which denies them a meaningful opportunity to participate in the educational program—all earmarks of the discrimination banned by the regulations."[41] The Court stressed that the Civil Rights Act of 1964 meant to ensure that no federal funds would subsidize or encourage discrimination. The Court also relied on a narrower ground: the school system was in breach of its contractual agreement when it accepted federal dollars.[42] The federal aid, thus, was conditioned on compliance with the regulations, which called upon recipient schools to provide affirmative instruction (and not discrimination) to students lacking English proficiency while receiving federal funds.[43]

Here, the problem was not segregation but mixing—in the absence of adapted instruction. The Court accepted the argument that including the Chinese-speaking students in the mainstream classroom with no accommodation amounted to discrimination on the basis of national origin because the Chinese-speaking students received fewer benefits from the classroom experience than did the English-speaking majority.[44] Ultimately, the San Francisco schools agreed through a consent decree to provide bilingual education for Chinese, Filipino, and Hispanic children.

Notably, the Court reached its decision based on the sheer impact of the existing curriculum and it required no proof of intentional discrimination as the measure of illicit discrimination.[45] In addition, the decision exposed a new version of the tension between integration and separate treatment.[46] Mixing students together without accommodating the newcomers denied the English language learners equal opportunity. The Court found that treating people who are differently situated as if they are the same is as much of a violation as treating people who are the same as if they are different.

The plaintiffs did not ask for, nor did the Court elaborate on, a specific kind of instruction the schools should adopt but agreed that schools needed to take some affirmative steps—changing their usual instruction—to respond to the different situation of students lacking English proficiency. Local school officials and advocates immediately disagreed over the best way to comply with the Court's decision. Some advocated bilingual-bicultural instruction, allowing students to learn English while maintaining cultural pride; others urged "maintenance" instruction in both their native language and in English throughout the students' school years. Still others stressed access to intensive instruction in English as a second language while criticizing programs that continued to separate students from their classmates long after they had learned English.[47] The named plaintiff himself, ten years after the decision, warned against teaching basic subjects in Chinese because then "you'll never learn English," although Kinney Lau thought it would be helpful if the teacher understood the students' native language.[48] His view emerged after long experience with disappointing initiatives.

When the litigation challenge was still fresh, a year after the *Lau* decision, the Office for Civil Rights, in the Department of Health, Education, and Welfare, announced a set of guidelines calling for more ESL instruction for elementary school students. The guidelines aimed to enhance students' esteem for their own cultures and knowledge of their home language while learning English. The agency monitored school districts and by 1980 negotiated 359 plans for compliance with its guidelines.[49]

Congress itself responded to the *Lau* decision with the Equal Education Opportunities Act of 1974, offering funds and directing recipient schools to take appropriate action "to overcome language barriers that impeded equal participation by its students in its instructional programs."[50] In essence, Congress required public school systems to do something but did not specify what would count as appropriate action. The statute codified *Lau*'s general conception of equal opportunity as compelling some official steps on behalf of students learning English but did not codify the agency's guidelines that pressed for bilingual, rather than merely English, instruction. Even before the *Lau* case, Congress also directed modest resources to developing educational programs, training teachers, and encouraging involvement of parents in addressing educational disadvantages of students lacking English proficiency and added to these resources in 1974.[51] Hence, Congress approved but did not require bilingual or bilingual-bicultural education.

Bilingual-bicultural education, according to its defenders, would help students maintain proficiency in a language other than English and support the development of positive self-conceptions for young people learning English.[52] This proved controversial over time. Opponents feared a new form of separatism and a perceived threat to English as the official and dominant language in the United States.[53] Critics noted that the choice of instructional method could have profound implications for the degree of integration and separation of students learning English from other students. Unless vigilantly guarded against, long-term separation of English language learners from their classmates could result from maintaining bilingual-bicultural competence; intensive ESL instruction could produce short-term separation; and English immersion could produce little classroom separation but leave students with the sense of isolation that Kinny Lau recalled years after the lawsuit bearing his name. Also, critics charged that bilingual education was an employment program for Hispanic teachers or an imposition on local decisionmaking.

A pivotal federal court decision preserved Congress's agnosticism on the subject of instructional methods for school systems addressing needs of students learning English. In *Castañeda v. Pickard*, the court of appeals for the Fifth Circuit ruled that districts could choose from among instructional methods recommended by experts but had to direct sufficient resources for implementation and also had to shift methods if an initial effort did not succeed.[54] The Mexican-American plaintiffs launched their class action suit in 1978 and charged that the Raymondville, Texas, Independent School District unlawfully discriminated against them by failing to adopt bilingual education adequate to enable their equal participation in the education offered by the district. The district offered no formal bilingual instruction after the third grade and instead offered only ESL instruction and access to the center dealing with remedial instruction in English and other subjects.

In addition to the language instruction claim, the suit alleged that the school district used an ability-grouping system for classroom assignment based on racially and ethnically discriminatory criteria, resulting in impermissible classroom segregation. The suit further alleged that the school district discriminated against Mexican Americans in the hiring and promotion of faculty and administrators. The plaintiffs thus claimed that the system retained vestiges of intentional, illicit racial and ethnic segregation and confused assignment based on knowledge of English with assignment based on ability. In this way, the plaintiffs explicitly tied the treatment of English language learners to *Brown* by questioning separation of students based on English knowledge and by challenging the absence of bilingual instruction in subjects other than language. The request for bilingual instruction relied not on the Constitution but on the enactments of federal legislation, regulation, and agency guidelines.

The district court rejected the plaintiffs' claims, and then the court of appeals partially reversed the decision, remanding to the district court for reconsideration of the Spanish language competence of teachers,[55] possible discrimination in the hiring of teachers, and the design and practice of the ability-grouping system against the backdrop of the district's prior de jure segregation.[56] As the most influential statement by a federal appellate court on the subject, the court's opinion in *Castañeda v. Pickard* struck a middle course between the plaintiffs' effort to have bilingual instruction mandated for all grades and the district's policy. The opinion did not call for English language learners beyond third grade in the substantive courses, other than intensive English language instruction and access to the remedial learning center.[57]

In the field, the case became known less for refusing to require bilingual education than for establishing that school systems must fund programs that actually ensure that students learn English or are reasonably calculated to do so.[58] At the same time, the *Castañeda* court preserved room for educational experts to determine the most appropriate method for particular students and particular circumstances. Under the Equal Education Opportunities Act of 1974, the court devised a three-prong test for assessing the "appropriateness" of a school system's approach to teaching students who are learning English. The school system plan must (1) reflect an educational theory that is either sound or a legitimate experimental strategy;[59] (2) include sufficient plans, resources, and personnel to be reasonably calculated to implement the theory;[60] and (3) be assessed and replaced if, after a sufficient trial period, it has not produced results overcoming the language barriers to student learning.[61] Evidence of success would be key.

The *Castañeda* court did not, however, address whether programs segregating English language learners would run afoul of existing school desegregation orders or the integrative ideal.[62] Bilingual programs could dramatically complicate school desegregation orders by separating Hispanic or Chinese students. Bilingual programs could also prompt English-speaking parents to seek other schools,[63] impairing the goal of mixing students. Or bilingual programs could promote a greater sense of belonging, as well as higher academic achievement, for Hispanic students and others learning English. The details of the language accommodation program and the attitudes of the school community would matter significantly in predicting the effect of separating and integrating different groups of students.

Experts in the field started to identify four basic types of programs but acknowledged that in practice the programs overlapped and often teachers drew from all of the models. "Transitional bilingual education" proceeds with most of the instruction in English but presents some of the school subject material in the child's home language. This enables progress while the child learns English and moves toward the program's goal, which is full transition to mainstream English classrooms, usually within two or three years.[64] "Maintenance bilingual education" seeks to preserve and deepen the student's knowledge of the home language and culture while the student learns English; almost always used within elementary schools, this model could involve students for many years.[65] In some versions, this program proceeds as a two-way bilingual program, integrating, for example, Spanish-speaking and English-speaking students with the goal of cultivating dual language fluency for both groups of students.[66] Eliciting simultaneous strong support and strong opposition, transitional bilingual and maintenance bilingual programs, when well run, afford real access to the curriculum for students learning English. But they also risk segregating students learning English from other students and undermining racial desegregation plans. "Immersion" teaches students English alongside other subjects while giving students cues and assistance with the language and is often accompanied by special intensive instruction in English through pullout sessions from the mainstream classroom.[67] Finally, "submersion" or "sink-or-swim" provides no particular special instruction. In light of these alternatives the *Lau* analysis is not sufficient under federal civil rights law in public schools receiving federal assistance but still finds defenders in Congress and in school systems.[68]

Toward the end of his time in office, President Jimmy Carter responded to bilingual education advocates with a proposal mandating bilingual instruction in any school with at least twenty-five English-language learners enrolled in two consecutive elementary school grades. The proposal triggered a backlash and new studies criticized bilingual instruction. Congress directed that federal bilingual programs should aim for transition and English competence, not cultural maintenance. In the early 1980s President Ronald Reagan's administration cut funding for bilingual education and encouraged alternatives, including English language immersion.[69] National debate erupted over making English the nation's official language and restricting bilingual instruction, with results pointing in several directions. President Reagan appointed the first Hispanic secretary of education. Congress and the courts helped preserve federal aid for bilingual education. However, under political pressure, the Office for Civil Rights withdrew the *Lau* guidelines favoring bilingual instruction and left the choice of appropriate services for English language learners to local districts.[70]

The keystone of President George W. Bush's domestic policy, the No Child Left Behind Act, addressed language instruction without public fanfare and, on its face, seemed to favor neither bilingual nor English-immersion instruction. Yet some critics warned that it was designed to reduce or eliminate successful bilingual programs and instead favor English immersion.[71] Signaling priority given to English rather than bilingualism, the Act replaced the Office of Bilingual Education with the Office of English Language Instruction, Language Enhancement, and Academic Achievement for Limited-English-Proficient Students.[72] It set aside no funds for English immersion and left control to the states to determine how to educate limited-English-proficient students, as long as the state relied on methods grounded on "scientifically based research."[73] Assessments of varied bilingual programs are difficult precisely because of the variety in the programs and in the students, as well as the politicized contexts for both the schools and the evaluators.[74] Political disagreements over studies reached a new level when the administration of President George W. Bush decided not to publish the results of a commissioned study that endorsed instruction in students' home language and entirely omitted bilingual instruction in 2006 federal guidebooks about options for teaching English language learners.[75] The administration explained that it dropped mention of bilingual instruction because some states had banned that form of instruction. These state bans themselves emerged from another strand of advocacy.

The politicized context may well affect competing scholarly assessments of the effectiveness of varied kinds of bilingual programs with immersion in English-speaking classrooms.[76] Uncontroverted evidence does suggest that the quality of the teachers is a more significant factor in student achievement than the choice between bilingual instruction and English immersion.[77] This kind of insight could lead some to defend continuing experiments with bilingual education on the grounds that it has never been given a fair chance and others to emphasize that separate instruction will never be equal, practically or symbolically. Yet both options may remain inadequate due to other factors—such as the economic class of the affected students and neighborhoods and limited parental educational backgrounds. Intense political pressures on both sides of the debate over bilingual education affect the quality and perception of evaluation efforts. In the meantime, the movement for legal bans on bilingual education took off. California entrepreneur Ron Unz successfully crafted, financed, and pushed for the passage of an initiative to eliminate bilingual education first in that state and then in Arizona and Massachusetts.[78] Colorado rejected a similar referendum. Florida, Illinois, New York, and Texas—all states with high numbers of limited-English-proficient students—continue to offer bilingual education programs.[79] California, Massachusetts, and Arizona have continued to allow parents under some circumstances to elect through annual written requests either bilingual education or immersion for their children,[80] but only if the child already has shown English proficiency or has special needs requiring the accommodation.[81] Courts rejecting these restrictions on bilingual education have pointed to educational expertise, just as courts resisting arguments for judicially imposed bilingual education have pointed to expert support for varied educational methods.[82] Quite apart from the debate over sites and forms of instruction, a fundamental legal question erupted that was crucial to students, their teachers, and their schools concerning the language used in required standardized tests of yearly progress. Controversy arose over the requirement of testing in English, as state and federal law often attached high stakes to tests, including denials of high school diplomas and threats of shutting down underperforming schools.

Besides legal and political disputes over forms of instruction and testing rules for students learning English, additional controversy has centered on selecting the ultimate location of decision-making. Choices include federal versus state, legislature versus courts. In a case emphasizing federal deference to state-level decision-making, the U.S. Supreme Court in 2009 reversed a decision requiring incremental funding for programs for English-language learners and allowed the state to fulfill its federal statutory equal education obligation through "structured immersion," essentially permitting no special assistance to students learning English.[83] A federal court had ordered Arizona to fund programs for English-language learners in fulfillment of its duties under the federal Equal Educational Opportunities Act of 1974, which requires a State "to take appropriate action to overcome language barriers that impede equal participation by its students in its instructional programs."[84] Subsequently, Arizona voters passed Proposition 203, which required statewide implementation of a "structured English immersion" approach, requiring all classroom instruction to take place in English and rejecting special instruction for students learning English.[85]

Citing these developments, in *Hornes v. Flores,* the Supreme Court allowed Arizona to get out from under the prior judicial order directing it to increase funding for instruction of English-language learners. The Court rebuked the court of appeals for "improperly substitut[ing] its own educational and budgetary policy judgments for those of the state and local officials to whom such decisions are properly entrusted,"[86] even though the Court's own five-person majority chose to enter into the debate. The Court declared that there is "academic support for the view that [Structured English Immersion] is significantly more effective than bilingual education,"[87] although the Court could point to only a selected few of the sixteen amicus briefs filed in the case for this proposition. The state's own trial witnesses were unable to verify that Arizona's system had produced significantly improved results.[88] The Supreme Court allowed the state to use its unsuccessful immersion program by accepting the state's claim that changed circumstances permitted modification of the prior order to fund English language instruction. The Court pointed to the intervening change in state law and to the enactment of the No Child Left Behind Act. Because the Act directs states to develop their own plans to ensure that schools and students make yearly progress, the Supreme Court justified alteration of the specific court order to fund programs for English-language learners.[89]

The Supreme Court's majority decision triggered a vigorous dissent by four justices. The dissenters argued that the majority's opinion obscured and undermined the commitment to equal opportunity in schools for students learning English.[90] Justice Stephen Breyer's lengthy dissenting opinion, joined by three justices, criticized the majority for treating the state's continuing "funding-based failure to provide English learning resources" as a changed circumstance sufficient to justify modification of the district court's order to fund English language instruction. Faulting the majority's convoluted procedural analysis, its treatment of the district court's factual findings, and its claim that the lower courts wrongly focused only on funding rather than outcomes, the dissent closed with a powerful statement of the stakes of the case as the four dissenting justices saw them:

The case concerns the rights of Spanish-speaking students, attending public school near the Mexican border, to learn English in order to live their
lives in a country where English is the predominant language. In a Nation
where nearly 47 million people (18% of the population) speak a language
other than English at home ... it is important to ensure that those children,
without losing the cultural heritage embodied in the language of their
birth, nonetheless receive the English-language tools they need to participate in a society where that second language "serves as the fundamental
medium of social interaction" and democratic participation.... In that way
linguistic diversity can complement and support, rather than undermine,
our democratic institutions....

Three decades ago, Congress put this statutory provision in place to ensure
that our Nation's school systems will help non-English-speaking schoolchildren overcome the language barriers that might hinder their participation in our country's schools, workplaces, and the institutions of everyday
politics and government, i.e., the "arenas through which most citizens live
their daily lives." I fear that the Court's decision will increase the difficulty
of overcoming barriers that threaten to divide us.[91]

Buried inside of technical discussions of deference to state authorities
and relief from prior judicial orders, the Court's decision generated little
public attention, even though it authorized a sharp reduction in educational support for students lacking English proficiency.[92] This time, the
issue was not a dispute over methods of instruction but over whether
there is a public duty—justifying federal involvement—to respond to
these students' needs. Far from public debate and expert assessments, the
Court seems to have closed the door on the *Lau* era and its declaration
that giving the identical education to students lacking English proficiency
is not giving them equal education.

Varied state and local initiatives addressing students learning English
continue. Many local communities see bilingual proficiency as a goal
for students from any background in an era when "globalization" is a
buzzword and here, dual immersion—in English and in the other language to be learned—can attract students of different backgrounds to the
same program. While Spanish is the most common language attracting
attention for bilingual instruction across the country, parents in some
regions have sought immersion in Arabic, Chinese, and other languages.
In 2009, a school district in New Jersey made plans to become one of the
first in the nation to create a Hebrew-language immersion program in a
public school.[93] Proposed as a Hebrew-language charter school, the idea
drew both from the long-standing bilingual education debates and the
room created by charter schools and school vouchers for special-mission
schools.[94] Changing legal attitudes about religion in schooling and the
use of multiculturalism to recast religious and ethnic claims on schools
have also created a climate conducive to Hebrew-language and Arabic-
language schools, with examples not only in New Jersey but also in New
York, Florida, and Minnesota.[95] Schools framed around these languages

could well attract self-selected student bodies, less heterogeneous than the enrollments at other schools. If this result emerges, such bilingual schools would increase the diversity of school offerings while decreasing the contact within schools among students from different backgrounds.

In contrast to the intensive work on English and academic subjects as a route toward assimilation in America, special bilingual schools have cropped up with the support of particular immigrant communities and a focus on combining academic quality with cultural preservation. In 2001, Minneapolis and St. Paul established two new schools, the Twin Cities International Elementary School and the Twin Cities International Middle School.[96] The schools' web site explained: "Founded by educational leaders in the East African community, the schools strive to provide a quality academic program, in a culturally sensitive setting, for immigrant and refugee children."[97] The schools "offer the best possible American academic program in a setting that respects and values community input."[98] Drawing students mainly from the large Somali immigrant population in the area,[99] the schools serve Hallal food, appropriate for their largely Muslim student population; the schools also teach Arabic, both because of the students' background and because the schools seek to prepare all students to live in a global society. The dress code permits head coverings, and all girls pictured in the schools' informational materials wear scarves or hijabs. New York City created an Arabic-language school as one of eleven ethnically themed public schools,[100] but it had to replace the initial head of the school after a comment she made was misread as endorsing radical Islamic violence.[101] Ethnic-themed schools could be conceived of as transitional institutions for newcomers to America. They can accord equal respect for distinctive groups and opportunities for groups of parents to pass on their own traditions; but, in the views of critics, they balkanize American identity.[102] Yet when designed inclusively, such schools can also offer chances for immigrant and other students to mix together while learning a language other than English.

Exclusion and Inclusion of Noncitizens

Overcoming barriers imposed by political branches, courts have guaranteed educational access for children who are not U.S. citizens—but current experiments push for separate schooling. The Supreme Court in *Plyler v. Doe* rejected the effort by Texas to deny a free public education to undocumented school-aged children in 1982.[103] California then proceeded through a citizens' initiative to exclude unlawful aliens from the public schools and to enlist school districts to investigate the legal status of each child.[104] A district court barred implementation of the initiative on the grounds that it interfered with federal immigration law.[105] Governor Pete Wilson appealed the decision, but the next governor eventually dropped the appeal and ended efforts to exclude noncitizen children from the schools.[106]

Meanwhile, many communities have created "newcomer schools": separate school facilities or programs for recent immigrants.[107] Intended to provide a comfortable transitional environment, these schools include bilingual and bicultural education and address issues for middle- and high-school-aged students who have not attended school or previously had little schooling or literacy instruction in any language.[108] School leaders worry that regular schools will frustrate adolescent immigrant children and lead them to drop out. High-school-aged Latino students who identify themselves as lacking English proficiency are more than four times as likely to drop out as their classmates who are proficient in English.[109]

By design, newcomer schools separate immigrants from other students for at least six months, although many call for one year, and at least one has a four-year program.[110] With tailored instruction, bilingual teachers, and supportive environments, the newcomer programs aim to boost graduation rates and prepare students for the mainstream. Several school systems have created entirely separate, freestanding newcomer schools with a full-day curriculum, making the English language content interesting and relevant. Many others involve part-day programs or place immigrant students and other students in the same building but in separate classrooms. The Bronx International High School in New York recruits limited-English-proficient students who have been living in the United States for five or fewer years and who fall into the bottom quintile on an English language competence assessment. This public school tackles not only language but also the entire situation of students who need to proceed with the usual high school subjects as well as learn English and provide translation and other assistance to their families.[111] Exceptional in its intensive program, philanthropic and federal funds, and assignment of students to the same four teachers for two consecutive years, this school requires much energy and extra resources. New York school officials take pride in its results; 70 percent of its students go on to four-year colleges.[112] (Thorough assessment of this statistic as a marker of success would require not only comparison with other schools but also other programs that invest the same degree of resources.) Programs like the Bronx International High School raise fresh issues about how to ensure equal quality and access to opportunities across separate school programs. One program closed after the federal government questioned its failure to provide after-school opportunities available at neighboring schools.[113]

These programs also reopen the debate over whether separate schools are inherently unequal. Newcomer schools and programs depart in the short term from the ideal of integration but essentially aim toward mainstreaming recent immigrants. Their lawfulness and desirability most likely turn on their implementation, and in the meantime, risks of stigmatizing segregation are reduced by the fact that enrollment in these programs is based on the choice of the student and the student's parents.[114] These schools and programs also typically generate their own diversity by drawing students from many different countries.[115] States that have passed English-only laws can exempt newcomer schools or press them to use English language immersion rather than bilingual instruction.[116]

A pressing problem is finding sufficient funds to provide the intensive investment that effective newcomer programs involve.[117]

Schools have struggled with the provision of the federal No Child Left Behind Act that requires states to include new immigrants in state standardized performance assessments. This provision could raise curricular expectations but could also lead to counterproductive experiences of failure, especially if the states fail to provide tests in the students' native languages.[118] California, for example, has an English-only testing policy for all California Standards Tests for grades K–12.[119] The federal government announced that new immigrants could be exempt from the English assessments during their first year in school in the United States; scores from their tests could also be excluded from the overall results for each school.[120] Even students attaining English proficiency could be excluded for two years from school-wide testing calculations.[121] Nevertheless, these students would still be expected to take the exams in mathematics, with help in their native language.[122] A deputy superintendent in Massachusetts commented that the previous policy was punitive: "It's a form of child abuse to require students to take this test when we know they're going to fail."[123] Many school officials remain worried about the moment when English-language learners must be counted within school-wide English assessments because their inclusion will distort what the schools have actually achieved with these students and with the students who already speak English. Under the No Child Left Behind Act, costly remedial efforts as well as stigmatizing sanctions are attached to schools with low performance scores—and backlash against the law has led states to seriously consider opting out of the funding that is attached to these assessment obligations.[124] Yet the alternative—having children take tests in their native languages—is also often a poor alternative, because it presumes literacy in that language, which the students often do not have.[125]

Poorly planned testing and school programs increase the risks of alienation and rising dropout rates among students who are immigrants or children of immigrants. Commentators increasingly attend to how schools' failures to help these individuals integrate into the larger society risk not only loss of human capital and defeat of individual dreams but also intergroup tension and national instability. On the other hand, effective schooling for newcomers can improve student performance and movement into college and employment.[126] Assuming that noncitizens and children of immigrants are included within the educational equality commitments of the nation, determining how to allocate funding, how these students should mix with other students, and what should be the content of the curriculum remain challenging issues.

Treatment of immigrants and differences in language and national origin in schools thus can be assessed in terms of effectiveness along many dimensions. English proficiency, bilingual proficiency, scores on standardized tests, high school completion, and college admission rates are obvious criteria for assessing schooling for English-language learners but also important are degree of contact and friendships with students from other backgrounds; development of positive views about one's own background and of the United States; and effects on both these students' and other students' senses of national identity and group membership.

The treatment of language and culture in American schools remains a hot and difficult subject for children in America whose families want to preserve cultural and linguistic roots, for recent immigrants eager to make it in America, and for English-speaking students looking for opportunities in a globalizing world. Equality is the touchstone; separation and mixing different students remain topics for experiment and debate.

Gender

Brown yielded swift and extensive repercussions for the treatment of gender in schools. The Court's decision, with the social movement and legislation energized by it, produced a federal legislative and regulatory apparatus that pressed for equal educational opportunities regardless of a student's sex or gender. Activists picked up the torch of advocacy first for girls but ultimately for both girls and boys. Conceiving of students in gendered terms helped advocates address disadvantages to girls and to boys from public school practices and to support specific educational programming. Advocates for equal education pushed initially for parallel but single-sex programs, then for integration, and more recently for revival of single-sex instruction—and a sharp assault on it. Current developments echo and modify complicated debates that have emerged since the 1960s over single-sex education.

Historic exclusion of girls from educational opportunities supplied an easy target for discrimination challenges and propelled advocacy not only for coeducation in the classroom but also for expanding resources for athletics and leadership for girls. Yet many proponents of gender equality also responded to the backdrop of long-standing exclusion of girls from elite boys' schools and the exclusion of women from elite male colleges, professions, and jobs by advocating all-girls instruction as a kind of remedial empowerment measure.[127] Advocates and public officials have explicitly made conscious references to *Brown* over several decades. Critics attacked educational regimes using gender to divide students as echoes of *Plessy* with "separate but equal" classrooms or schools. Surprising, paradoxical, and sometimes painful coalitions and debates emerged over single-sex educational initiatives for poor African-American boys, which foundered legally against the template of gender neutrality pursued by women's rights advocates; single-sex initiatives for girls had an easier time bridging an older sex-segregated practice with newer ideas of equalizing options because of the continuing popularity and apparent success of elite private and parochial schools for girls. Ultimately, single-sex schools and single-sex classes have gained federal approval (and both public and private support) under the framework of diversifying educational options to enhance equal opportunity, even as they renew scholarly and popular concerns about sex stereotyping. The framework of individual and parental choice has taken the sting out of single-sex education when compared with its mandatory precursors. Since 2002, single-sex classrooms and schools have multiplied, reflecting a complex confluence of political and legal arguments and passionate advocates, all pursuing their visions of equal educational opportunity.

Histories of Gender and Education

The historical background for the developments in single-sex education in the United States reaches back centuries before *Brown*. Justifications for distinctive treatment of girls and women stem from historical ideologies that accorded girls and women (really, white girls and women) a special place in the home and family, imagined as a sphere separate from the public realms of boys and men.[128] Those justifications conveyed an attitude of protection against the harshness of politics, workplaces, and military duties reserved for men (historically, for privileged white men). As a result, legal efforts to include females in male settings have in some ways implied a loss of privilege or protection, even when the prevailing rules spelled exclusion from settings of power and opportunity.[129] Civil rights initiatives tackled barriers to women's participation in schooling, employment, and politics. These initiatives have succeeded in expelling old rationales for excluding girls and women from various kinds of education; equal opportunity is now the consensus ideal.[130] But justifications for separate schooling have resurfaced, advancing ideas about how best to prepare girls and women to overcome legacies of discrimination and also raising old and new claims about real differences between males and females. Separate instruction remains a lawful alternative and is an increasing practice, garnering public policy and some vocal public support.

Thus, single-sex education grew up before *Brown* and its notion of equal educational opportunity; schools for girls also found defenders after *Brown* who sought to remedy discriminatory or disparate effects of coeducation on girls. Most recently, single-sex programs have grown as people have sought the claimed benefits of single-sex education for both sexes.[131]

In the seventeenth century, education for girls rarely moved beyond home instruction or, at best, primary schools; both colleges and the schools preparing students for college excluded girls.[132] A few boarding schools were started for girls in the late eighteenth century, but these efforts tended to focus on refinements like music and art rather than the subjects pursued by boys. When Emma Willard created her seminary for girls in 1821 to teach the subjects available at men's colleges, she provoked controversy, but even Willard framed the enterprise in traditional gender terms by calling it preparation for motherhood.[133] The idea of private seminaries for girls gradually gained support. With the advent of public education through the "common school" movement, which emerged in the 1840s, cities and towns debated whether to make it coeducational. Opponents warned that boys would be too coarse and would corrupt girls. Some argued that single-sex instruction better suited the real differences between boys and girls. During the late nineteenth century, ostensibly scientific and moral rationales for excluding women from legal and medical education persisted in many institutions. And even where separate elite exam schools existed, some deployed higher admission criteria for girls than their counterparts required for boys.[134]

Early women's rights reformers Susan B. Anthony and Elizabeth Cady Stanton argued in the 1850s for coeducational public schools as the means to achieve equality. Coeducation also won the support of many teachers who claimed that the presence of girls would reduce the rudeness of boys.[135] Over time, as communities established public schools, most became coeducational rather than single sex for the simple reason of economy. A coeducational school is cheaper than building and running two school systems. Some historians suggest that coeducational schools in the nineteenth century actually offered more freedom from gender-role expectations than other institutions in operation at the same time.[136] By the end of the nineteenth century, reformers expressed more emphatic arguments for single-sex education, and the most elite private schools and colleges remained single-sex—and typically excluded blacks, Jews, and recent immigrants.[137] A few schools for Negro girls emerged as projects of abolitionists or racial uplift reformers.[138] Nonetheless, coeducation remained the norm for public schools throughout the twentieth century, as they expanded beyond the elementary grades to include high school courses. Single-sex education remained dominant only in the most prestigious public and private elementary and secondary schools even though it was prevalent in higher education. Even there, coeducation grew from less than one-third of colleges in 1870 to half in 1910 and three-quarters in 1957.[139]

Single-sex Education after Brown

After 1954, *Brown* inspired advocates for women and girls to challenge the remaining single-sex educational institutions. A civil rights framework influenced schooling for girls starting in the 1960s, even before the women's movement actively organized to pursue litigation and reforms.[140] The 1964 Civil Rights Act (Title VII), as enacted, included sex as a forbidden ground of discrimination, even though it was not included in the draft of the legislation. In retrospect, the Act's inclusion of sex helped to reinvigorate movements for gender equality that had stagnated after World War II.[141] Initially proposed by an opponent of the Act, apparently as an effort to defeat it, the amendment adding "sex" was quickly endorsed by women in Congress and in the country as a much-needed and much-deserved recognition of gender inequality.[142] A growing movement for women's rights successfully pushed for the 1972 Education

Amendments to the Act, producing Title IX, which conditions the use of federal funds for educational programs on individual legal protections against gender discrimination.[143] Advocates used the law to move school systems to equalize resources across academic and athletic programs for boys and girls and also to open up male-only settings, including all-male exam schools within public high school systems. Women's rights advocates brought highly visible and successful challenges to disparities in funding and opportunities for college and high school athletics,[144] but had more mixed results in confronting the operation of all-male schools. Title IX itself excluded from its coverage the admissions policies at secondary schools[145] as well as public colleges traditionally enrolling only students of one sex.[146]

This exclusion of school admissions from protections against gender discrimination hints at the enduring belief that differential treatment by gender is not necessarily derogatory or negative even when explicit and intentional. Even advocates and scholars committed to combating discrimination have disputed the analogy between race and gender, especially around the issue of whether separate can ever be equal.[147] The courts historically accepted gender categorization by government as reflecting some "natural differences,"[148] such as smaller size and muscle strength for the average girl compared with the average boy.[149] Some commentators challenge even these exemptions from sex-neutral practices.[150] Unless temporary or carefully constructed, single-sex educational programs may seem to perpetuate the physical, legal, social, or economic inferiority of females.[151] But the ultimate access to opportunities and rates of achievement that would signal gender equality is not the only issue at stake in this debate. Scholars and activists have targeted gender-based stereotypes, the reliability of ostensibly empirical evidence about gender differences gathered by people who are themselves influenced by cultural images, and the level of judicial scrutiny to be applied to gender distinctions in law and policies.

In the 1970s, after her own encounters with unsupportive treatment at Harvard Law School and in her early professional experiences, Ruth Bader Ginsburg planned a litigation effort at the American Civil Liberties Union (ACLU) to contest gender inequality in public policies. With a strategy similar to the NAACP's challenges to racial segregation, Ginsburg pursued gender neutrality in government programs.[152] This initiative selected lawsuits that attacked instances of special treatment for females and sought "strict scrutiny" by courts of any gender distinctions drawn by law or government programs, just as judges applied the same principle to any race-based legal distinctions.[153] Although the Court did not adopt "strict scrutiny" for equal protection challenges to gender-based legal classifications, over time (in cases brought by Ginsburg), the Court articulated an "intermediate scrutiny" requiring an important government purpose to justify such gender classifications, and the Supreme Court invalidated government programs benefiting women and not men.[154] After Ginsburg became a court of appeals judge, the Supreme Court rejected single-sex education in nursing, a traditional women's field.[155] Finally, after Justice Ginsburg joined the Supreme Court, the Court rejected a male-only admissions policy at a state military academy. Justice Ginsburg's opinion for the court in *United States v. Virginia* (VMI—the case involving Virginia Military Institute [the Institute]) the Institute articulated an even more searching level of judicial scrutiny demanding "exceedingly persuasive" justifications of gender-based classifications.[156]

Only one federal court challenge to a male-only public high school has reached the Supreme Court, and it arose before these later developments. The justices could not come together with a majority view, so the issue remains unsettled. That case, *Vorchheimer v. School District of Philadelphia*, involved an elite college preparatory public high school that was restricted to boys.[157] Central High School in Philadelphia, founded in 1836, used high admissions standards, and its graduates included distinguished professionals, businessmen, academics, and government leaders. The separate, neighboring Philadelphia High School for Girls ("Girls' High") began as a training school for teachers; it evolved into a college preparatory school but lacked the endowment, science labs, and distinguished history of Central High. The very contrast between the names Central High and Philadelphia High School for Girls signaled a historic ordering, elevating the boys' opportunities over the girls.'

Susan Vorchheimer, the plaintiff, indicated that she preferred Central High and believed it held its students to a higher standard than did Girls' High.[158] The district court in 1975 identified disparities in resources, academic offerings, and prestige between the two schools. Although it concluded that the education at the two schools was "comparable," it acknowledged the lack of a coeducational option for students seeking an academically rigorous public school program and hence agreed with the plaintiff's challenge to the exclusion of girls from Central High.[159]

The appellate court reversed and essentially approved a "separate-but-equal" approach, permitting the exclusion of girls from Central High School. A majority on the court found a 1974 amendment to the Elementary and Secondary Education Act of 1965 equivocal on the subject of single-sex admissions because it rejected student assignment solely on the basis of sex[160] yet left out "sex" in its ban on segregation in schools by race, color, or national origin.[161] The appellate panel also concluded that because of potentially real differences between the sexes, government policies could pursue differential treatment, including single-sex instruction, which it deemed to be a traditional and respected educational strategy. Given the availability of similarly excellent single-sex educational opportunities for boys (at Central High) and for girls (at Girls' High),[162] the court of appeals rejected Vorchheimer's challenge to the exclusion of girls from Central High. A dissenting judge objected that the court's decision established "a twentieth-century sexual equivalent to the *Plessy* decision" by approval of a separate-but-equal interpretation of the Fourteenth Amendment's equal protection clause and that it misconstrued

Congress's language, rejecting student assignments on the basis of sex.[163] The dissent also questioned the majority's treatment of sex segregation at the two elite public schools as voluntary, given that the public system in the city lacked any option of an academically excellent but also coeducational high school.

Vorchheimer pursued the case to the Supreme Court in 1977. There her claim received support from a brief prepared by Ruth Bader Ginsburg and her ACLU project on gender equality, which had not participated in the prior stages of the suit.[164] Before the Court, Vorchheimer's lawyers challenged the "separate-but-equal" approach on the grounds that "[i]n the context of the subordinate place so long assigned to women in society, no school 'sister' to Central can supply an educational experience genuinely equal in character, quality, and effectiveness."[165] The petition reflected work by sociologists Christopher Jencks and David Riesman suggesting that single-sex schools in a male-dominated society carried messages associated with the traditional gender hierarchy. After argument, the justices split four to four, producing no decision and leaving in place the appellate decision affirming the single-sex policy.

After that result, the Court faced further litigation challenging gender distinctions in other contexts and began to articulate a more searching inquiry into the reasons for official distinctions between males and females. Meanwhile, in the shadow of the Court's 1982 decision rejecting the exclusion of men from a state nursing college,[166] three plaintiffs brought a challenge in Pennsylvania state court to the single-sex admissions policy of Central High School in Philadelphia in 1984. The state court found Girls' High and Central High unequal in light of evidence of striking inequalities in the range of subjects available for instruction, qualifications of teachers, and campus size and resources. Interpreting both the federal and the state constitutions, the state court also found that the single-sex instruction served no important government objective and directed that Central High become coeducational.[167] Intense debates emerged within the school board over whether to appeal the decision halting single-sex admission at Central High. Ultimately, the board decided not to appeal, by a vote of five to three.[168]

If Central High could not exclude girls, it would seem logical that Girls' High could not exclude boys. But symmetry neither dictated the result nor commanded popular appeal; people seem to have the view that symmetrical treatment of historic boys' and historic girls' schools does not remedy sex-based educational disadvantages. At least in the short term, argued advocates and school administrators, boys-only institutions should become coed, but girls-only institutions should be retained so that girls can gain special attention and support. As the challenge to Central High unfolded, alumnae, teachers, and students of Girls' High organized to defend the school as a place that empowered girls. With little apparent interest on the part of boys in going to Girls' High, it has retained its de facto single-sex admissions policy and its related mission of advancing women's success.[169] In 1992, the federal Department of Education investigated Girls' High and found no violation, because boys could apply for admission even though none apparently did.[170]

Nationwide, the federal court of appeals decision in *Vorchheimer* allowing single-sex education in public high schools remains the last judicial word on the subject.[171] As of 2010, that decision still permits public single-sex education in the United States if the options for each sex are similar.[172] Yet the issue remains controverted and the result unstable, perhaps due to instances linking race and sex.

In the wake of *Vorchheimer*, but also clearly affected by the intersection with race, a federal district court in 1991 issued a preliminary injunction halting efforts to create three Afrocentric, all-male academies in Detroit for at-risk students.[173] This action stopped an experiment that was under way not only in Detroit but in Milwaukee and other cities that were trying to address a widely perceived crisis of school failure for urban black boys. Inspiration for these initiatives had come in part from sociologist Spencer Holland, who argued that male role models and discipline could engage inner-city minority boys in education in ways that female teachers could not; he urged schools to address issues of low self-esteem and alienation among boys who often had no adult men in their lives.[174] With more than half of African-American males dropping out of high school, the majority of male students in the city's high schools failing academically, and 60 percent of drug offenses in one Michigan county attributable to school dropouts, drastic measures seemed worth considering.[175] Detroit's City Council and Board of Education investigated the context in which 80 percent of the males in Michigan's criminal justice population had attended the Detroit public schools and black men in Detroit were dying at almost fifteen times the national average for all men in the country.[176] Led by a school board task force, Detroit's public school system planned to offer 560 seats in specially designed all-male academies; twelve hundred applied.[177] As designed, the academies would restrict enrollment to boys and were aimed at black boys specifically; they were to offer not only male role models but also African-American teachers, a curriculum directed at African-American experiences, and rites of passage from boyhood to manhood, counseling, and career development.[178]

With 90 percent of the public school students in Detroit being African American, this racial and ethnic focus did not seem exclusionary and instead reflected the racial realities of the city. Yet however abominable the situation of black boys in Detroit appeared, the situation of black girls was also poor, and all-male academies would do nothing to address the lack of good opportunities for impoverished African-American girls in the city. Hence, all-male academics drew the attention and ire of national women's rights groups. The combination of race and gender in the all-male academies evoked further controversy and national debate over when, if ever, racial as well as gender segregation is justified in schools.[179] Still, the school initiatives received considerable local support. Even local organizations that were initially opposed decided to withdraw before the lawsuit proceeded. As a result, the challenge to the academies was framed by white-led national women's rights groups, revealing and producing real tensions over national versus local attitudes. Led by the National Organization for Women's Legal Defense Fund, national opposition to the schools focused on gender equality, while local debates focused on racial and economic disadvantage that seemed to require a drastic remedy.[180]

The district court predicted that the initiative for boys would violate the federal and state constitutions as well as federal and state statutes and regulations. The court emphasized the school district's failure to develop comparable alternatives for girls, as well as the lack of evidence to show the need to depart from coeducational settings.[181] After the court halted the boys-only admissions policy with a preliminary injunction, the Detroit school board settled the case before trial on the merits, of reserving spaces in the schools for girls. The district court and the Detroit school board all assumed that a final decision and appellate review would reject the all-male schools.[182] A similar result emerged for African-American schools planned at the same time in Milwaukee.[183] In these instances, the combination of gender, race, and class defied simple answers about what equality in education entails.

During the 1980s and 1990s, public school districts increasingly admitted girls into all-boys schools where no comparable opportunities existed in all-girls schools. But public systems also preserved existing all-girls schools and promoted the creation of new all-girls schools through a combination of community traditions, use of informal policies, and "success in warding off the handful of boys who express[ed] interest."[184] This asymmetrical approach, allowing all-girls schools but disallowing all-boys schools, continued as a kind of a temporary remedial response to local and national histories of male preferences and benefits in public education.[185] That is how many people, and especially many feminists, rationalized the coincidence of two notable developments affecting single-sex education in the summer of 1996: the Supreme Court rejected the exclusion of females from the Virginia Military Institute (the Institute) just as New York City announced plans to create an academically rigorous all-girls public high school for low-income families in East Harlem.[186]

By then, President Bill Clinton had appointed Ruth Bader Ginsburg to serve as an associate justice of the Supreme Court. Clinton compared Ginsburg's role in the women's rights movement to the role of Thurgood Marshall in the struggle for civil rights for African Americans.[187] The invalidation of the male-only admission policy at the Institute marked Justice Ginsburg's apotheosis, perhaps even more than her appointment to the Court. Bearing more symbolic than practical significance to the development of gender equality,[188] the decision in *the Institute* rejected exclusion of women by a school that defined masculinity often in terms of male superiority and female inferiority.[189] Ginsburg herself commented about the decision: "To me, it was winning the *Vorchheimer* case twenty years later."[190]

Her opinion for the Court assessed a separate women-only institution that had been created by the Commonwealth of Virginia in the face of the lawsuit challenging the exclusion of women from the historic Institute, much as the Supreme Court assessed separate black-only institutions hurriedly created in the face of pre-*Brown* challenges to white-only institutions of higher education in the 1930s and 1940s. As a lawyer, Ginsburg had worked to establish sex-based distinctions as worthy of the same judicial vigilance as race-based distinctions, and she achieved partial success in cases calling for "intermediate scrutiny," although not strict scrutiny, of sex-based classifications by government. Something closer to "strict scrutiny" emerged in her opinion for the Court in *the Institute*.[191] The Court reasoned that Virginia failed to show an "exceedingly persuasive justification" for the exclusion of women, nor could it satisfy a "separate-but-equal" approach with the hastily developed alternative women's program. The Court concluded that this program, the Virginia Women's Institute for Leadership, launched during the litigation with state assistance at a small private liberal arts college near the Institute, would not offer the same rigorous military training, faculty, courses, facilities, financial opportunities, reputation, and connections with distinguished alumni that the Institute provided its male students; indeed, the alternative for women did not even try to offer key elements of the Institute program.[192] Hence, the exclusion of women from the Institute failed to meet requirements of the equal protection clause.[193] The state failed to offer an equal opportunity for women. The effects of past discrimination and the risk of future discrimination persisted with Virginia's defective gender-based policy.

But the decision did not resolve whether the "separate-but-equal" approach remains a lawful option for satisfying equal protection review of gender classifications in public schooling. Because Virginia offered a patently inferior alternative to the women excluded from the Institute, the Court did not need to resolve whether single-sex education could ever be equal.[194] In his separate concurrence, Chief Justice William Rehnquist defended the possibility of separate single-sex schools, noting that it was "not the 'exclusion of women' that violated the Equal Protection Clause, but the maintenance of an all men school without providing any—much less a comparable—institution for women."[195] Indeed, one commentator contrasted the petition to the Supreme Court that Ginsberg contributed to in *Vorchheimer* with the opinion she crafted as a justice in *the Institute*: "Unlike her position two decades earlier in *Vorchheimer*, in *the Institute*, Justice Ginsburg seems intellectually open to the possibility that a public single-sex school can pass constitutional muster. Indeed, conspicuously absent from the Court's *the Institute* opinion is *any* reference to *Brown*."[196] Instead, the Court explicitly contrasted Virginia's defective approach with single-sex schools that "dissipate, rather than perpetuate, traditional gender classifications."[197] And the Court in *the Institute* noted that "[s]ingle-sex education affords pedagogical benefits to at least some students…and that reality is uncontested in this litigation."[198] Nina Pillard, who as assistant to the U.S. solicitor general drafted the Supreme Court briefs for the United States in the case, later concluded, "[b]y requiring that any educational institution designed separately for women and men be equal in every material respect, *the Institute* also assures that single-sex education will not be used as a ruse for inequality, or as a training ground in separate, different, and unequal gender roles."[199]

Even as the Court was debating *the Institute*, plans for what became the Young Women's Leadership School in Harlem unfolded, but they reflected a very different point of origin than either the male-only the Institute or the Virginia Women's Institute for Leadership alternative. The Harlem initiative was a dream hatched after a national correspondent for NBC news, Ann Rubenstein, interviewed a teen-aged mother at the day-care center for teen parents in a Milwaukee high school in 1985 and asked where she imagined herself five years later. When the girl started weeping silently, Rubenstein realized that

> "[s]he knew she was doomed. . . . She knew she was locked in a cycle that happens when a teenager has a baby, particularly an underprivileged teenager. She knew, and I knew. That had a profound impact on me. I knew based on that moment that we were not doing enough. The day-care center wasn't enough. We had to get these young women on a different path."[200]

Rubenstein had the idea of launching a public high school that would engage at-risk girls and open up college and better futures as an option for them. After Rubenstein married into the wealthy New York Tisch family, she and her husband devoted money, social networks, and media access to create the Young Women's Leadership School of East Harlem, which not only succeeded in its own terms but became a model for other urban school systems and a spur to philanthropic and public investment in all-girls schools. Ann Rubenstein Tisch sought legal advice from Rosemary Salomone, law professor and advocate of single-sex education. Salomone suggested a remedial approach predicated in part on a 1994 report by the New York City Department of Education that showed girls, and especially African-American and Hispanic girls, performing worse than boys in math and science.[201] Mirroring the effort in Detroit and Milwaukee to use single-sex education to create a special learning environment with high aspirations for impoverished students of color, the Young Women's Leadership School nonetheless departed from the halted Detroit all-male academies precisely by focusing on girls, not boys—and also by proceeding with the backing of well-placed, well-financed white leadership. Implying an asymmetrical approach—single-sex schooling for girls but not for boys—the initiative appealed to many white liberal civil rights advocates, even though judges could find it difficult to justify all-girls but not all-boys schools if faced with a court challenge.

In an effort to avoid perceptions that it is exclusive or selective, the Young Women's Leadership School's recruitment materials emphasize that it is not designed for or restricted to gifted students.[202] As a public school, it also receives financial and programmatic assistance from a private foundation headed by Ann Rubenstein Tisch, which has effectively lobbied for federal and local aid for similar schools elsewhere.[203] After ten years of experience, the Young Women's Leadership School of East Harlem could report 100 percent attendance, compared with 60 percent citywide, and 100 percent college admission for its graduating students.[204] The National Association of Secondary High School Principals named the school one of the ten National Breakthrough High Schools of 2005.[205]

However, at the time of its founding in 1996 (three months after the ruling in *the Institute*), the school triggered significant controversy and splintered civil rights groups.[206] Salomone has commented about this period:

> Some [women's rights advocates] who had passionately denounced all-male admissions at state military academies...were suddenly rallying to support public single-sex schools for inner-city girls in the name of affirmative action. Others, despite their avid support for [single-sex education], were condemning [such schools] with equal resolve.[207]

Given its origin and location, the school's development revived debates over how best to advance opportunity for poor students of color and over when single-sex education would be compatible with federal and state equality norms. Its founders emphasized that their goal was to offer low-income minority students an educational option similar to elite private and parochial all-girls schools. Nonetheless, the New York Civil Liberties Union, the National Organization for Women, and the New York Civil Rights Coalition challenged the use of gender as an admissions criterion, and the U.S. Department of Education's Office for Civil Rights indicated informally that it was reaching a preliminary finding that the school's policy appeared to contravene Title IX.[208] This was in keeping with the judicial rejection of the all-male academies in Detroit five years earlier.

With challengers representing key constituencies of the Democratic administration in Washington, members of the Clinton administration met with civil rights groups who opposed the new single-sex initiative. The administration postponed and temporized, torn between the competing arguments over gender neutrality and enhancing opportunities for low-income girls of color.[209] Staff members in the Clinton administration may also have been mindful of First Lady Hillary Clinton's own positive experiences at Wellesley College, or perhaps some just hoped to wait out the clock without taking a position on the issue. Despite the importuning by the civil rights groups, no boy seeking admission to the East Harlem school could be found, and no lawsuit ensued.[210] Eventually, the federal Department of Education's Office for Civil Rights switched direction and indicated that the school might be viewed as an affirmative action remedy and hence advancing rather than violating Title IX.[211]

The 1990s thus marked a time of transition as educators, feminists, and government officials considered single-sex education. Salomone, while advising local and federal single-sex initiatives,[212] wrote a leading book on the subject: she contrasted the historic feminist struggle to open up all-male educational institutions with emerging conceptions of single-sex education as the remedy for unequal education.[213] She pointed out that ideals of feminist empowerment had combined with traditional ideas of elite schools for girls to support initiatives such as the Young Women's Leadership School, while white feminist battles against exclusive male schools and perhaps national discomfort with an Afrocentric focus contributed to the halting of the all-male academies meant to assist African-American boys in Detroit.[214] Yet it seems a bit arbitrary to conceive of the East Harlem all-girls school initiative as remedying the effects of past disadvantages and exclusions when its rationale echoed that of the all-male academies in Detroit. Each sought to address apparent cycles of failure for impoverished urban children of color; each sought to mimic elite institutions that had used a sense of mission and a single-sex format to elevate student aspiration and achievement.

Nonetheless, while concerns about low-income children of color animated the creation of the Young Women's Leadership School, its founders tapped into broader claims of risks to girls across racial and class groups, documented in studies starting in the 1970s and continuing into the 1990s.[215] Studies indicated gender bias in the way teachers treated students: teachers waited longer for boys than girls to answer questions and on average gave more attention to boys compared with their treatment of girls.[216] In addition, studies suggested that girls feel inhibited when in the presence of boys; evidence also showed that girls in coeducational schools face sexual harassment from boys.[217] The context of such reports of gender bias across racial and class differences proved favorable to defending single-sex education for girls under a kind of affirmative action rationale. At the same time, the persistence of all-girls private schools affected discussions about public schools. If all-girls schools would be desirable for those able to select private schools, then they would be desirable as an option in public schools. The setting of the all-girls school would provide a supportive environment for enhancing girls' achievements; an ethos of belief in their capacities; freedom from the potential harassment, putdowns, or distractions of being in classes with boys; and a sense of special mission. The development of the Young Women's Leadership School matched the asymmetrical approach to single-sex education already epitomized by the coeducational Central High School and Philadelphia High School for Girls. The rationale predicated on remedying gender discrimination would leave all-male schools impermissible.[218]

By the end of the 1990s, further complicating treatment of gender in schools, some scholars and popular writers reported research indicating that under at least some circumstances, boys faced greater educational disadvantages than girls.[219] Boys faced more school disciplinary measures, high levels of truancy and expulsion, lower academic performance, higher dropout rates, and lower college attendance than girls—and seemed less likely to ask questions if girls were around.[220] A decade after the failed initiative to create all-boys academies in Detroit and Milwaukee, increasing numbers of social scientists, educators, and parents identified concerns about boys failing in school. Authors of popular books argued that schools are organized for girls in terms of the emphasis on "good behavior" and in the benchmarks for cognitive and social development, with girls developing earlier than boys.[221] Boys lagged behind girls in many standardized test results[222] and other indicators.[223]

As part of his push for standards in K–12 education, President George W. Bush included statutory language permitting the use of federal funds in "same-gender schools and classrooms (consistent with federal law)."[224] By including the proviso "consistent with federal law," this statute avoided taking a stand on the unresolved status of all-boys schools. The federal court rejection of the Detroit academies plus the Supreme Court's rejection of the Institute's male-only admissions policy put a burden on states wishing to use single-sex public schools or classrooms, even with the *Vorchheimer* precedent still standing. Especially unclear was whether a program offered to students of one sex had to be accompanied by a "comparable" program offered to students of the other sex. In any case, the Bush administration and Congress made clear an intention to signal federal encouragement of and potential financial support for school systems seeking to explore single-sex classrooms or schools. The administration and Congress also thereby opened the possibility of changing the existing Title IX regulations that generally prohibited single-sex programs with limited exceptions.

In 2002, the Department of Education took a further step by announcing its intention to expand the room for single-sex instruction in programs receiving federal funding.[225] Whatever the ambivalence in the Clinton administration, this initiative received bipartisan support, including endorsements by senators Hillary Rodham Clinton and Kay Bailey Hutchinson.[226] In presenting its proposed rule in 2004, the Department of Education pointed to evolving equitable treatment for girls as a reason for granting more flexibility around single-sex education.[227] The Department issued a rule announcing new flexibility: allowing more room for single-sex instruction and schools in order to increase the diversity of educational options and to meet the needs of specific students.[228]

The government had been signaling since 2001 its encouragement of single-sex schools before issuing a final rule that could be challenged in court.[229] Proposing a rule and leaving it in that proposed state may reflect a political strategy. The administration gains points from supporters for pursuing the policy, avoids court challenge to it, and generates potential support from both experimentation and research efforts that could bolster the policy if and when it does reach a final rule and subsequent court challenge. The delay also allowed the facts on the ground to change, as the number of single-sex schools grew—with the green light offered by the proposed rule itself.

In October 2006, the Department of Education announced a final rule that became effective on November 24, 2006, and permitted instruction in single-sex classrooms and schools.[230] This rule clarified that these single-sex options had to be entirely voluntary and that evaluation of substantially equal opportunities for boys and girls should include intangible features and reputation of faculty.[231] The Department acknowledged comments raising potential constitutional challenges to the rule and explained that no Supreme Court decision had invalidated elementary or secondary single-sex education and that concerned school systems should consult legal counsel.[232] The Department also emphasized its evenhanded approach,[233] even while it authorized schools to offer single-sex classes to students of one sex only if they could show lack of interest or special needs among students of the excluded sex.[234] Similarly, the Department made clear that provision of a single-sex school would not require provision of a corresponding single-sex school to the excluded group.[235] Instead, consistent with No Child Left Behind's Innovative State Grants Program and structured on the language of the intermediate scrutiny standard, the Department encouraged recipients of federal money "to make an individualized decision about whether single-sex educational opportunities will achieve [an] important objective and whether the single-sex nature of those opportunities is substantially related to the [objective's] achievement."[236]

The *New York Times* reported that observers characterized the rule as "the most significant policy change on the issue [in] more than 30 years."[237] Instead of forbidding single-sex instruction with public dollars other than in exceptional circumstances, the federal government would permit such instruction to increase diversity of educational options and to meet specific needs of students.[238] The school system would no longer have to provide a similar option for members of the other gender.[239] The Department rejected objections that single-sex instruction would reinforce negative stereotypes.[240] With the focus on improving educational outcomes, justifiable diversity should apply to the types of educational options, not merely to the characteristics of the members of a particular class.[241]

The release of the final regulations has generated diverse reactions. Paul Vallas, chief executive officer for the Philadelphia school district, shared Leonard Sax's contention that the regulations' release would produce growth, stating, "You're going to see a proliferation of these [single-sex schools]....There's a lot of support for this type of school model in Philadelphia."[242] Many civil rights groups, meanwhile, argue that the regulations violate both Title IX and the equal protection clause.[243] Coupled with unanswered constitutional considerations, the recent Title IX regulations have already been targeted for litigation challenge.[244] On May 19, 2008, the ACLU Women's Rights Project challenged the sex-segregated classroom practices of the Breckinridge County Middle School, a public school in Kentucky.[245] The suit couples arguments about defects in the regulatory procedure and violation of the federal antidiscrimination statute[246] with allegations that the regulations violate equal protection by allowing intentional sex discrimination without demonstrating—as the *the Institute* Court required—an exceedingly persuasive justification or substantial relationship with an important state interest.[247]

Social Science about Gender: Problematic Knowledge

The reliability of social science evidence as a justification for public school separations of students by gender has begun to receive more stringent judicial review. Echoing the NAACP's reliance on social science evidence in litigating *Brown*, advocates and opponents of single-sex education cite research, and each side has been able to find research to support their views.[248] While it is tempting to imagine that social science research provides answers about equality and education, most notable is the inconclusiveness of empirical research about schools and gender.[249] Social science findings about girls and boys are ambiguous and complex. Even studies seeking to summarize the studies are inconclusive.[250] Indeed, advocates on each side can and do rely on the empirical uncertainty to support their own side of the single-sex education debate, given the absence of reliable evidence that such revival of gender classification will work better or worse than coeducation.[251] Lawyers and policy-makers also may exaggerate or mischaracterize findings, as in the brief using research on all-girls schools to justify all-boys schools[252] and advocates' tendency to use data on colleges and universities to address issues in elementary and secondary education.[253]

The reliability of empirical findings is itself weakened by selection bias in studies based on parochial and other private schools and failure to account for differences in parental involvement and socioeconomic status.[254] Reliance on parochial school data is understandable; the most numerous and long-established single-sex schools are Catholic institutions. Yet the self-selection of the families in those schools renders generalizations about the result problematic, and even these results give rise to scholarly disputes. For example, one study by Valerie Lee and Anthony Bryk and another by Cornelius Riordan used the same data on 1,807 students in a Catholic single-sex high school; both found that the academic achievement of boys and girls improved in these settings.[255] But Riordan concluded that the improvement was greatest among girls and minority boys and that the critical factor explaining the higher test scores was not that the schools in question were single-sex but that they had a rigorous academic orientation.[256] Then, another researcher reanalyzed the same data along with a new data set and found no differences in academic achievement between the coeducational and single-sex settings. This latter study took into account factors of school selectivity and socioeconomic status.[257] Another two researchers reanalyzed and overturned their own initial findings of benefits in single-sex settings.[258] Different findings can result from treating the schools under study as the same when in fact they differ in terms of the quality of teacher-student relationships and in resources, as another study found.[259]

There are further defects in the reliability of research on single-sex education, especially as used in policy debates. Many studies emphasized by advocates of single-sex education come from other countries, which makes extending the findings to the United States complicated.[260] The claims that single-sex education empowers girls and that single-sex instruction reinforces gender stereotypes do not easily lend themselves to rigorous empirical assessment.[261] And the attitudes and cultural presuppositions held by the researchers are difficult to disentangle from the questions they ask and their interpretations of findings.[262] Historical context and the goals of the stakeholders affect findings as well.[263] One does not have to believe charges that a political backlash against the women's movement underlies research asserting a crisis of education for boys[264] to conclude that political context and funding sources also infiltrate research questions and results.[265]

When the focus is on student achievement, research results can convey a mixed picture. All-male environments may actually hinder the achievement of white boys but improve the achievement of black and Hispanic boys.[266] Single-sex programs for racial minority boys can represent a new infusion of resources, better teachers, or a clearer mission than what such boys may otherwise encounter, but it is possible that the same elements could work without requiring a school to be single-sex. Existing studies are not fine-grained enough to tell. Stephanie Monroe, the assistant secretary for civil rights at the Department of Education presiding over the federal policy shift, has acknowledged the inconclusive state of social science findings while trying to put a positive spin on single-sex education: "Educational research, though it's ongoing and shows some mixed results, does suggest that single-sex education can provide some benefits to some students under certain circumstances."[267] The level of scrutiny required by courts in addressing challenges to single-sex schooling could make the quality of the evidence pivotal to the legality of these schools. If courts were to apply searching scrutiny to the use of gender classifications in creating single-sex classrooms or schools, neither generalizations nor ambiguous social scientific results would likely be sufficient to sustain the distinctions against equal protection challenge.[268]

Most notably, gender gaps running in either direction do not approach the divide in school performance between economically advantaged and disadvantaged students.[269] This fact explains some of the interest in single-sex education as a strategy for improving opportunities for poor students of color, as they tend to be among the most disadvantaged students, yet the special educational needs of this population swamp assessments of the single-sex dimension of reforms targeted to this group. Perhaps the gender framework allows for coalitions beyond the usual advocates for poor children of color, and the focus on sex differences elicits funding and attention by researchers, reformers, and policy-makers.

The most recent direction in empirical research revives old radioactive issues of inherent gender differences. At the turn of this new century, the spread of neuroscience and the easy availability of brain scans for social science research has fueled new work analyzing differences between the brains and bodies of boys and girls. Books aimed for popular audiences claim to build on the new neuro-science research while leaping beyond the findings to claim justification for separate classrooms and schools.[270] Marketed to mass audiences, books for parents and teachers have reported biological differences in how boys and girls process information—even differences in the optimal classroom temperature for boys versus girls.[271] This kind of work is described by critics as a revival of ideas about biological gender differences already debunked by science.[272] When Lawrence Summers made a remark entertaining the possibility of real gender-based differences, he triggered a firestorm that precipitated pressures to remove him from his post as president of Harvard University.[273] Debates over cultural and biological bases for gender differences persist.[274] The biology-based research proffered to justify single-sex education is especially galling to feminists who have long attacked biology-based claims of gender difference in the process of challenging assumptions of women's inferiority, vulnerability, or essential difference from men. Feminists have advocated single-sex schools by arguing that sexist social attitudes harm girls. Because many of those attitudes depended on claims of natural differences, arguments about biological difference risk reanimating ideas about inevitable constraints on girls—and on boys. Salomone, well known as a supporter of single-sex education, nonetheless told a reporter: "As one of the people who let the horse out of the barn, I'm now feeling like I really need to watch that horse.... Every time I hear of school officials selling single-sex programs to parents based on brain research, my heart sinks."[275]

The revival of outmoded gender stereotypes by new single-sex educational initiatives is not a mere flight of the imagination.[276] A Louisiana middle school proposed single-sex classes based on stereotypic views of boys as hunters and girls as mothers, but the ACLU's threat of suit halted the plan.[277] Reviving older gender stereotypes may be especially risky with all-boys schools. One study of single-sex academies in the 1990s in California found that they perpetuated traditional gender stereotypes and reinforced "macho" cultural attitudes.[278] Even all-girls schools, however strong the educational experience, may appear to outsiders to confirm gender stereotypes.[279] Gary Simpson, professor at Cornell Law School, expressed this skepticism about the revival of single-sex instruction:

> In a society in which gender stereotyping is hardly a thing of the past, do coordinate single-sex schools send a message that girls and boys are best kept separate because girls cannot compete effectively with boys? Even if the all-girls school is no less rigorous and competitive than the all-boys school, will the girls' accomplishments at their school be undervalued by college admissions officers, employers and others because of preconceived notions about all-girls schools, as compared to all-boys schools?[280]

However much single-sex schools feed gender stereotypes, the problem of gender stereotypes also persists in coeducational settings. One review of empirical evidence identifies sexism in both coeducational and single-sex classes.[281] This kind of finding indicates that sexist societal attitudes put girls' equal educational opportunities at risk and require alteration in either kind of setting. Opponents of single-sex education contend that its very existence not only exacerbates stereotypes but also alleviates the burden on coeducational schools to promote gender equality in all classrooms,[282] just as heralding majority-minority schools as places where blacks and Hispanics can succeed could lessen the obligation of other schools to ensure the success of students of color.[283] Indeed, even many who worry about unequal opportunities for girls oppose expansion of single-sex education. Education professor David Sadker published *Failing at Fairness: How Our Schools Cheat Girls* in 1995 but in 2004 objected to the federal Department of Education's proposal to expand single-sex education as a "perverse anniversary of the *Brown* decision.... Here, 50 years after *Brown*, we're actually codifying segregation. The problem is fixing the coed[ucational] classroom, not escaping from it."[284] A focus on social attitudes constraining gender roles supports single-sex education not by pointing to inevitable inherent differences between boys and girls but by seeking to revise attitudes held by teachers, by parents, and by the children themselves that artificially limit children's efforts, learning, and behavior. In this spirit, a letter to the *New York Times* pointed out that single-sex schools allow girls to "become noisy instigators, impish troublemakers, charismatic school-wide leaders—niches that disproportionately may fall to boys in coed[ucational] schools."[285]

Making Sense of the Revival of Single-sex Education

The legacy of *Brown* hovers in debates over single-sex education, with equal opportunity asserted both by those defending and those opposing such instruction. Legal challenges to single-sex education at the postsecondary level may bear more symbolic than practical significance to the development of gender equality;[286] yet the related debates over gender and public compulsory education affect thousands of students directly and millions more in terms of attitudes and aspirations. Litigation addressing these issues in the context of athletics is emblematic of the competing meaning of equal educational opportunity for girls. Schools that fail to offer a girls' team in a given sport must allow girls to try out for the boys' team, with the exception of contact sports. With separate girls' and boys' teams allowed, courts also accept exclusion of boys from girls' teams in order to preserve opportunities for girls.[287]

The Department of Education's revised Title IX regulation, which provides greater flexibility to recipients to establish single-sex classrooms and schools, followed an intense debate over single-sex education. The agency's rule-making process both reflected and spurred the creation of an increasing number of single-sex educational options. Reportedly, public single-sex schools increased from a handful in 1995 to perhaps hundreds in 2007.[288] In addition, many public schools have introduced single-sex classrooms, generating at least 445 of them nationwide.[289]

Although it may help some students, single-sex education seems only acceptable when pursued on a voluntary basis; otherwise, it is too redolent of historic practices of exclusion.[290] Offered as one of many school choices, single-sex instruction seems difficult to oppose; even doubt about empirical benefits from single-sex education can warrant experimentation,[291] and the rhetoric of individual choice is the solvent of many confusing and divisive issues in America. The availability of school choice relieves school systems from having to make a definitive judgment about single-sex education for all students, and at the same time presses for inclusion of at least some single-sex schools, to afford parents and students the option.[292] Some commentators elide the difference between the education value of diverse student bodies with the potential benefit from having a variety of school options from which to choose.[293] This just goes to show that "diversity" has a positive ring in American education, especially when combined with individual choice. Whether in coeducational or single-sex settings, the watchwords for girls' education are equal opportunity and choice. Yet issues raised by single-sex education, like the danger of exacerbating sexual stereotypes, occur not just for individual students but also at the societal level. To many advocates for gender equality, single-sex education may have seemed for a time less justifiable for boys, given the historically higher status and greater resources devoted to educational opportunities for boys and not girls. At the same time, advocates have often supported girls-only education as a vehicle for empowerment and pride. Ginsburg's struggle to overcome legal distinctions drawn on gender made headway but achieved more success in elevating the commitment to equal opportunity than in demanding gender neutrality. This is especially apparent in the survival and resurgence of single-sex education.

The intersection between gender and other social markers profoundly affects the educational debates. Single-sex education initiatives aimed at inadequate educational options for poor students of color have faltered for boys but have succeeded for girls. Nowhere did the idea of single-sex options have more legs than as an avenue out of failing schools for poor children of color. For advocates and policy-makers after 1954, *Brown* supplied a template for addressing gender and education: identifying equality as the measure of schooling; casting doubt on whether "separate" could ever be "equal," and pressing for integration, here known as coeducation. But in a vivid glimpse of shifting views, the online community behind Wikipedia in 2008 prefaced the entry on "coeducation" with an invitation to debate whether "this article or section [should] be merged with *single-sex education*."[294] The term "coed" remains in use to refer to a female student, demonstrating the continuing view of the female student as different and as the carrier of gender integration in schooling. The racial frame from *Brown* risks distorting concerns about gender that persist for students, communities, and the law. A central goal behind *Brown* was to eliminate the idea that race signified any inherent difference between people, but gender continues to be viewed as a marker of real and natural difference between human beings, and one that easily falls into two distinct categories.[295] Courts, schools, and communities continue to emphasize gender differences, whether to celebrate them or account for them in other ways. Many who support opening boys' schools to girls suggest that the asymmetrical treatment of separate schooling for girls can be justified for purposes of pride, remedying past disadvantage, and preparation for a still-discriminatory larger world. These suggestions mirror discussions about the value of Afrocentric schools or schools devoted to children of color.

A focus on gender, especially in the context of debates over single-sex education, risks obscuring the continuing significance of race. When the National Organization for Women's Legal Defense Fund successfully challenged the proposal for all-male academies in Detroit, Michigan, the theory of gender equality halted an initiative to address a widely perceived racial crisis: the school failure, dropout patterns, and criminal justice involvement of African-American males. And when the Young Women's Leadership School took off as a successful initiative in East Harlem, New York, it inspired the creation of similar schools elsewhere and supplied support for new federal governmental incentives for single-sex education. The all-girls format advantageously resonated with the success of elite girls' and women's colleges and secured the support of upper-class whites who were hoping to improve the opportunities for poor students of color but with no particular goal of racial or class integration in the elite schools themselves. Yet, at the same time, rightful concern about woefully inadequate educational opportunities for poor children of color could retain unreflective uses of old gender stereotypes while producing different opportunities for girls than for boy.[296]

Given uncertainty about the relevant constitutional standard and inconclusiveness and unreliability in the empirical assessments, the motivation and resources believers plowed into single-sex education have built a hospitable statutory and regulatory framework (pending judicial review) and provided real resources to build more single-sex options. Consider the reaction when a state legislative initiative established twelve single-sex public schools to address the needs of low-income and minority students and gave districts $500,000 to operate the academies.[297] One principal in the state acknowledged: "Why do I go for the single-gender [schools]? . . . It's a great opportunity. It's also money. I can do something."[298]

Perhaps such initiatives will generate better, more reliable empirical evidence. Studies of single-sex schools may even identify factors like teacher-student relations to benefit coeducational settings as well. With the apparent flowering of public single-sex schools, clarifying the criteria for evaluation should become a greater priority. Will and should these schools be assessed primarily in terms of graduation rates, achievement on standardized tests, and college admission rates—or also on attitudes toward members of the other sex and durability of gender stereotypes, racial integration, students' capacities to take the perspective of another, character development and community service and civic engagement? Although current social science research may not be equipped to answer this question, these schools should also be assessed in terms of their impact on civic equality—the perceptions and treatment of individuals as equal participants in local, state, and national governance regardless of gender, race, class, or other group identities, including disability, sexual orientation, religion, and economic class.

Making Waves

Schooling and Disability, Sexual Orientation,
Religion, and Economic Class

> *You gotta understand our differences are the same.*
> —Lupe Fiasco

The historic treatment of students with disabilities in many ways resembles racial segregation in schools. *Brown's* influence in this field is clear but complicated. Also complicated are debates over equal treatment of students who identify as gay, lesbian, bisexual, or transgendered. Religious students—and religious schools—elicit further variations on the educational equality debate with consequences for social integration and intergroup relations.

Disability

Compulsory education laws in the United States for many years exempted students with mental and physical disabilities, and many school systems excluded such students or assigned them to separate institutions well into the 1970s.[1] Before *Brown*, court challenges to this treatment of students with disabilities failed either on the assumption that the child's impairments made schooling inappropriate or that the presence of the child with disabilities would harm the best interests of other children and the school.[2] Even schools set up for students with disabilities could exclude a student by asserting that the child's limitations would prevent educational progress.[3] During the 1920s, communities established separate schools for students who were blind, deaf, or severely retarded,[4] and many schools established separate classrooms for students who were considered to be slow learners.[5] Misclassifications assigning students to separate classrooms or schools was not uncommon, and especially affected students who were immigrants or members of minority groups.[6] This process of segregating persons with disabilities often relegated such persons to squalid residential institutions and imposed forced sterilization, justified in terms set by the eugenics movement.[7] Those children with disabilities who did receive services did so largely in classrooms or schools removed from their peers.

Parent advocacy organizations and civil rights activists challenged these practices, often with explicit references to *Brown v. Board of Education*.[8] Parents and educators pressed for both more funding and experiments placing students with disabilities in regular educational settings.[9] Integration, also called "mainstreaming" and "inclusion," became a central goal through litigation, legislation, and advocacy for individual students, but for some children, advocates also pursued specialized instruction in separate settings.[10] Intertwined with failures in the treatment of students with disabilities was the problem of racially discriminatory treatment. Two distinct problems became clear over time: (1) faulty classifications of students of color as disabled produced an overrepresentation of students of color in special education settings often remote from the mainstream classroom, and (2) schools failed to provide adequate services and programming for students of color and others who had disabilities.

Since the 1980s, changing and evolving understandings from medicine, psychology, and more recently from cognitive science altered and improved the knowledge base about how different students learn. Research illuminates the bases of and constructive responses to varied disabling conditions and the extent to which social settings affect what once were viewed as inevitable and natural features of certain disabilities. For reformers, the civil rights paradigm offered a framework for litigation and legislation, elevating equal educational opportunity, while the backlash against racial desegregation and evolving understandings about disabilities combined to make specialized instruction and related social and health services further features of equality in education. Parents and advocates sought protection against misidentification of students as disabled and development of appropriate placements of and services to those rightly identified. As in the other contexts discussed in this book, parents, teachers, and school systems have engaged in ongoing conflicts over whether equality in the context of students with disabilities demands integration or separate instruction.

From Litigation to Legislation

Julius Hobson, an economics researcher who became a civil rights activist in the District of Columbia, conducted several years of statistical analysis of the District's schools after the end of formal racial segregation and mounted a federal court challenge alleging continuing violations of the constitution.[11] Represented by the prominent progressive lawyer William Kunstler, who later called this his most gratifying case,[12] Hobson's suit fortuitously landed before Judge J. Skelly Wright. Judge Wright himself supplied a vital link to the civil rights movement and *Brown*. Before his 1962 appointment to the Court of Appeals for the District of Columbia Circuit, Wright served as district court judge in the Eastern District of Louisiana as an appointee of President Truman. There, his racial desegregation orders implementing *Brown* produced sharp opposition and social ostracism from business and political leaders in the community.[13] After he ordered desegregation of the public schools in New Orleans in 1960, Wright was vilified and hung in effigy.[14] Wright himself explained: "As I came to these problems, I had no particular moral convictions. I was just another Southern guy who didn't give a lot of thought. But it became clear to me that not only was it legal, but it was also right."[15] Lolis Elie, a local black lawyer, later commented: "The only man I know who stood hard and fast for change was Judge Skelly Wright, the federal judge. He was forcing the city to face the reality of having to integrate the school system."[16] Southern politicians blocked Wright's appointment to the Court of Appeals for the Fifth Circuit, governing Louisiana.[17] President John F. Kennedy therefore nominated him to the Court of Appeals for the District of Columbia, where he served for more than two decades.[18] In the Hobson case, Judge Wright was sitting by designation as a trial judge and issued comprehensive findings of impermissible racial discrimination in the District of Columbia schools. He rejected the use of IQ tests to place students in separate educational tracks as impermissible de facto racial segregation.[19]

When presented with Hobson's challenge to the use of ability tracking in the District of Columbia schools, Judge Wright wrote an opinion applying *Brown* and its companion *Bolling v. Sharpe* and found that the tracking system violated the Fourteenth Amendment of the U.S. Constitution because of the racial segregation it produced.[20] This decision was the first to identify the way individual schools in effect created racial segregation by labeling and sorting students, allegedly by ability. The decision helped to inspire advocates for children identified as having disabilities to end the exclusion of these students from mainstream schooling and halt their consignment to inferior educational settings. Noting the context of a school system that had previously deployed explicit racial segregation, the court cited unequal resources for and no compensatory educational benefits to the students placed in the lower tracks.[21]

Two years later, a Utah court ruled against the complete exclusion of students identified as "trainable" mentally disabled from regular public school classrooms.[22] In this first reported case explicitly analogizing students with special needs to black students, the court mirrored the language in *Brown*:[23]

> Today it is doubtful that any child may responsibly be expected to succeed in life if he is denied the right and opportunity of an education.... Segregation, even though perhaps well intentioned, under the apparent sanction of law and state authority, has a tendency to disregard the educational, emotional, and mental development of the children. The setting aside of these children in a special class affects the plaintiff parents in that... they have been told that their children are not the same as other children of the state of Utah.[24]

As of 1970, a year after the Utah court ruling, only seven states provided education for more than half of their children with disabilities.[25] No state until the mid-1970s provided educational services for all of its children with disabilities.[26] Attorney Thomas Gilhool developed a class action challenge to Pennsylvania's practice of excluding from public schooling any student labeled by the school system "uneducable and untrainable."[27] Gilhool, too, modeled the theory on *Brown*,[28] and in retrospect Gilhool's work was "pivotal in establishing the constitutional right of children with disabilities to a public education."[29] He organized expert testimony, again echoing the *Brown* strategy. For example, Ignacy Goldberg, secretary of the International Association for the Scientific Study of Mental Deficiency, provided evidence to counter the assumption that children with mental retardation could not learn.[30] After one day of testimony put forward by the plaintiffs, the defendants agreed to negotiate a settlement, later embodied in a consent decree enforceable by the federal district court. The court wrote that Pennsylvania's willingness to settle "reflects an intelligent response to the overwhelming evidence against their position."[31]

In the consent decree reported in 1971 as *Pennsylvania Association for Retarded Children v. Commonwealth (PARC)*,[32] the Commonwealth of Pennsylvania agreed to provide free and appropriate education and training for every child, including those identified as "exceptional" or having special needs. The consent decree acknowledged the testimony that even profoundly developmentally delayed students could learn and directed a preference for teaching such students in a regular school classroom over a special education classroom—and a preference for a special education classroom over other alternatives outside the regular classroom.[33] The consent decree thereby modeled a preference for mixing students together that has endured in national policies.

Reaching a similar result, also in 1972, the federal district court in *Mills v. Board of Education* issued a summary judgment rejecting the exclusion of children with disabilities from the District of Columbia schools[34] and calling for publicly supported education "suited to the [student's] needs."[35] Styled as a class action, the complaint identified each of the named plaintiffs not only as disabled but also as black, and the combination of race and disability drew the court's attention.[36] The court noted that "though all of the named minor plaintiffs are identified as Negroes the class they represent is not limited by their race. They sue on behalf of and represent all other District of Columbia residents of school age who are eligible for a free public education and who have been, or may be, excluded from such education or otherwise deprived by defendants of access to publicly supported education."[37] The court found that there was no genuine issue of fact because the defendants conceded that they had failed to provide either education or periodic review of the educational situation for the named plaintiffs and others in their situation. Citing *Brown, Bolling v. Sharpe,* and *Hobson v. Hanson,* the court built on these racial desegregation and antitracking cases to conclude that

> the defendants are required by the Constitution of the United States, the District of Columbia Code, and their own regulations to provide a publicly-supported education for these "exceptional" children. Their failure to fulfill this clear duty to include and retain these children in the public school system, or otherwise provide them with publicly-supported education, and their failure to afford them due process hearing and periodical review, cannot be excused by the claim that there are insufficient funds.[38]

The court declared that the burdens from any shortfall of funds would have to be shared by all the students, not assigned simply to the children with disabilities. The court accepted the defendants' proposed plan for identifying children's needs and matching them to educational placements and retained jurisdiction to monitor the implementation of the plan. Following the decree in the *Mills* case, the school system held three hundred hearings to reassign students in the first nineteen months.[39]

These two cases encouraged a national movement. By 1975, advocates across the country filed forty-six cases[40] pursuing equal protection and due process objections to the educational treatment of children with disabilities, and more than thirty federal courts endorsed the *PARC* and *Mills* principles.[41] Some forty-five states enacted legislation to deal at least in part with education for students with disabilities.[42] No federal statute existed to govern the matter. The category of "disability" was not included in the 1964 Civil Rights Act. As a first foray into federal legislative protections, advocates secured a provision to be known as Section 504 of the Rehabilitation Act Amendments of 1973. Signed into law by President Nixon, this provision conditioned the receipt of federal funds by schools and other programs on a guarantee that "no otherwise qualified individual with a disability" would, solely on the basis of the disability, be excluded from or discriminated against in the programs supported by the federal aid.[43] More limited than the 1964 Civil Rights Act because it applied only to recipients of federal funds, Section 504 nonetheless marked a sharp shift in the federal legal treatment of persons with disabilities to a framework of rights rather than support or care.[44]

Before Section 504, in an illustrative case, a school refused to include a student with spina bifida in the mainstream classroom unless the child's mother attended to the child's physical needs.[45] In a case filed under Section 504, the court rejected the school's position and emphasized that the school needed to include children even at serious expense because of the value of the integration experience: "A major goal of the education process is the socialization process that takes place in the regular classroom, with the resulting capability to interact in a social way with one's peers. It is therefore imperative that every child receive an education with his or her peers insofar as it is at all possible."[46] There was a general financing issue. Regulations implementing Section 504 pointed to the *PARC* and *Mills* court decrees, but Congress itself offered no additional funding for supplementary aids or services to meet the needs of students with disabilities in mainstream classrooms or in other settings.

Family associations, such as the Arc,[47] connected parents of children with disabilities and proved an effective lobbying force for state and federal support.[48] Among the key individuals who advocated powerfully for a more comprehensive response to the educational needs of children with disabilities, Marion Wright Edelman proved especially effective. The first African-American woman admitted to the Mississippi bar, Edelman headed the NAACP Legal Defense Fund and Education office in Jackson, Mississippi, after her graduation from Yale Law School. She later served as counsel for the Poor People's Campaign, launched with Dr. Martin Luther King, Jr. (just before his assassination), in an effort to mobilize a mass movement around poverty issues. In 1973, she founded a new organization, the Children's Defense Fund, with the clear model of the NAACP Legal Defense Fund in mind and an original focus on poor African-American children. To Edelman's own surprise, an early Children's Defense Fund survey revealed that rural communities with predominantly white populations had the largest number of children between the ages of seven and thirteen listed as not attending school, and that disabled children composed a large proportion of those out of school.[49] After discovering that schools rejected students with developmental and physical disabilities,[50] Edelman made legislation guaranteeing education for all children a top priority for her nascent organization. She drew on lessons from the civil rights movement in mobilizing parents, using media, and linking with other organizations to press for congressional action.

When Congress held hearings in 1973 about the education of children with disabilities, it found that 3.5 million children with disabilities were not receiving an appropriate education and nearly another million received no education at all.[51] With overwhelming majorities in both houses,[52] Congress then enacted and President Gerald Ford signed into law a federal grants program offering the carrot of federal funding on the condition that states provide a free appropriate education for all students with disabilities and a fair process for identifying and monitoring the proper placement for such students. Initially called the Education for All Handicapped Children's Act, or Public Law 94–142, the law was renewed and renamed the Individuals with Disabilities Education Act (IDEA) in 1990.[53] To receive funding, states and local school districts needed to devise systems to locate and evaluate all students who could be disabled, develop individualized education plans for each of these students, set standards for the educational placement of the students, and provide procedural options for parental participation in and review of the educational plan. Both this law and Section 504 of the Rehabilitation Act secured bipartisan support and the signature of President George H. W. Bush. Given the fact that disabilities arise regardless of race, gender, or socioeconomic background, widespread and bipartisan support contributed to the success of these legislative movements.

From the start, the federal law recognized the value of integration. The statute required that, to the maximum extent appropriate, the school system place the child with disabilities in the "least restrictive environment,"[54] defined as the school setting most integrated with the mainstream class or closest to it. Variations on this process are known as mainstreaming or inclusion. At the same time, the law demanded that the placement be appropriate for the particular student's needs and ensure the benefits of tailoring programs to meet the needs of the individual child.[55] Especially against the backdrop of the civil rights movement's challenge to racially segregated schools, a commitment to inclusion framed the legislative response to the evidence that schools around the country either excluded millions of students with various disabilities or assigned them to separate classrooms or institutions. Another important legislative element gives protections against faulty identification, which could produce stigma and misallocation of resources.[56] The IDEA offers participating states money in exchange for plans to ensure appropriate education and related services and administrative procedures for creating individualized education plans with parental participation and opportunities for review.[57] At once an entitlement program and an equality commitment, the special education law has become a major focus of attention for schools and parents struggling over resources and balancing the interests of individual children and groups of children. It has also become a focal point in assessing when equal opportunity calls for integration and when instead it calls for specialized, separate instructional settings.

Congress meant to tilt placements of students with disabilities toward the mainstream classrooms where possible. Congressman George Miller put it as a presumption: "I believe the burden of proof...ought to rest with that administrator or teacher who seeks for one reason or another to remove a child from a normal classroom, to segregate him or her from non-handicapped children, to place him in a program of special education."[58] Acknowledging the impact of integration on students without disabilities, Congressman C. D. Daniel suggested that "the opportunity to share learning experiences with handicapped children will broaden the personal growth of classmates who are not handicapped. Lessons of patience, understanding, and the ability to provide peer encouragement are just as valuable as traditional educational lessons to the future citizens of this nation."[59] Teachers and administrators have also emphasized the potential benefits of inclusive classrooms for everyone. Inclusive classrooms can enlarge the circle of concern and capacities for empathy among those without disabilities. Inclusive instructional styles offer social connections, collaborative learning, and a sense of membership to students with disabilities; they can reduce unnecessary supervision and assistance by family members and paraprofessionals for students with disabilities; they can bring more resources into the mainstream classroom, including more teachers and aides who in turn lower the teacher-student ratio; and they can trigger the development of classroom and school-wide approaches that offer more individualized and collaborative learning, respecting the strengths and challenges of every student.[60]

Although appropriations never matched the authorized funding levels or the needs registered by the states,[61] the federal law has profoundly influenced the placement of students with disabilities, bringing about greater integration with nondisabled peers. Before the adoption of the law, nearly 70 percent of children with disabilities who received education did so in separate classrooms or separate schools.[62] As a result of the law, the advocacy, and the related changes in educational philosophy, over 70 percent of students with disabilities spent at least part of their day in the regular classroom with other students by 1996.[63] Nearly half—47 percent—of students with disabilities now spend all their time in mainstream classrooms.[64] Courts initially ordered mainstreaming only if shown to be beneficial, but over time judges began to read the statutory call for mainstreaming to "the maximum extent appropriate."[65] Judges read the statutory language this way perhaps because educators increasingly took advantage of new instructional techniques supporting the inclusion of students with disabilities in regular classrooms. A leading court opinion declared, "inclusion is a right, not a privilege for a select few."[66] But the tilt toward including students with disabilities in classrooms with other students also reflected intensive litigation efforts. A line of court decisions favors mainstreaming, but courts, educators, parents, and scholars continue to disagree over precisely when integration is wise and when, instead, separate instruction affords equality.[67]

Continuing Debate over Integration and Separation

In favor of inclusion are these considerations: (1) the recognition that socializing with nondisabled peers offers real academic and nonacademic benefits to students with disabilities, both in the present and in preparation for navigating life in the future;[68] (2) learning alongside students with disabilities also can benefit nondisabled students by enhancing their understanding and appreciation of the struggles and talents of others and their ability to see their classmates as individuals rather than embodiments of stigmatized categories;[69] and (3) the creation of inclusive schools and classrooms can provide greater responsiveness to the range of individual strengths and challenges experienced by all students and can bring in more resources for and knowledge about diverse learning styles.[70] Fundamentally, each of these opportunities reverses what are widely viewed as the negative consequences of segregation: (1) the stigma and isolation felt by students with disabilities when separated from the mainstream;

(2) the stereotyping and discomfort with "difference" that arises among nondisabled students when they are separated from students with disabilities; and (3) the potentially enormous difficulties individuals have in moving from the category of "disabled" to "nondisabled" or in the other direction, despite errors in the identification process.[71]

Yet several factors compete with and weigh against integration through inclusive classrooms. First, placement in the mainstream classroom would not be the ideal setting for many disabled students. The goal of devising educational programs and services tailored to the individual student's needs must be pursued even when that points toward separate classrooms for some or all of the time. Second, even with considerable efforts by adults, students with disabilities risk becoming the objects of bullying, harassment, or exclusion by other students within the mainstream settings. Further, the educational opportunities of the nondisabled classmates in some circumstances can be jeopardized because of disruptions or distractions caused by the students with disabilities or disproportionate teacher attention that they require.[72]

The first of these concerns is a topic of disagreement within schools and among school experts, teachers, parents, and advocates. Disagreements center on what kinds of students with special needs can and should remain in the mainstream classrooms and what kinds of supports are reasonable and feasible to bring into these classrooms.[73] States and localities vary in their approaches especially to inclusion for the most severely disabled students. The risk that the mainstream classroom will not be safe or hospitable for students with disabilities is real and is verified by many students' experiences.[74] Yet this risk also indicates the importance of efforts at inclusion to altering societal attitudes and cultivating maturity and compassion in the wider community. As one education scholar put it:

> Though it is understandable that parents and students may reach for segregation as a solution, given horrific experiences and prejudicial behavior, it cannot be the long-term solution to discrimination and lack of acceptance. We want to create schools in which all children are welcome, in which it is safe to be different or perceived as different, without fearing for the physical or emotional safety of some....
>
> If we think we can solve the problems of teasing, exclusion, and bullying by removing the targets, we will embark on an endless series of removals and segregations.[75]

The final and perhaps weightiest concern—and the one commonly expressed by parents—is that students without the disability label will suffer under a policy of inclusive classrooms. Many parents worry that teachers' attention will be diverted from the children without disabilities or the class will be "dumbed down." Studies do not confirm these fears. Research indicates that academic performance of "typical" students equals or exceeds the performance of comparable students taught in noninclusive classes.[76] Other studies indicate that teacher attention is not diverted, nor are disabled classmates disruptive.[77] Successful examples of inclusive instruction, however, show what can be accomplished by teachers with flexible teaching styles, opportunities to collaborate or team-teach with others with specialized training, and use of effective techniques such as positive behavioral supports rewarding constructive behaviors and involvement of the class in identifying and valuing good conduct.[78]

Commentators warn that the influence of *Brown* contributes to a simplistic embrace of mainstreaming for all children.[79] An inappropriate placement in the regular classroom does not afford equal educational opportunity if the student cannot gain benefits from it. Thus, for some students with serous cognitive impairments, learning "life skills" such as shopping for groceries or even dressing oneself are central, so the mainstream classroom is a poor fit for them.[80] Yet even this sentence echoes historic assumptions that students with physical disabilities are unteachable, assumptions that are often easier to shield from challenge when the students with disabilities remain separated from other students. Students with serious cognitive impairments may get some educational and social benefits out of being in a class with other children, and with appropriate supportive services they may receive more than they would in an entirely segregated setting.[81] At the same time, segregation or exclusion does not seem to trouble parents, especially of children with learning disabilities, who view the IDEA as a way to obtain special assistance and advantages.[82] This should serve as a reminder that integration is not the only way to achieve equal opportunity; treating people the same who are different is not equal treatment.[83] Yet the presumption of integration may still be necessary to counter the legacy of exclusion and contrary bias.[84]

Especially challenging are placements and services for students with emotional and behavioral disorders. These students can disrupt the classroom and learning opportunities for other students, can require frequent school discipline, and may need to be placed away from mainstream classrooms.[85] When should the suspension of a student with emotional or behavior disorder be seen as a kind of segregative treatment and when, instead, should it be understood as the punishment matching the response meted out to any other student engaging in the same acts?[86] Should a school system's decision to shift a disabled student away from the mainstream classroom be viewed as the appropriate placement or instead as a failure to promote integration in the mainstream classroom? Some researchers cite evidence that whole-school supports and behavioral management instruction for teachers reduce disciplinary problems and argue that schools should pursue these approaches in order to enhance their ability to keep students with emotional and behavioral disorders in mainstream classes.[87] Others question whether regular classrooms can supply enough trained and experienced personnel and a low enough pupil-to-staff ratio to have demonstrable success in improving the achievement and conduct of students with emotional or behavioral impairments.[88]

A related line of contention affecting mainstreaming debate concerns the allocation of financial and other resources that can directly and indirectly affect prospects for inclusion of students with disabilities in mainstream classrooms. Given that students with disabilities typically require more resources whether they are placed in the mainstream or in special classrooms,[89] local communities and the national policy scene have erupted in debates over funding formulae and mechanisms. The impact of existing and potential funding on inclusion and separation is complicated. Some people may assume that mainstreaming will be cheaper, but when it is implemented with appropriate supplemental aids and supports, it may well be as costly as separate classrooms with specially trained teachers. Pushing against decision-making that is tied solely to students' needs, state funding formulas can create incentives for moving students with disabilities out of the mainstream classroom into separate educational settings in order to shift costs to another budget or source of funding.[90] In addition, difficult and disruptive fights over the allocation of resources between disabled and nondisabled programs can create political and professional conflicts while raising potentially unsolvable ethical issues about entitlement and fairness.

The difficulties of mobilizing extra resources and managing extra burdens on teachers often pose obstacles to inclusion as an educational approach. In practice, inclusion often requires collaboration between regular education teachers and special education teachers and sometimes special training and the provision of classroom aids to assist the regular teacher. Some students need "related services" such as transportation, physical therapy, and assistance managing a catheter or other medical equipment. The law was designed to cover these features as well, but the term "related services" itself gives no sense of scope and provides no formula or additional funding for these extra services for students with ongoing physical care needs. District courts and courts of appeals have produced conflicting interpretations.

Ultimately, the Supreme Court clarified that all students with disabilities have a right to attend school when they are medically able to do so, regardless of the kind or extent of health-related services they may require in school, so long as a physician is not needed to provide those services.[91] In *Cedar Rapids Community School District v. Garret F.*,[92] the Court concluded that cost and administrative burdens could not justify denial of continuous nursing care needed by a ventilator-dependent student so that he could attend the regular school, where he was otherwise performing well. This decision was justified on the grounds that "Congress intended 'to open the door of public education' to all qualified children and 'require[d] participating States to educate handicapped children with non-handicapped children whenever possible.'"[93] The IDEA thus directs schools to provide nursing or other health services during the school day in cases where students cannot attend school without those services, whether or not the service is covered by Medicaid or private insurance and regardless of the schools' interests in keeping costs down. Yet questions about other kinds of related services—and who pays for them—persist.

Courts continue in varying degrees to defer to the expertise of school officials who oppose placing students with disabilities in mainstream classrooms, even as the Supreme Court has recognized the law's dual demand for appropriate placements and placements that permit children with disabilities to attend school alongside nondisabled peers to the extent reasonable.[94] Combining deference to educators with the statutory preference for the least restrictive alternative remains a challenge for both courts and school administrators, and no single clear legal test exists for measuring state compliance with the law's "least restrictive environment" provision.[95] No simple test or analysis is likely to emerge any time soon, given the variety of disabling conditions, competing views about the purposes of education and value of integration in serving those purposes, and shifting expert ideas about the capabilities of children with certain conditions.

Brown inspired the litigation and legislation addressing education for students with disabilities. It provides the template for demanding both equal opportunity and integration for such students. Working out what that means for individual students will continue to require complex assessments, subject to review. Discerning how to provide education that is both appropriate and as close to nondisabled students as possible requires especially thoughtful treatment of students with disabilities under regimes of mandatory statewide assessments. Including students with disabilities in mandatory statewide assessment could be at least as crucial to equalizing educational opportunities as classroom integration. Teachers and administrators are more likely to become committed to improving the educational performance of these students as much as that of other students when these accountability measures are extended to them.[96] Yet when there are "high stakes" attached to those assessments—such as denying high school diplomas to students who do not meet a minimum score on the standardized test—students with disabilities may be punished for their own incapacities and denied recognition for the progress and work they have achieved.[97]

The challenge of testing academic performance by students with disabilities raises the enduring problem of quality of instruction.[98] Some truly gifted teachers may be able to teach heterogeneous classes effectively, while other teachers may find it impossible and instead turn to special education to identify disabled students and remove them from the classroom or require classroom aids or other assistance. Examples of successful inclusive instruction can be inspiring but also daunting, given the challenges many teachers find in even relatively homogeneous classrooms in the context of yearly assessments based on standardized tests.[99] Even advocates of inclusive instruction acknowledge that it can be difficult and requires more planning and flexibility.[100] Whether legal strategies can bring about an increase in the number of talented teachers or generate better preparation for teachers of heterogeneous classes remains a vital, difficult question, and one that underscores the urgent need for quality instruction for students across racial, class, and geographic divisions.

Race and Disability

No fact more pointedly connects the treatment of disability with the legacies of *Brown* than widespread evidence of overidentification of disabling conditions by race, often with the effect of removing black students from the mainstream classroom and creating a new form of segregation.[101] The racially disproportionate pattern in special education was the very situation that gave rise to *Hobson v. Hansen*—the first decision that rejected a school's use of ability tracking to sort and separate students. The tracking system itself produced racially separate classrooms, just as the courts ended racial segregation in the schools.[102] Overrepresentation of African Americans in special education apparently escalated after courts ordered racial desegregation.[103] Although the overrepresentation occurs across the country, of the seven states today with the highest disproportion of African Americans who are labeled mentally retarded, five (Mississippi, Alabama, North Carolina, South Carolina, and Florida) are states that had de jure segregation until *Brown*.[104] As special education has been expanding—from about 3 percent to about 6 percent over the past two decades[105]—so has the continuing overrepresentation of black children in such programs.[106]

Perhaps the intersection of poverty and race contributes to a real disproportionate incidence of disabilities—although courts presented with this argument have rejected it.[107] Disabilities, including physical disabilities, do appear to accompany poverty, and poverty correlates with race, so some degree of overrepresentation of African Americans in special education can be foreseen.[108] Yet African Americans are not overrepresented in special education on the basis of hearing impairments, visual impairments, or other medically based conditions. They are, however, overrepresented in the categories of mental retardation and severe emotional disturbance—categories in which individualized judgments rather than uniform tests are required for the identification process.[109] The numbers are striking. By one account, black children make up about 17 percent of total public school enrollment, and of that number, 33 percent are labeled mentally retarded;[110] by another, African-American students are nearly three times more likely than white students to be identified as mentally retarded.[111] Dramatic variations across states also suggest that the assignments reflect factors other than objective determinations of underlying conditions.[112] Once identified as disabled, these students are much more likely to be separated from the mainstream classroom and to have inadequate and inappropriate services as well.[113] African-American students are also underrepresented in classes for "gifted" youth.[114]

Studies suggest that institutional bias, inadequate training of teachers, language barriers, and cultural miscommunication, as well as the individual biases of referring teachers and evaluators, contribute to the misclassifications of students of color.[115] Scholars and social scientists widely report the impact of cultural differences and racial stereotypes on this phenomenon.[116] Black students may face disproportionate placement in special education programs because they disproportionately receive low-quality education before referrals. But the processes of identification and assessment also contribute to the disproportionate placement of black students in special education programs.[117] Further problems of misclassification arise for students whose first language is not English.[118]

Although identification of a disability can bring added resources to help a child learn, this label also usually carries a stigma, making misclassification a real burden. The consequent misplacement too often means a lost opportunity for more appropriate instruction. The stigma itself reflects racial and class dimensions of the special education population. White students are more likely to obtain the label "learning disabled," which bears less stigma than the label "mentally retarded." In addition, both these labels influence the actual educational opportunities that follow. One study suggests that "[u]pper middle-class white boys receive discretionary resources in low-stigma settings that might better be used by other students with learning difficulties. African Americans get shunted, too often, into dead-end classes."[119] African-American students are more likely than other students to be put in restrictive segregated settings remote from the general classroom and with a less challenging curriculum. They are also less likely to challenge the placements and less likely to prevail when they do so.[120]

Overwhelming evidence of a national pattern of overrepresentation of children of color in special education has prompted studies and journalists to identity a "crisis" and a "national problem,"[121] and Congress has required schools to report on the racial patterns of special education identification and placements.[122] It remains unclear whether state and federal civil rights officials will seek to alter these patterns, as, indeed, it remains unknown whether civil rights enforcement will be justified by statistical patterns rather than by demonstrated discriminatory intention by government employees.

Gender segregation is also a problem here. Overrepresentation in special education affects chiefly African-American boys and has generated serious grounds for concerns that the NAACP and other groups have raised.[123] There are potential problems of racial and gender disparities leading to underidentification of students in some categories of disability as well. By some reports, Latino students tend to be underrepresented in some special education programs and overrepresented in others.[124]

Some observers propose loosening the presumption of integration into mainstream classrooms for students with disabilities;[125] others urge scaling back special education as such while increasing individualized instruction without the special education label.[126] Adopting a single, across-the-board approach is unlikely to match the needs of students who have cognitive impairments, students with learning disabilities, and students with emotional or behavioral disorders. Particularized assessments and placements of students based on their own unique constellation of strengths and weaknesses and on the array of options in the particular school system may be the most promising approach for avoiding prejudicial mistakes and for enhancing the students' learning. Yet individualized assessments contribute to the wide variations in treatment of students who arguably have similar situations and needs and make room for the exercise of unconscious bias by teachers and evaluators. The ambiguity and potential distortions of the empirical data about incidence of disabilities and about effective instruction make this yet another area where reliance on expert social science knowledge is attractive and yet fraught with difficulties.

Sexual Orientation, Religion, and Poverty

Echoing *Brown* in unpredicted ways, many students, parents, schools, and communities are occupied with equality in schools for students who identify with or explore lesbian, gay, or transsexual orientations. Perhaps even more surprising are the uses of equality arguments on behalf of religious students—a category of students newly claimed to suffer from discrimination—and religious schools. Reformers' efforts to define and pursue equality of opportunity for low-income students failed as a matter of federal constitutional law; advocates later secured state court victories but achieved limited accomplishment in practice.[127] Each of these contexts confirms the dominance of an equality framework launched by *Brown* in organizing school improvement efforts; each recapitulates, in different ways, disputes over integration as the sole or best way to achieve equality.

Gay and Lesbian Students

The New York City public school system, in conjunction with a private organization established to support gay and lesbian youth, founded the Harvey Milk High School in 1985 for gay and lesbian teenagers.[128] Its goal was to create a supportive, safe place for students who faced violence, harassment, or intimidation in mainstream schools.[129] Enrollment from the start has been voluntary. Students apply to transfer to the school, which includes transgendered teens and teens who may be perceived to be gay, lesbian, bisexual, or transgendered.[130]

The legal protections for students on the basis of sexual orientation remain ambiguous and subject to local rules, although federal courts have read Title IX of the federal Education Amendments of 1972 to encompass harassment on the basis of sexual orientation.[131] Although some academic theorists question the analogy between race and sexual orientation for purposes of antidiscrimination law, legal advocacy organizations have followed the path carved out by the NAACP in advocating for legal protections for gays, lesbians, and transgendered people.[132] Test case litigation is the familiar strategy, and it paid off in this area. In June 2003, the U.S. Supreme Court struck down as unconstitutional a Texas statute criminalizing homosexual sodomy.[133] The majority opinion, written by Justice Anthony Kennedy, explained that "two adults who, with full and mutual consent from each other, [engage] in sexual practices common to the homosexual life-style...[enjoy] a right to liberty under the Due Process Clause...to engage in their conduct without intervention of the government."[134] An amicus curiae brief had analogized contemporary prejudices about sexual orientation with racial prejudices prevalent in the 1950s and 1960s.[135]

Shortly after the decision in *Lawrence v. Texas*, the New York school board authorized an expansion of the initial Harvey Milk High School program from two classrooms with 50 students to eight classrooms with 170 students and a full four-year high school. This decision triggered protests, especially by conservative religious groups.[136] When state Conservative Party chairman Mike Long attacked the school's existence, he echoed critics of racial segregation: "Is there a different way to teach homosexuals? Is there gay math? This is wrong.... There's no reason these children should be treated separately."[137]

Critics also include gay rights supporters who warn that the separate schooling fails to equip these schools' students for the real world and fails to dismantle discrimination.[138] One critic said: "Through long, painful years we reached a consensus that we couldn't allow segregation. This is a short-term gain and we need to look at the long-term, larger issues."[139] A Michigan newspaper that took up the issue opposed the separate school as well: "Advocates say that by having their own school, gays will feel more comfortable and won't be subjected to the intimidation that many of them now face in public schools. That argument comes uncomfortably close to racial segregationists in the 1950s and 1960s who insisted that black students did best when they were 'among their own.'"[140] Yet advocates point out that because of harassment and violence, adolescents who identify as gay, lesbian, bisexual, or transgendered are much more likely to drop out or attempt suicide than other students—and hence need a special school.[141] Given evidence that calling someone "gay" remains a common insult among teens,[142] sorting out how best to address prejudice and cruelty aimed at lesbian and gay students will undoubtedly pose challenges for some time to come.

A voluntary, separate school along the lines of the Harvey Milk High School may seem more acceptable in a large system, like New York's, that includes citywide special schools in science, fashion, and other topics. Perhaps a special school for gay and lesbian students could be viewed as part of the city's project of developing excellent magnet schools with special themes.[143] Yet it remains troubling to conceive as "voluntary" the transfer of a student to a special school in order to escape harassment at the regular school. Whether separate instruction can be equal seems less urgent than determining how to make integrated education safe. The very existence of the separate school may reduce pressure for policies of zero tolerance for harassment and violence in any school. This task is challenging legally, normatively, and practically, given that some students and parents claim that freedoms of expression and religion lie behind their critiques of homosexuality[144]—even as other students claim they face harassment for being gay, lesbian, bisexual, or transgendered or for supporting such students. Abusive

treatment of any fellow student should not be tolerated within a school setting. One court agreed with a student who claimed protection under Title
IX after being harassed for advocating tolerance of gays and lesbians.[145]
New issues arise as younger students come out in middle schools that have
not anticipated how to ensure their safety and well-being.[146] Although some
people object to any public school acknowledgment of the sexual orientations of students, the commitment to equal opportunity for gay and lesbian
students animates most of the arguments on both sides of this issue.

Religious Schools

The architects of *Brown* did not have in mind educational opportunities conceived in terms of religion. Yet legal treatment of both public
aid to religious schools and public school treatment of religion have
changed since *Brown* as concerns about equality have reframed preoc-
cupations with separating church and state. Lawsuits in the 1950s and
1960s contested whether equality required public aid to private religious
instruction or whether equal treatment—or the constitutional ban on
any official establishment of religion—instead required the creation of
a strictly secular realm.[147] Directly attacking integration of religion and
public spaces, some advocates successfully campaigned against the use of
nuns and priests as teachers in public schools.[148] Reformers' effectiveness
in pointing out a Catholic presence in public schools ended up fueling
movements to eliminate all religion from public schools.[149] The federal
courts came to conceive of a "wall" between religion and government,
especially in the context of schooling.

The alteration of that legal regime is one of the most notable constitutional shifts of the past two decades. Reformers successfully pursued
neutral—meaning equal—treatment of religious and secular schools and
equal treatment of religion with other topics in public schools. During the
1960s and 1970s, lawyers advised public schools to exclude any reference to
religion. In recent years, given shifts in Supreme Court treatment of religion
in public places, schools have been allowed to introduce symbols of religious
holidays as long as there is evenhanded treatment of different religions.[150]
Public dollars may now reach private religious schools, as long as these, too,
reflect an evenhanded, neutral approach.[151] A principal architect of this
shift from insistent separation to equal treatment is Michael McConnell, an
accomplished law professor who served as a distinguished federal appellate
court judge in the 1980s and 1990s and has now returned to an academic
post. In his scholarship and advocacy, he argued in favor of full and equal
rights for religious individuals in the public sphere, instead of the maintenance of separate public and private spheres with the relegation of religion to
the private sphere.[152] It surely is no accident that McConnell has also written
extensively on the Fourteenth Amendment and racial desegregation.[153] His
deep scholarship on the subject has informed his effective advocacy for equal
treatment of religion and individuals seeking religious schooling.

As counsel for a group of students seeking state university funding for their Christian publication, McConnell successfully persuaded five justices of the Supreme Court to focus on the unequal treatment of different student groups by the state university when it denied funding for the religious publication while subsidizing other student publications.[154] Although freedom of speech rather than equal protection provided the constitutional hook for McConnell's case, his conception of equality reframed what the Court itself had previously treated as a question of separating public aid from religious activities. The reframing worked.[155] The Supreme Court rejected as unconstitutional the exclusion of a religious student newspaper from eligibility for state university funding, ruling that such exclusion amounted to impermissible viewpoint discrimination under the guarantee of freedom of speech.[156] Similarly, a plurality on the Supreme Court reasoned that it would be illegal viewpoint discrimination for a public school to deny space to a religious after-school program.[157] This argument, likely to obtain a majority with the new members of the Court, shrinks concerns about government establishment or endorsement of religion and in effect brings religious students and their families as a new group into the ranks of groups whose needs must all be considered in the pluralist, multicultural world created by *Brown* and its advocates.

In his scholarly writings, McConnell has also articulated a generous view of the constitutional duty to accommodate religious believers.[158] The 1981 Supreme Court decision in *Widmar v. Vincent* injected into constitutional analysis concerns for equal treatment and for the inclusion of religious groups in public school settings.[159] The Court reasoned that a policy excluding religious groups from access to campus facilities when other groups have such access amounted to content discrimination, impermissible under the constitutional guarantee of freedom of speech.

In an earlier era, giving religious groups space in a public school would have seemed to violate the duty to steer clear of government endorsement of religion or any particular religion. The new, prevailing legal view directs that offering religious groups access to public school facilities outside of class time would not amount to a violation of the establishment clause when the school accords similar access to other groups. However refusing access to a group because of its religious identity or message would violate the free speech clause by disfavoring one message or viewpoint.[160] Furthermore, a state university regulation that prohibits religious worship on school property would violate the guarantee of freedom of speech. Congress embraced this trend by enacting the Equal Access Act, extending to religious groups whatever access to public elementary and secondary school sites was afforded to nonreligious groups. When a public school denied after-school use of school facilities to a Christian student group, the group prevailed in a claim under the Equal Access Act, overcoming the school's defense that their decision avoided an establishment clause problem.[161] The Supreme Court used the occasion to revisit its prior decision in the university context and interpreted the federal Equal Access

Act as posing no establishment clause problem when it required public secondary schools receiving federal funds to give equal access to religious and nonreligious student groups.[162] The Court subsequently found a public school district in violation of the Free Speech Clause when it denied a church access to school facilities during after-school hours to show a film that presented a religious approach to childrearing.[163]

McConnell testified before the Senate Judiciary Committee in favor of the general idea of a religious equality amendment that would allow prayer in public schools.[164] Equality as well as freedom would be at stake, in his view, and he drew an analogy to racial equality in defending the need to recognize the rights of individuals to exercise their religious beliefs without fear of discrimination or denial of benefits. Thus, after a court of appeals found it within the discretion of a ninth-grade teacher to disallow a student's proposed research paper on Jesus Christ, McConnell stated: "I have little doubt that the case would have come out the other way if a racist teacher had forbidden a paper on Martin Luther King, Jr., or an anticommunist teacher had forbidden a paper on the evils of capitalism."[165] Mindful of the comparison between race and religion, advocates like McConnell have successfully extended the legacy of *Brown* to embrace the treatment of religious students in public schools.

Even when it comes to public financial support for parochial schools, lawyers and scholars have persuaded courts to shift the legal framework from establishment clause and also free exercise claims to considerations of equal treatment. McConnell pointed to the fact that working-class and poor families could not effectively choose religious schools for their children due to the cost of tuition and the barrier against public aid to religious schools.[166] He has also explored (without resting the case for public aid to religious schools on it) a theory of equal protection for minority religious groups that feel the need to create schools apart from the public schools.[167] Advocates before the courts have recast earlier concerns about public funds contributing to religious activities, setting aside the 1960s and 1970s jurisprudence that rather incoherently divided acceptable and unacceptable public aid to religious schools.

As a result, the Supreme Court has recently turned to asking whether aid programs afford neutral treatment of religious and nonreligious schools. In line with the Court's emerging focus on neutrality, nondiscrimination, and equal treatment in assessing claims under both the establishment and free exercise clauses of the Constitution,[168] the Court has started to analyze challenges to public aid for religious schools by asking whether the aid comes through a general program with neutral, secular criteria that neither benefit nor disadvantage religion. Under such a test, in the 2000 case of *Mitchell v. Helms*, the Court upheld a voucher program enabling parents to select private parochial schools for their children,[169] as well as to use public dollars to pay for books, computer software, and other secular materials for their children's use in a private religious school.[170]

Members of the Court have also warned that excluding religious schools from generally available aid could present a violation of the free exercise clause.[171] In this view, not only is there no constitutional violation when a government program includes religious schools within the eligibility criteria for otherwise generally available public funds; the courts could find a constitutional defect if religious schools generally are excluded from public aid.[172] Commentators expressly describe these developments as ending second-class treatment of religious schools.[173] The traditional "separation of church and state" becomes unacceptably unequal in this light.

This last point resembles an equal protection argument, but the influence of *Brown* is even more direct than that. In the majority opinion in *Zelman v. Simmons-Harris*—the voucher decision—the Court emphasized the explicit justification for the voucher experiment in Milwaukee as improving educational opportunities for low-income minority children.[174] In his separate concurring opinion, Justice Thomas, holding Justice Thurgood Marshall's seat on the Court, stressed that *Brown*'s promise remained distant because of the deterioration and continuing segregation of urban schools.[175] Justice Thomas embraced the irony that although vouchers seemed a tool to promote white flight after *Brown*, nearly fifty years later, vouchers could open quality instruction for students otherwise trapped in failing public schools.[176] Justice Thomas cited *Brown*'s declaration of the importance of schooling to an individual's success in life while pointing to the failing Cleveland schools that prompted the voucher program.[177] He also stressed that minority and low-income parents express the strongest support for vouchers and rejected opposition as preoccupied with formalistic concerns far from the core purposes of the Fourteenth Amendment.[178] Both Milwaukee and Cleveland, the first cities enacting contemporary experiments with vouchers, explained that their policies sought to open access to quality educational opportunities for predominantly poor African-American and Hispanic children.

A majority of African Americans report positive views of vouchers and school choice programs in public opinion polls.[179] African-American parents supporting school vouchers view them as a promising avenue for better educational opportunities.[180] Law review commentators celebrated the voucher decision as a step toward fulfilling *Brown*'s vision of equal educational opportunities for students of color,[181] while social scientists and racial justice advocates debate whether parochial schools are more segregated than public schools[182]—and whether real academic opportunities for students of color more likely remain within the public system.[183] Their debates offer a hint of the highly controverted character of scholarship in this area, affected by funding from politically identified research organizations as well as national political campaigns staking out positions on school vouchers and school choice.[184] As very few districts have gone ahead with school voucher programs, limited experience makes it difficult to draw conclusions about their effects on racial integration or school achievement. Instead, most of the arguments draw on experience with private scholarship programs and varieties of public school choice.[185]

The policy debates concentrate nearly exclusively on whether directing public aid to allow poor students to attend private religious schools can enhance opportunities for disadvantaged students, who are primarily African American and Hispanic. The legal debates emphasize equal treatment of religious and nonreligious schools but do not focus on religious and nonreligious *students*. Indeed, a central question is whether the inducement of public subsidy for parochial schools will put undue pressure on families who are not religiously affiliated or do not share the religions of the available parochial schools.[186] Political and legal debates over vouchers focused on treatment of religious schools and have not addressed equal treatment of religious and nonreligious students equally, although that may have been in part the motivation of voucher advocates. Notably, this has often meant working to open Catholic schools to low-income, urban, Protestant African-American students unable to enroll in successful suburban schools. This policy goal may explain why even constitutional concerns to keep public funds from private religious schools have dissipated as communities have pursued school vouchers for those still waiting on the promise of *Brown*. Pro-free-market conservatives, pro-parochial-school traditionalists, and civil rights advocates could join in a cause—equal educational opportunity—that *Brown* made righteous while giving up on *Brown*'s means of achieving racially integrated public schools.

Concerns about government involvement with religion have not disappeared.[187] Some people caution that because financial need may induce parents to send their children to religious schools that may seek to indoctrinate them in their religions or compel them to perform religious practices that are not their own, public school voucher programs should be understood as violating the establishment clause.[188] Still others have launched antidiscrimination challenges to state constitutional bans on public aid to religious schools on the grounds that they are animated in part by anti-Catholic sentiments.[189] Nonetheless, the Supreme Court's green light for voucher initiatives was itself couched primarily in terms of equality both for religious and nonreligious institutions and for low-income students of color.

With advocates and courts reframing the most important question as being not about aid to religious schools but about equal treatment for religious students and religious ideas, the legacy of *Brown* may also encompass a broader social commitment to pluralism—or with greater room for religion in the public sphere.[190] The Christian Right pursues arguments for inclusion that expand space for religious expression in public schools even as gay rights lawyers seek to curb religious expression in public schools where it undermines respect for and tolerance of those with a minority sexual orientation.[191] Legal commentator Jeffrey Rosen puts it this way:

> Americans have always been deeply religious and deeply suspicious of state-imposed uniformity. In an era when religious identity now competes with race, sex, and ethnicity as a central aspect of how Americans define themselves, it seems like discrimination—the only unforgivable sin in a

multicultural age—to forbid people to express their religious beliefs in an increasingly fractured public sphere. Strict separationism, during its brief reign, made the mistake of trying to forbid not only religious expression by the state, but also religious expression by citizens on public property.[192]

Whatever one may think about the turn to equal treatment to frame constitutional analysis of religious establishment and free exercise claims,[193] the equal treatment approach to religious issues could produce new kinds of school segregation and new kinds of integration. By enabling more students to enroll in parochial schools, the new approach diminishes the ability of public schools to serve as the meeting place for all students.[194] Yet in urban areas, the parochial schools may become the integrated schools. Vouchers and subsidies for private schools may well draw non-Catholic students into Catholic schools and continue the diversification of the urban Catholic school system that has proceeded for the past several decades.[195] Meanwhile, specific accommodation of religious students in public school facilities and programs make public schools more hospitable for them—but there are risks of introducing new forms of peer exclusion and hierarchies where religious activities and affiliations are divisive. The paradoxes and challenges of religious accommodation in American schools take on an eerie mirror image of France's decision to ban noticeable religious apparel in state-supported schools. Amounting to a ban on Muslim girls' head scarves, this ostensible commitment to reinforcing the inclusive features of French republican identity symbolically exclude some and may actually drive observant Muslim girls into self-segregated religious schools.[196]

Poverty and Economic Disadvantage

Reformers worked to secure equal educational opportunity for children from low-income families before and after *Brown*. From the early challenge to unequal resources spent on the segregated schools, the NAACP focused on equalizing resources across not only racial but also economic groups. Yet even the limited successes of the desegregation movement seemed to help middle-class African Americans more than impoverished ones.[197] One response came in President Johnson's War on Poverty, yielding as a legislative success the Elementary and Secondary Education Act, which extended federal aid to assist low-income students.[198] Overcoming historic resistance to federal involvement in public schools, Title I of the Act directed federal resources to schools as a way to address educational disadvantages associated with poverty.[199]

Title I from the start never made clear whether the goal was to provide educational services specifically for poor students—warranting "pullout" programs, computers designated solely for their use, or other separate treatment—or instead to use the number of impoverished students in a given school system as a benchmark for allocating federal funds to improve all schools.[200] Many districts used the resources to identify for separate instruction those students who scored below a cutoff point on standardized tests. Experts often found these tests counterproductive for those students and for larger goals of whole-school improvement.[201] The 1988 reauthorization of the law introduced greater flexibility by allowing schools with more than 75 percent low-income students to use the funds to improve the entire educational program rather than simply target the identified students, and subsequent reforms pushed even further in the direction of whole-school improvement.[202] Treating student poverty as an indicator of risks for school failure, these initiatives did not, however, identify isolation, segregation, or stigma associated with children in poverty as issues deserving educational reform.[203]

As an even more direct repercussion of *Brown*, reformers waged an ultimately unsuccessful campaign to secure strict judicial scrutiny under the U.S. Constitution of state reliance on local wealth in the allocation of school funding.[204] Although state school finance plans vary, almost all states rely heavily on local property taxes, with some state-level funding based on general tax revenues, to finance public schools. This means that resources for local school districts are vulnerable to differences in local property values. Locales with more valuable properties can more easily generate high revenues with lower taxation rates than can locales with less valuable properties.[205] Reliance on property taxes historically has produced wide variations in the per-pupil expenditures within each state. If poorer children are more likely to live in communities with a lower tax base, the system confines these children to systematic educational disadvantage.[206] At the time of a 1994 lawsuit in Arizona, the assessed valuation per pupil in the wealthiest districts in the state was seven thousand times that in the poorest ones.[207] In 2003, the school districts identified with the highest levels of child poverty (the top 25 percent of child poverty levels) received less funding than the schools with the lowest levels (those ranking in the bottom 25 percent).[208]

The leading federal case challenging such systems involved poor Mexican-American students whose lawyers asked the courts to recognize relative poverty as a suspect class for purposes of equal protection analysis. The litigation strategy targeted reliance on local property taxation to finance schools and thus challenged policies that only indirectly classified or affected low-income students.[209] Moreover, although motivated by concern for poor children, the challenge to state school finance based on local property taxation shifted attention to school districts with lower taxable wealth.[210] Advocacy for poor children through school finance litigation faces the added complication that poor children may live in commercial and industrial areas with valuable property tax income.[211] The highest California court found defects in the state's school property-tax finance scheme because "districts with small tax bases simply cannot levy taxes at a rate sufficient to produce the revenue that more affluent districts reap with minimal tax efforts."[212] The California court reasoned that as a result, the state's finance scheme impermissibly used wealth distinctions without accomplishing a compelling state interest—and the California court declared education to be a fundamental right, protected by the Constitution. (Public backlash against the suit contributed to the passage of a tax revolt proposition, reducing the total revenues available for schooling.)[213]

By contrast, the U.S. Supreme Court, in a five-to-four decision, refused to accord heightened scrutiny when it found no evidence that the Texas school financing system discriminated against any distinct category of poor people.[214] Hence, the large reliance on local property taxes, reflecting property wealth within each district, remained permissible, according to the majority decision in *San Antonio Independent School District v. Rodriguez*. The Court further ventured that the wealth of school districts did not match a "suspect class" warranting strict scrutiny and instead permitted the state's reliance on district-level property taxes as a reasonable approach. Finding no violation of the Fourteenth Amendment's guarantee of equal protection, the Court left education and educational funding to the states.

Justice Thurgood Marshall in dissent noted that no one denied the disparities in educational funding produced by the contrasting taxable property wealth in different districts.[215] Noting that impoverished children and members of racial minorities disproportionately lived in the poorer districts, Justice Marshall reasoned that the wealth disparities in the districts alone should be enough to trigger strict scrutiny by the courts under the equal protection clause.[216]

Ironically, perhaps, the very refusal of the Court's majority to treat wealth as a suspect class permits school districts and other government actors to this day to use income or wealth indicators in assigning students to schools even as the Court closes avenues for race-based voluntary integration plans.[217] Richard Kahlenberg has developed extensive proposals for socioeconomic integration, taking advantage precisely of the room permitted for student assignments on this basis.[218] Redrawing district boundaries, including socioeconomic class as a factor in preferences for spots in schools within a school choice student assignment system, and simply distributing students to schools on the basis of their income status (using subsidized meal eligibility) are all tools available for promoting socioeconomic integration. A handful of school systems have pursued these avenues as a proxy for racial integration as a way to reduce real and perceived disparities in resources and achievement across schools with predominantly poor and predominantly wealthier students.[219] Mixing students from different socioeconomic backgrounds into the same school stands for some as the best recourse now that neither courts nor private choices make racial mixing a national priority.

Yet very few districts, despite the absence of legal barriers, have adopted this strategy of socioeconomic integration. *Brown* inspired the effort for equity in school finance but not a movement for socioeconomic integration in schools. Rather than establishing equal educational opportunity across socioeconomic class as an ideal—in the way that equal educational opportunity has emerged to help students regardless of their race, gender, language, national origin, disability, or religion—legal and political debates over issues of poverty and economic disparity have shifted toward minimum standards and clustered around the notion of "adequacy."

Much of the reform work in this area takes place within individual states, given the Supreme Court's decision to turn away a federal claim in *San Antonio Independent School District v. Rodriguez*. Reformers began to pursue the legacy of *Brown* on behalf of economically disadvantaged students by litigating for educational "equity" under state constitutional education guarantees.[220] An initial round of suits advanced the equity argument under state constitutions, but more than half of them failed. Even those that secured positive judicial results generated disappointing results in terms of actual remedies ordered and genuine effects for children.[221] If a remedy called for equalizing expenditures on a per-pupil basis, it would likely encounter opposition from parents in wealthy districts who wanted not only excellent but also superior schools for their children.[222] New Jersey's Supreme Court, relying on the New Jersey Constitution, mandated in *Robinson v. Cahill* school finance reform thirteen days after the decision in *San Antonio Independent School District*.[223] *Robinson* gave rise to dozens of further suits in New Jersey alone, as the state struggled to devise a workable system for redistributing resources across its schools.[224] Conceptual and political hurdles abound. If equity means "the same" expenditures, it might require caps on spending in wealthier districts. Raising expenditures for poorer districts would require distribution of portions of revenues from wealthier districts. Both strategies could be likely to mobilize opposition from politically savvy, influential middle-class and wealthy communities. Consider the focus and resources that upper-middle-class and wealthy parents typically devote to their children's education. Besides the advantages offered at home, wealthy parents pursue for their two- and three-year old-children early education programs that are known as the "Baby Ivies" because of the intensive admissions competition.[225] Even if reformers could surmount political opposition to redistribution of school resources, simply equalizing expenditures would not address the potentially greater needs in schools with high levels of low-income students, with high numbers of students learning English, and with many others with special needs.[226]

Hence, even when a school finance suit produced a court victory, the remedy of equalizing funding often appeared insufficient, as it would not necessarily yield the same quality of educational opportunities, given the often more complex needs of disadvantaged students attending schools with high concentrations of poor students.[227] Similarly, equity for taxpayers—so that communities willing to make the same taxation effort yield similar funds for their schools—would not directly lead to the same educational opportunity for students, especially if the resulting system pushed wealthier families toward private schools or other public systems.[228] Fundamentally, plaintiffs found remedies disappointing when courts ordered reduction of disparities in per-pupil expenditures or per-district resources but the actual level of expenditures in many instances did not increase. As a result, school finance litigation has shifted over time from an effort to reduce disparities between per-pupil expenditures in wealthy and poor districts to other strategies to assist the most disadvantaged.[229]

State-based efforts have turned to assure minimum levels of educational quality. State courts often piggybacked on developments in state legislatures and the federal government, which started to recommend and then require regular performance standards and standardized student testing.[230] Lawsuits seeking state constitutional backing for adequate education have prompted modest changes in the allocation of resources to schools, including how teachers and students spend at least some of their time, but with modest evidence of improvements in the quality of teachers or elevation of achievement for disadvantaged students.[231] The effectiveness of school finance and adequacy suits are, like most matters dealing with school finance and student achievement, subjects of disputes among researchers.

In fact, an academic debate has persisted for decades over how or whether money matters to student achievement. Some evidence suggests that spending on better trained and more experienced teachers can matter but other choices may not.[232] Social scientists debate whether changes toward more equitable funding produce better educational outcomes, measured by test performance, especially for the lower income students.[233] Researchers also write about the politicization of school finance research.[234] Greater attention to the educational needs of impoverished children on the part of lawyers, reformers, and state officials is indeed a legacy of *Brown,* but this greater attention has brought no sustained consideration of mixing students of different socioeconomic status. There has been a shift from claims of "equity" to a focus on "adequacy," with limited evidence of improved educational opportunities or outcomes. Thoughtful observers stress that real educational opportunity for children from impoverished families requires reform of housing and early childhood education and redressing the racial segregation that so highly correlates with disparities in school finance and with the isolation of the children of the poor from other children.[235] In only 15 percent of the highly segregated white schools in the United States are more than half the students eligible for free or reduced-price meals, while in 86 percent of the highly segregated black and Latino schools more than half of the students fall within those income groups.[236]

With echoes of the litigation strategy preceding *Brown,* advocacy groups in California in 2000 challenged chemistry labs with no chemicals, literature classes with no books, and computer courses where students discussed what they would do if they had access to a computer.[237] Settled at the time of *Brown*'s fiftieth anniversary in 2004 by the newly elected Republican governor Arnold Schwarzenegger, this suit secured $138 million in additional state funding for instructional materials for schools identified in need and $50 million for implementation costs and other oversight-related activities.[238] Critics who had once supported the suit later charged that the settlement had gained inches rather than yards and had dropped the ball on broader pursuit of adequate educational opportunities for poor students.[239]

Working through the promise of equal opportunity in schools without embracing integration across lines of difference, reformers have pursued one strand of *Brown* in seeking resources for low-income students, even-handed treatment of religion, and protection of students regardless of sexual orientation. What happens when unequal—or oppressive—treatment on the basis of culture, language, disability, race, religion, and politics combine? Reformers struggling over equal educational opportunities for Indians, Native Hawai'ians, and others draw on the legacy of *Brown* while confronting the significance of social hierarchy and group identity.

4

Reverberations for American Indians, Native Hawai'ians, and Group Rights

People are not only exploited and oppressed in similar ways, they are exploited and oppressed in different and specific ways.

—Mike Cole

Usually left out of discussions of school desegregation, the historic treatments of American Indians and Native Hawai'ians in the development of schooling in the United States was a corollary of conquest and colonialism.[1] As late as the 1950s, forced assimilation and eradication of indigenous cultures pervaded what was considered the "education" of students in these groups.[2] The social, political, and legal civil rights initiatives surrounding *Brown* helped to inspire a rights consciousness among Indian and Native Hawai'ian reformers and activists, who embraced the ideal of equal opportunity while reclaiming cultural traditions. Between the 1960s and 2007, complex fights over ethnic classification, separation, integration, and self-determination emerged for both American Indians and Native Hawai'ians.

Their struggles, crucial in themselves, also bring to the fore a challenging underlying problem: are distinct individuals or groups the proper unit of analysis and protection in the pursuit of equality?[3] The centrality of the individual to law and culture in the United States tends to mute this question. Yet in this country as well as elsewhere, equal treatment or equal opportunity has two faces: promoting individual development and liberty, regardless of race, culture, religion, gender, or other group-based characteristic, and protection for groups that afford their members

96

meaning and identity. Nowhere is the tension between these two alternatives more apparent than in schooling, which involves socialization of each new generation in the values and expectations of their elders. Will that socialization direct each individual to a common world focused on the academic and social mobility of distinct individuals or will it inculcate traditions and values associated with particular groups?

Even in the United States, devoted to inclusive individualism, the Supreme Court rejected a statute requiring students to attend schools run by the government and created exemptions from compulsory school fines when they burdened a group's practices and hopes for their children. In *Pierce v. Society of Sisters*, the Court respected the rights of parents to select private schooling in order to inculcate a religious identity or other "additional obligations."[4] To advance the same chance for every individual to succeed academically, schools may be advised to acknowledge and even strengthen the influence of group-based experiences on the students' preparation and aspirations. In *Wisconsin v. Yoder*, the Court exempted Amish parents from the compulsory school law fine after the litigants explained how the social integration of their high-school-aged children would interfere with the manual labor, religious reflection, and participation in the separate cultural community that these Amish parents wanted for their children.[5] Both decisions can be reconciled with a central commitment to the individual only if the individuals of interest here are the parents, allowed in each instance the latitude to shape their children's futures and to sustain the cultural pluralism that they find meaningful. Even in this view, equal treatment for groups and preservation of cultural diversity contends with demands of individual opportunity. For when the group affiliation gains respect as a feature of a distinct individual's life, tricky questions about the status of group membership for legal and policy purposes arise, especially in the context of schooling. Can people claim rights of full inclusion in the society's mainstream without giving up their identities as members of religious, cultural, ethnic, or racial subgroups? Can forms of schooling preserve group identities in ways that support rather than undermine a national project of ensuring individual opportunity and equality? What degree of attention to group traditions best cultivates a new generation of productive, self-governing, and mutually respectful individuals?

Brown can be enlisted to assist competing claims over individual and group rights, for it demands freedom from governmental sorting of individuals into schools by identity at the same time that it offers a model of group mobilization to demand equal treatment of individuals who identify with particular religious, cultural, ethnic, or racial groups. And because the tension between individual rights and respect for groups is so often inflected by struggles against group-based oppression, the group-based remedies can seem essential. Degradation of students because of the language they speak at home, their skin color, the religion they practice, or the sexual orientation they claim may make it seem necessary to provide school resources that honor these identities and practices. This explains why some of the motivation for private religious schools, Afrocentric schools, and Arabic-language and culture schools is similar to the arguments for schools exclusively for girls and schools designed for gay, lesbian, bisexual, or transgendered students.[6] An alternative route toward equality would be to create inclusive schools that center on the diverse life histories and experiences of all students—both as unique persons and as members of various groups.[7] A chronicle of the struggles over the education of American Indians, Native Hawai'ians, and other cultural groups offers instruction about failures to redress historical oppression on the basis of group membership.

American Indians

Over much of U.S. history, the U.S. government forced American Indians off the land they inhabited, so that white settlers could take possession of it and then drive the Native Americans into isolated territories. Some 120 of the 400 treaties the federal government negotiated with Indian tribes before 1871 included terms providing for the education of Indian children in English.[8] In most places in the country, Indian children were sent to specialized separate schools, if any school at all. The federal government paid to school Indians in Catholic missionary schools until 1900. At that time, reformers opposed to Catholicism pressured the federal government to create its own schools for Indian children. In the peak of the fervor for Americanizing Indian children, reformers sought to remove them from their native cultures and tribal traditions and even removed them from their families.[9] More extreme than the school segregation of blacks and Hispanics, the public policy of Indian removal sought to restrict white-Indian contact, as did the reservation system after the Civil War.[10] Missionaries and government agents alike pursued the assimilation and eradication of tribal culture, and used boarding schools as a chief vehicle.[11]

Richard Henry Pratt, founder of the first Indian boarding school outside of a reservation, summarized the philosophy of the "civilizing" function of these schools with the memorable phrase "Kill the Indian and Save the Man."[12] Viewed at the time as an enlightened "friend of the Indians" because of his commitment to integrating them into the general society, Pratt himself authorized beatings when Indian students spoke in their native languages, restricted students' contact with their families and communities, and devised a model for boarding schools that others pursued by kidnapping children and keeping them in schools plagued by disease, despair, and sexual abuse.[13] Following on the government's treatment of Indians throughout the nineteenth century, marked by subjugation, deceit, theft of lands, and cruelty,[14] reformers in the twentieth century sought to redeem the promise that had been made in exchange for the land taken from the Indians: "civilization"— that is, that they would be able to become like whites.[15]

Reports on government schools for Indians since the 1920s have documented repeated failures in these schools. At the same time that they inflicted abuse on students, they failed to educate and instead produced high dropout rates and low achievement.[16] The federal government preferred boarding schools between 1879 and 1917, but then it reduced reliance on them and pushed for the education of Indians in local public schools.[17] By the 1930s, the federal government was promoting the organization or reorganization of tribes in a spirit of cultural pluralism.[18] But then came a policy of "termination"—pushing rapid assimilation and seeking to end the "special relationship" between the tribes and the federal government. The current policy followed, reflecting the mood of the civil rights era after *Brown* and favoring tribal self-determination and self-governance.[19]

Brown, the civil rights movement, and then the bilingual education movement contributed to the push for reforming schools for Indians in the 1960s and 1970s in a way that would respect their languages and customs both as worthy of preservation and as a way to enhance Indian students' comfort and success in school.[20] New attention to the education of all minorities after the *Brown* decision stimulated inquiries by Congress. Some Republicans from the West and Southwest picked up the cause of rights for Native Americans as a civil rights issue of their own.[21] Public officials and Indians joined in condemning the reportedly poor academic achievement, high dropout rates, and forced assimilation occurring in Indian schools, as well as their failure to devote any schooling time to passing on Indian cultures and languages.[22] A 1969 Senate report concluded that the federal education policy for Indians "was a failure of major proportions."[23] The report called for involving Indian parents and communities in education planning, turning curricular attention to bicultural and bilingual programs, and adopting best practices in teaching disadvantaged students.[24]

In the early 1960s, President John F. Kennedy authorized expanded educational programs as part of enlarged federal services for Indians. President Lyndon B. Johnson appointed an Indian to serve as commissioner of Indian affairs, the first in over a century.[25] President Richard M. Nixon's 1970 statement to Congress concerning the accomplishments and contributions of America's Indians led to wider federal support for Indians' self-determination in directing their children's education.[26] Since the 1970s, this focus on self-determination and cultural preservation, rather than integration, has dominated federal educational policy for Indians. The U.S. Commission on Civil Rights, prompted in part by the growing confrontationist claims of the American Indian Movement, issued a report criticizing the exclusion of Indians from power over schools for their children. This report paved the way for the Indian Self-Determination and Education Assistance Act of 1975, which supported Indian control (rather than federal Bureau of Indian Affairs control) in governing and running schools for Indians.[27] This initiative reinforced the rationale for separate schools while also expanding employment opportunities for Indians on reservations, where unemployment can reach more than 80 percent.[28]

In addition to the Indian Self-Determination and Education Assistance Act,[29] Congress, over time, enacted the Tribally Controlled Schools Act of 1988,[30] the Indian Education Act (which includes Alaskan Natives), and the Native American Languages Act.[31] In addition, the Johnson-O'Malley Act shifted federal resources to Indian control, authorizing federal contracts to provide for the education of Indians.[32] Each of these efforts recognized Indian children as having particular educational needs and authorizes federal support not just for individuals with backgrounds as Indians but for tribes and linguistic groups. Taken together, these federal statutes and the ongoing work of the Bureau of Indian Affairs have maintained the practice of treatment of Indians as groups, entitled to degrees of self-governance and deserving cultural preservation.

Although much of federal policy addressing Indians focuses on reservations and tribal governance, since 1924 the United States has accorded Indians the rights of citizens, free to live and attend schools anywhere. The vast majority do not live on reservations set aside for Indians and most American Indians attend public schools.[33] The federal government has continued to fund schools on reservations while working to support greater tribal control of those schools. Nationwide, Indians compose only 1 percent of the student population, but they form larger percentages of local public schools where Indian communities are clustered, chiefly in rural communities in the West and Southwest, and especially in Oklahoma and South Dakota.[34] Some educational experiments have pursued greater integration of Indians with whites,[35] but in the late 1970s reformers turned to separate instruction in order to enhance Indian culture, language, and identities.[36] Some reformers developed a new kind of separate boarding school, designed not to terminate Indian culture but instead to cultivate Indian identities in an environment separate from both whites and from Indian families and communities.[37] Typically single-sex, these boarding schools separated family groups not only by gender but also by age.[38] Ironically, these schools mixed students from different tribes and contributed to the development of a pan-Indian consciousness, enabling a broader alliance for the preservation of Indian identities and cultures, now forged as much through resistance as through continuity with long-standing heritage.[39] By 2009, the seven federally funded off-reservation boarding schools became oversubscribed.[40]

Continuing with the policy of cultural preservation, in 1990 President George H. W. Bush signed the Native American Languages Act,[41] intended to preserve and promote Native American languages and language instruction.[42] For many, sending children to schools outside the reservations recalled the stigma associated with the forced assimilation of the boarding school era.[43] Yet due to declining resources, national pressures for higher academic achievement, and the dimming of negative views of the past assimilation policies, many Indian families looking for quality education now pursue education outside reservations and beyond Indian country.[44] Public school systems, which themselves often seek to boost enrollments and the associated per-pupil expenditures of public dollars, are more likely than in the past to welcome those students, even though some unwritten rules of ethnic separation may persist in the off-reservation public schools.[45]

In recent years, tribes have increasingly used federal funds to devise a system of private college-level programs,[46] mainly community colleges, where Indian students perform better and stay in school longer than they do in other colleges.[47] Thirty community colleges serve Native Americans in thirteen states.[48] Boosted by federal funds, philanthropy, and modest improvements in the economic conditions of some Indian communities, these institutions are a source of pride due to the cultural activities they pursue and the students' academic success.[49] Eligible for federal funds if controlled by a federally recognized tribe, these schools must be open to all Indian students; and they may admit non-Indians, although they do not have to do so.[50] American Indian education here pursues the path of separation and the strengthening of group pride.

Native Hawai'ians

Missionary education permeated Hawaii during the nineteenth century and continued even after American colonialists overthrew the monarchy of Hawaii in 1893. Policies to segregate Native Hawai'ians from other students accompanied the creation of the first "common schools." After the end of legally enforced segregation, separate patterns persisted informally, and Hawai'i remains the state with the highest percentage of students—chiefly non–Native Hawai'ians—enrolled in private schools.[51] A unique initiative is the prestigious private school system founded to serve Native Hawai'ians. Its exclusion of others has produced high-profile legal challenges in which both sides claim inspiration from *Brown*.

The admissions policy at the Kamehameha Schools in Hawai'i gives preference to students with Native Hawai'ian ancestry.[52] Created under a trust established by Bernice Pauahi Bishop, the last descendant of the line of Hawai'ian royalty, the private Kamehameha schools are supported by an endowment that was valued at more than $9 billion in 2007, with approximately $127 million spent that year on campus-based programs.[53] The trust subsidizes 95 percent of the educational costs at the schools, which enroll sixty-seven hundred students of Hawai'ian ancestry at K–12 campuses on Oahu, Maui, and Hawai'i and thirty preschool sites statewide.[54] An unnamed non-Hawai'ian student challenged the school's admissions policy, stating that it violated section 1981 of the 1966 Civil Rights Act; the plaintiff lost in federal district court and won in the court of appeals, only to lose when that court reheard the case en banc. The fifteen-person panel split eight to seven in upholding the school's Native Hawai'ian preference policy.[55]

In this unique context, a majority of judges on the federal Court of Appeals for the Ninth Circuit, sitting en banc, concluded that the preferential admissions policy was valid. The majority reached this conclusion because the enterprise was wholly private and had been established when Hawai'i was still a sovereign nation with the intent of counteracting the significant, ongoing educational deficits of Native Hawai'ian children in Hawai'i. In addition, the majority's decision was based on the fact that Congress had itself enacted legislation meant to address the educational disadvantages experienced by Native Hawai'ian students.[56] A concurring opinion reached the same result by viewing Native Hawai'ian as a political rather than a racial classification, more like Indian tribes than African Americans, and thus given more latitude for the use of group preference.[57]

The contrast between the majority and the dissent in addressing the Kamehameha schools illuminates the clash between the remedial commitments represented by Congress's National Hawai'ian Education Act of 2002, which aims to address the "near-annihilation of the Hawai'ian people," and the "color-blindness" approach to equality.[58] Neither of these approaches recognized diversity as a potentially compelling public interest, even though the Supreme Court has treated diversity as compelling enough to permit race-conscious elements in college and graduate school admissions. Encountering people from different backgrounds may seem not quite the point for the elementary and high school programs at the Kamehameha schools, although the schools' defenders are quick to note the ethnic, racial, and religious diversity of their student bodies, due to intermarriage.[59] On a potential collision course with their admissions policy is the position taken by recent members of the Supreme Court who oppose race-conscious elements in assigning students to public school classrooms from kindergarten through high school.[60] If the Native Hawai'ian category is viewed as a racial category, it could indeed fall before the Supreme Court's restrictions on the use of race in school admissions.

The Native Hawai'ian situation is, however, sui generis. Several civil rights advocates have emphasized the historical uniqueness and distinct purposes of the schools:

> The Kamehameha Schools were created in 1883, 15 years before the United States annexed Hawai'i, by the private trust of Princess Bernice Pauahi Bishop, the last direct descendant of Hawai'i's first king. The princess created the trust to uplift Hawai'ian children through education because the forces of Western encroachment had nearly decimated the Hawai'ian people and foreshadowed the American takeover of the Hawai'ian government. The princess sought not to exclude others by labeling them inferior or unworthy (a classic civil-rights violation) but rather to rebuild her own people (an act of restoration and self-determination).[61]

Similarly, a conservative commentator noted: "Congress has repeatedly acknowledged the continuing need for remedial race-based legislation, having passed more than eighty-five laws that include preferences for Native Hawai'ians."[62] Despite the uniqueness of this history, the most unusual feature of the situation is the attractiveness of schools that have historically been restricted to a disadvantaged minority. In this dimension, these schools resemble but still are not the same as some all-girls schools whose excellence or special programs have drawn male applicants.[63]

While it was pending on petition for certiorari in the United States Supreme Court, the case was settled for $7 million.[64] A future suit may arise, however, if a non–Native Hawai'ian wishes to attend the schools and is willing to pursue a challenge all the way to the U.S. Supreme Court. Such a future suit is an unlikely but not unimaginable prospect. Prospective students of all backgrounds could desire places in the Kamehameha Schools because of the resources the schools can devote to education. Tuition is a mere 6.2 percent of the costs of the excellent education there, and financial aid assists those for whom that charge is too high.[65] With relatively highly paid teachers, excellent facilities, and arts and sports programs, the schools are highly attractive and offer quality private schooling at a fraction of the price of comparable schools. The charitable trust also supports aid for the schools' alumni as they pursue higher education.[66]

The cultural dimensions of the schools have changed over time. The content and focus on instruction at the schools shifted back and forth over the years from an initial goal of Americanizing students and providing vocational education (from 1887 to around 1924),[67] to a dual-track program including a competitive academic track,[68] to a period without admissions tests, and now as a "symbol of educational excellence for Hawai'ians."[69] Organized as a Christian school, intended to ground students in Christian values, the initial private school originally banned the hula until the 1950s but participated in a renaissance of Hawai'ian culture in the 1960s.[70] The preschool programs, educational outreach programs, teacher training, and other initiatives offered beyond the campuses include Native Hawai'ian cultural programs and literacy support. Yet by retaining the requirement of Native Hawai'ian ancestry for admission, Kamehameha Schools represent a distinctive symbol of excellence and a continuous link to the past, even for Native Hawai'ians who do not have a formal affiliation with the schools.

In a notable development, the Kamehameha Schools in recent years offered support to the public schools with the goals of raising educational outcomes for Native Hawai'ians in those schools and also assisting in the startup and conversion of Hawaiian-focused charter schools and Native Hawai'ian "immersion schools."[71] Hawaii authorized the creation of twenty-five charter schools in 2001, and twelve of these pursued Native Hawai'ian educational programs, culture, and language. Native Hawai'ians comprise about 93 percent of the students enrolled in the Native Hawai'ian–focused charter schools, while about 26 percent of the entire student population is Native Hawai'ian.[72] Native Hawai'ian students attending Hawai'ian-oriented charter schools perform better on standardized tests than do Native Hawai'ians in the other public schools, although both groups fall at least ten points below statewide averages.[73]

If the primary purpose of the schools was to maintain and pass on Native Hawai'ian traditions,[74] or even to boost academic performance by Native Hawai'ians through culturally responsive teaching, the Native

Hawai'ian charter schools might seem an adequate substitute. They proceed without an admissions requirement pertaining to ancestry while attracting predominantly Native Hawai'ian student bodies. This approach would seem a prime example of indirectly achieving what would be illegal if the courts or legislature banned admission criteria limited to those with Native Hawai'ian ancestry.[75]

Meanwhile, the Native Hawai'ian Education Act, originally enacted in 1988 and reauthorized in 2002 as part of the No Child Left Behind Act, supports innovative educational programs for Native Hawai'ians and seeks to redress their pattern of an achievement gap compared with other students. Under this program, the federal Department of Education has disbursed about $30 million in annual grants to support initiatives from prenatal to postsecondary schooling for this population since 2002, with ongoing efforts to devise assessments about the impact of such efforts.[76]

Reflecting distinctive histories and battling cultural domination, American Indian and Native Hawai'ian schools may embrace self-segregation in order to enhance political control of their children's schooling or to elevate attention to traditional culture and language or to increase the chances their children will attend schools run by teachers committed to the students' success and well-being. Separate instruction, once imposed, may be embraced as preferable by those who have been disadvantaged. The fact that both Native Americans and Native Hawai'ians have often been racialized—treated as nonwhite—contributes to their historic subordination. If understood as political groups, they legally could proceed in distinctive schools; if viewed in racial terms, legal concern under the stringent scrutiny of any racial classification that the Supreme Court has come to impose would be triggered. The question remains whether the embrace of self-segregation by large numbers of Native Hawai'ians avoids legal challenge and also overcomes the historical inequalities in educational opportunity—or whether the civic equality represented by minority groups choosing essentially separate schooling perpetuates separation in schools, society, and politics.

Caution about identity-based schooling, even when apparently chosen by members of minority groups, must remain as long as people remember the forced exclusion of Native American and Native Hawai'ian students, the officially imposed racial segregation of African Americans and Mexican Americans, and the exclusion of entire Japanese and Japanese-American communities during World War II.[77] Yet the dimensions of self-determination that are present in contemporary schools identified as Indian or as Native Hawai'ian raise possibilities for the assertion of power by minority groups.

Assessing the Legacies for Groups and Individuals

Brown is held up in the United States for many propositions, but the central ones are that (1) educational opportunity is so crucial to any individual's realistic chances of success in life that it must be made available to all on equal terms,[78] and (2) given the nation's history of mandated segregation, separate educational facilities are inherently unequal.[79]

Yet, as with race, in the contexts of each of these other dimensions of different identities, mixing students who are different remains an elusive, contested, or even rejected goal. Accepting schools that do not mix students of different backgrounds and identities may be a concession to failed integration efforts. But in many settings, education organized around students' group-based identities rallies supporters who believe better outcomes—on standard educational measures or other criteria—will accompany identity-based schools. Researchers supply some (often mixed) empirical support to justify separate instruction in terms of academic achievement or student self-esteem in a way that no modern evidence could be used to justify education for students officially sorted by race. Explicit defenses of separate instruction grow more difficult when the resulting classrooms look like the racially segregated classrooms before *Brown*. Hence, the Supreme Court's recent rejection of voluntary uses of racial classification to promote integrated schooling is particularly unfortunate, as there is no possible good reason for racial segregation, while still potentially defensible reasons are proffered for Native Hawai'ian education, single sex education, classrooms for students with learning disabilities, and programs for immigrants.[80] Might some of these reasons some day come to be viewed as being as antiquated and mistaken as old claims that inherent racial differences justified racial segregation?

Protecting individuals as individuals but also ensuring freedom of individuals and groups to affiliate around a shared identity, culture, or tradition are simultaneously important values. Reconciling the two is difficult enough, but the difficulty is compounded when the two values also arise against the backdrop of historic exclusion or subordination of individuals on the basis of a group trait. Add to this the possibility of two different histories of exclusion and subordination, associated with two groups, and what appears is the kind of unusual Supreme Court case that suggests truth is often stranger than fiction (or a law professor's exam hypotheticals).

The case is *Board of Education of Kiryas Joel Village School District v. Grumet*.[81] In this 1994 case, the Supreme Court struck down a New York state statute that created a special public school district exclusively to educate students with disabilities in a community populated entirely by ultra-Orthodox Jews. Issues of religious, linguistic, and cultural identity for descendants of Holocaust survivors motivated the community's advocacy for the special school district; the parents pursuing the statute also invoked rights of students with disabilities to the free, appropriate public education won as a victory for another historically excluded group.

The case became a contest between narratives of exclusion and the pursuit of equality. From the perspective of members of the Satmar Hasidim, the largest, most traditional subgroup of the Hasidic strand of ultra-Orthodox Judaism, the special school district was their entitlement as members of the political community, just as any other town could apply for a public school. They only needed it for their children with disabilities because they provided private, single-sex religious schools for their other children. The disabled children needed extra services and specialized education—and were entitled to federal and state funds for those purposes.[82] During the 1980s, the state had provided special publicly funded services on the sites of the religious schools, but the Supreme Court, at the height of its enforcement of separation between state and religion, had ended that practice.[83] Some of these Hasidic parents had then sent their disabled children to the public schools in the next town, only to find that their children experienced "panic, fear and trauma" in response to their encounters with people so different from themselves and alleged insensitivity to their cultural and linguistic differences.[84] Some might criticize the Village of Kiryas Joel for failing to include disabled children in their private religious schools, either as a matter of religious duty or as a means to maximize the experience of inclusion for those students. Yet if they did so, then the disabled children would be isolated from the larger secular world and its opportunities.

Like the larger Satmar community, the twelve thousand individuals living in Kiryas Joel had resisted the assimilation offered by modern secular Europe and by the economic and civic opportunities in the United States.[85] They had established themselves in the United States to honor the memory of those murdered during World War II by creating separate communities resembling the eastern European villages that survivors had fled. They had transported their way of life from Hungary to Brooklyn, and then some had moved to the place they named the Village of Kiryas Joel. The Satmar in Kiryas Joel speak Yiddish; they dress in clothes more typical of medieval communities than late twentieth- or twenty-first-century America; they segregate the sexes outside the home; and they eschew television, radio, and English-language publications.[86] Initially an unincorporated area, Kiryas Joel eventually was formally incorporated, with Satmar Hasidim comprising 99 percent of the population. At the urging of town residents, the New York legislature then authorized it to create public schools. It was that authority that the community used to create schools, but solely for their children with disabilities.

Beyond the school context, many outside observers have criticized the authoritarian Satmar religious leadership and the community's internal schisms; some accuse members of the community of using devious tactics of appeasement, bribery, and manipulation.[87] But the sharpest criticism has been that the Satmar are self-segregating and are using public funds to pay for an essentially private school, solely for their own disabled children and separated from the rest of the world.[88] There is some basis, outside the court record, for viewing the Satmar community as intentionally separating themselves from others. One Satmar Hasidic man residing in New York City was quoted as saying: "If we have our kids learning with [others], they'll be corrupted. We don't hate these people, but we don't like them. We want to be separate. It's intentional."[89] Another member of the Satmar community in Williamsburg, Brooklyn, warned of outside influence on children—as a defense of an assault on a Lubavitcher rabbi after he offered lessons to an eighteen-year-old Satmar.[90]

Whatever views toward separatism some members of the community hold, the community set up for their special needs children a public school administered by a non-Hasidic superintendent with twenty years of experience in the field of bilingual-bicultural education and teachers from outside the community to offer entirely secular instruction.[91] The village also made this school coeducational, in contrast to the single-sex private schools used for the other children in Kiryas Joel. And members of the neighboring community were apparently not displeased to avoid having to educate the Yiddish-speaking special needs Satmar Hasidic children.[92]

The New York School Board Association challenged the state's authorization of the school as a violation of the establishment clause, and the Supreme Court agreed, although the case triggered multiple opinions and rationales.[93] The state legislature responded to the decision by drafting new legislation crafted as a general statute granting every local community that meets certain neutral criteria the right to carve out its own school district—and redrafted the law twice more until it finally withstood challenges in state court. The Supreme Court later allowed state-funded special education services on the sites of private parochial schools; hence the private schools of Kiryas Joel could have such services provided on-site. Nonetheless, the Kiryas Joel Village School District continues to operate its one school, serving 250 special needs students drawn from within Kiryas Joel and from other neighboring Hasidic communities.[94]

This case illustrates judicial discomfort with self-segregation, even though the homogeneity of the community stems from private choices. Elsewhere, private choices often avoid constitutional scrutiny. The Supreme Court itself has refused to authorize remedies for a city's intentional racial segregation if those remedies cross municipal borders into a community without proof of its own intentional racial discrimination.[95] The most telling issue, though, from the vantage point that values inclusion and social integration, was raised by Justice Stevens in a concurring opinion. He rejected the assumption pervading the case that the only available choices were to expose the disabled Hasidic children to "panic, fear and trauma" in the neighboring school system or to create a special school district for them.[96] Instead, "the State could have taken steps to alleviate the children's fear by teaching their schoolmates to be tolerant and respectful of Satmar customs."[97] No one at the Court or apparently elsewhere put a sufficient value on social integration to turn to this alternative. Ultimately, the religious group creating its own separate town and its own separate school system proved more acceptable than social integration. Unwanted by the Satmar Hasidim and also unwanted by their neighbors, social integration was neither mandated nor pushed.

Because of its association with state-backed discrimination, any government educational policy that separates students by identity, even when it is in some sense "voluntary," should be scoured for evidence that it actually promotes equal opportunity for each individual to have real success in life. Special-identity schools—organized by gender, disability, immigrant status, cultural heritage, sexual orientation, or religion—may well invite highly motivated students, teachers, and parents and help attract the kind of committed teachers and public and private resources that build successful schools. Special-identity schools may also provide an environment where the students feel cared for, believed in, and safe from the harms of either low expectations or harassment. Yet such schools may also contribute to misunderstandings about different identities or may fail to develop students' abilities to navigate and thrive in more diverse settings.

If a school district, or state, or nation has the opportunity to start from scratch, should it promote or restrict special-identity schools? This is the very question that is seldom discussed yet is directly presented by the emergence of school choice initiatives as public magnet schools, charter schools, and vouchers enabling private school choice multiply around the country. School choice initiatives, explored in the next chapter, pose challenges and opportunities for equality and integration across the lines of students' identities and backgrounds.

School Choice and Choice Schools

Resisting, Realizing, or Replacing **Brown?**

If school choice is to enjoy a brighter future than wave upon wave of supposed school reforms of the past, it is time for reformers to fight not just for choice but for good choices.
—Frederick M. Hess[1]

To school desegregation activists in the 1960s, school choice plans represented one of a series of tactics of avoidance or obstruction.[2] Yet choice programs became part of school desegregation remedies and then became initiatives for varied school reforms. Political alliances and clashes around the issue of school choice color public perceptions even more than the actual effects of school choice on students' achievement or social integration. School choice can enable both self-segregation or student mixing across many lines of difference. As a tool of school reform, school choice continues to hold promise and risks for those seeking equality and integration within schools while enhancing pluralism and respect for differences in society as a whole. Yet some forms of school choice could undermine equality goals unless they are accompanied by direct efforts to maintain and enforce these goals.[3]

Widespread perceptions that American schools are failing have fueled a major nationwide movement for school reform since the early 1980s.[4] At the forefront have been business leaders who—worried about American competitiveness and the qualifications of the workforce for jobs requiring increasing technical skills—have brought conceptions of competition and innovation to the school reform initiatives. Parents and teachers, seeking greater control of local schools, have also energized the movement. Challenging established school bureaucracies and political arrangements, these reformers have pushed for performance standards, voucher systems to promote competition and consumer choices, site-based management, and other opportunities for innovation at the level of the individual school rather than the district or statewide system.

One of the key themes pursued by a range of parents, teachers, business leaders, and other advocates as a motor for reform is parental choice.[5] This concept combines a market-style consumer sovereignty idea with notions of personal liberty. School choice stimulates competition among providers, as parents look for benchmarks for assessing quality. As a result, states and localities have initiated institutional innovations.[6] These include magnet and pilot schools, which draw students from an entire district by offering a special focus. Vouchers permit poor students to use public funds to pay tuition in private schools. Charter schools allow groups of teachers, parents, or others to propose their own ideas for running individual public schools and to secure public aid to do so.[7] By the end of the 1990s, publicly subsidized schooling options increased sufficiently that people could no longer assume that government just assigned students to their elementary, middle, and high schools.

Yet in a more basic sense, "school choice" in principle has always existed in the United States. Those with sufficient economic means have always been able to select schools either by choosing to live in a district with the desired public schools or by paying for private schooling. The first option, moving to a specific district, exists because student assignment to public schools has traditionally tracked residential areas. School expenditures and quality in large part reflect local property taxes and local administrative decisions. The quality of local public schools in turn affects local property values, with the result that family income and wealth have deeply influenced the actual range of public school choices available to particular children. The end of racial and religious restrictions in residential housing covenants marked the demise of those barriers to this kind of residential-based school choice.

Private schooling, an option that existed even before the rise of public, government-subsidized schools, remains available to those who can afford the tuition or obtain a scholarship. Despite a legislative initiative to restrict school-aged children to public schooling, the U.S. Supreme Court in the striking 1925 landmark case *Pierce v. Society of Sisters* interpreted the Constitution as ensuring parental choice for private options, whether religious or secular.[8] In that case, the Court rejected a law enacted by an Oregon referendum launched by the Ku Klux Klan and the Oregon Scottish Rite Masons to undermine Catholic schools by eliminating private schooling as an option for satisfying the state's compulsory schooling law. The Court ruled that Oregon's law impermissibly restricted the liberty of parents to direct the upbringing and education of their children. By ensuring constitutional protection for private parental choice of children's schools, the Court preserved schools with religious, military, or other missions, with the stipulation that they also satisfy the governing state's basic requirements for compulsory schooling.[9]

"Homeschooling" received a major boost after the Supreme Court permitted Amish families to bypass the high school attendance requirement of Wisconsin's compulsory schooling statute in 1972.[10] Although the case itself involved the limited and specific claim that state-enforced attendance at a regional public high school was contrary to the religious beliefs and way of life of the Amish parents, the Court more generally invoked the rights of parents to guide their children and noted the expert testimony that the Amish parents offered an "ideal" vocational education to their adolescent children.[11] The Supreme Court ruling stimulated homeschooling by evangelical Christian parents, antiestablishment parents, families worried about drugs and negative peer pressure in schools, and high-achieving parents who might have objections to mainstream public schools.[12] By 2007, parents in the United States chose to homeschool some 1.5 million students.[13]

Families without economic resources to pay for private schools or devote parental time to homeschooling typically had only the option of their neighborhood public school. In most urban, economically impoverished areas, the only real alternative would be a local Catholic school, and even the relatively low tuition at these schools, subsidized by the Church, would remain out of reach for many families. Perhaps this is why the "school choice" movement in the 1980s and 1990s drew support from parents frustrated by the poor educational outcomes, high dropout rates, and violence at many urban schools. The movement also capitalized on the rhetoric of market-based competition, the interest of philanthropists, and the support of Catholic leaders and members of some other religious groups.

Yet school choice initiatives had come even earlier—from the conservative think tanks and advocacy groups that orchestrated the research studies, litigation and legislation initiatives, and public relations of the school choice movement. Amid news accounts and commission reports identifying a national educational crisis, reformers advocated a variety of reforms under the banner of "choice," including public vouchers to pay for private schooling, magnet and pilot schools open to any student within a particular public system, and public charters inviting entrepreneurial groups to propose and implement innovative schools. Such charter schools would be funded with public dollars but often with fewer restraints from public educational bureaucracies and with the ability to bypass the terms of teachers' collective bargaining agreements. Advocates of these initiatives argued that school choice would let parents and guardians exercise their own preferences in selecting schools, would generate competitive pressures to improve the quality of education, and would grant low-income parents some of the latitude of choice experienced by parents with more resources.

Critics raised doubts on each front. Empirical evidence about actual effects is limited and unreliable, given that studies are usually funded by politicized sources. Nonetheless, no one doubts that school choice initiatives since the 1980s have spurred an era of school innovation, enabling the creation of a variety of schools with special missions. Many magnet, charter, and private schools in turn are marketed to appeal to specialized constituencies and to segment student bodies along lines of identity or affiliation. Given the Supreme Court's recent decisions constricting the use of race in student assignments, the one kind of school not permitted now is one that uses students' racial identities—even if the goal is to produce a racially integrated school.[14]

This chapter, after considering the politics, scope, and effects of school choice, looks at the rise of varied special-mission schools and considers their potential for separating or combining students along lines of identity and affiliation. But first, the definition, history, and scope of school choice deserve attention.

Defining and Tracing School Choice

"School choice" here will refer to initiatives authorizing the use of government resources to enable parents and school-aged children to select a school rather than simply be assigned to one by the government, although choice over schooling of a fundamental sort exists for parents with sufficient resources to pay for private school, to move to a district with desirable public schools, or to homeschool their children. Magnet and pilot schools within public systems, school transfers, charter schools, and vouchers for private school tuition offer choices.

Magnet schools. This type of school offers a specialized curriculum or program and admits students through a lottery or as one option among all of the public schools in the district where a student resides.[15] Magnet schools originally developed as a mechanism to promote racial integration and invited students of all races to select from among schools within districts previously marked by segregation. Districts interested in developing magnet schools received a boost from federal funding amounting to $955 million between 1984 and 1994.[16] Intended to attract students because of their special qualities, magnet schools often identify themselves in terms of special curricular offerings in science, math, and technology, visual and performing arts, or studies of a particular foreign language or geography. The use of magnet schools to achieve racial balance within and across districts persisted until 2007, when the Supreme Court halted explicit use of race even as one factor in assigning students to public schools, absent a prior judicial finding of official intentional racial segregation.[17]

Testing and transfers. The centerpiece of President George W. Bush's domestic policy, the federal No Child Left Behind Act, extended previous federal, state, and local initiatives giving parents with students in low-performing schools the option to transfer their children to other public schools and providing public reimbursement for transportation costs—although minimal funding, bureaucratic barriers, and limited spaces in better schools limit this option to very few students.[18] The Act's requirement of annual achievement testing for students in grades 3–8, according to plans developed by each state, pushed for consequences for schools that do not demonstrate progress on these measures.[19] Such testing is intended both as motivation for individuals and schools and to provide measures for comparison—and competition—among schools and even among states. The idea, not yet realized fully in practice, is that with multiple competing schooling options and information from standardized test results, individual parents could make more informed choices about their children's education and public and private funders could decide the best use of their educational dollars. Failing schools would be expected to close or change their methods.

Critics charge that the tests, which focus on limited math and reading skills, narrow instruction in ways that do disservice to genuine learning and critical thought[20] and that inadequate funding for teachers, tutoring, and other supports undermines the Act's goals and violates the rule against unfunded federal mandates.[21] The focus on tests concentrates attention on students' meeting of certain threshold scores rather than students' progress and confuses state and federal standards, producing waste and undermining intended accountability.[22] Yet even with these many problems, the push for national accountability in education has both encouraged and enabled the proliferation of different types of school settings and educational strategies. Given performance measures and outcome goals, everyone concerned with schooling can propose alternative ways to achieve the goals and advocate competition among the alternatives as a strategy for overall success. Hence, as paradoxical as it may seem, the increasing federal role in education represented by the No Child Left Behind Act supports rather than displaces the plural and diverse approaches emerging within local and regional school systems through charter school initiatives and vouchers for private education.[23] These options can engage parents and students in the very process of selecting schools and thereby promote greater family involvement, a strong factor in student achievement. The pluralist framework can also draw talented people into schooling who otherwise would not have pursued teaching or educational administration.

Charter schools. School choice as a movement jumped to a new level in 1991 when Minnesota adopted the first state law authorizing individuals and groups to seek state approval and public funding to launch "charter schools." By 2004, forty states, the District of Columbia, and Puerto Rico had enacted charter school laws and deployed chartering agencies to authorize these new schools.[24] Between 1992 and 2005, the number of students enrolled in charter schools rose from zero to more than one million; still, despite this rather steep growth, this number represents less than 2.3 percent of all students in public school.[25] Charter laws authorize public funds to be distributed to groups of teachers, parents, or other community members who propose and develop school subjects and allow a degree of ongoing public monitoring. James Foreman, Jr., Law Professor at Georgetown University, has suggested that the forerunners of the contemporary charter school movement were the summertime "freedom schools" and the year-round experimental "free schools" that civil rights advocates initiated during the 1960s to raise academic achievement for African-American children, develop racial pride, and dramatize the inadequacies of public schools.[26] Ray Budde, a retired school teacher, and Albert Shanker, the past president of the American Federation for Teachers, each contributed to the idea of school choice by advocating for schools chosen by both teachers and students.[27] Budde coined the phrase "charter schools," and Shanker used the phrase in a proposal to restructure school districts to give teachers control and responsibility for instruction. Minnesota picked up the idea, and other states quickly followed. Most charter laws proceed at the state level, but some initiatives, such as Boston's pilot schools, promote educational innovation by offering charters within a single district.[28] According to their authorizing laws, charter schools typically operate apart from the usual state and local bureaucracy and often proceed outside the collective bargaining terms of the teacher unions.[29]

Vouchers. School choice initiatives also include vouchers: transfer payments that enable parents to select a private school and pay its tuition with public dollars. Voucher programs in the United States, thus far all targeting low-income students, have been launched in Milwaukee, Wisconsin, Cleveland, Ohio, and the District of Columbia while other communities offer vouchers for special needs students.[30] Other public policy tools could promote school choice by offering parents tax credits for private school tuition and other expenses or by permitting and facilitating transfers to schools within a student's public school district or to other public school districts.[31] Companies creating scholarships for low-income students to attend private school might receive tax credits and further boost school choice.[32]

Missing options. Although privately funded scholarships and specialized public schools admitting students by exam expand options for students and families, they do not represent government policies. Another option that almost never exists in practice would be to open up good suburban schools to students who live in urban and rural communities that lack effective schools. For example, METCO-Boston, launched in 1965, was designed to open good but racially isolated suburban schools to urban students, who commute daily to the suburban schools. Its capacity is restricted, though, both by the limited number of open spaces and by the inadequacy of public funding to cover the actual costs of the suburban schools.[33]

Vigorous efforts to relocate low-income families of color from inner cities to middle-class suburbs would be another school choice tactic. One dramatic effort, the Gatreaux Assisted Housing Program, overcame problems, including the discomfort of participating families, and ultimately proved effective in opening up educational and employment opportunities.[34] Congress followed with legislation to support geographic mobility for low income families; it affects small numbers but shows promise.[35]

More broadly, "school choice initiatives" should be located as one resolution to enduring debates over who decides whether and how to educate children. This question has prompted intense struggles among parents, communities, and governments in many eras. Nothing less than the political, cultural, and economic future of a society is at stake in the answers. In choosing among designs for schools, parents, communities, and governments cultivate specific national, cultural, or religious identities, as well as develop individual children's capacities for success as adults. In the United States, struggles over "Americanization" of children also engage contests over implicit and explicit religious education. It was these struggles that ultimately prompted the Supreme Court to elevate the right of parents to select private schools—including religious schools—as a constitutionally required option for fulfilling a state's compulsory schooling law.[36] Hence, school choice of a sort (the private school option without public subsidy) is constitutionally protected.

The movement for common schools that was initiated in the 1830s attracted reformers seeking social improvement. Horace Mann advocated common schools for boys and girls, as well as for immigrants and long-standing American residents, in order to promote political stability, equalize conditions, equip more people to earn their livings, and enable people to follow the law and respect private property.[37] Mann expressly and controversially argued for education that transcended the sectarian differences of different branches of Christianity.

The common school ideal initially excluded slaves and children with disabilities. Tensions over curricular content erupted as nativist Protestants sought to Americanize immigrant Catholics.[38] As industrialization created a demand for more educated workers and child labor displaced that of adults in factories, a coalition of labor and social reformers successfully pushed for compulsory statewide school laws across the country by the turn of the twentieth century. Joining the fight, the American Legion and the Daughters of the American Revolution pushed for instruction in American history; this is the moment when the Ku Klux Klan in Oregon claimed that only public schools could be trusted to Americanize immigrants.[39] Lawmakers enacted compulsory school laws with the idea that allowing parents to decide when and whether to educate their children would, in too many instances, force parents and young people to choose between children's wages and their education.[40] Some parents also resisted schooling arranged by the government in favor of education reflecting their own religious views or cultural practices.[41] Run locally, public schools nonetheless converged around standardized texts and curricular expectations, following the lead of professional teachers and curriculum developers.[42] Increasing standardization emerged also after 1970 as state and federal authorities directed the establishment of curricular requirements and rules meant to assist students with disabilities, English-language learners, and students in impoverished communities.

Parental choice about where and how to educate a child remains. Liberal societies like the United States, which value both the opportunities represented by schooling and the freedom of individuals to raise their children and pursue their religious and cultural practices, face potential tensions between laws mandating school attendance and laws guaranteeing parental choice. The solution, in the abstract, is to ensure education but preserve parental choice over the particular kind of education. This resolution is well summarized in the Universal Declaration of Human Rights, drafted and ratified by the United Nations General Assembly in 1948. Article 26 of the Declaration declares simultaneously that "everyone has the right to education. Education shall be free, at least in the elementary and fundamental stages. Elementary education shall be compulsory" and "Parents have a prior right to choose the kind of education that shall be given to their children."[43] Read together, these provisions imply that even private elementary education options selected by parents must be free, imposing no financial costs to the family. However, it is possible to conclude, consistent with practice in the United States, that governments satisfy the fundamental right to an education by providing a free public school option and ensuring that private options satisfy the compulsory schooling requirement while leaving such alternatives to private funding.

In the United States, public funding has historically been confined to schools organized and run by local or state governments. Parents preferring religious or other private schools tried legislative actions to secure public aid, but largely effective constitutional challenges barred such aid from the 1970s through the 1990s. Then scholars, advocates, and judges explored new interpretations of the establishment clause, culminating in the Supreme Court's approval of a public school voucher program in 2002.[44] These developments cannot be separated from the broader history of school choice advocacy.

The Politics of the Twenty-first-century School Choice Movement

"School choice" is a familiar item in any quick scan of the agendas of politically conservative think tanks in the 1990s and 2000s. The Heritage Foundation and the Cato Institute, for example, pursued a proposal for competition and parental choice that was introduced by the free-market economist Milton Friedman.[45] Friedman, who had already won the John Bates Clark Medal for outstanding achievement in economics, first proposed publicly funded school choice in 1955. Basic microeconomics supports the idea that consumer choice among competing providers of any item will produce improved products, although the application of this idea to schooling requires viewing schooling as a product and preserving the state's role in disbursing funds and ensuring minimum standards. Friedman later included a version of the school voucher proposal in his 1962 book *Capitalism and Freedom*, and he ultimately created a philanthropic foundation that advocated for school choice through research, assistance to local groups advocating school choice, and grants for educational innovation.[46] From the time of his initial proposal, Friedman emphasized the benefits of vouchers to promote a free society as well as to produce competition that could remedy deficiencies in schooling. His work did not, however, propose elimination of public funding. It instead justified continuing public financing because of the vital role schools play in passing on the common values and literacy skills needed to sustain a democracy.[47] Some degree of public control in setting baseline expectations always remained implicit in his work.

Fifty years after his initial proposal, Friedman reported that it had not been spurred by any contemporaneous events,[48] although *Brown* had just been decided. In fact, at the time of the 1955 publication, Friedman explained that he had drafted the paper presenting his proposal before he had learned that several southern states were exploring public funding of private schooling "as a means of evading the Supreme Court ruling against segregation."[49] Noting that he deplored racial prejudice and initially thought that the risk of exacerbating "class differences" would count against the proposal, he reasoned that government-forced desegregation was only slightly less objectionable than government-forced segregation, as both involve the use of government to force individuals to act in accordance with views not their own.[50] Publicly funded parental choice of schools—including all-white, all-black, and racially integrated schools—struck him as the best solution both for addressing racial segregation and for improving the quality of schooling.[51]

In actual practice, school choice policies emerged shortly after the Supreme Court's 1954 and 1955 decisions in *Brown* as a form of white southerners' resistance to court-ordered desegregation. Many white parents withdrew their children from the public schools and enrolled them in private schools that excluded nonwhites rather than participate in court-mandated desegregation. Existing private schools expanded, and brand-new private schools opened up for this purpose. Virginia went so far as to offer state tuition grants and county tax credits to enable white children to pay for private schooling in all-white settings. Prince Edward County even closed the public schools, but the Supreme Court rejected this effort as a patent defiance of court-ordered desegregation.[52]

During this period, "freedom-of-choice" plans in education became a euphemism for resurgent racial segregation. Some public systems explored the possibility of simply lifting student assignments to particular public schools and allowing students to opt out of desegregated schools.[53] In 1968, the Supreme Court rejected a "freedom-of-choice" plan as insufficient to meet the district's obligation to desegregate.[54] The plan at issue assigned students to their previously segregated schools while offering them transfer options. White families almost uniformly selected the historically white schools, and blacks almost uniformly chose the black-identified schools.

As a result of this experience, "school choice" in many quarters became tainted as an antidesegregation phrase. By the 1970s, however, some liberals and progressives began to support the idea of school vouchers to support school options for students otherwise stuck in ineffective ghetto schools.[55] An initial experiment with school vouchers in Alum Rock, California, proceeded with federal funding with hopes of racial and socioeconomic integration.[56] Controversial at the time, the initiative did not continue after its evaluation by the RAND Corporation indicated mixed results.[57] Nonetheless, even that experiment seemed to show that parents who initially preferred neighborhood schools eventually became more open to distant schools; the experiment had no clear effect on student achievement or racial integration, although Hispanic parents preferred bilingual programs.[58] In the 1970s and 1980s, some courts included elements of choice in judicially ordered school desegregation plans; this time, school choice was intended to promote racial integration and depended on close public monitoring of school enrollments to guard against desegregation.[59]

In 1990, John Chubb and Terry Moe of the Brookings Institute renewed arguments for school choice. They claimed that parental preferences would reflect children's real interests and produce improved opportunities by drawing schools into competition with one another.[60] Critics warned that racial segregation would again return. School choice, they argued, would disadvantage children of less educated parents, students with disabilities, and students learning English while rewarding children whose parents had the time and sophistication to seek out information and select the better schools.[61] To ensure adoption in urban areas, advocates needed to recast school choice as a benefit for the disadvantaged rather than a way for the advantaged to opt out of mainstream schools. Critics and supporters alike noted that school choice initiatives could face constitutional challenges if they directed public dollars to private religious schools or foreseeably segregated students by race or ethnicity.[62] The inclusion of private religious schools required not only a political coalition but also legal change.

The Legal Strategy for School Choice

Clint Bolick, who initiated a litigation campaign in the late 1980s to pursue school choice in Cleveland, Milwaukee, Arizona, and Florida, got his professional start with the Mountain States Legal Foundation, funded by conservative businessman Joseph Coors and led by James Watt, who later headed the Department of the Interior under President Ronald Reagan. Bolick then worked for the Equal Employment Opportunity Commission under conservative Clarence Thomas (whom President George H. W. Bush later appointed to the Supreme Court). With his colleagues, Bolick developed a plan to launch conservative public interest law firms that would mimic the long-term strategies of the NAACP Legal Defense Fund but in the pursuit of libertarian aims.[63] Bolick explained his conscious effort to draw on the Fund's efforts as a pursuit of "a principled incremental, long-term agenda, expressing the cause in the most universal possible terms, and forging nontraditional alliances."[64] He left his government post to launch the Landmark Legal Foundation, where he developed a framework for recasting civil rights through libertarian ideas. His 1991 book, *Unfinished Business: A Civil Rights Strategy for America's Third Century*,[65] argued that the conservative civil rights agenda would benefit African Americans.[66] Departing from the usual conservative criticism of "judicial activism" in the pursuit of civil rights, Bolick also urged judicial action, but to counter liberal policies. He next advocated a strategy of representing low-income parents to "place urban public schools on trial and clearly identify choice as a low-income empowerment solution."[67] He later explained that success in advancing school choice would build public support for economic liberty and private property rights.[68] In 2005, he stated: "School choice gives disadvantaged families some of the clout that middle- and upper-income families have, through the power to exit the system. School choice provides an educational life preserver for children who desperately need it, and creates a competitive incentive for public schools to improve."[69]

Bolick continued to act on this strategy as the first director of the Alliance for School Choice, a national organization launched in 2004 on the anniversary of *Brown*. Its state chapters advocated for legislation, litigation, and organizing efforts to enlarge and implement school choice. Its strategy directly tackled a central legal obstacle to any school choice policy extending government financial assistance to religious schools: federal constitutional decisions during the 1970s and 1980s finding violations of the establishment clause in statutes reimbursing private schools for secular textbooks and teachers' salaries[70] and in programs providing remedial instruction and guidance services by public school staff to religious school students at these schools.[71] The Supreme Court had also rejected tax credits and tax deductions for tuition paid to nonpublic schools as violations of the establishment clause.[72] These decisions stood in the way of public vouchers to pay for religious schooling.

Bolick and other advocates took advantage of inconsistencies in the Supreme Court's checkered doctrine. The Court actually had permitted public aid to students enrolled in religious schools in cases where public school personnel offered students standardized tests and speech, hearing, and psychological services[73] outside the campus of the religious school.[74] The Court also allowed some tax deductions for children's school tuition, textbooks, and transportation associated with public or private schools.[75] Advocates seeking school choice joined forces with others who found the Court's treatment of government aid to religious institutions unfair and unpredictable. The litigation campaign proved effective. The Court issued a series of decisions in the 1990s receptive to ideas of neutrality and permitting inclusion of religious schools in programs involving government support.[76]

Bolick initially framed several unsuccessful lawsuits advocating school vouchers or public stipends for students attending public schools.[77] He lost a challenge to Maine's exclusion of religious schools from a program granting state-paid tuition for private schooling to families living in towns lacking any public school.[78] A similar effort failed in Vermont.[79] Staff at the John M. Olin Foundation nonetheless concluded that even when such litigation efforts failed, they warranted support in order to put urban schools "on trial" and cast doubt on increases in public school funding.[80]

Following such initial failures, law professor Michael McConnell and others helped frame litigation pursuing school choice and secured victories in the supreme courts of Wisconsin, Ohio, and Arizona.[81] In 1997, in a case in which Bolick coauthored an amicus curiae brief, the U.S. Supreme Court explicitly overruled prior decisions to allow public employees to provide services on the campuses of religious schools where the programs supported the same kinds of services offered to public school students.[82] That decision paved the way for the Court's dramatic turn in 2002, when it approved a voucher plan in Cleveland offering financial assistance to allow low-income parents to select religious schools.[83] Revising prior interpretations of the establishment clause, the Court noted that the private parental choice to use a public voucher to pay for a religious school separated the public funds from direct expenditure at religious schools. The Court emphasized the availability of public alternative and magnet schools and private religious and secular schools under the city's plan.[84] The Court's decision depended on the promise of the participating private schools to neither discriminate on the basis of race, religion, or ethnic background nor teach hatred of any person or group on the basis of race, religion, national origin, or ethnicity.[85] Hence, *Zelman v. Simmons-Harris*, often called the "school voucher case," lifted barriers against aid to religious institutions and stands as a major victory for advocates of school choice.

Larger political changes, contributing to a shift in the makeup of the courts in general and the Supreme Court in particular, enabled this constitutional green light for school choice. Yet another crucial facilitating factor came with the success of intellectual entrepreneurs who reframed establishment clause analysis and school choice questions to take advantage of the legacies of *Brown*. Prior to this reframing, the constitutional prohibition against state establishment of religion produced numerous court decisions ruling that government resources should not reach religious schools. Advocates and scholars worked to recast the refusals of public aid reaching religious schools in terms of discrimination against religious students and religious ideas and thereby displaced the separation-of-church-and-state framework that had dominated in the past.[86]

Reimagined in terms of the allegation of discriminatory treatment—government exclusion from otherwise available public aid for schooling—advocates put the spotlight not only on the treatment of religious schools but also on the treatment of religious students and religious speakers. Advocates planned and produced a line of precedents that inch by inch opened public schools to religion, beginning with after-school programs held on public school sites and student-initiated activities at public schools. This successful strategy worked rhetorically, resonating with the concern over exclusion and subordination voiced in *Brown,* and doctrinally, by switching from a focus on the establishment clause to concerns about government-imposed viewpoint discrimination under freedom of speech. Switching the discussion to the free speech clause of the First Amendment,[87] advocates successfully directed judicial attention to policies that subsidized some but not other student speech. The Supreme Court concluded that a public university could not exclude a student publication with a religious orientation from the funds available to other student organizations, nor could a public school exclude a religious after-school program from using public buildings available to other after-school programs.[88] The same concern over government aid to religion that had previously generated the bar against religious activities in public settings now animated the defenses offered in these cases. Relying on then-existing precedents, school officials explained that public funding of a religious publication or inclusion of a religious after-school program on public school property would amount to an impermissible establishment of religion.[89] Yet the Supreme Court rejected these defenses as insufficient to overcome the discrimination against religious speech.

These cases provided the backdrop to the Supreme Court's consideration of Cleveland's voucher plan. Because Cleveland included religious schools in the pool of options available for public funds, challengers argued that the city's program had the forbidden "effect" of advancing religion, even though it was defended with the permissible secular purpose of providing educational assistance to poor children in a demonstrably failing public school system. The city maintained that the program advanced equal treatment, ensuring neutral policies that neither favored nor disfavored religion. The argument worked. With the permissible and indeed admirable purpose of improving education for poor children, the backdrop of increasing social acceptance of religious voices in public educational settings, and the explicit commitment to equal, or neutral, treatment of religious and nonreligious programs, the majority of the Supreme Court allowed prior court decisions banning direct public subsidies for religious indoctrination to fade in importance.[90]

Justice Clarence Thomas, who took Justice Thurgood Marshall's place as the sole African American on the Court,[91] noted the irony that choice plans had promoted white flight and segregation at the time of *Brown* but now, fifty years later, represented perhaps the only avenue for better opportunities for poor students of color in a city like Cleveland.[92] Justice

Thomas chided those who would hold up an ideal of common public education over this practical option of private schooling to provide better instruction for children trapped in failing schools.[93]

Clint Bolick's strategy thus paid off. Identifying poor black and Hispanic children as beneficiaries and aligning school choice with civil rights rather than against it seemed to work. Bolick later commented: "How could the court have ruled otherwise, given its sacred promise in *Brown* nearly a half-century earlier that all children are entitled to equal educational opportunities?"[94] Public attitudes about school choice depended in no small part on the framing of the issue. Hence, in a single poll given in 2002, 46 percent of respondents favored "allowing students and parents to choose a private school to attend at public expense," while 52 percent favored "allow[ing] parents to send their school-age children to any public, private, or church-related school they choose. For those parents choosing nonpublic schools, the government would pay all or part of the tuition."[95] School choice initiatives, in appearance and often in reality, became associated with more opportunities for poor children of color rather than with exit strategies for well-off white children. For this reason, school choice advocates claim to be the rightful heirs of the civil rights struggle for equal education. In an editorial published in the *Wall Street Journal*, Alveda King, a niece of Dr. Martin Luther King, Jr., endorsed school choice as a remedy for inadequate schools and unequal parental resources.[96]

Yet many traditional civil rights groups continued to challenge school choice as endangering equal opportunity, especially for poor children and children of color. They charged that voucher programs would skim from failing mainstream public schools the most informed and motivated parents, whose vital involvement and advocacy made the schools better for all those enrolled.[97] Some people, still concerned about public aid to religion and diversion of public funds to private institutions, defended state-level restrictions on public funding of private schooling even in the context of special needs instruction.[98] They argued that school choice, unless closely regulated to ensure a mix of race and ethnic background in each school, was likely to produce class stratification and racial segregation.[99] Debating Bolick's school choice views, law professor Laura Underkuffler argued that voucher proponents not only seek to offer low-income children places in successful private schools but also push for "the complete dismantling of the idea of public education, to be replaced by a market in vouchers."[100] Questioning the motives and effectiveness of voucher programs for private religious education, Underkuffler contrasted them to Minnesota's Open Enrollment Public Schools Plan, which allows students the opportunity to apply for enrollment in any public school in the state, including ones outside the student's own district, and covers transportation expenses for low-income students.[101] Bolick in reply disputed whether sufficient high-quality public schools exist to serve all students and defended the inclusion of private schools as a way to break up the bloated and inefficient public system, much as private mail service had challenged the U.S. postal service.[102]

The progressive advocacy group People for the American Way questioned Bolick's asserted interest in assisting low-income families and pointed to his own statement that he planned to put public schools on trial.[103] The group also pointed to briefs he had filed in opposition to school desegregation, racial balancing of teaching staff in school, and affirmative action.[104] With similar suspicion of deeper unstated motives on the other side, some defenders of school choice have criticized teachers' unions, which have vested interests in existing public schools and less success in organizing teachers in private and alternative schools, for resisting options designed to help disadvantaged children.[105] These charges and countercharges about real motives notwithstanding, the fact remains that the legal strategy for school choice successfully cleared the path for school choice plans that include private religious schools.

Yet, for the core supporters of private and parochial school choice, the victory proved insubstantial in practice. The politics and policies that have emerged have taken other directions. The rise of for-profit school management companies, deployed both by public and private systems, advanced some people's hopes for market efficiency and competition as a means for educational improvement but invited criticism for creating new kinds of waste and for jeopardizing the ideal of common and democratic public schooling.[106] Conservatives who endorsed the market and attacked government provision of schooling and other social benefits confronted a resurgent defense of government in service of the public good. In addition, the excesses of private contractors in the U.S. wars in Afghanistan and Iraq and the incompetence of outsourced emergency relief providers following Hurricane Katrina contributed to renewed support for government regulation and government provision of services. The financial and stock market shocks of 2008–9 further soured many people's views regarding unfettered markets.

By 2008, the vouchers movement halted, while charter schools and other forms of public school choice continued to expand. Mixed results in the voucher programs set up for low-income urban students and resistance on the part of suburban parents who liked their public schools stalled voter support for voucher initiatives, despite massive campaign funding by voucher advocates.[107] Voters defeated five state school choice referenda in a row, and none of the results were close.[108]

A sign of the change in mood is apparent in the demise of the single federal school voucher program. From the start of his time in office, President George W. Bush encouraged Congress to authorize a small initiative in the District of Columbia schools extending a $7,500 subsidy to about seventeen hundred students each year as the sole federal voucher program. An initial assessment of this initiative (the D.C. School Choice Incentive Act of 2003) found no statistically significant difference in the test scores of the students in the program compared with others and no greater student satisfaction, although parents of participating students reported greater satisfaction with their children's schooling and higher perceptions of school safety.[109] After the election of President Barack Obama, Congress enacted a spending bill that effectively terminated the program.[110] In the face of criticism, President Obama worked out a compromise allowing students enrolled through the voucher program in participating schools to graduate from those schools; the compromise softened the effect of the termination but triggered a further round of partisan debate.[111] By 2009, public vouchers to support private schooling had receded from the public stage, leaving entrepreneurial school reformers engaged with charter, magnet, and pilot schools and other forms of school choice within existing school districts.[112]

The Effects of School Choice

As indicated by the debate over the voucher experiment in the District of Columbia, assessment of school choice initiatives is clouded by political passions and personal interests. Studies undertaken by government agencies yield ambiguous results; studies sponsored by think tanks and advocacy groups, unsurprisingly, reflect the views of their sponsors.[113] The most thoughtful observers conclude that the context and details of the plans and school programs reflect the particular demographic and attitudinal characteristics of specific communities and render generalizations about the effects of school choice inconclusive and unreliable.[114] Ensuring that each school operates within an ecology of committed and engaged parents and teachers seems more important for educational outcomes than choice per se.[115] Choice mechanisms may increase the number of such schools, at least temporarily, but the jury remains out.

Debates over school choice center on student achievement. This is not surprising, given supporters' claims that school choice initiatives will improve school quality by promoting innovation and introducing competitive pressures. The actual effects of vouchers, charters, and other school choice efforts on student achievement are complex, unclear, and disputed. Individual charter schools, including schools enrolling entirely low-income children of color, have reported improvements in academic achievement; so have portions of public systems that include choice dimensions.[116] Critics suggest that the families involved in such initiatives are self-selected and thus affect results.[117] There is no measurable difference between the reading scores of charter school students and other public school students, but female students enrolled in charter schools, on average, have produced lower scores than female students in other public schools, according to one major study.[118] Some studies find that school choice is associated with positive influence on student achievement.[119] Others emphasize that the results reflect conditions more specific than participation in a school choice scheme.[120] Still others attack the use of standardized tests to measure and compare student performance and to assess school reforms.[121] Even some conservative commentators have concluded that the free market alone would not produce better schools for disadvantaged students.[122]

Perhaps the key effect of recent school choice is to draw some new players—teachers, administrators, advocates—into entrepreneurial educational activities. When the school system in New Orleans was devastated by Hurricane Katrina, President George W. Bush's secretary of education, Margaret Spellings, awarded the school system $24 million for the development of charter schools, advancing the administration's commitment to school choice and attracting teachers and administrators from across the country to promote educational recovery and improvement of a system that had long been desperately inadequate.[123] The initiative prompted some to warn of opportunism and jeopardy to the mission and accountability of public schooling, but the urgency of establishing functioning and effective schools has silenced most critics.[124]

Less discussed by school choice advocates are the effects of school choice on the composition of student bodies nationwide. Does school choice alter the patterns of racial separation affecting much of American schooling? Does it produce more or less single-sex instruction or more or less inclusion of disabled students in classrooms with nondisabled students? More or less mixing of immigrant and nonimmigrant children or English-language learners and native English speakers? Catholics, Protestants, Moslems, Jews, Hindus, and children from secular families? Poor, middle-class, and wealthy students? Straight and gay, lesbian, bisexual, or transgendered students? Native Hawai'ian, American Indian, and students of other background? No prejudgment of the benefit of integration versus separate instruction along any of these lines is necessary to see value in knowing how school choice mechanisms affect the composition of student bodies, both within the choice alternatives and the mainstream public schools where students not participating in school choice programs remain.

Race and Ethnicity

Neither public nor private schools can take into account the race of individual students in school assignments, except as a remedy for judicially determined racial discrimination by government actors;[125] yet school officials can influence the racial composition of individual schools through many kinds of policies. School choice initiatives can increase racial and ethnic mixing in schools, but they can also produce schools that are more racially imbalanced than the existing public schools in the same community. At the same time, voucher programs can produce greater racial mixing in the private schools by enabling poor students of color to enroll in private schools with predominantly white student enrollments.[126] School choice programs can enable students from racially segregated neighborhoods to enter schools that are more racially diverse than their neighborhood schools.[127]

Public systems, using "controlled choice" plans, have tried in the past to take advantage of voluntary school enrollments while monitoring the racial composition of individual schools to produce racial mixing.[128] Under this type of system, students list several choices of schools, and officials make assignments based on student preference, while also ensuring that the student enrollment within each school approximates the racial and ethnic composition of the larger community. Official attention to racial composition of schools even as part of a voluntary choice plan is now largely forbidden, however. The Supreme Court's decision in *Parents Involved in Community Schools v. Seattle School District No. 1* forbade official use of individual students' racial identities to ensure racial balance absent a prior judicial finding of intentional racial discrimination.[129] Four members of the Court agreed that the way to halt racial discrimination was to stop using racial classifications. This view would seriously chill the consideration of race as a factor when school systems invite students to choose among educational options.

Schools can still use residential neighborhoods and household income levels to produce school assignments promoting diverse student bodies and may thereby be able to preserve some degree of racial mixing. Justice Kennedy's separate opinion that supplied the required fifth vote for the verdict in *Parents Involved* expressly approved efforts to undo racial isolation (unlike the four justices supporting the opinion of Chief Justice Roberts).[130] Justice Kennedy's opinion left room for schools to "devise race-conscious measures to address the problem in a general way"[131] though not by means of individual student assignments by race. Justice Kennedy's opinion suggested "strategic site selection of new schools; drawing attendance zones with general recognition of the demographics of neighborhoods; allocating resources for special programs; recruiting students and faculty in a targeted fashion; and tracking enrollments, performance, and other statistics by race."[132] Communities thus can try to produce racially integrated schools through these indirect means. Mindful of the Supreme Court's guidance, a California court upheld a plan that included consideration of the racial composition of the neighborhood as a whole. The plan avoided classifying individual students by race but nonetheless could generate racially mixed schools.[133] The NAACP Legal Defense Fund has developed a manual to support careful but still race-conscious uses of special admission programs and voluntary transfers in addition to the options listed by Justice Kennedy as tools for creating and maintaining racially integrated schools.[134]

School choice programs that pay no attention to the racial composition of the schools may end up reducing racially mixed enrollments.[135] Cambridge, Massachusetts, was long a site of controlled choice, enacted voluntarily at a time when Boston erupted in conflict over court-ordered school desegregation. The school system in Cambridge had begun to assign students on the basis of socioeconomic status rather than race even before the Supreme Court's decision in *Parents Involved*. This tactic has benefits, but it has noticeably altered the racial composition of the schools, producing disparities between majority-minority and majority-white schools.[136] The results may reflect different patterns of parental preferences for particular curricular programs or for schools near their homes. The convenience of a school's location is an important factor for parents and students. Parents who favor neighborhood schools, though, may also feel comfortable with the racial composition of their neighborhood school if it reflects the racial composition of the neighborhood, and neighborhoods vary considerably in a city like Cambridge. Parental preferences, then, may consciously or unconsciously reflect racial attitudes. Minority group members may be attracted by the ethnic or racial inflection of a school's mission; whites may be repelled by a characterization of a school as being "in the wrong neighborhood" or not having "enough" white students. A study of magnet schools in Maryland found that white parents tended to select schools with fewer minority students, and black parents were motivated more by the desire to keep their children in predominantly black schools than to put them in more challenging academic programs.[137]

Several studies indicate that when left to the individual preferences of families, charter schools can generate either more or less racial and ethnic diversity than the neighborhood schools.[138] Comparing schools by region shows similar results.[139] Nationwide, charter schools enroll a higher percentage of nonwhite students than do conventional schools.[140] This reflects a higher concentration of charter schools in urban areas, but it does not indicate the degree of integration taking place at the level of the individual school or classroom. Moreover, general patterns like this need to be disaggregated to be interpreted. Across the country, blacks are overrepresented in charter schools, whereas Hispanics are overrepresented in some states and underrepresented in others.[141] There is something complicated going on. This variation does not, however, mean that school choice has no effect on the racial composition of schools. Actual patterns are obscured by national-level statistics, often cited by advocates of school choice. For although it is accurate to note that charter schools across the nation enroll a higher percentage of minority students than do traditional public schools,[142] when compared with the schools in their own districts, charter schools' racial and ethnic composition is nearly identical[143] or less mixed.[144]

One possibility is that school choice allows both white flight from neighborhood schools and self-segregation by families of color in specialized charter schools.[145] Charter schools in Arizona "disproportionately skimmed white non-Hispanic students" from traditional public schools, according to one study that controlled for median household income and other factors.[146] In particular communities or particular schools, Hispanic parents disproportionately select thematic charter schools, such as the Cesar Chavez Academy in Pueblo City, Colorado.[147] Specialized curricular programs also appeal to other particular communities, such as Hmong or Somali immigrants, Native Hawai'ians, Hispanics, and African Americans.[148] Parents in each of these groups may be drawn to a school organized to celebrate their own cultural heritage.[149] One such school in Illinois is the Betty Shabazz International Charter School, named for an advocate for African Americans and designed to offer cultural affirmation with references to the contributions of Africans and African Americans across the subjects in the curriculum.[150] A notable increase in the number of racially segregated schools in Michigan can apparently be traced to the impact of charter schools as black families sought out alternatives to failing conventional public schools.[151] At the same time, minority students used choice options to exit conventional Minneapolis schools at higher rates than did whites, leaving the standard schools with a higher white enrollment.[152] One scholar has suggested that black parents may seek out charter schools in order to reduce the disenfranchisement they feel in highly racially isolated urban schools; this scholar found that higher proportions of black families living in districts with notable racial separation in the conventional schools were more likely to seek out charter schools than those living in districts with more racially balanced conventional schools.[153] In order to overcome this racial isolation, black parents may even choose to send their children to charter schools that have lower test scores than the schools in the districts their children exit.[154]

Details in the designs of individual schools and of school choice programs can tip parental preferences and ultimately school enrollments toward or away from racial and ethnic integration. Triumphant Learning Center and Los Milagros Academy are each charter schools seeking to serve all students in the same Arizona town, and each offers a college-preparatory curriculum. Yet their names, locations, founders, schedules, expectations of parental involvement, and meals attract different student populations, with Triumphant Learning Center appealing to white families (producing 90 percent white enrollment) and Los Milagros Academy appealing to Hispanic and Catholic students (53 percent Hispanic enrollment).[155] Designed to appeal to particular segments of the population, with foreseeable disparate applications across racial and ethnic groups, schools with specialized ethnic, cultural, or bilingual programs are likely to reduce racial mixing, absent concerted efforts to generate diverse enrollments. If the use of such schools involves foreseeable segregative effects, it could generate legal challenges to charter schools that target one group.[156] Charter schools and other school choice options could promote racial and ethnic integration if students of all backgrounds are recruited and they get to enroll in the schools they choose. But inadequate transportation, differential distribution of information and knowledge about options, and admissions criteria (such as mandatory parental involvement) skew enrollments in specialized schools toward disproportionately white and wealthier families.[157]

Striking opportunities for racial mixing would arise if the choices bridged districts and crossed the lines between cities and suburbs or between towns and rural areas. School districts need not be coterminous with municipal borders, and historically many were not.[158] State procedures for consolidating and annexing school districts would allow inclusion of neighborhoods that would diversify the racial and economic mix of students.[159] As Taryn Williams has argued, "[d]ividing up urban districts and consolidating them with surrounding middle-class districts would create opportunities for socioeconomic integration. By arranging those new districts like flower petals emanating from the center of the city, the distance students and teachers would have to travel if they were assigned to a new school could be kept reasonable."[160] This approach could enable school choice to cross suburban and urban lines while offering suburban parents the choice to share the tax base of urban areas. Yet the early example of Cleveland, an innovator in school vouchers as a response to notable failure of the city's schools, gives little encouragement to those who hope for school reforms bridging urban and suburban communities. As Stephen Macedo commented: "The upshot of this drama is that the Ohio Legislature, the courts, and the suburban school districts have put many Cleveland parents and children eager to take advantage of school choice in a cruel situation. The real problem with the Scholarship Program...is that Ohio has failed to require suburban public schools to participate in the program and give parents a real choice among schools."[161] The crucial point to acknowledge is that as long as good options remain relatively scarce, "school choice" will allow schools to pick students as well as parents to pick schools—and parents with financial means or savvy may most likely benefit.[162]

Gender

When the federal Department of Education enacted its new regulation easing restrictions against gender differences in education, it not only encouraged the development of single-sex schools but also ensured even greater flexibility for charter schools. If the charter school is not vocational and is established on its own rather than part of a larger collection of schools, it avoids the requirements to provide a justification for and undergo an evaluation of its program that traditional public schools must meet.[163]

Single-sex classrooms and schools have exploded in the years since the federal government first considered permitting them. Only 11 public schools offered single-sex programs in 2002, while at least 542 public schools did so by 2009, including 32 charter schools and 12 magnet schools.[164] Single-sex programs within traditional public schools may be a response to competition from charter schools.[165] For example, school superintendent Walter Milton in 2009 explained plans for two new gender-based academies in Springfield, Illinois intended in part "to preempt expected growth in independent charter schools in central

Illinois."[166] Charter schools may then offer an option for families seeking coeducational classrooms in communities where initiatives for single-sex instruction sweep through the public schools.[167] Voucher programs have authorized public funding for participating single-sex schools, whether religious or not, and magnet schools can experiment with single-sex classes and offer them as a special feature.

Disability

In the abstract, school choice could help students with disabilities by allowing parents to select schools that best accommodate them and by encouraging schools to compete on this ground. Parents could select among schools with greater or weaker commitment to including students with disabilities in mainstream classrooms, or among schools that focus on a particular disability, such as blindness, autism, or attention deficit hyperactivity disorder. On the other hand, educating students with disabilities often involves additional expenses, and the funding formulas used for vouchers, charters, and other school choice options typically offer no additional resources to cover these costs.

Students in charter schools and in magnet schools are eligible for accommodation and related services under federal and state law in the same way as students in any other public school, yet distribution of public funding may keep ordinary public schools more attractive for some students with disabilities.[168] Students using vouchers to attend private schools might be able to tap into public special education funds if any money remains after the demand within the public schools is satisfied. One study suggests that some families turn down vouchers because of the dearth of public funding to facilitate accommodations, yet the same study reports relatively high parental satisfaction with private school accommodation of students with special needs.[169] Where vouchers can pay for a school that specializes in teaching students with one or more particular disability, parents of disabled and parents of nondisabled students may find common cause in preferring specialized schools for disabled students rather than the inclusion model that mixes students. Political support as a result may be greater for vouchers focusing on students with disabilities than for the general student population.[170] Parents using vouchers could then select schools with specialized services for students with disabilities or even for private schools without special accommodations but small classes responsive to different learning needs.[171] School choice mechanisms might support increased tailored instruction or improved outcomes for students with disabilities but might instead fail to afford specialized services and procedural protections that are available to students in public schools.

The emergence of charter schools with special missions to serve students with disabilities could also produce greater separation of these students from others and undermine the goal of mainstreaming these students. Informal practices discouraging students with special needs from enrolling in other kinds of charter schools may produce schools with fewer students with disabilities when compared with neighboring public schools.

The degree of inclusion for students with disabilities presents design questions for charter schools. Do charter schools make clear that they are as open to students with disabilities as to other students? Do individual charter schools operate as mainstream programs with accommodations and designs that include students with disabilities? Instead, should particular schools run programs that specialize in meeting needs of students with some or many kinds of disabilities—and produce student enrollments that are largely or solely made up of students with disabilities? Aggregate national data about charter school enrollment obscure these choices.

Even national data, while ranging in specific figures, indicate that charter schools serve a somewhat smaller proportion of students with special needs than do regular public schools. A pilot study for the 2003 National Assessment of Educational Progress reported that 8 percent of charter school fourth-grade students had disabilities, whereas 11 percent of regular public school fourth graders had disabilities.[172] Similar disparities appear in comparisons of charter and other public schools within particular states.[173] According to one recent study, special education students made up 10.8 percent of charter school enrollments across the country in 2005, while such students made up 13.4 percent of regular schools.[174]

So charter schools do not yet on the whole offer equitable access to students with disabilities at the level of the individual school with state-level differences in charter school opportunities specializing in serving special needs students, compared with inclusive instruction with heterogeneous student bodies. Some charter schools have provided specialized instruction and supports, attracting a disproportionately high enrollment of students with special needs.[175] Some states interpret federal and state law to preclude the creation of charter schools specifically designed to serve students with disabilities; sixteen state charter laws prohibit individual charter schools from restricting admissions to students with disabilities.[176] Other states allow a programmatic focus on disability inclusion as long as all interested students are eligible for admission.[177] Some states promote charter schools for at-risk or academically low-achieving students, and four states specify that "at-risk students" include students with disabilities.[178] Nevada's charter law explicitly permits the creation of schools specifically designed for students with disabilities.[179] Ohio authorizes charter schools designed for students with autism;[180] other states may follow suit.[181] Although only 71 out of 3,632 charter schools across the country in 2008 were designed specifically for students with disabilities, 34 of these schools were chartered between 2004 and 2006, so there may be a trend toward such specialized schools.[182]

Charter schools may also be accorded discretion over which students can enroll in ways that allow exclusion of students with disabilities or overrepresentation of such students. For example, Texas charter schools are authorized to exclude students with a history of behavioral problems, even when those problems are traceable to a conduct or emotional disorder.[183] New Hampshire's charter school statute permits the schools to "select pupils on the basis of aptitude, academic achievement, or need, provided that such selection is directly related to the academic goals of the school."[184] So charter schools may be able to avoid the presumption of inclusion otherwise operative in traditional public schools. At the same time, some parents may seek out charter schools in order to avoid the "special education" label already or potentially assigned to their child because of stigma, while taking advantage of more individualized instruction or extra resources available in some charter schools.[185]

As for the students' actual experiences, even more fine-grained detail is required to determine how much time students with disabilities spend with other students in charter schools. Here, there is some indication that students with disabilities in charter schools spend more of the school day in the same setting with other students (71 percent spend 80–100 percent of their time in the general classroom) than do students with disabilities in traditional public schools (where 50 percent of such students spend 80–100 percent of their time in the general classroom).[186] The day-to-day experiences of disabled students, then, may involve more mixing with other students in charter schools than in traditional public schools.

Students with particular disabilities may benefit from concentrated resources that are not available in individual charter schools. Some traditional public school systems have located coordinated resources for students with a particular disability, such as hearing impairment, in a specific school within the system. This approach shares costs across the system and would be difficult for a charter school to achieve, operating on its own.[187] Charter schools may not be able to take advantage of such approaches, and the result might be greater underrepresentation of students with those disabilities in the charter schools. Yet these very approaches may also produce higher concentrations of students with disabilities in particular public schools. General conclusions about the impact of school choice on the degree of inclusion for students with disabilities in classrooms with other students must await close study of state and local variations in laws, practices, and funding incentives. It is already clear, though, that school choice mechanisms considerably increase the potential for separate or substantially separate schools for students with disabilities when compared with conventional public schools, governed by federal and state law preferences for inclusion. The intervention of parental choices can bypass the inclusion mandate.

Religion

School choice options could produce more integration across religious lines as vouchers open access to parochial schools to low-income students who may not share these schools' religions. An Arabic-language school could draw students from varied backgrounds, including Muslim and non-Muslim students, for such a school could attract students interested in learning a language that is of great importance historically and is greatly needed in the United States military and foreign service.[188] Specialized schools enabled by choice initiatives could therefore be framed in terms of opening access to a foreign language or culture while effectively appealing to and operating as centers for students of a particular background or religion.

Yet school choice could instead facilitate self-segregation by religion. Perhaps because the subject is so controversial, one prime example has been given a pseudonym for purposes of policy discussions. The so-called Valley Charter School was launched in 1994 to supplement the education of homeschooled children in a California community where most of the participating families are conservative Christians.[189] Such a "school" is entirely composed of self-selected families, using the charter device to obtain public funds for enrichment of homeschooling.

In another example, charter programs appear to have yielded self-segregation by an immigrant group in the name of accommodating their needs—but it may also signal how easy it is for the majority to proceed without mixing with these immigrant students. The Twin Cities of Minneapolis and St. Paul established the Twin Cities International Elementary and the Twin Cities International Middle School in 2001, responding to the needs of a particular immigrant community.[190] The schools' web site explains: "Founded by educational leaders in the East African community, the schools strive to provide a quality academic program, in a culturally sensitive setting, for immigrant and refugee children."[191] The schools offer an American academic program in a setting respectful of and attentive to community input. Drawing students mainly from the large Somali immigrant population in the area,[192] these schools serve Hallal food, accommodating their largely Muslim student population, teach Arabic because of the students' background, and seek to prepare all students to live in a global society, permits head coverings. In a 2001 study by the American Muslim Council, American Muslims ranked school choice their top political priority.[193]

In Milwaukee, the Clara Muhammad School, along with a variety of other religious schools, participates in the city's public voucher program. A Hebrew-language charter school in Florida emphasizes the benefits of its bilingual, bicultural curriculum, but proposals for additional Hebrew-language charter schools raise questions about violations of the establishment clause if religious instruction as well as language skills are the focus.[194] Charter legislation in some states allows religious leaders to sit on charter schools' governing boards and accommodates students' religious schedules and after-school religious instruction.[195]

Some of these charter school arrangements raise a complex and unresolved constitutional question: do charter schools violate the prohibition against government establishment of religion if they have or could be perceived by reasonable observers as having religious dimensions? The answer may ultimately turn on details in the design of the charter system, given that the Supreme Court has already approved the use of publicly funded vouchers to pay for private religious schools where the parents make genuine and independent private choices from among an array of options within a program that is neutral with respect to religion.[196] The government may seem less neutral when it specifically approves a particular proposal for a charter school than when it includes a particular private religious school in the mix of schools eligible for public vouchers. The distinction is subtle, and courts will likely face this question in the future,[197] even if program designers may become quite sophisticated and develop purely secular and general materials for public use while still marketing the program to members of a particular religion.[198]

An even more technical legal problem arises in the thirty-one states that allow charter schools but ban the conversion of private academies to public charter schools.[199] Some may nonetheless consider redeploying the sites and teachers of parochial schools—and notably Catholic schools that are closing due to costs—as the basis for new public schools.[200] New York City's mayor, Michael Bloomberg, announced a plan to convert parochial schools into charter schools by using provisions under the law to create new boards of trustees, hire new teachers and staff, and admit students who did not attend the preexisting parochial school.[201] Public charter schools have already emerged in other states on the sites of religious schools that have closed.[202] Legal considerations have contributed to the denial of conversions of parochial schools in other locations.[203]

Assessing Choice

"Choice" has emerged at five moments of legal, political, and cultural conflict over schooling in the United States. In the first part of the twentieth century, the Americanizing push behind Oregon's compulsory school law triggered a successful challenge lending constitutional protection to parental choice of parochial and other private schooling.[204] But the decision produced a system in which only public schools received funding, leaving parental choice of private schooling to private philanthropy and families with economic resources. White communities resisting the desegregation mandated by *Brown v. Board of Education* after 1954 turned to the "choice" of private schools—with the most extreme version closing the public schools until the Supreme Court intervened.[205] "Freedom of choice" transfers emerged as failed strategy for ending official racial segregation in public schools.[206] School choice for a time became a tool for school desegregation as systems created city-wide magnet schools, aiming to overcome de facto as well as de jure racial segregation, but the Supreme Court ultimately curbed such plans.[207] And publicly funded vouchers subsidizing private school tuition emerged in response to spectacularly failing urban schools—with the Supreme Court clearing the way even when the public dollars in large measure went into religious schools.[208] By the turn of the twenty-first century, a mix of public and private schooling options, including entrepreneurial public charter schools, have grown under the banner of school choice that mobilizes business people, school reformers, proponents of religious schools, critics of state-run services, and parents desperate for better education for their children. The persistent if capacious notion of "school choice" thus has encompassed efforts to defeat or avoid mixing students of different backgrounds, efforts to promote integration, and other varied forms of educational improvement.

Charter school legislation, school vouchers, and choice options within mainstream public school systems invite groups of people to develop individual schools with specific themes. Some aim to attract population subgroups, inviting self-segregation by religion, ethnicity, language, or disability. Recognition and support for schools organized along these different lines could be understood as an embrace of differences, a form of system-wide or society-level inclusion, or, to use Heather Gerken's term, "second-order diversity": enabling an institutional practice that involves variation among, not within, a particular setting or group.[209] Expressing tolerance or appreciation at some level, a system facilitating special-identity schools can also create a focal point for particular communities and an endorsement of pluralism.[210] Yet enacting pluralism without renovating structures and attitudes of exclusion and hierarchy can forseeably perpetuate or exacerbate patterns of inequality or social distrust—or simply fail to promote individual social mobility and integration into a society with sufficient cohesion and mutual respect to enable democracy and advance public welfare.

The prospect of special-identity schools enabled by school choice should prompt questions about what, if any, guidelines school systems, local communities, states, or the federal government should establish. Should local, state, and federal authorities encourage or discourage special-identity schools or school choice initiatives that promote self-segregation by race, ethnicity, or religion? The capacity of parents and students to use school choice arrangements to self-segregate is a feature that school systems can curb or promote, and then the officials involved in the system bear some responsibility for the results. Frankly, choice initiatives in practice simply may equalize the ability of groups other than well-off whites to self-segregate. Seeing this fact should alert public policy-makers to the effects of the system they design. How much should choice promote single-sex education, special schools for students with particular disabilities, or other particularized schools aiming to serve subgroups in the school population? Should school systems instead use school choice to increase mixing and integration across the lines of race, ethnicity, religion, socioeconomic status, sex, disability, and culture, and if so, how? Absent regulations, choice initiatives will prompt at least some new degrees of self-segregation and perhaps knowing use of the system by families and even by public officials to enable this result.

If this is the effect, then the choice movement will end up undermining a central goal of *Brown*, the goal of mixing different kinds of students in the same schools to overcome prejudices and to prevent inequitably allocated educational resources. Yet ending public and private oppression based on individuals' group traits and enabling individuals to achieve academically and succeed in society is another aspiration of *Brown*. For this goal, increasing the number and effectiveness of schools that teach respect and tolerance is crucial, regardless of the composition of the student body. School choice initiatives and public support for private schools do not necessarily undermine tolerance, civic engagement, or social integration. In fact, some studies indicate that students at Catholic and nonsectarian private schools give greater indications of tolerance and civic involvement than students in public schools.[211] These schools may also draw heterogeneous populations, accomplishing some mixing as well.

Of course, the sheer fact of mixing students of different identities and backgrounds does not necessarily produce the desirable effects of tolerance, civic identity, or social integration. The experiences of other liberal democracies with forms of school choice show a pattern of broad social tolerance that offers public support for religious pluralism while also regulating government-subsidized private schools.[212] At the level of the individual institution as well as in the whole society, what is essential is building schools with a strong sense of community and a mission to inculcate the values of equal respect. Jay Greene's research in the United States indicates that more crossracial friendships and fewer instances of racial fighting occurred in private schools than in public schools, but the finding is confounded by the high proportion of religious schools in the private sector.[213] Shared religious background or religious teachings could affect friendships, fighting, and school climate, as could self-selection by participating families.

Looking back over fifty years, the striking irony is that school choice, once a term implying an exit from desegregated schools, has generated a legal campaign modeled on the NAACP's *Brown* strategy and yielded important legal and policy innovations. Motivated initially by efforts to increase competititon and include parochial schools in the pool eligible for public support but coming to include public charter schools, pilot schools, and magnet schools, school choice has altered the landscape of American schooling by dislodging the assumption that most students simply attend the school assigned by the local district. But the school choice movement, perhaps to the surprise and disappointment of many key advocates, has created more alterations within public school systems than changed through access to private schools. Charter, pilot, and magnet schools and other vehicles for local experimentation and innovation direct public resources to support parent selection of schools and encourage innovation and specialization. Drawing talented people into roles as teachers, investors, board members, parental leaders, and policy-makers, charter schools in many communities have become centers of excellence, excitement, and initiative. Some offer a chance for a kind of committed partnership between parents and teachers in governing local schools that can resemble the best examples of private schools and historic black schools.

One consequence is the increased chance for parents and students to opt for education in settings that do not seek to mix students across races, genders, disability status, or religions. Indeed, it may be easier and cheaper to differentiate and market individual school programs in terms of gender, disability, and culture than in terms of demonstrated successes in pedagogy. Should there be any limits on the use of public schooling resources to promote instruction that sorts students explicitly or implicitly by gender? By disability or ability status? By language or immigrant status? Ironically, given the history of *Brown,* the only explicit constraint is the one that prohibits the use of individual students' racial identity—a constraint that in effect limits voluntary integration efforts by local school systems. Of course, otherwise existing prohibitions on exclusions on the basis of race, gender, disability, and national origin do and should apply. But the programs schools offer can implicitly steer students toward and away from particular schools, and growing latitude for experimentation can permit single-sex schools, schools for English-language learners, schools for students with learning disabilities, and other areas of focus that yield relatively homogeneous student bodies on one or more dimension. Federal, state, and local governments could do much more to expressly require charter school systems to promote racial and economic integration; they could support interdistrict transfer programs; they could enhance magnet schools designed to generate student bodies that are diverse in terms of race, ethnicity, disability status, and other characteristics; they could use socioeconomic categories to mix students; they could charge each school receiving public support to demonstrate how it advances social integration (whether across racial, ethnic, gender, language, or other lines of difference) through school enrollments, curricular content, and ties to varied communities. Should schools be charged with social integration anymore? If not, should other social institutions pick up this task? The social science of social integration, itself a legacy of *Brown,* is a central resource for addressing these questions.

6

Social Science in *Brown*'s Path

Social Contact and Integration Revisited

*[S]ubstantial bettering of social relations waits upon the growth of a
scientific social psychology.*

—John Dewey[1]

The architects of *Brown v. Board of Education* soldiered through long
struggles and many obstacles, but even they would probably be surprised
by the state of affairs emerging half a century following the decision.
Brown influenced expanding use of social sciences by lawyers pursuing
social change and especially educational reforms. The state of racial integration in education might be stunningly disappointing, but *Brown* has
also produced unexpected dividends addressing historic educational disadvantages based on gender, disability, language, immigrant status, poverty, sexual orientation, and religion. This dual legacy of disappointment
and promise raises profound questions about the priority the nation gives
not just to equal opportunity but also to social integration, the movement
of individuals from previously excluded or subordinated groups into the
social mainstream where they can join others in pursuing opportunities and enriching society. Because this aspiration gained support from
social science evidence in the *Brown* litigation itself, this chapter considers the strengths and limitations of social science research on social
integration, including research launched in the wake of the *Brown* litigation. The boost *Brown* gave to the field of social psychology to advance
racial equality has some irony, given the reliance by defenders of racial

segregation on eugenics and other "scientific" theories of their day. The contribution of social psychology to the cause of racial justice is particularly contested, as many critics have contended that its use contributed to narrowing policy debates to a focus on psychological damage rather than structures of racial oppression and the role of community supports in academic success.[2] It might even be fair to conclude that when it comes to racial relations in the United States, there is more success in the growth of the research field studying social integration than there is success in actual social integration.

Hence, paying attention to contemporary social science in assessing how social integration affects academic achievement, social cohesion, individual development, economic and social opportunities, and civic engagement and democracy means remaining mindful of the limitations of research and continuing to subject its assumptions to scrutiny. Research methodologies have improved and offer insights into other possible social institutions or practices—including afterschool and summer programs for young people, military and national service, and integrated workplaces—that could advance social integration if public schooling no longer pursues it as a central task. The chapter closes by revisiting the prospects for enhancing social integration through schooling, while inviting continuing reassessment of the reach and limitations of social science as a tool to address such issues.

Social Science in *Brown*

"Since its inception, American social science has been closely bound with American Negro destiny. Even before the Civil War the Southern ruling class had inspired a pseudoscientific literature attempting to prove the Negro inhuman and thus beyond any moral objections to human slavery," wrote Ralph Ellison in 1944.[3] *Brown* marked a turning point in social science, or claims in its name. In the decades before the litigation, advocates proffered social science to justify racial segregation, and studies in turn supported prejudice and stereotyping on the basis of race, gender, ethnicity, and disability.[4] The tide began to turn when the Carnegie Corporation commissioned a study by Swedish economist and lawyer Gunnar Myrdal. His 1944 book *An American Dilemma* provided massive economic and sociological data and condemned racial segregation for preventing African Americans from fully participating in American society and for sustaining the prejudices that reinforced their exclusion.[5] The lawyers working with the NAACP explored potential sources of social science evidence to support their challenges to segregated schooling. Thurgood Marshall recollected in 1977 that his use of social science represented an effort to prove actual damages from segregation: "I went to the basic principle that if you had an automobile accident and you are 'injured,' you have to prove your injuries—you had to put on [the stand] a doctor, and the doctor will explain what your injuries are and how you are damaged. So I said that these Negro kids are damaged, we will have to prove it. Everybody said, 'You're crazy.' I said, 'How can you prove it?'"[6] Marshall and the NAACP team drew on not only Myrdal's work but also testimony that Robert Redfield, an anthropologist from the University of Chicago, had given in the NAACP's 1946 challenge to the whites-only admissions policy of the University of Texas law school in *Sweatt v. University of Texas*.[7] Redfield emphasized that no racial characteristics were relevant to either the education at issue or to the reaction of the Negro student to the learning environment.[8] Redfield joined other social scientists in offering testimony in subsequent cases challenging state-mandated racial segregation in public elementary and high schools.[9]

The NAACP lawyers most famously relied on studies conducted in the 1930s and 1940s by Kenneth B. Clark and Mamie Phipps Clark (stemming from Mamie Clark's master's thesis) that indicated how Negro children internalize negative ideas about their race.[10] In their study, the Clarks presented black children with dark-skinned and light-skinned dolls, asked them to choose "the bad doll," and found that most of them picked the dark-skinned doll.[11] Thurgood Marshall and Robert Carter at the NAACP Legal Defense Fund drew the Clarks and other social scientists into the litigation not only as witnesses but also as participants in the entire assault on segregated schools argument.[12]

In the planning stages of *Brown*, many of the NAACP lawyers resisted using the doll studies. According to one observer, Spotswood Robinson "thought it was crazy and insulting to persuade a court of law with examples of crying children and dolls," and William Coleman was heard to comment: "Jesus Christ! Those damned dolls! I thought it was a joke!"[13] Testifying for the Commonwealth of Virginia, psychologist Henry Garrett castigated the doll studies for relying on students who themselves were resisting segregated schooling.[14] Law professor Edmond Cahn and a student coauthored a note in the *Yale Law Journal*[15] that questioned the Clark study's methods and findings,[16] immediately after the study was presented in the NAACP briefs.[17] Dr. Henry Garrett, the sharpest critic of the NAACP's social scientists' position, was particularly invested in the political project. He organized a group of scholars devoted to preventing racial integration and promoting the ideas of eugenics and "race hygiene."[18] He also openly and avidly participated in neofascist and ultra-right-wing groups.[19] His views were treated as mainstream; he served as president of the American Psychological Association in 1946 and chair of the Psychology Department at Columbia University from 1941 to 1955. Yet what was mainstream remained so up for grabs that Garrett's criticisms of the Clarks' work ultimately proved no challenge to Kenneth Clark's own professional stature. The shift in prevailing views was complete by the time Clark assumed the presidency of the American Psychological Association in 1970.

The doll studies, while salient to many observers, in fact played a modest role in the evidentiary base for the litigation. While *Brown* was pending,

Kenneth Clark published a 1953 essay presenting many potential uses of social science in contesting prevailing social assumptions and in bolstering the legal challenges to racial segregation. According to Clark, the doll studies were relevant in that they showed how racial segregation interfered with the personality development of both Negro and white children and communicated the inferior status of Negroes. This focus on the harms done to black children neglected harms done to whites and others, offered no insights into the social psychology or material effects of racism, and failed to acknowledge how stereotypes can be self-fulfilling prophecies.[20] Clark noted that social science could demonstrate that racial classification should be viewed as irrelevant to schooling because there are no psychological or biological differences inherent in racial identity; racial segregation harms society as a whole because it impairs communication and increases mutual hostility and suspicion across racial groups; desegregation improves interracial relations and social stability; and successful desegregation in elementary and secondary schools is even easier than in graduate and professional schools because younger students are even more flexible than older students in attitudes and behavior.[21]

Introduced in four of the five trials ultimately combined into *Brown,* this social scientific analysis drew cross-examination but faced contrary social science testimony in only one of the suits.[22] In that suit, the state of Virginia called three experts (a psychiatrist and two psychologists) who testified that personality effects of segregation could not yet be determined through social science studies and that residents of Virginia were not ready to give up their segregated schools. Yet even these experts for the state testified on cross-examination that segregation would be stigmatizing and produce feelings of inferiority.[23] Clark concluded: "Now that the precedent of admitting social science testimony has been established, it is certain that social scientists will be used in similar cases in the future."[24] The research and testimony of the social scientists offered a way to question widespread assumptions not only about segregation but also about the inevitability or naturalness of attitudes held by whites and blacks about race. Raising such questions would challenge the state defendants' efforts to justify racial segregation as natural, inoffensive, or socially beneficial.[25]

Swimming in a sea of contests over social practices and their meaning, Clark sought to anchor social science in the hard sciences. He explained how the social scientist pursues the collection and interpretation of data with care and objectivity, while also being "clear and courageous in his social values."[26] This apparent tension between objectivity and social or political commitments could be resolved, he argued, through adherence to the duty to pursue the truth, despite potential conflict with dominant community beliefs. Competent social scientists could produce conflicting testimony, as had already occurred with competing psychiatric testimony about the sanity of particular criminal defendants.[27] But social scientists could also describe consensus when it emerged; and in that spirit, the Society for the Psychological Study of Social Issues produced a report that was later reworked into a brief filed in *Brown* on behalf of prominent social scientists.[28]

By the time the Supreme Court considered the constitutionality of "separate but equal" schooling, the Court itself had already produced a sufficient set of legal precedents to provide legal doctrine to support the rejection of racially segregated schooling under the equal protection clause. The Court had concluded that deprivation of access to peers and the social networks in which they do and will operate violated constitutional requirements in the context of law school education in Texas.[29] The Court directed that an African-American student pursuing graduate studies in education in a state university was entitled to the same instruction and opportunities as other students—and that this entitlement is not fulfilled through separate facilities.[30] Having rejected separate facilities in graduate and legal education, the Court left open what the courts would do about the "separate but equal" doctrine as applied to elementary and secondary schools or other social institutions. The Court did not explicitly overturn *Plessy v. Ferguson,*[31] the key precedent holding that equal protection of the law could be secured through "separate but equal" facilities.[32] Even though five members of the Court seemed ready to overturn that doctrine, there initially was no rationale around which they or the rest of the justices could unite.[33] As newly appointed chief justice Earl Warren stepped into *Brown,* put over from the prior year for reargument, he told his colleagues that segregation could only be defended on the belief that blacks were inferior to whites.[34] Justice Frankfurter considered how history refuted allegedly scientific grounds for viewing blacks as inferior.[35] Chief Justice Warren's unanimous opinion rejecting *Plessy* and segregated public schooling was short in length and short on doctrinal analysis. It responded to concerns about public resistance and postponed the remedial question until the following year.

In this context, Chief Justice Warren included the famous footnote 11, listing seven works by social scientists to his opinion's rejection of *Plessy*'s separate-but-equal doctrine.[36] The offering of social science evidence to the Court provided an additional and potentially legitimating ground for the decision,[37] while also creating fodder for more public debate. Scott Brewer characterized *Brown*'s use of the footnote as "a remarkable culmination of the legal realist project of taming abstract legal propositions with the whip of social science."[38] The defendants and many later commentators criticized the Supreme Court's reliance on the social science evidence in footnote 11[39] by citing flaws in the research, especially the studies by the Clarks.[40] Many, of course, were just waiting to pounce on any possible grounds for attacking the landmark decision. Whatever the actual influence of specific social science research on the justices, the sociological flavor of their decision struck many as more salient than its legal basis. The *New York Times* entitled a story on the opinion "A Sociological Decision: Court Founded Its Segregation Ruling on Hearts and Minds Rather Than Laws."[41]

In his book *The Warren Court,* Morton Horwitz deftly read the famous footnote 11 in *Brown* as a window onto conflicting theories of constitutional interpretation. According to one theory, constitutional requirements change as society changes; according to another, the Constitution is constant, but cases can announce previous errors in judicial understandings of the world. Horwitz thus argued that the citation to "modern" psychological and sociological studies pointing to injuries that segregation inflicted on the self-esteem of black children allowed the Court in *Brown* to emphasize changes to society's understanding of the meaning of forced racial separation through time.[42] Yet at the same time, in ruling that "separate educational facilities are inherently unequal," the Court announced that state-imposed racial segregation had always violated and would always violate the guarantee of equal protection. Reliance on social science in this sense involved exposing the nature of an unchanging reality even as people needed new research studies to come to new understandings of that reality.

Using social science to challenge prevailing views is difficult if we think of social science as simply providing neutral tools for discerning reality. Human judges will inevitably at times make mistakes, whether they rely on fresh social science findings about new realities or instead on evidence supporting new understandings of unchanging reality. Even worse, social science findings themselves can be wrong when announced or wrong when reconsidered later. Some of the studies cited in footnote 11 in *Brown* have been challenged by subsequent research and improved research techniques, even as the footnote itself boosted reliance on social science in equal protection and civil rights litigation. Recently the Supreme Court considered but treated social science as inconclusive when it rejected the use of racial classifications to achieve voluntary school desegregation.[43] These uses of social science all partake of the view that the project of this kind of research is to discern a knowable social reality. Social science offers, then, an imperfect but important lens on that reality, which is germane to judicial assessments of the constitutional meanings of equality and liberty.

A contrasting approach treats social science itself as a project of social interpretation, a project informed by values and politics rather than value-neutral discovery.[44] Even though this conception puts at risk the authority that litigators may hope to obtain by relying on social science research, it offers insight into the project of meaning-making at work in constitutional litigation.[45] Nowhere is this project more evident than in constitutional litigation over schooling where the fights among lawyers and experts reach into the very distinction between law and society, with certain understandings of society themselves at risk of being illegal.[46]

Social Psychology in *Brown*'s Wake

Despite or perhaps even because of its controversial role in the *Brown* litigation, social science has emerged as a key arena for pursuing the project of social integration.[47] With the development of social science applications to not only race relations but also social relations across lines of language, culture, gender, and disability, the discipline emerged as a growth industry. But it is also a contested terrain and a resource equally available to public officials and advocates with competing views of what law and policy should require and permit.[48]

The key figure in the development of the social science of social integration was Gordon Allport. Despite Kenneth Clark's suggestion, he initially declined to get involved in *Brown*,[49] but he eventually joined thirty-four other eminent social scientists in the brief submitted before the Supreme Court.[50] Already famous for his work on the concept of personality, Allport supported the role of psychologists in social reform and emerged as a leader of applied social science in these efforts.[51] At that time, Allport served as chair of Harvard University's Department of Psychology. He had been elected president of the American Psychological Association in 1938 and moved the field toward greater attention to political and social issues.[52]

Just before the Supreme Court issued its decision in *Brown*—three years after the initial underlying cases began—Allport published his book *The Nature of Prejudice*.[53] The book spurred decades of research into the dynamics of intergroup relationships and launched a period of ascendancy for the field of social psychology in addressing prejudice and intergroup relations, alongside other disciplines, including history and economics.[54] Allport's focus on prejudice reflected both the social context of his own youth, which included American racial relations, the Holocaust, his own work during World War II with refugees, and his supervision of graduate students studying prejudice.[55] He urged attention to "ethnic" rather than racial categories in order to acknowledge treatment of group differences in terms of "physical, national, cultural, linguistic, religious, or ideological" traits.[56]

The 1954 publication of *The Nature of Prejudice* drew broad attention. Soon heralded as a classic, Allport's book examined the sources and dynamics of in-group and out-group relations. Allport argued that casual contact between people is not likely to overcome prejudices but maintained that "[p]rejudice (unless deeply rooted in the character structure of the individual) may be reduced by equal status contact between majority and minority groups in pursuit of common goals" and sanctioned by the institutional supports of law, custom, or local culture.[57] This idea, soon called "the contact hypothesis," informed desegregation efforts by positing that interracial attitudes improve through contact across racial lines when organized as cooperative activities among people of equal status. In a later edition of his book, Allport commented on the efforts to desegregate public schools and offered a critique of the gradualism adopted by the courts in light of the "all deliberate speed" standard offered by the Supreme Court in 1955. Allport suggested that while many white communities generated opposition in the face of the gradualist approach, swift change could reduce opposition by presenting the status of a fait accompli and leaving less time for opposition to build.[58]

Critics who may not have even read Allport's work argued that court-ordered desegregation oversimplified the steps necessary to overcome attitudes associated with centuries of raced-based social hierarchy. The problem seems to have been anticipated and well described by Allport. He contended that if contact occurs in the midst of hostility or with no change in the status differential between groups, it can reinforce and deepen negative stereotypes. Allport had been clear from the start of his work that the contact must take place under favorable circumstances for hostile attitudes to diminish.[59] Contact is a necessary but hardly sufficient predicate for reducing prejudice.

Allport's own work predicted that simply mixing students without eliminating the hostile environment would yield little positive change in attitudes. So he would not have been surprised that the first decades of school desegregation produced a mixed record on the dimension of improving intergroup relationships and decreasing negative racial stereotypes. Researchers found the initial results of desegregation orders disappointing even when they yielded lessons for improving future efforts.[60] One review of the initial decade of controversial court-ordered desegregation observed that "in 16 percent of the desegregated schools examined, the attitudes of whites toward African Americans became more favorable over time or were more favorable than those in comparison schools that were segregated. In the remaining schools, there were either no changes over time or no difference between desegregated and segregated schools (36%) or attitudes became, or were, more negative (48%)."[61] Yet over a longer time frame, studies show that blacks who attended desegregated schools were more likely to work in integrated settings and have white friends, live in integrated neighborhoods, and send their children to desegregated schools than blacks who attended segregated schools. Relatedly, whites who attended desegregated schools were also more likely to work in desegregated settings.[62]

Although Allport's book did not itself appear before the decision in *Brown*, it oriented academics and journalists to the factors affecting prejudice and increased attention to the role social science could play in the process of reforming schools. His work is widely seen as the foundation for generations of research and remedial social programs.[63] Scholars following in his footsteps have pursued the lines of inquiry he opened into the social cognitive processes people use in categorizing others, the motivations of self-enhancement and material gain behind prejudices, social process such as language that maintain and transmit biases, and potentially useful social interventions to reduce bias.[64] Newer research emphasizes the interactions between social environments and an individual's psychological structures in the development, maintenance, and modification of bias.[65] It also shows how conflicts over resources interact with intergroup biases.[66] *Brown* itself spurred interest in these topics and inspired scholars to examine the processes of internalized prejudice, unconscious dimensions of prejudice, and variations in how individuals respond to group-based ideologies.[67] Other studies illuminate how efforts to eliminate social categorization and to develop overarching identities spanning subgroup membership can reduce prejudice.[68] Multicultural education efforts, diversity training, intergroup dialogues, and cooperative learning efforts each can be traced to insights from the contact hypothesis.[69]

In the wake of *Brown*, then, social scientific research has become a central medium for evaluating desegregation and other equality initiatives and even for working out which potential legacies of *Brown* are worth pursuing in theory and in practice. There is a risk of some circularity in citing research that is itself a subject of inquiry. This chapter considers critiques of social science even as it turns to its products for evidence and analysis. This strategy acknowledges how the pervasiveness of social science data in legal and public policy discussions is itself one of the repercussions of *Brown*.

Legislative and judicial uses of social sciences since *Brown* invite close analysis of their frames of reference and the political projects implicit in the work. To see the political projects in the work is not to debunk the social science or the legal arguments as shams. Instead, both law and social science emerge as tools for struggles over meaning and social interpretation, and ongoing scrutiny of the assumptions and effects of expert work remains an important task.

Assessing *Brown*'s Effect on Social Integration in the United States

A frank assessment must credit the landmark *Brown* decision with helping to launch judicial and legislative initiatives to end official racial segregation in schools, Southern backlash and the governmental failure to produce racially integrated schools, but also mars mobilization in response. However disappointing the patterns of school enrollments had become more than a half century later, the same historical distance shows how *Brown* initiated a dramatic change in day-to-day practices in the United States around race, for example, the ending of Jim Crow laws. In the first decade of the twenty-first century, some African Americans, Hispanics, and members of other racial minorities have reached the pinnacles of academic, economic, social, and political achievement, including the presidency of the United States. Yet the "color line" in more subtle ways still matters significantly to the life chances and social worlds of individuals in the United States. Racial divides in the country persist and grow as 49 percent of incarcerated individuals are African Americans, although they comprise only 13 percent of the general population.[70] Mexican Americans remain concentrated in particular residential neighborhoods and in blue-color jobs; mobility for subsequent generations is impaired by every setback in the larger economy.[71] This is the context supporting the conclusion that "throughout the twentieth century America was, as it remains, one nation divisible, with liberty and justice for some."[72] The NAACP lawyers targeted schools in the *Brown* litigation, so the remaining and growing racial separation in American schools is especially sobering. The most separated students are white students, who, due to residential segregation by race and class and white flight from officially desegregated schools, on average attend schools that are composed mainly of other white students.[73]

Honest evaluation of *Brown* should also catalogue how, in its wake, advocates undertook similar efforts to achieve equality in schools on the basis of types of diversity beyond racial identity. In each context, advocates encountered ambivalence over whether equality calls for separate instruction or integration across lines of difference.[74] Social separation or integration across these lines also affects the life chances of individuals and the character of the society and the polity.

Amid widespread disenchantment with racial desegregation and ongoing concerns about shortfalls in student achievement, political movements for "school choice" gained speed and accelerated the development of experiments with varied forms of separate instruction based on various lines of student identities and interests.[75] Rather than realizing the dream of the "common school" where students of all backgrounds would join together in shared preparation for the tasks of citizenship, school reforms at the turn of the twenty-first century challenged the very ideal of a common-school experience. And the Supreme Court's distaste for racially conscious measures produced a world in which the only explicit restriction on the kind of school that can be supported through a public charter, public magnet, or voucher for private school tuition is the prohibition on taking individual students' race into account, even if the goal is to create a racially integrated school.[76]

Equal opportunity remains the undisputed goal for American schools, and in that respect, *Brown* endures. Despite the Supreme Court's own refusal to declare a federal constitutional right to an education,[77] the Court extended *Brown* when it rejected the state exclusion of the class of undocumented students from public schooling, and state and federal governments have elaborated the meaning of and commitment to equal educational opportunities for all children.[78] When a conservative Republican president embraced the phrase "No child left behind" as the new mantra, he only prompted a dispute over credit for the phrase, not over the ideal, and he came under criticism only by those who questioned whether the resources allotted betrayed an insincere commitment to that ideal.[79]

As a public goal, the No Child Left Behind Act represents a national commitment to minimum levels of opportunity for each child to succeed, as measured by standardized tests established by the states. The Act has also supplied an organizing focus for the work of schools around the country. The Act has yielded mixed results, even in terms of only the narrow measurement of scores on tests that each state can prescribe and modify—and those states can and do lower their standards to try and boost results. The stark variation in the quality of schooling in America is most striking. The disparities in school expenditures and governance ensure that students' racial and socioeconomic profiles continue to skew their chances for access to the best publicly provided schools.

Advances in the educational and economic opportunities for girls and women are notable yet are often more constrained than those for boys and men. Still, in some communities—notably among African Americans and Hispanics—girls and women reach greater educational and economic attainment than boys and men, and nationwide more women are pursuing postsecondary education than men.[80] Hence, gender equality remains elusive yet complicated. Individuals with disabilities, assisted by shifts in public policies, have more educational and employment opportunities than in the past but nonetheless often face social misunderstandings, isolation, and, more recently, backlash against the social policies designed to help them.[81] Immigrants face periodic waves of resentment and have varying patterns of success in joining the educational and economic mainstream in the United States.[82] Political reactions against bilingual instruction and the public use of Spanish reflect tensions between different communities, even as Spanish rather than English had become the dominant or exclusive language in many neighborhoods in the United States.[83] Some who predict increasing global interdependence seek fluency for themselves or their children in Mandarin Chinese, Arabic, and other languages. Dramatic growth in the number of Islamic and Jewish parochial schools and the size of their enrollment proceeds (still involving small absolute numbers), even as Catholic schools, often serving low-income students of diverse religious backgrounds, struggle for sufficient resources to remain open.[84] In fact, Catholic school enrollments have dropped by half (from a high of five million) since the 1960s.[85] Attending to evidence at the level of basic facts—what are the patterns of social mixing in schools and allocation of educational opportunities—remains a valuable undertaking, for advocates, policy-makers, parents, and the larger community.

Diversity and Social Integration

A national public culture exhibited in laws and popular media has come to emphasize the value of diversity in education, work, and society. Intermarriage across racial and religious lines in the United States has increased, and same-sex marriage is lawful in a growing number of states. Yet many individuals do not have personal friends or connections with people who differ from them in terms of race, immigrant status, socioeconomic status, disability status, sexual orientation, or religion. Strikingly, one researcher suggests that increased diversity in a society is associated with increased levels of disengagement and distrust, not only across groups but within groups.[86]

Given this background, school choice policies that increase educational opportunities for elementary and secondary students could advance the commitment to equal opportunity but could also exacerbate patterns of separation along lines of group identity. Whether the school is public or private seems less important to educational opportunity than whether more seats are open at good schools with effective teachers, especially for families who otherwise could not afford good options. If this means growing schools with specialized missions—such as gateways to medical careers or Arabic language and culture—and drawing self-selected students, it may be worthwhile. Public charter schools, vouchers for private schools, and other initiatives prompting smaller, mission-focused schools can draw new talent and keep gifted educators in the often exhausting work of teaching. Some current school reforms bring energy, focus, and resolve and show promise for generating high achievement and pathways to college and successful careers.

With energy and resources flowing to school choice initiatives, what then is and should be the fate of the vision—and experience—of a common public school with students of all backgrounds? School choice can worsen the already high levels of racial and economic separation among American schoolchildren.[87] Charter schools also draw in students with disabilities in significantly smaller percentages than do traditional public schools. Those students with disabilities who attend charter schools often find themselves at institutions that are substantially separate from mainstream populations,[88] as such schools choose either to specialize in accommodating students with disabilities or broadcast their inability to do so.[89] Some parents appreciate the schools specializing in educating students with autism or learning disabilities, while others question the growing segregation of their children through such schools.[90] English-language learners may also be sharply underrepresented in charter schools.[91] School choice, through charter schools especially, is working at least sufficiently that districts at risk of declining enrollments turn to marketing to try to win students back to the mainstream public schools.[92]

Many dismal schools remain. Even among those schools with new mission and purpose, what happens to social integration and shared preparation for the tasks of citizenship if they are no longer the responsibility of schools? The fundamental divide between schools for wealthy and for poor communities persists, and that divide resists reforms, given the tradition of local control. Racial separation emerges now "de facto," as a result of "choices." Many white families make choices simply assuming that suburban schools in relatively expensive communities offer better opportunities for their children, and the continuing economic, social, and cultural constraints confine more families of color to urban schools.

Jennifer Hochschild and Nathan Scovronick explain in their book *The American Dream and the Public Schools* that Americans believe that each child "should have an equal chance to succeed" but parents "will continue to try to use the fruits of their labor to secure an advantage for their own children."[93] Perpetuating difference and inequality while expressing the ideal of equality, American schools profoundly reflect and extend socioeconomic differences. The tension between equality and parental choice goes even deeper, for the public commitment to educate each child at times conflicts with the constitutional assurance that all parents can pursue the education that fulfills their priorities for their children in terms of identities and affiliations.[94]

For decades, private school enrollments in the United States have hovered around 10 percent of the school aged population, and now this group is joined by those taking advantage of publicly subsidized school choice. Diminished opportunities for social integration arise with each new deliberate experiment of separate schooling, since each draws a self-selected group more homogenous than the society as a whole.[95] But new schools could also be constructed to draw in diverse student bodies and promote mutual appreciation and cultural competence.

Mixing students of different backgrounds and identities may improve their academic achievement. Obtaining better information about when and why this is true is a complex and promising task for policy-makers. But mixing students across lines of difference and helping them forge a sense of shared purpose and experience carries distinctive values that are captured by the ideal of integration. That ideal moves beyond sheer presence in the same schools to participation in a shared community of mutual respect and common goals within a diverse student body.

Social integration at its best (1) overcomes and prevents stereotyping and dehumanizing; (2) promotes not just tolerance for those who are different but mutual engagement, mutual appreciation, and the ability to take the perspective of another; (3) assists individuals in relating well to diverse others and in working together in mixed groups to solve problems and perform other tasks; (4) advances the resource of social capital and networking across different groups; and (5) reduces conventional lines of division through the creation and support of crosscutting groups, overarching identities that nurture a sense of solidarity and civic membership, and reduction of the lines of social hierarchy that have constrained individual opportunity in the past. If education from kindergarten through high school neither accomplishes nor aspires to pursue social integration,[96] this goal could be pursued through children's after-school and summer programs, military and national youth service, and workplaces. Each of these alternatives represents efforts worthwhile in their own terms as well as potential avenues for integrating people from different walks of life. Yet none would be as universal or potentially effective as schooling. The integration ideal deserves to be revisited and defended as a crucial element of preparing individuals for successful and productive lives as workers, parents, and civic participants in a pluralistic, democratic society.[97]

Benefits of Social Integration

Academic Achievement, Socio-economic Mixing, and the Example of Department of Defense Schools

Recent work by social scientists helps address the correlations between mixing different kinds of students and academic achievement in different kinds of schools. Researchers also explore when and how mixed groups improve the ability of individuals to feel connected with and able to take the perspective of others, although this research may reflect societal assumptions still in flux. Further scholarship identifies the value of diversity to team-work and creative problem solving. A review of all of this work must be tempered with the reminder that data gathering, model building, and other tools of social science can be flawed and in need of revisiting. Social science research projects must always be understood as works-in-progress trying to interpret the world.

Student achievement patterns differ markedly across schools in the United States. These variations may correlate with patterns of parental socioeconomic class status, but they may also correlate with the racial composition of the school or with concentrations of students in the statutorily mandated "individual education plans" to address disability issues, language learning, or single-sex instruction. The causation behind differences in student achievement is notoriously difficult to pin down, but it may well reflect differences not only in teachers' abilities but also in teachers' expectations of different kinds of students. When teachers have unconscious stereotypes and prejudices about the capacities of students based on their race, ethnicity, gender, disability, or other characteristics, students respond; teacher expectations are robustly associated with student performance, as are students' senses of belonging in the class and in the school.[98] Student achievement patterns also tend to echo different kinds of engagement by parents in the school, as well as different levels of parental education and income.[99]

Although the evidence is partial, achievement, measured on standardized tests, seems to improve for many students in settings that are racially integrated and in settings that mix middle-income and lower-income students. White students' test performance has been unaffected or improved by racial desegregation, while the performance of black students has demonstrably increased in desegregated schools.[100] Black and Hispanic students showed the greatest gains in academic achievement from racially mixed schools, with results apparently connected to school integration rather than increased funding.[101]

Richard Kahlenberg's argument for assigning students to schools by socioeconomic status reflects another kind of issue used to justify social integration to boost academic achievement.[102] Identifying predominantly middle-class schools as the ones where most students succeed, Kahlenberg traced the influences of peers, parents, and teacher expectations found in middle-class schools as strengths that could be extended to economically disadvantaged students.[103] Moreover, assigning students to schools on the basis of socioeconomic characteristics, unlike assigning them based on the racial identity of individual students, is permitted, because the Supreme Court has rejected heightened judicial scrutiny of wealth-based distinctions.[104] Class-conscious politics could be less divisive and more effective than racial politics in building winning coalitions.[105] Still, political opposition is likely, and flight of the middle class would be a serious risk.

Kahlenberg addressed this risk without commenting on what it indicates about the attitudes of middle-class parents toward social integration. He predicted that a school reaching 50 percent enrollment of low-income students would hit a tipping point prompting middle-class parents to remove their children. On that basis, he recommended that no more than 50 percent of students in any given school be eligible for reduced-price lunch.[106] He also proposed a choice-based school assignment scheme that would allow parents to list first, second, and third choices from among district schools in order to allow the school administrators to achieve an appropriate socioeconomic balance for each school.[107] And he described three school districts that already pursue this kind of policy with educational and political success.[108]

There is much to admire in the pursuit of socioeconomic integration in schooling. First, it is constitutional. Kahlenberg correctly anticipated that the Supreme Court would object to voluntary plans to produce racially mixed schools.[109] In addition, a focus on socioeconomic integration in grades K–12[110] could guarantee every student access to a middle-class school—in terms of the predominant student body and characteristics of school culture—as a route to school equality. The overrepresentation of blacks and Hispanics in the most impoverished settings makes targeting socioeconomic disadvantage a strategy of racial as well as redistributive justice.[111] Yet issues posed by legacies of racialized exclusions, stereotyping, and disadvantage remain. Socioeconomic mixing would not necessarily increase the degree of racial mixing. Most analysts conclude that because the lion's share of impoverished people are white, socioeconomic integration in fact would not by itself produce racial diversity.[112] The simple focus on socioeconomic integration, without thoughtful attention to race, is unlikely to halt segregation in a world where white parents, given the choice, select public or private schools enrolling many nonwhites.[113] Kahlenberg himself advocated racial mixing as long as it was lawful, although his emphasis on this point sought to combat prejudice rather than to boost student achievement.[114] Yet white parents may be choosing predominantly white schools because they want their children to be with children who perform well on tests, children who, given the racial gap in school testing, are disproportionately white.[115]

A deeper problem pertains to the step from mixing to integration: from sharing the same space to sharing the same communal dreams, respect, friendship, and sense of membership. Kahlenberg assumed that simply being in the same school with middle-class students will produce a sense of membership and shared aspirations for poor kids. A strong positive school culture may produce this collective identity—if other barriers do not exist. Unfortunately, racial differences remain a barrier in too many settings. The racial achievement gap persists even in integrated middle-class schools, even among African Americans and Hispanics who are themselves middle class, and among academically motivated and focused students of color.[116] To alter current patterns of racial and cultural differences in school achievement, the solution of socioeconomic mixing must be combined with counterprogramming, challenging the assumption that it is a white middle-class school that makes room for non white low-income kids and drawing also on the critical perspectives and experiences of children of color and poor families to make an inclusive school. Further work is needed to create truly inclusive cultures of achievement and respect.[117] Pedro Noguera, an expert on the racial gap in achievement, concluded from his research: "I fundamentally believe that educating all children, even those who are poor and non-White, is an achievable goal, *if* we truly value all children. Of course, that is the real question: Does American society truly value all of its children?"[118]

Teaching methods, communication styles, and basic assessments of students' motivations need to change if each student is to feel really valued and to perceive equal opportunities. White teachers in one study proved effective in assessing the motivation and interest levels of their white students, but their perceptions of their students of color failed to match those students' own understandings of their interests and motivation levels.[119] Devising culturally relevant pedagogies, acknowledging the persistence of racial and ethnic stigma, and openly demonstrating commitments to respect and ensuring equal chances for all students could be crucial steps beyond mere mixing of students if the racial gap in achievement is to be closed.[120]

Absent careful attention, socioeconomically mixed schools too often are already settings for renewed racial segregation through academic tracking, special education assignments, and students' own divisions in lunch tables and cliques.[121] In a racially mixed school with racial tension, nonwhite peers harass studious nonwhite students for "acting white,"[122] and white peers can exacerbate perceptions of "stereotype threat." Socioeconomic mixing could make a difference in the educational opportunities available to many students and could produce some racial mixing, but on its own it will neither produce racial mixing in every district nor overcome the patterns of racial disparity in educational aspiration and achievement.

The record of schools run by the U.S. Department of Defense is instructive here.[123] Governed and financed by federal legislation, 223 schools enroll 105,000 students, with 70 percent of them overseas and the rest attending Department of Defense schools in the United States.[124] Resembling the composition of student enrollments in the state of New York, about 40 percent of the students in these schools are members of racial minority groups.[125] These students are 58 percent white, 22 percent black, 10 percent Hispanic, and 9 percent Asian or Pacific islander; 7.9 percent are of limited English proficiency, and 8.8 percent are in special education plans.[126] In 2007, the fourth-grade math achievement gap between black and white students in Department-run schools was nineteen points, compared with a national average of twenty-six points.[127] Of the three schools with comparable or smaller gaps, the Department-run schools reported the highest average scores for white students and the second highest for black students.[128] Similar results appeared with the eighth-grade math test and the reading tests for both fourth- and eighth-grade students. A recent report concluded that if the Department of Defense schools made up a state school system, "its 1998 National Assessment of Educational Progress (NAEP) reading and writing test results would rank it number one in the nation for minority students."[129] In terms of absolute results, only one state (Connecticut) ranks ahead of the achievement levels of the Department of Defense domestic schools, and only two (Connecticut and Maine) rank ahead of its overseas schools student achievement levels.[130]

This record of achievement would be notable under any circumstances, but it is especially compelling because the Department of Defense schools produce scores on standardized tests that are much higher than those predicted on the basis of students' parents' levels of education, occupational prestige, and income.[131] Factors contributing to the accomplishment of the Department of Defense schools include a clear mission, clear standards and accountability, rich and varied instructional methods,[132] and after-school homework programs at all schools.[133] The schools make heterogeneous classes the norm in terms of student achievement rather than using ability groups or tracks. Hence, these schools integrate low- and high-achieving students and students with disabilities in the same room.[134] A staff member told an evaluation team: "If we expose all of our kids to rigorous courses, this will go a long way toward bridging the minority gap. Especially in middle school, kids' bodies and brains take them out of action for a while but they are still sponges. They are absorbing a lot around them. You don't want to drop expectations for anyone."[135] In terms of resources, the Department of Defense has sufficient but not unusual levels of spending; while the Department's schools spend 22 percent more per pupil than the national average, they spend less than the average high-minority-enrollment school district.[136] They do compensate teachers at a level slightly higher than the national average,[137] and the schools are "communally organized," with high involvement by teachers and parents.[138]

Given the high level of transience as parents of children in these schools move, the same methods hold real promise for regular public schools that face similarly high rates of mobility. In fact, the student population turns over on an average of 37 percent each year in the Department of Defense schools, a higher rate of turnover than that in many troubled urban schools.[139] Notably, the Department of Defense schools require parental involvement, including participation in parent-teacher conferences. That requirement could be pursued in public schools, although the structure of requirements and sanctions is obviously different for families involved in the military. The duties of military personnel with school-aged children include attending parent-teacher conferences and reporting back to supervising officers about participation in the educational programs of their children.[140] Also harder to duplicate is the value placed on education and training that permeates the military community as a whole.[141] Yet some of these steps could be copied in public schools, such as the Pentagon directive that teachers and principals at Department of Defense schools include parents in lunch-time concerts and reading nights.[142] Given that the average enlisted person in the military has no more than a high school education and earns a modest salary, the academic success of their children reflects the combination of instructional methods, parental involvement, and cultural attitudes about personal accountability within the closed community making up the schools.[143]

The relatively successful level and quality of racial integration of the U.S. military, in addition, could play an important role in these schools. Although the overall racial composition of the Department of Defense schools resembles the composition of the public schools in the state of New York, almost 70 percent of the African-American students at the Department schools attend schools in which 60–80 percent of the students are white or Asian American. In public schools across the country, only 16 percent of African-American students attend schools with that high a proportion of white and Asian-American students.[144] By ensuring high expectations for all students, reducing distractions from tension over group membership and status, and operating within the most racially integrated sector of American society,[145] the schools run by the military reflect benefits from social integration. This is the only sector of American society where whites are routinely supervised by African Americans and Hispanics. Evaluators of the Department schools acknowledge the benefits of being "nested within a tightly-knit community life on U.S. military installations," without illicit drug activity or gang violence, and with only 6.2 percent single-parent households, compared with the national average of 27 percent.[146] The military culture and community and the commitments of teachers to ensuring that each student learns may be the most critical factors in the success of the Department schools.[147]

Social integration in the service of academic achievement takes a different turn with the issue of gender, given the varied findings of studies of coeducation versus single-sex education.[148] The reliability of such studies with regard to girls' academic achievement is hampered by the politicized context and limited settings for comparison.[149]

Assessing academic achievement for students with disabilities is complicated by the wide variety of disabilities, barriers to testing, ongoing disparities in access to the curriculum used for other students, and challenges ensuring the comparability of disabilities among students learning in different settings. Even given these limitations, there is evidence that for many students with disabilities, joining classrooms with their nondisabled peers is associated with higher levels of academic achievement, as is indicated by a metaanalysis of fifty studies.[150] Another analysis found that those with physical disabilities who experienced integrated rather than segregated education were 43 percent more likely to be employed upon leaving school.[151] One study showed improvement not only for the students with disabilities enrolled in the regular classroom but also for those without disabilities when compared with their counterparts in separated classrooms.[152]

The experiences and risks of harassment, bullying, and social stigma interfere with academic achievement. The targets tend to be members of racial minorities, girls, children with atypical gender presentations or who are perceived to be gay or lesbian, members of minority religious groups, students with disabilities, students learning English or speaking English with an accent, and immigrants. Bullying and peer harassment, in addition to interfering with academic achievement, bear potentially devastating experiences for the victims.[153] Shifting demographic patterns could create new occasions for members of these groups, or for white students as they become less dominant in particular communities, to have to endure harassment or stigma, accompanied by risks of backlash and economic anxiety.[154]

Promoting Perspective-taking, Reducing Stereotypes, and Improving Individual Experiences

Communities and the nation as a whole cannot wait for racial integration to be achieved before they pursue equal educational opportunities. But putting integration aside risks perpetuating the stereotypes and disadvantages that hamper too many African-American and Hispanic students. School reforms that do not involve racial mixing can work to boost academic achievement for African Americans and for Hispanics, but then they deprive students from different racial and ethnic backgrounds of access to one another. Segregation during childhood predicts segregation during adulthood in work and home, and discomfort with integrated settings.[155] Societies that organize schooling to reproduce lines of social division risk exacerbating these divisions and also create the danger that students in substantially separate schools will come to hold very different views of their society and polity.[156] The waves of research on contact hypothesis indicate the effectiveness of cooperation toward common goals, the development of a common affiliation to reduce the salience of subgroup identities, and equal participation in activities to overcome stereotypes based on subgroup membership.[157]

Decades of social science research since *Brown* have shown how schooling children from different groups together can prevent social stigma.[158] In particular, improved relationships are associated with interdependence and shared goals rather than competition.[159] Racially diverse classrooms organized into cooperative learning groups tend to increase friendships, empathy, and liking for others of different races.[160] A review of 515 studies involving 250,000 participants in 38 nations found contact between members of an in-group and an out-group reduced prejudice by (1) enhancing knowledge among the in-group about the out-group, and

(2) encouraging people to empathize with and take the perspective of others.[161] One scholar reviewed studies testing the contact hypothesis and concluded that "the research suggests that the contact should be voluntary, non-superficial, interpersonally oriented, have a high potential for friendship development and provide opportunities for informal interaction," while emphasizing overarching group membership and common goals.[162] Yet proximity—sharing the same school and the same classes—remains both necessary to and associated with the development of cross-racial friendship and reductions of racial prejudice.[163] Students attending schools using team-based learning reported significantly more friends of other races than students attending traditionally organized schools.[164]

Research showing generally positive effects from contact with others extends to ethnic minorities and immigrants,[165] groups separated by language and culture,[166] students with disabilities,[167] gays and lesbians,[168] and people with different religions.[169] Still, larger social narratives may dominate people's experiences so that negative views persist despite intergroup contact.[170] Sophisticated research is attentive to the interactions among social narratives, political power, individual psychological experience, and student achievement and can help explain how prejudicial assumptions and behaviors often continue despite contact when there is failure to establish equal status relationships. This may illuminate the debate over whether coeducation combats gender hierarchy. The prevailing social narratives about gender may be too strong for any actual contact to subvert them. There is some evidence for this explanation in the finding that teachers need to impose structure on classroom collaborations to guard against the likelihood that male students will take the lead in discussion and suppress dissenting views.[171] Similar understandings animate arguments that single-sex classes can challenge gender stereotypes better than coeducational settings can, which can accentuate gender differences in students' performance and even in their reported academic interests.[172]

Complicating matters here, the very scholarship advancing such views can itself be criticized for employing gender stereotypes and emphasizing girls' emotional adjustment over academic achievement.[173] On the basis of a metaanalysis of 713 samples used in 515 studies, two scholars validated the success of contact in improving attitudes across differences in racial, ethnic, gender, and disability status. This analysis underscored the importance of equal status, collaboration, authority involvement, and positive norms if contact is to yield a positive result.[174] Even under these conditions, changes in attitudes are often gradual and may proceed through stages, including denial of difference and continued assertion of superiority, before moving to acceptance, valuing others who are different, and reassessing the status of one's own group.[175]

Effects on academic achievement and group-based stereotypes are not the only measure of success from classrooms that mix students boys and girls and students who differ from one another along other dimensions. Promoting students' ability to take the perspective of others who differ from themselves is another worthy and measurable goal.[176] This ability, important for social relationships and ethical judgments,[177] can be notably enhanced when students with disabilities learn alongside nondisabled peers.[178] An advocate of inclusion classrooms described how Chris, a friend of Jack, a child with cerebral palsy, "noticed that Jack needed help getting his coat put on: his arms were stiff and the coat wasn't flexible enough. Chris designed a coat for Jack that had zippers all the way down the sleeves, so Jack's arms didn't need to be bent to get his coat on."[179] Chris entered the coat into the State Young Inventors Contest and won a first place gold medal and a savings bond. Yet according to one poll, 70 percent of elementary school principals agreed that integration of students with disability has been pushed to undesirable extremes, with negative effects for all kinds of students.[180]

Both observational and experimental studies have found positive effects of educational exposure to racial and ethnic diversity, particularly on the development of more complex cognition.[181] Law professor Emily Buss has interpreted recent psychological literature to show that a child's interaction with "unlike peers" can facilitate personal and moral development.[182] Exposure to numerous points of view and ways of life may seem like a crisis to a child who is overwhelmed by possibilities and forced to select among them, but over time such exposure can enhance personal development of autonomy.[183]

Experiences in schools with diverse student bodies may change something more fundamental than attitudes and stereotypes. By creating a sense of safety and inclusion, diverse classrooms can reduce harassment and experiences of victimization—but this requires altering the school culture and the implicit messages about who "owns" the school and who belongs there. African-American and Latino students in seventy diverse sixth-grade classrooms reported feeling safer, less harassed, and less lonely than their segregated peers.[184] A sense of safety enhances academic achievement and personal well-being. Looking back on their experiences in diverse high schools, students in one study reported discovering later how comfortable and well-prepared they had become for living and working in a diverse society.[185] Done badly, social mixing in schools can produce anger and distrust across groups; done well, it can promote mutual accommodation, shared values, and alteration of larger social patterns of structural inequality.[186]

Diverse Teams, Problem Solving, and Creativity

Another body of social science research is inspired by employers interest in the "twenty-first-century" skills of teamwork and creativity. Here, studies from both natural experiments and laboratory exercises indicate the power of diverse groups of people to work together, generate new solutions to problems, and exhibit other forms of creativity.[187]

For example, Scott Page's research has drawn on the notion of "smart mobs" or "the wisdom of crowds." This work shows that diverse groups are better at solving a variety of problems in work settings than homogeneous groups, even when rated higher on standard ability measures.[188] Differences in socioeconomic class and schooling background matter here as much as differences in race and gender. Each of these dimensions of diversity demonstrably produce different perspectives, different knowledge, and different inferences about cause and effect, contributing to improvement in teams' understanding, efforts, and results. Page emphasized that diverse groups "sometimes start out performing worse but end up performing better than homogeneous groups" if the members have felt that their identities have been validated and their contributions valued.[189] Page has been careful to reject any claim that people's social or demographic traits determine their cognitive tools or perceptions and instead has emphasized cultural and experiential differences as the source of differences in perceptions and approaches.[190] His research may help to explain why cities with diverse populations across time and place so often create economic growth, artistic surges, and other indicators of productivity and creativity.[191] The challenge for both small teams and large communities is to guard against tensions and mistrust across lines of racial, ethnic, religious, or other differences that risk undermining the gains from diversity. Other researchers addressing the value of diversity in classrooms have examined how individuals' work in teams surmounts or bypasses intergroup tensions and holds promise of effective working relationships among adults in diverse settings.[192]

Social Capital, Networking, and Building a Sense of Commonality

Besides boosting creativity, friendships, social and political equality, and real opportunities for academic excellence, inclusive schools can increase social capital—the collective social networks that enable people to do things for one another. Connections enable people to find and keep jobs and to gain access to other social, cultural, and economic resources.[193] Working together and sharing cultural experiences in school affects school retention and success and also promotes positive intergroup relationships in workplaces.[194]

These ideas about social connection echo long-standing claims about the common school ideal, even as they are backed by substantial empirical research. Robert Putnam has emphasized that the largest site of social capital in this country is in religious organizations, which depend on homogeneity with regard to at least one, and often multiple, dimensions of identity.[195] His work also notes that this kind of within-group, or "bonding," social capital risks keeping marginalized groups isolated from the mainstream.[196] Even new immigrants to the United States build their social networks and their understanding of civics and how the nation works through coreligionists, as Peggy Levitt found in her studies of recent immigrant experiences.[197] Many immigrants learn what is to be

American by claiming their religious identity[198] and acknowledging and tolerating difference.[199]

Schooling influences the range and depth of social bonds. This fact preoccupied the architects of public schooling in the United States, who aimed to foster a sense of national identity and craft within schools the communities that would support democracy. Horace Mann and other leaders of the common school movement in the 1820s through the 1840s thought that a religious but nonsectarian foundation for morality would provide the common base of social relations for an otherwise diverse population. Although Mann deposited his hopes in schools, he noted: "It may be an easy thing to make a Republic, but it is a very laborious thing to make Republicans."[200] Creating open, public schools would build a democracy in ways the exclusive elite private schools could not. The common school advocates sought to establish a Christian but nonsectarian foundation that would nurture a shared morality as a means of cultivating a nonpartisan understanding of civic duties and a common culture and set of virtues to equip people to engage in self-government.[201] The public schools they created have been fairly seen as devoted to "Americanizing" immigrants. This Americanizing element triggered opposition and resistance by Catholic leaders, who in turn launched the successful movement for separate, private Catholic schools.[202] Ironically, then, the movement for common schools set in motion the creation of separate schools and started the now-familiar gap between the rhetoric and the reality of inclusiveness in American education. As a further irony, urban Catholic schools at the end of the twentieth century were pursuing a mission of civic education that produced racially and religiously diverse student bodies, while urban and suburban public schools were becoming increasingly divided by race and class. With this inclusive mission, Catholic schools at the same time can offer the sense of belonging within a community in which parents, teachers, and other adults share commitments to the success of the students. These qualities are characteristic of other successful institutions—like schools run by the U.S. military.

The newer movements for charter schools and public schools organized around specific language or ethnic groups worry a variety of critics who fear that social divisions will grow and schools will fail to promote common identities and social ties. Charter schools, vouchers, and other innovations now shift schooling in America to multiple and varied options. The emerging question is whether school communities should be overtly divided along the lines of religion, race, disability, or ethnicity or should revive the aspiration to greater inclusiveness and commonality. If school choice produces school communities that reflect cleavages in the larger society, the strategy will risk undermining social solidarity and true equal opportunity even if it seems to strengthen prospects for individual student success.

Separate instruction often occurs simply because it enables teachers to focus on students with particular needs or interests. Hence, it often seems easier to pursue language instruction separately from instruction in other curricular content, yet such separation often leaves students who are learning English behind their peers in other fields while yielding high levels of ethnic, economic, and linguistic segregation, and missing the option of dual immersion, helpful to kids learning either English or another language.[203] Separation of students by class and religion may also grow as nonimmigrant families react to the growing diversity within public schools. David Tyack suggested that as public schools became more pluralistic and egalitarian in the 1980s and 1990s, conservative groups reacted with the movements for vouchers and school prayer.[204] This reaction recapitulated claims that modern schooling in practice marginalized traditional Christian groups.

Jonathan Kozol objected that small schools organized around racial or ethnic identities represent new forms of segregation and that even short-term improvements do not translate into long-term successes in test scores, much less in real learning.[205] Kozol quoted a former principle who described an Afrocentric school as a local version of " 'your own Liberia but even with the pride the people feel, it hasn't been successful.' "[206] Richard Bernstein struggled with the discipline and spirit of high expectations that some Afrocentric schools may create but worried that such schools treat pride as external to school success and mastery, while other multicultural schools, in his view, lack serious study of cultures and instead propagate messages of difference and identity politics.[207] Special classes or schools for students with disabilities, Steve Taylor argued, do not prepare people for living and engaging in competitive work in the larger community.[208]

Yet constitutional law scholar Kenneth Karst has argued that expanding the connections individuals have to groups defined by race, religion, family, occupation, sports, and hobbies can create new kinds of commonalities that could help to unify a nation otherwise subject to cultural divisions.[209] Multiple crisscrossing connections can build a variety of ties that in turn soften what otherwise could be one or two deep social cleavages. Danielle Allen has suggested that friendships between people of different backgrounds in settings like schools affect the larger society because people carry those friendships into the political realm.[210] She explained: "If a citizen sees the institutions of which he or she is already a part as a medium in which to exemplify the citizenship of trust-building, institutional reform will already be underway."[211] Given the multiple lines of differences within society, perhaps the key is to ensure schools produce shared experiences across at least some of them and over time enable students to develop ties with others unlike themselves.

Even if the ties are not individually powerful, they can foster identification with others and offer ingredients for the complex sense of self that all people use in creating their futures.[212] As Peggy Levitt has noted, recent immigrants have discovered that asserting a religious identity is an acceptable way to be different and be American at the same time, and transnational religious identities are long-standing elements of the American scene.[213] Close and sustained educational and social experiences can enlarge people's sense of mutuality and appreciation for others from different backgrounds and alter old patterns of hierarchy and unequal status.[214] If schools, increasingly separated by race and experimenting with separations by gender, language, immigrant status, and other identities, do not provide the locus for ties across difference, what other social institutions will?

Pursuing Social Integration Outside of Schooling

After-school and Summer Programs for Young People

If students do not attend schools or classes with others who differ from themselves, opportunities for such contacts could be created through after-school and summer activities. Within a district or across a region, after-school programs could draw students into organized activities such as sports and the arts, or they could offer academic enrichment and homework assistance. Both kinds of programs could be developed in settings that allow students of different backgrounds to interact in teams with shared goals. Using racial integration in sports as an example, the key is to allow students of different races to be on the same team, not to compete in a league where each team is racially homogeneous. The discipline and mission of military organizations and similar elements of voluntary youth service efforts are associated with high degrees of success in fostering not only the mixing of people from different racial, religious, and ethnic backgrounds, but also strong practices reflecting and strengthening mutual respect and solidarity. Military and national service organizations may achieve similar results across the differences of sex, sexual orientation, disability status, and socio-economic status. To date, though, it is in the area of racial integration that notable success has been achieved, with a key contribution stemming from the visibility of black leaders.

Military and National Service

Military service can also create socially integrated settings. Nations with mandatory military service often experience benefits from the creation of a common sense of purpose and identity, although circumstances of national jeopardy or aggressive military policies present drawbacks from these experiences. Military service can be a path for social integration even within a society divided by religion.[215] The U.S. military, unlike the military in some other nations, has resisted efforts to embrace integration in terms of gender or sexual orientation.[216] Increasing gender integration and the uneasy accommodations of the "Don't Ask, Don't Tell" policy are changing the U.S. military, although these developments do not yet offer powerful promise of military leadership across differences of gender and sexual orientation. President Barack Obama has indicated a commitment to ending "Don't Ask, Don't Tell" and moving to full integration of gays and lesbians in the military, although this will require an act of Congress. The capacity of the military to implement a new policy may offer the nation a powerful lesson about inclusion.

In the United States, the army remains the leading national example of intentional racial integration within a public institution.[217] More than one million African Americans served in the segregated U.S. military during World War II. President Harry Truman's 1948 executive order terminating segregation in the armed forces produced swift change in the leadership and organization.[218] Not without difficult times, the process of racial integration in the armed services demonstrates the possibilities of major, positive change involving training and assessment of benchmarks to improve racial relations. In their landmark 1996 study, Charles Moskos and John Butler reported that blacks were three times more likely to say that race relations were at that time better in the army than in civilian life and whites were five times more likely to report the same conclusion.[219] Officers are assessed in part on their ability to create an environment free of racial bias.[220] Officers also rotate through positions of responsibility to ensure equal opportunity and a productive racial climate.[221]

Clear commitments to uncompromising standards of performance, combined with multiple opportunities for education, training, and mentoring, also seem to be important elements of the army's success with racial integration.[222] Involving participants in a common overarching cause that is itself a source of pride and fuel for a common identity no doubt contributes as well.[223] Moskos and Butler note how fusing black identity, the civil rights struggle, and national identity in military discourse recognizes Afro-Anglo culture as core to American culture and has contributed to the military's successful racial integration.[224] Moreover, the sheer number of African Americans in the military ensures that "a sufficient pool from which to recruit black leaders...allows for the acceptance of features of Afro-American culture that enhance the organizational climate, and ensures that whites recognize the diversity among blacks."[225] Military experiences do more than mix diverse people; they integrate them into a team with a sense of common purpose, strong group affiliation, and measurable effects on intergroup attitudes.[226] Nowhere has this been more dramatic than in the context of racial integration in the U.S. military.

The U.S. military has also demonstrated success in involving individuals with disabilities. Many notable American military figures, including General George S. Patton, a pivotal leader during World War II, and General William Westmoreland, who served as commander of the U.S. military advisors in South Vietnam and as the army's chief of staff, had learning disabilities. The Reserve Officer Training Corps specifically accepts students with disabilities if they can handle the physical, medical, and academic requirements without assistance.[227] The civilian workforce of the armed services and private contractors under contract with the military are governed by the Americans with Disabilities Act; and federal law mandates that at least 10 percent of the civilian workforce of all U.S. military bases be made up of people with disabilities.[228] The U.S. navy reports that it has been ranked as the fifth best employer, including private sector companies, in employing individuals with disabilities.[229] Perhaps the military's tradition of racial integration since 1948 helps the services take a leadership role here; perhaps the military's respect for disabled veterans contributes to an inclusive attitude. Further, the commitment to developing educational programs that work for a wide variety of recruits contributes to military schools' success in teaching students of all backgrounds.[230] Yet, in a society with a voluntary military, the military experience only reaches a portion of the population.

National civilian service could reach larger numbers and thereby advance the goal of social integration across racial, gender, class, disability, and other distinctions.[231] Periodic proposals for national service beyond military service have cropped up in American politics.[232] During the New Deal, the national Civilian Conservation Corps brought together young men (all U.S. citizens) from varied backgrounds to work on widely hailed environmental projects such as reforestation, but the racial segregation of the era persisted in this program.[233] Some people have proposed mandatory civilian service with hopes that a universal program would enhance social integration and civil engagement and command response to domestic needs. To date, Congress has authorized only voluntary programs, coupled with the incentive of college aid. In 1989, Senator Sam Nunn and Representative Dave McCurdy proposed tying federal financial aid for college to service requirements.[234] During his first presidential campaign, Bill Clinton embraced national service but as president faced considerable opposition to the cost and bureaucratic effects; so instead he launched AmeriCorps, a modest program that annually draws about fifty thousand college-aged participants, who engage in tutoring, building low-income housing, and supplying other free labor to local communities.[235] After 9/11, with an emphasis on national security and patriotism, President George W. Bush and Senator John McCain briefly supported a larger national service program, but their efforts fell apart in the face of partisan politics.[236] Senators McCain and Barack Obama both made national service a priority during the 2008 presidential campaign,[237] and in April 2009, President Obama signed the Edward M. Kennedy Serve America Act, which reauthorized and expanded the AmeriCorps program started by President Clinton but did not elaborate on the particular goals to be advanced.

Explicit among the goals of AmeriCorps since its founding has been enhancing the civic ethic and developing cooperation and understanding among racial and ethnic groups.[238] The program's supporters often mention the chance to bridge racial, ethnic, and social divides in American society as one of its key benefits, along with the goals of enhancing civic engagement, advancing participants' personal growth, strengthening communities, and meeting local needs.[239] AmeriCorps encourages diversity in its participants. Approximately three-quarters of them have been female, matching the pattern of employment in the nonprofit sector (and mirroring the gender composition of the military in reverse). Most participants have had some college experience, and many have college degrees, and their racial and ethnic demographics appear to duplicate those of the country as a whole.[240]

Supporters of the more controversial idea of mandatory national service have emphasized its potential to provide cohesion and to acculturate diverse individuals, as well as to meet social needs, develop individual responsibility, and promote patriotism.[241] Representative Charles Rangel promoted mandatory military service as a way to remedy the overrepresentation of members of racial minorities in the armed services and to produce a common experience of service.[242] A similar argument would extend to civilian service. Supporters of voluntary national service suggest that positive incentives and the development of a cultural norm of service as a rite of passage would accomplish the goals of social integration and civic engagement without relying on coercion.[243] National service as a rite of passage is a familiar notion in countries with mandatory military service. South Africa pursues a broader program, encompassing community service and aiming to foster social cohesion, promote nation-building, and develop participants' technical and social skills.[244] A similar proposal is under consideration in Great Britain.[245]

The rite-of-passage notion suits national service aimed at high school students as a transition to adulthood. Some national service proposals that seek to engage midcareer and retired individuals could attract mature people to offer their experience and skills to help address social needs while also advancing social integration among older populations.[246] Research on existing national service programs emphasizes increased civic engagement and social trust among participants, though studies differ about whether participants develop a significantly increased appreciation of cultural and ethnic diversity.[247] One doctoral dissertation found that participation in AmeriCorps increased social integration across different groups in communities that already had strong levels of social capital within homogeneous groups, which suggests that it is easier to extend existing social capital within groups than to generate it from scratch.[248]

Volunteer service has increased in recent years for both men and women, across ethnic and racial groups, and across age ranges; nearly sixty-two million Americans gave eight billion hours of service in 2008.[249] Voluntarism among young adults (aged sixteen to twenty-four) is particularly on the rise. By making national and community service a priority during and after the 2008 campaign and election, President and First Lady Michelle Obama have sought to mobilize the energy of individual volunteer and organizations to tackle local and national needs. A new national norm of expected civic service could be a fruit of difficult economic times. Besides creating clearinghouses to connect individuals who want to serve in volunteer work settings, public and nonprofit organizations could use this moment to increase opportunities for individuals from different backgrounds to work together, building bridges across racial, ethnic, economic, and other differences.

Workplaces

National service, however promising, would for most people involve a relatively brief commitment rather than a transformation of day-to-day activities. The U.S. army has become the most racially integrated institution in the country;[250] yet the coercion and discipline involved in the military is not likely to offer a model for racial relations in the larger society. Other workplaces in the United States do not substantially mix people across racial and ethnic lines—yet they do so more than schools or residential neighborhoods do, according to the analysis of Cynthia Estlund.[251]

When hierarchical relationships at workplaces mimic traditional racial hierarchies in society, they perpetuate traditional racial biases. But workplaces may also generate experiences of shared purpose and shared community that help people to mute or overcome racial biases.[252] Workplaces could promote solidarity and build social networks across differences such as race, immigration status, gender, religion, disability, yet employment experiences usually occur after individuals have developed attitudes about their own identities and the identities of others. Gender segregation at work persists, even with women's expanded workplace participation and increasing presence in supervisory and professional jobs.[253] The prevalence of sexual harassment and sexual innuendo in workplaces reveals that some cultural myths and images are so persistent that they are not overcome simply through contact.[254]

Employees can come to feel interdependent when they perform tasks together and when their achievement of those tasks generates shared rewards. But racial, ethnic, and other differences are associated with workplace divisiveness when the workplace lacks a continuing commitment to solidarity or when shared rewards do not track joint work across lines of difference.[255] Even when a team member intends to behave in a way that promotes group solidarity, others may read that action differently in response to the salience of different demographic markers dividing the members of the team.[256] Simply working alongside one another does not alter structural inequality and stereotypes if the larger narratives, concrete rewards, and actual values of the work-setting fail to challenge social divisions and structural inequality in the larger context.

Schooling (Again)

Workplaces, compulsory service, and afterschool and summer programs may enhance experiences of connection across lines of social difference but each is limited and partial as a vehicle for social policy. If social integration matters as a public purpose, it should be included within the design and operation of compulsory schooling from kindergarten through high school, for education is the only universal portal through which everyone in the nation travels. In the absence of mandatory military or national service and given the variation in employment settings, education is the sole shared vehicle for socialization. Even schools that are relatively homogeneous in terms of race and ethnicity, immigration status, or other student characteristics can promote civic awareness and address prejudices through the content of the curriculum and the pedagogy.[257] Yet mere curricular content about social integration is an inferior substitute for actual day-to-day contact, which, if framed to develop a sense of common purpose and mutual respect, can change attitudes and experiences of social division.

School choice—whether through charter schools, public vouchers for private school tuition, or initiatives formally within a public system—could stimulate schools designed to promote diversity and social integration within the classroom experience. Schools organized with these purposes in mind can use diversity to enhance students' learning and achievement in conventional academic terms, in the development of problem-solving abilities, and in intergroup relations and social skills.[258] The demand for racially integrated opportunities is evident in the waiting lists for diverse regional magnet and charter schools in Connecticut and for the METCO program in Boston and Springfield, Massachusetts, which opens up suburban schools to students residing in urban districts.[259] Inclusion schools, which integrate students with and students without disabilities, also often have waiting lists because they offer a lower-than-average teacher-student ratio and individualized instruction.[260] Reformers could use school choice to pursue culturally relevant pedagogy, teachers committed and equipped to support to the success of all the students, and other means to increase conditions that foster students of diverse backgrounds. Parents and citizens could seek explicit legal and programmatic commitments so that charter schools, magnet schools, and other innovative programs pursue integration, inclusion, and social solidarity within their walls.

Relying on vouchers, charter schools, and other specialized schools for integration and inclusion may seem like outsourcing a key social goal rather than hard-wiring it into mainstream schools. Yet school choice options offer a motor for change. It may seem ironic—though the possibility is increasingly plausible—that charter and parochial schools are the heirs of the original common schools of the nineteenth century seeking to include all kind of students. The goal of building common experiences lay at the root of public schooling as it was first advocated in America by Horace Mann and others.[261] Shared school experiences involve not only sitting side by side but also learning and common narratives, identities, and purposes—or as political scientist Rogers Smith calls them, "stories of peoplehood." Such stories, he has written, "do not merely serve interests, they also help to constitute them," inspiring trust and worth among diverse individuals.[262] He concludes: "politically, we probably cannot hope to shape communities that can long endure unless people see them as expressing more than their procedural agreements and senses of abstract justice"; hence communities need to combat particularism and, in the United States, give special attention to alleviating deeply entrenched racial inequalities.[263] Mixing and joining students of different races, ethnicities, socioeconomic status, immigrant backgrounds, and religions matter for the character of the increasingly diverse and fractured polity, as well as for the sense of mobility and opportunity that individual students experience over time.[264]

Yet, paradoxically, the dominant narrative of the American national ideal offers paths to American identity through the embrace of particular subgroup experiences. Becoming American by asserting a subgroup identity allows people to feel community in their differences and distinctively American in their embrace of difference.[265] Immigrants who seek to preserve their traditions appeal to the American commitment to diversity and tolerance.[266] This is the case for recent immigrants who are Hindus and Muslims just as it has been for Catholics and Jews who have immigrated to the United States in the past. Learning what that commitment entails, however, calls for experiences of social integration that are designed to prevent stereotyping and dehumanization. America at its best promotes mutual engagement with and valuing of people who are different and the social capital that builds through criss-crossing networks. None of this will work without larger efforts attacking structural inequalities in the resources available for education and in the status of the adults of different races, religions and cultures. Renewed social integration efforts could multiply social capital networks across different groups while reducing conventional lines of division. Successful social integration in schools would demand but in turn contribute to renovating attitudes and concrete resources so that every child could be assured chances to learn in settings with diverse adults committed to their success. Belonging to crosscutting groups and participating in overarching identities would nurture people's sense of solidarity and civic membership. And social scientists will continue to use their tools to study such efforts, to try to influence legal and political practices, and to reassess their own efforts to make sense of a potentially shared and meaningful world.[267]

On Other Shores

When Is Separate Inherently Unequal?

Brown belongs not to the United States but to the world.
—Steve Adams, Superintendent,
Brown v. Board of Education National Historic Site

Even before it was decided by the U.S. Supreme Court, *Brown v. Board of Education* had a global profile.[1] Swedish economist Gunnar Myrdal in a work that the Carnegie Corporation commissioned in 1944 in search of an unbiased view of American race relations, supplied a searing indictment of America's treatment of the "Negro," and his work, *An American Dilemma*, became a key citation in the Court's famous footnote eleven.[2] Initially, President Dwight D. Eisenhower showed no sympathy for the school integration project and expressed suspicion that the United Nations and international economic and social rights activists were betraying socialist or even communist leanings in supporting the brief.[3] But as the United States tried to position itself as a leader in human rights and supporter of the United Nations, the Cold War orientation of President Eisenhower's Republican administration gave rise to interest in ending official segregation, lynchings, and cross burnings in order to elevate the American image internationally. The Department of Justice consulted with the State Department on the drafting of an amicus brief in *Brown* that argued that ending racially segregated schools would halt the Soviet critique of racial abuses tolerated by the U.S. system of government and thereby help combat global communism.[4] Ending segregation emerged as part of a strategy to win more influence than the Soviet Union in the "Third World." African-American civil rights leader and journalist Roger Wilkins later recalled that ending official segregation became urgent as black ambassadors started to visit Washington, D.C., and the United Nations in New York City.[5]

Tracking the influence of *Brown* in other countries is thornier than tracking its influence inside the United States where the topic has motivated a cottage industry in academic scholarship.[6] As this book has considered, the litigation has by now a well-known and complicated relationship to actual racial integration within American schools. Some argue that the case exacerbated tensions and slowed gradual reform that was already under way. At the same time, *Brown* and reactions to its backlash helped galvanize the social movement around school reform that then developed and that enabled major legislative and social change— and produced notable change in the racial composition of schools by the 1970s. Further backlash against *Brown's* enforcement then returned schools to considerable racial separation by the decision's fiftieth anniversary.[7]

Inside the United States, *Brown* may turn out to have more influence on racial justice outside the context of schooling, more influence on schooling outside the context of racial integration, and more significance to law outside of both race and schooling.[8] *Brown's* rejection of "separate but equal" schools spurred the end of segregation in retail stores, theaters, swimming pools, and employment, though often only after a struggle and legislative or litigated reforms.[9] The steps from Jim Crow segregation to the election of President Barack Obama were many and nonlinear, but *Brown* played a role in mobilizing changes in ideas as well as in practices and opportunities. The reported attitudes of white Americans toward African Americans and day-to-day interracial relations at work and in families have shifted notably toward acceptance, though hierarchy and discrimination remain, sometimes subtly, and sometimes not.[10] *Brown's* influence inside schools but outside of the context of race has profoundly altered the discussions and treatment of gender, disability, language, ethnicity, and national origin, with further changes in the way educational and life opportunities of students are affected by their sexual orientation, religion, economic class, or status as Native Hawai'ians or Native Americans.[11] Well beyond schooling, *Brown* and the efforts surrounding it have created the model for social and legal reforms in the United States—deploying social science research, and social movement activism—on behalf of girls and women, persons with disabilities, members of religious minorities, and advocates for economic justice, environmental protection, and other issues.[12]

Without systematically cataloguing the reverberations of *Brown* outside the United States, it is still striking to note the varied explicit references to the decision. As in the United States, the case and the struggle behind it have served as an evocative reference point for advocates pursuing equal opportunity and social change in Northern Ireland, South Africa, India, and eastern Europe and even for initiatives addressing social hierarchy and exclusion without connection to race or education.[13] Although single-sex education is common and unquestioned in many parts of the world, contemporary efforts to ensure that separate instruction for girls and boys is actually equal echoes the U.S. post-*Brown* arguments.[14] In addition, *Brown* and its surrounding social and legal movement have supplied authority for the broad judicial remedial power used to reject the South African government's failure to distribute the drug nevirapine to HIV-positive pregnant women and to create a process to develop housing for the homeless.[15] The case has also been used to bolster efforts to achieve fairness in negotiations of land allocations affecting Arabs in Israel.[16]

As advocates pursue equality in many parts of the world, *Brown* offers a hopeful symbol of traditions of legally imposed or socially maintained hierarchy, exclusion, or degradation based on group membership. Yet in the midst of struggles for equal educational and other opportunities, it does not take long to find that forced assimilation can produce its own form of degradation and exclusion. The UNESCO Convention Against Discrimination in Education thus simultaneously rejects discrimination impairing equality of treatment in education on the basis of "race, colour, sex, language, religion, political or other opinion, national or social origin, economic condition or birth" yet protects "separate educational systems or institutions for pupils of the two sexes," if they provide equivalent access to opportunity, and "separate educational systems or institutions" on the basis of religion or language if in keeping with the wishes of the pupils' parents or legal guardians.[17] Similarly, reflecting the distinctive histories of mistreatment of national minorities in Europe, the Council of Europe's Framework Convention for the Protection of National Minorities directs member parties "to promote the conditions necessary for persons belonging to national minorities to maintain and develop their culture, and to preserve the essential elements of their identity, namely their religion, language, traditions and cultural heritage."[18] In addition, the European Charter for Regional or Minority Languages protects and promotes the continuing use of traditional languages within member nations (though not languages of new immigrants)[19] and specifically calls for making education from preschool though university available in these languages. These explicit protections for group rights contrast with the approach in the United States which nonetheless grapples with issues of group identity in the contexts of bilingual education and schooling for Native Hawai'ians and Native Americans.

Schooling accentuates potential tensions between on the one hand conceptions of equality that are focused on individual opportunity, inclusion, and commonality and on the other hand conceptions of equality that are focused instead on group rights, group autonomy, and multiculturalism.[20] Overcoming group-based discrimination could demand treating each child as a distinct individual, entitled to social mobility and full inclusion in the larger society, or instead could summon respect for parents and groups of adults who wish to pass on their own traditions and perhaps even separate their children from others and foreclose social mobility. A compromise or alternative approach would pursue accommodations (of language, religion, culture) within a mainstream school. Yet difficulties achieving this ideal of integration, premised on mutual respect, may lead some to prefer separate schools, where teachers and parents imbue the students with pride and avoid day-to-day chafing against social attitudes that do not welcome the minority identity. In this dynamic, Justice Clarence Thomas's defense of majority-African-American schools may mirror arguments for Muslim or Jewish schools in France or the Netherlands or even for Afrikaans schools in South Africa.[21]

These struggles grow even more acute where violent conflict, past or incipient, hovers in the society. For nations with a history of genocide, civil war, or intergroup violence, even contemplation of school integration across group differences is fraught with risk. Asked about prospects for integrating schools across racial and ethnic differences in Iraq, a government official replied: "We would go to war to stop that."[22] In an experiment in integration, the first such school in Bosnia enrolls both Muslim Bosniak and Catholic Croat students, but the two groups attend different classes inside the school.[23] A journalist explained: "In keeping with the national government's official stance of separate education— with each student having the 'right' to be taught in his or her own language, and to learn his or her own religion and history—the gymnasium separates students according to nationality."[24] Students do come together for sports and other extracurricular activities—and in a science lab paid for by a donor who restricted its use to integrated groups of students. Co-existence is a first step before a sense of commonality or solidarity can emerge.[25]

Communities struggling with the issues of equal schooling outside the United States have encountered problems familiar to Americans since *Brown,* such as overrepresentation of disadvantaged minority groups in separate schooling for students with disabilities, barriers to social integration posed by separate classrooms for immigrants or subgroups without fluency in the nation's dominant language, and flight of dominant or privileged groups from schools undergoing integration efforts. Similarly, debates exist in other countries over whether proof of intentional discrimination is a necessary predicate for a legal remedy, over local versus central control, and over the reliability of the contact hypothesis. Also resonant are struggles over whether ending segregation is enough or more affirmative efforts at integration are needed, required, or possible.[26] Examples from South Africa, Northern Ireland, France, and the Czech Republic reverberate with *Brown* and the complexities in its wake. The variations in responses reveal not only the evolving, multidimensional meanings of *Brown*'s insights but also the diverse situations in which it resonates.

Equal Respect and Unequal Schooling after Apartheid:
South Africa

The apartheid regime in South Africa began segregating students by race
in 1905 and deliberately excluded black South Africans from real educational opportunities. Hendrik Frensch Verwoerd, then senator and later
prime minister, shaped the Bantu Education Act of 1953 to enforce segregation at all levels of education in the country. He explained: "There
is no place for [the African] in the European community above the level
of certain forms of labour. It is of no avail for him to receive a training
which has as its aim, absorption in the European community....Edu-
cation must train people in accordance with their opportunities in life,
according to the sphere in which they live."[27] By the 1970s, per capita,
schools for black students were spending one-tenth of the resources allocated to white schools.[28]

In 1958 Britain's prime minister, Harold Macmillan, cited *Brown*
while critiquing apartheid in an address to South Africa's Parliament.[29]
During the 1970s, two lawyers who had worked closely with Thurgood
Marshall on *Brown* assisted lawyers in South Africa to develop judicial
strategies to terminate apartheid.[30] Even since the fall of apartheid and
the creation of a new constitutional regime, the South African Constitutional Court has repeatedly cited *Brown* in cases. For the case of *In
re The School Education Bill of 1995,* the Constitutional Court relied
on *Brown* in discussing the important role of education in developing
and maintaining a democratic society but looked to the history of South
Africa and the global human rights movement in rejecting the claim that
the government had a constitutional duty to establish or fund Afrikaans
schools. At the same time, the South African Court recognized the right
of private groups to maintain such schools.[31] One author has argued
that the tensions over school desegregation and affirmative action in the
United States influenced the drafters of the South African Constitution
in their decision to shield remedial uses of racial categories from constitutional challenge.[32]

The racialized disparity in educational opportunities had modestly
diminished by the time apartheid ended, but legacies of the apartheid-
era segregation and disparate allocation of resources continue to such
a degree that some predict the postapartheid era is producing another
"lost generation" missing chances to learn and achieve.[33] Current educational disparities seem to entrench racial and class divides for the vast
majority, leaving many in rural areas so ill-educated that the best they can
hope for is a menial job. They otherwise become unemployed or engage
in criminal conduct.[34] Studies of South African schools highlight the
gap between desegregation and integration by reporting just how many
schools continue to proceed with separate programs for black and white
students and the pervasive negative stereotyping of black students. At the

very least, these studies reflect the persistent racial separation in residential communities.[35]

One thoughtful analysis traces continuing racial separation and disadvantage for black South Africans despite passage of the 1996 South African Schools Act and other reforms.[36] With reformers pressing for decentralized control and enhanced parental participation, teachers and principals have gained influence in many historically black schools, while white middle-class parents have taken greater control of the governance of their still mainly white schools.[37]

Meanwhile, in a recent case, the Constitutional Court worked to accommodate language rights while tackling legacies of hierarchy and exclusion. In response to a shortage of classroom space for English-speaking students in the Ermelo region, the Department of Education sought space in Hoërskool Ermelo, an Afrikaans-language school. The school offered use of an extra building but asserted its right to instruct only in Afrikaans. The Department of Education then displaced the governing board of the school and established an interim committee that changed the school's language policy to include both English and Afrikaans.

The school successfully challenged this action. The Constitutional Court unanimously found that the Department lacked authority to appoint a committee to determine the school's language policy. The Court acknowledged the constitutional right to be taught in an official language of one's choice. At the same time, the Court identified the likely demand for instruction in English in the community and indicated that the school's own governing body should revisit its language policy in light of the interests of not only current students but also the community. The Court ruled that the imposition of a language policy by a committee foisted on the school was unlawful, but the school's own governing body had to reassess its language policy. The Court emphasized the need for change, given the dwindling numbers of students seeking instruction in the medium of Afrikaans and the great demand from students preferring English as the medium of instruction. The Court also directed the Department to pursue sufficient spaces for English learners for the following school year.[38] Affirming equality conceived as respect in this case involved protecting a minority language of a historically privileged group;[39] affirming access to education for all in the region, the Court found itself poised over the possibility of enacting state-enforced mixing of students speaking different languages and, likely, of different races. The economic and racial context for the case is in fact obvious to all involved and carries echoes of the Soweto uprising, a key antiapartheid protest over the elevation of Afrikaans as the language of academic instruction, to the disadvantage of English speakers.[40]

The Constitutional Court noted that the school's language policy effectively excluded learners wanting to be taught in English—who, in this case, turned out to be exclusively black learners.[41] The usual reliance on decentralized control in postapartheid South Africa hit a limit here, as the racial impact of local governance in this case was unacceptably unresponsive to the needs of black students, who continue to have far fewer resources than white students. The Court expressly pointed to the Constitution's intention to transform both public education and South African society by addressing unequal access to educational resources.[42] The decision voiced the Court's deference to local control of education but set limits to that deference.

Schooling in a Divided Society: Northern Ireland

Education in Northern Ireland has long been divided between "controlled" schools—which are government run, have Protestant roots, and serve about 50 percent of the students—and "managed" schools, which are maintained by Catholic organizations and educate about 45 percent of the children. Historically, these separate school systems have taught contrasting versions of regional history and as a result have not reduced but instead contributed to the tensions and violence of "the Troubles," which begin in the 1960s and have continued even after the Belfast agreement of 1998.

Aiming ultimately for government support, the movement for integrated schools started in the 1980s. A group of parents started the Northern Ireland Council for Integrated Education as a voluntary organization to develop schools that would bring together students from the two communities. With government aid, the Council allows parents to launch new, integrated schools; the Council also developed a procedure by which parents could vote to convert an existing school into an integrated school.[43] These schools give general instruction in Christianity rather than more specific instruction in Protestantism or Catholicism.[44] The Department of Education incorporates such schools only after they show sufficient enrollment and a waiting list among the preschool cohort.[45]

By 2009, the Council had produced, with aid from English charitable trusts, nineteen integrated nursery schools, forty integrated primary schools, and twenty integrated second-level colleges—showing impressive growth, but reaching barely 5 percent of the population.[46] The program at the integrated schools specifically aims at fostering mutual respect and involving parents and undertakes efforts toward these ends, rather than simply mixing the students.[47] A steady stream of social science studies has examined the effects of contact on intergroup attitudes and relationships in Northern Ireland and largely suggests positive effects from contact.[48] Across the country, integrated schools have generated considerable parental demand, with long waiting lists. Perhaps by having a strategy of integrating schools only with supportive parents and starting such schools on a small scale, the project ensured from the

start a base of support rather than conflict—even before the larger community conflict quieted down.

After a decade of relative peace following a process producing political power-sharing, Northern Ireland experienced a spike in intergroup
violence in March 2009. The murder of a Northern Irish police officer in
Ulster occurred two days after the murders of two British soldiers, and a
resurgence of acts of terror committed by dissident groups wracked the
region.[49] Johann Hari, a British journalist, warned that the peace process
had only occurred at the top, among politicians, without touching the
distrust and roots of violence in the community:

> Ian Paisley and Martin McGuiness have been sitting together—inspira-
> tionally—but in the streets and estates beyond Stormont, Northern Ireland
> has been becoming even more divided. Dr Peter Shirlow, of the University
> of Ulster, has conducted the most detailed survey of inter-communal rela-
> tions in Northern Ireland—and found an almost completely segregated
> society. Only 5 per cent of the workforce in Catholic areas are Protestants,
> and vice versa. Some 68 per cent of 18- to 25-year-olds had never had a
> meaningful conversation with a single person from "the other side."...We
> have been fixing the ceiling, while the foundations fracture.[50]

Hari wrote: "Northern Ireland needs its own version of *Brown v. Board
of Education*."[51] Citing a six-year study by Queen's University, Hari noted
that individuals who attended the integrated schools were "significantly
more likely" to oppose sectarianism, had more friends across the divide,
and identified as "Northern Irish" rather than as "British" or "Irish."[52]
Stressing that "[i]t's difficult to caricature people you've known since you
were a child: great sweeping hatreds are dissolved by the grey complexity
of individual human beings," Hari marveled that "82 percent reported that
they personally support the idea of integrated schooling. Further, 55 percent of parents say the only reason their kids do not attend an integrated
school is because they cannot get into one." Obstructing school integration, in Hari's view, is the domination of the school system by religious
sectarians, both Catholic and Protestant. The decline in the school-aged
population is placing pressure on the sectarian schools to merge. And taking one more page from U.S. history, this British journalist concluded:
"Who knows—a hefty push for school integration could yield, in a few
decades, a Northern Irish Obama, carrying both sides in his veins."[53]

It remains puzzling why polls indicate overwhelming support for
integrated schools yet there is no policy shift toward them or for altering control of the school system by religious sectarians. Perhaps a
more concerted push toward integrated schools would prompt backlash. There remains a genuine dispute over whether and to what extent
the government should pursue integrated schools in Northern Ireland.
The ideal has gained a popularity never realized fully in practice as
in the United States but with a very different pattern of public and
private action. The waiting lists for the integrated schools seem like a
resource of social hope awaiting concrete action.

Eastern European Treatment of Roma Children:
D. H. versus Czech Republic

Often called Gypsies in the past, the Roma (part of a larger group called Romani, and with other groups known as Sinti and Kale), who are the largest, poorest minority group in central and eastern Europe, are subjected to varied forms of social and political exclusions.[54] One survey of social attitudes in three European countries found that 78 percent of those responding held negative views of Roma.[55] With roots traced to Northern India, languages composed of mixtures of Sanskrit and European languages, and centuries of semi-nomadic living in tribes and clans, many populations identified as Roma have long lived at the margins of communities in Europe. They have typically had low levels of employment and little formal education. After the demise of Soviet control of eastern European countries and with the increasing integration of Europe, conflict between the social marginalization of Roma individuals and new normative European commitments to equality and free movement of peoples escalated, first in the countries in eastern Europe and then in western Europe as well.

Besides poverty, a pervasive sense of "otherness," exacerbated by prior failed assimilation efforts, attaches to the Roma in many parts of Europe.[56] Some people blame Roma individuals and communities for the increase in crime that has followed the collapse of the communist regimes.[57] When eastern European countries applied for membership in the European Union, public attention turned to the economic and social disadvantages experienced by Roma in those countries—and fears of a flood of Roma immigrants to western Europe.[58] National governments, the European Union, and nongovernmental organizations identified problems surrounding Roma communities and launched reform initiatives. Yet the usual European reforms pursuing rights for minority groups proved ill suited to the situation of the Roma. The minority rights regimes emphasize preservation of minority cultures and languages, while the Roma's problems have mainly to do with poverty and segregation, often combined with attenuated connections to traditional culture and language following communist-era suppression and centuries of migration.[59] In addition, Europe-wide initiatives spurred stringent protections enabled by the European Union's ability to impose conditions on eastern European countries seeking admission.[60]

A major participant in efforts to ensure protection for the Roma has been the Hungarian-born Jewish immigrant (first to Great Britain and then to the United States) George Soros, who has followed up his extraordinarily successful career in business, currency speculation, and investments with major philanthropic initiatives around the world, estimated to involve more than $6 billion in contributions since 1979.[61] Creator and chair of the Open Society Institute, Soros began his philanthropic efforts in the 1970s, when he aided black students in enrolling at the University of Cape Town in apartheid-era South Africa and funded dissident critics of communism in eastern Europe. The Open Society Institute launched and ran the Roma Participation Program between 1997 and 2007, aiming to support grassroots efforts and reforms to improve the inclusion and status of Roma populations.

With Open Society Institute support, the European Roma Rights Center in Budapest, Hungary, joined with others, including Czech attorney David Strupek, in 1999 to challenge student placement practices in the Czech Republic, where a disproportionately large number of Roma children were being placed in schools for students with mental or learning disabilities rather than mainstream schools.[62] Lawyers and others working on behalf of the Roma students explicitly discussed *Brown* and the movement surrounding it.[63] They initiated a case known as *D.H. and Other v. Czech Republic* as the centerpiece of the Roma rights movement's litigation strategy,[64] which was designed to pursue cases that could change existing practices "through liberal and far-reaching judicial interpretation, as well as to trigger comprehensive reform of legislation."[65] Although styled as a complaint by eighteen students, *D.H.*—like the cases combined into *Brown*—focused on systematic discrimination and mindsets perpetuating second-class status for an entire group of people. Lawyers from the United States, Great Britain, and many European nations contributed to the advocacy strategy and commentary about it.[66]

The Constitutional Court of the Czech Republic dismissed the suit. Then in 2000, on behalf of the same eighteen Roma students, the lawyers filed a new complaint with similar allegations before the European Court of Human Rights and alleged violations of the guarantee under the European Convention on Human Rights ensuring freedom from racial discrimination in education.[67] The complaint argued that the Czech practices produced de facto segregation on the basis of race, with Roma students largely assigned to special schools for students with disabilities while the regular primary schools were used by the majority of the population. In *D.H.*, the allegation of indirect discrimination argued that the practice of placement in the special schools had a disproportionate and negative impact on the Roma community. Mirroring experiences in the United States and elsewhere, classification of minority students as having a disability resulted in discrimination and disadvantage for the affected Roma students.[68] Hence, the case turned to social patterns and statistical evidence. Studies of the region of Ostrava showed that a Roma child was twenty-seven times more likely to be placed in a special school than were other children; Roma students composed between 50 and 70 percent of the students in the special schools although they ᵔde up about 2 percent of the population.[69] The complaint also argued ᵔe special schools used an inferior curriculum that prevented their from transferring back to the regular primary schools or gaincient background to pursue any secondary schooling other than nal education.[70]

Before the European Court of Human Rights, the Ministry of Education of the Czech Republic defended its practices by reference to the individualized assessments of each child's intellectual capacity prior to placement and by indicating that Roma parents consented to the placement of their children in the special schools.[71] The Roma complainants responded that the process for placing students into special schools relied on unreliable intelligence testing with no accommodation of the linguistic and cultural backgrounds of the Roma students, who often had insufficient command of the Czech language.[72] Meanwhile, in 2000, the European Commission Against Racism and Intolerance observed that Roma children were channeled into special schools in a quasi-automatic fashion and attributed poor performance on the placement tests in part to the fact that most Roma children did not attend kindergarten.[73] While the D.H. litigation unfolded, the government adjusted its testing methods, ostensibly to be more responsive to the Roma students' cultural backgrounds—but this yielded little change in results.

The Second Chamber of the European Court of Human Rights rejected the complainants' claims,[74] but in 2007 on review the Grand Chamber ruled in favor of the Roma applicants by a vote of thirteen to four.[75] Finding the special schools offered an often inferior curriculum and with diminished educational and employment prospects,[76] and finding that the placement in special schools likely increased stigma for Roma children, the Grand Chamber quoted, with approval, the European commissioner for human rights, who said that "segregated education denies both the Roma and non-Roma children the chance to know each other and to learn to live as equal citizens."[77] The Grand Chamber noted that regular schools showed reluctance to accept Roma students. Quoting the European Commission Against Racism and Intolerance, the Grand Chamber acknowledged that Roma parents often "favoured the channeling of Roma children to special schools, partly to avoid abuse from non-Roma children in ordinary schools and isolation of the child from other neighborhood Roma children, and partly owing to a relatively low level of interest in education."[78] The Grand Chamber cited research from the United States about racial inequity in special education,[79] noting the negative effects of early tracking.[80] It located its judgment in the context of sources from the Council of Europe,[81] including European Community law and practice concerning indirect discrimination and disparate impact of policies on minority populations;[82] United Nations materials;[83] and a set of "other sources," including the U.S. Supreme Court's interpretation of the 1964 Civil Rights Act, allowing evidence of the disparate racial impact of a test as evidence of racial discrimination.[84]

The Grand Chamber relied centrally on article 14 of the Convention for the Protection of Human Rights and Fundamental Freedoms, which states: "The enjoyment of the rights and freedoms set forth in [the] convention shall be secured without discrimination on any ground such as sex, race, colour, language, religion, political or other opinion, national or social origin, association with a national minority, property, birth, or other status."[85] The Grand Chamber reaffirmed its view that discrimination includes differential treatment of persons in relevantly similar situations without objective and reasonable justification, as well as its view that discrimination on the basis of ethnic origin is a form of racial discrimination.[86] Breaking new ground, the Grand Chamber accepted "that a general policy or measure that has disproportionately prejudicial effects on a particular group may be considered discriminatory notwithstanding that it is not specifically aimed at that group."[87] The treatment of the Roma children could not be approved, even though the Czech government argued that the separate schools are separate but not inferior—an argument rather like the U.S. Supreme Court's separate-but-equal doctrine in *Plessy v. Ferguson*.[88] The Grand Chamber found that a prima facie case of different treatment was established and that the Czech government had failed to prove objective and reasonable justification.[89] The psychological tests used to assign the students could not supply such a justification given the risk of bias;[90] the assignment of Roma students to the special schools seemed "quasi-automatic,"[91] producing the disproportionately high overrepresentation of Roma children in the special schools, resulting in less favorable educational treatment of Roma children.[92] No proof of discriminatory intent was required to shift the burden of proof to the government to identify, if it could, an objective and reasonable justification for the differential treatment that did not stem from the students' ethnic background.[93] The government's effort to point to the consent of Roma parents to use the special schools and to the needs of the Roma children failed to satisfy the Grand Chamber, because the right to be free from racial discrimination cannot be waived, and even if it could be waived, informed consent would be needed and was not shown in this case.[94] With awareness perhaps of some irony, and over the emphatic objection on this point by a dissenting judge,[95] the Grand Chamber also acknowledged that the Czech Republic had undertaken more efforts at social and educational integration of Roma children than other European states, where as many as half of the Roma children attend no school at all.[96]

A strong dissent by Judge Karel Jungwiert of the Czech Republic emphasized that most of the Roma population in the country had arrived after World War II (when the domestic Roma population had been destroyed by the Nazis).[97] Therefore, he argued, the Roma represented an immigrant population largely lacking local language competence, and he stressed that the Czech Republic had pursued a course of positive discrimination to favor the Roma and involve them in the schooling process on a far greater scale than other European countries with Roma populations.[98] Not mentioned in his dissent is the 2000 report by the High Commissioner for National Minorities of the Organization for Security and Co-operation in Europe that found that among four countries where high numbers of Roma students were being sent to schools for disabled students, the Czech Republic had the worst record.[99] Another dissenting judge objected to the majority's refusal to credit the Roma parents with making informed choices about their children's education and characterized the majority's treatment of this point as insulting and its own kind of racism.[100]

Like *Brown,* the case of *D.H.* is itself a landmark decision. Marking the first time the European Court of Human Rights recognized a national pattern of discrimination, the case made new law protecting an historically despised group. In recognizing the principle of indirect discrimination and in finding discrimination on the basis of disparate impact of testing, the European Court of Human Rights went further than the U.S. Supreme Court in *Brown* as it authorizes findings of a violation without requiring evidence of intentional discrimination.[101]

Jack Greenberg, one of the original lawyers in *Brown* and later head of the NAACP Legal Defense Fund, consulted on the struggle to integrate Roma in eastern European schools. He found great success in Bulgaria, where social workers assisted integration efforts and teachers received special instruction to equip them to teach the integrated classes.[102] He reflected that *Brown* served as an ice-breaker, enabling America "to chart a course toward racial equality," and wrote hopefully about the positive reception of integration by the president of Bulgaria.[103]

A more sobering connection between *D.H.* and *Brown* arises as advocates for the Roma express dismay over how little has changed for the Roma students themselves since the decision,[104] much as little changed in terms of racial integration in schools in the decade following *Brown.* Two years after the judgment, the Roma continued to be largely segregated in the Czech educational system. Two nongovernmental agencies have reported that Roma children remain vastly overrepresented in the schools for students with disabilities.[105]

Little changed after *D.H.* in no small measure because the European Court of Human Rights required little by way of remedy. The Court refrained from requiring specific reforms, whether statutory or administrative.[106] It did mandate an end to the violation and redress "so far as possible,"[107] but it issued modest damages and directed no specific action. In a report dated April 2009, the Czech government continued to refer to "academic underachieve[ment]" of Roma students rather than discrimination experienced by them.[108] The Czech government continues to use separate schools with a curriculum designed for students with mental retardation and to direct many more Roma students there than any other students.[109] Surveys released by the Czech government as well as studies by nongovernmental organizations indicate that Roma students remain much more likely than non-Roma students to be placed in the separate schools.[110]

While the litigation was pending, the Czech legislature formally abolished the category of "special schools" and eliminated the statutory explicit bar to the enrollment of students from the special schools in academic secondary schools,[111] but these changes have had little actual effect. The "special schools" remain, simply with the new name "practical primary schools."[112] The legislature created a new category of "socially disadvantaged children" and allows different education for them than for other children in the country. The result puts advocates in a delicate position, for the continued existence of a lawful basis for sorting Roma children contributes to continuing risks of separate and stigmatizing treatment of Roma students,[113] even though it may also help to recognize needs for Czech language classes or other special accommodations.[114] Lifting the explicit bar of students from the separate "practical primary schools" entering secondary schools has not altered the practical barriers posed by entrance exams, given the inferior education offered at the separate schools.[115] Approximately 1 percent of Roma students educated in the special schools have been able to switch to the mainstream schools and complete the diploma that serves as a prerequisite for admission to a university.[116] The vast majority of schools included in government surveys had no plans for integrating students from the special schools into the mainstream programs, and more than 50 percent of the sampled teachers in mainstream schools expressed apprehension about the integration of socially disadvantaged children into mainstream education.[117] The Court's decision offers scant specific guidance for tackling these problems.

D.H.—like *Brown*—has motivated both backlash and forward political changes. The president of the Czech Republic vetoed comprehensive antidiscrimination legislation as unnecessary and poorly drafted. This action actually put the nation at risk of sanctions from the European Union, which had required such domestic legislation as a condition for admission. The legislature eventually approved the act over the president's veto.[118] Observers and advocates predict the case will have influence well beyond the Czech Republic.[119] The government of Slovakia adopted a five-year program intended to improve living standards and education for the Roma minority, with a goal of compulsory nursery school for all five-year-olds by 2013 and tighter limits on the placement of Roma children in special schools. Slovakia also expressly banned school segregation by ethnic identity.[120]

D.H. itself captures the reverberations of *Brown* beyond race to ethnicity, language, national origin, and disability status as categories salient in struggles for educational equality, even as it also marks the new frontier of civil rights as human rights advocacy. Identifying students as disabled could lead to appropriate, tailored instruction or instead could replicate a line of social cleavage and disadvantage. And, as in the United States following *Brown*, special treatment on the basis of disability or language could have the effect of separating students of different ethnic and socioeconomic class backgrounds.[121] In the Czech Republic, giving students the same test, in the same language, amounted to unequal treatment because they came to the test from different backgrounds and with different abilities.[122] Some advocates believed that the test was a mere excuse to permit the placement of Roma children in special schools. In the United States, this argument would have drawn inquiry into the intention of the officials running the system. By contrast, in *D.H.*, the European Court ruled that demonstration of invidious intention was not necessary to show a pattern of separation and disadvantage for children from one background. In this way, the European Court struck out on a path quite different from the constitutional interpretation of the U.S. Supreme Court, which demands proof of intentional discrimination to establish a violation of the U.S. Constitution. U.S. Courts have interpreted civil rights statutes enacted in the wake of *Brown* to authorize remedies where official acts produce disproportionate racial impact, but the trend in the United States is against this approach.[123] Despite its avoidance of a discriminatory intent proof requirement, though, the European Court has not reversed the system of separate instruction for the Roma children. Here, as elsewhere, conflicting views about when equal opportunity calls for separate instruction and when instead it calls for inclusion and integration reveal not only evidence of different needs of particular students but also the effects of the different positions of power and stigma associated to particular groups. Negative attitudes toward particular groups—like the Roma in contemporary Europe—reflect and feed their disenfranchisement. Either educational strategy, separation or mixing, can echo that pattern. Sheer contact will not overcome entrenched attitudes and constricted opportunity structures. Tailored instruction may seem the best way to meet the needs of Roma students, but it seems likely to call for separate instruction that in its very form leaves in place the inferior social status experienced by most members of the Roma communities.

Even a community celebrated for enhancing educational success for Roma students—Veldhoven, in the Netherlands—deploys specialized and separate instruction. In Veldhoven, the local government ended separate instruction for Roma students at the primary level but maintained separate classes in secondary school so that Roma students could ask questions in their language and receive special attention—and achieve sufficient academic mastery to move on to more advanced instruction.[124] But even this apparently successful strategy may reflect efforts to avoid negative reactions from mainstream Dutch parents to the inclusion of Roma children in mainstream classrooms.[125]

Some may wonder whether *D.H.* in fact harms Roma children. The existence of this high-profile judgment can allow government officials to assert that the discrimination issue has been addressed; any shortfall in student performance can then be said to reflect students' underachievement rather than government failures to ensure opportunity. Observers have maintained as much in the context of the United States, where the passage of over fifty years since *Brown* and many years of varied remedial efforts permit government officials and members of majority groups to say "We've dealt with this already, we've done our part."[126] Yet such claims can also lead advocates to redouble efforts to achieve the promise of equal educational opportunity and to end discriminatory treatment. Civil rights lawyer and law professor Sherrilyn Ifill has drawn this lesson, countering arguments by some that opportunities for black students and educators declined because of *Brown*:

> *Brown* began with great promise—one that has yet to be fulfilled. But let's not blame *Brown* for the failure of our schools. Instead, *Brown* should serve as our inspiration to demand that our states do what the Supreme Court demanded they do 55 years ago: provide quality education to our students regardless of race. Even more that the electing a black president, the commitment to educate black children would represent a truly historic, transformative and long overdue moment in our country's history.[127]

Authority for Change

Notwithstanding the ongoing debates over the long-term effects of *Brown* and its tie to the mass movement for legislative and social change around racial equality, the significance of *Brown* should not be underestimated. *Brown* has inspired important legal initiatives in and beyond the United States addressing inequalities of opportunity. Advocates pursued equal schooling along lines of gender, disability, language, immigration, class, religion, and sexual orientation with *Brown* as the vital example and touchstone. It triggered a movement for school choice—first as a mechanism to avoid racial desegregation, then a technique to pursue it, and finally, as a motor for educational reform. It stimulated social science research about the influences of contact across lines of social difference; it offered narratives and exemplars of social change entrepreneurs that elevated the image of law as a beacon for change and bolstered new initiatives.

Granted, *Brown*'s applications have generated ongoing disagreements over when mixing in the same classroom achieves or interferes with equal opportunity for girls and boys, for students with disabilities, immigrants, and others marked by apparent differences. Some of those disagreements echo conflicts over racial integration while others reflect issues over effective instruction with heterogeneous versus homogeneous student groups. So many of the controversies over equal educational opportunity summon reformers to make classrooms that transcend patterns of social exclusion or prejudice while also exposing the constraints on school reform in the absence of larger social change. *Brown*, in its promise of equal opportunity, and its refusal to allow the past to prevent a better future, inspires legal and policy arguments in schooling and beyond. Some hint of its legacies—and the complicated nature of the issues it engages—appear in the claims of those who seek to defend newcomer schools for recent immigrants, those who oppose separate bilingual classes, those who challenge assignment of minority students to programs for students with disabilities, those who seek accommodation of religious minorities in the public school dress codes, and those who press for gender equality in private religious schools. *Brown* holds out the vision of schools that reject and thereby remake social stigma associated with markers of individual and group difference, even while launching more than a half-century of debates over whether instruction separating students inevitably communicates inequality or instead can be used to remedy disadvantage and social attitudes assigning inferior status.

What kind of schooling can enhance opportunities for and achievement of varied kinds of students while renovating social hierarchies? This very question, inspired by *Brown,* has given rise to mountains of social science research about the influences of intergroup contact, the effect of different forms of instructions, and the consequences of varied social policies on desired public ends. Hence, another testament to *Brown's* influence and complex legacies is its boost to social science research and its use in civil rights cases and other kinds of litigation and law reform.[128] No less notable, though, is *Brown's* own reminder that social science itself must be tested so as to guard against biased or other faulty assumptions. For proponents of segregation once preferred studies; NAACP-inspired research has generated its own waves of revision and critique. Advocates, policy-makers, and parents should be sobered by both the need for evidence and the contested reliability of studies about gender and education, language instruction, and other dimensions of educational reform. Yet even this chastening light reveals the impact of *Brown* and its attendant movements on efforts to study and improve educational initiatives for immigrants, students learning English, girls, boys, students with disabilities, gay/lesbian/transgendered students, students who identify as religious, Native Hawai'ians, Native Americans, Catholics and Protestants in Northern Ireland, Roma students in Eastern Europe, and Black South African and Afrikaaner students.

It is against this apparently wide wake of *Brown* that its failure to eradicate racialized educational separation and disadvantage in the United States is so disappointing. Perhaps even more disheartening to many than this failure is the fact that racial integration no longer appears to be an important agenda in American schooling, despite the powerful evidence of the academic success that was achieved when it was seriously (though briefly) enforced. This apparent abandonment of racial integration as a crucial goal in the United States seems to be taking place despite significant social science research about the benefits of such integration to individuals and to society in terms of academic achievement, social capital, creative problem solving, and reduction of negative stereotyping. The retreat from racial integration in schooling as a goal in the general population is all the more striking given the successes of schools run by the U.S. military. The achievements of the Department of Defense schools in closing the racial gap in academic performance underscores the power of high expectations, flexible pedagogical approaches designed to reach varied students where they are, parental involvement, community support, and schooling in the larger context of successful racial integration among adults.[129] If schools across the country do not pursue racial integration, the important goals it advances might be undertaken in part in workplaces, the military, afterschool programs and national youth service. These institutions could also be sites for pursuing social integration across other lines of difference, including immigrant status, gender, religion, ethnicity, sexual orientation, and disability. There, as in schools, mere contact is insufficient. Equal opportunity and true integration require shared goals and rewards, a surrounding context of leaders and broader communities embracing co-existence, solidarity, and vigorous revision of the attitudes and social structures that exclude and subordinate along lines of difference.

Even if society implicitly turns to workplaces, afterschool programs, military and national youth service to chase the goals of equality and social integration, what happens to the dream of equal opportunity and social integration in schools? School choice, once used to avoid racial desegregation, increasingly captures hopes in the United States as a mechanism for improving the quality of schooling and the sense of school mission; school choice can draw new teacher talent and engage parents and communities in the tasks of education. In this country, school choice is perhaps the key site of reform and hope for equal opportunity. Yet, unless carefully framed, school choice regimes open new risks of separatism and even increased fears about different social groups.[130]

Choice initiatives, when designed well, offer new possibilities not only for societal-level appreciation of differences but also for drawing together students from different backgrounds in schools where all of them can thrive and succeed.[131] A special focus on game design, civic leadership, internships, or other features can attract students of different races, ethnicities, religions, genders, abilities, and social classes. Even schools focused on particular identity-linked traits, such as the Arabic language, new immigrant status, autism, or girls' leadership, could promote mixing different kinds of students if the individual schools are developed to have broad appeal and if student enrollment policies can take diversity into account.

For purposes of producing a diverse student body, public school systems in the United States are almost always barred from taking race into account,[132] although assignments based on geographic diversity may achieve racial diversity in communities with residential segregation,[133] and cross-district school choice programs could produce schools with substantial racial and socioeconomic diversity. Charter and magnet schools can be organized as single-sex schools if comparable opportunities are available to students of the other sex, and these schools can yield racial, ethnic, and religious diversity, as well as mixing students with and without disabilities. Important decisions remain about the extent to which school systems should make room for special-identity schools (organized around language—including dual language programs, ethnic or cultural traditions, immigrant status, disability, or other identity traits). If these kinds of schools become significant numerically, they may come to cultivate respect and appreciation for differences, but they may also exacerbate social divisions and the sheer lack of shared experiences that is conducive to stereotyping and distrust.[134] School systems, local communities, states, and the federal government can establish regulatory frameworks with more or less encouragement for special-identity schools and more or less attention to civic education and cultivation of respect for others in the curriculum and the extracurricular opportunities. At stake is nothing less than the character of the society and the polity a generation hence.[135]

Advocates and opponents of special mission schools can both find support in *Brown* as they pursue the promise of equal opportunity and the end of state-mandated segregation along lines of difference. The protean quality of *Brown* as a symbol of equality and justice has something to do with this, but so does the irreducible tension between the goal of equality understood as access to mainstream success regardless of personal identity and the goal of pluralism understood as latitude for adults as individuals and groups to pass on the traditions and identities that matter to them. The creation of special-identity schools—to address the needs of students with autism or other disabilities, to promote opportunities for girls (and for boys), to facilitate the academic and social success of new immigrants, Native Hawai'ians, and American Indians, to ensure safety for gay, lesbian, bisexual, or transgendered students—may advance individual equal opportunity while muting the goals of social integration, overcoming group-based hierarchy, and promoting a strong sense of "we" that can be owned by people of different backgrounds and identities. Overcoming forced assimilation and oppression of individuals due to their racial, religious, linguistic, or cultural backgrounds may call for according more room for charter schools devoted to passing on Native Hawai'ian traditions, for example, but then opportunities for individual success require redoubled efforts to ensure high academic quality and access to broad social networks. *Brown*'s ideals can be mobilized both against forced assimilation and for expanding intergroup contact.

Despite efforts by some to reduce the case to concern for individual psychological injuries due to racial classification, *Brown* will forever offer people a tool for questioning and challenging the abusive use of power to confine educational and life opportunities. It is a tool now deployed by advocates and critics in Northern Ireland, South Africa, eastern Europe, and elsewhere. *Brown* now belongs to the world. It is a flag marshalling challenges to government imposition of status hierarchies, the confines imposed by prejudices and stereotypes, and the formal and informal practices of separating some groups from others or hoarding resources by some while denying access to others. It is a banner for social inclusion, solidarity, and the vigorous struggles inevitably required for people from different backgrounds to forge a common world, respectful of individuals and of group differences. The iconic status of *Brown* may explain why courts cite it for propositions far beyond the contexts of educational equality and racial justice. It turns out to be germane to the treatment of gender in calculating pension benefits;[136] to the duty of state officials to obey the Constitution when dealing with extradition;[137] and to the issues of children's rights and voting redistricting.[138] According to one book, *Brown* has become the "yardstick" for measuring legitimate constitutional interpretation.[139] Confirmed in its iconic status, described as the "finest modern moment" of the U.S. Supreme Court,[140] *Brown*, perhaps "for different reasons and for different purposes," remains a touchstone for struggles for justice.[141] It is a resource for individuals—like Ruth Bader Ginsburg, Michael McConnell, Clint Bolick, and George Soros—who mobilize legal and political support as they pursue their own divergent visions of justice.[142] *Brown* offers hope to those who combat social hierarchies and political divisions and those who want to marry ideals and practice in assaulting state-enforced constraints.

Perhaps the most powerful legacy of *Brown* is this: opponents in varied political battles more than fifty years later claim to have ties to the decision and its meaning. For example, President George W. Bush invoked *Brown* in opposing race-conscious college admission practices.[143] The success of *Brown* in reshaping the moral landscape has been so profound that we do not fully comprehend its legacies—and may fail to attend sufficiently to continuing controversy and complexities in its wake.[144] One underexamined legacy may be a conception of integration that requires pluralism, rejecting the elevation of any one subgroup as the ideal for a society and remaking the identity of the larger society in order to open avenues for individuals and subgroups to feel and be equal.[145] Another legacy may be continued attention to psychological experiences of disadvantaged individuals to the near exclusion of discussions of structural inequality and the distribution of material resources across different groups.[146] Still another is expansive use of social science in policy and legal debates. Yet no less significant here is heightened awareness that social science remains influenced by its social context even as it is used as a tool to assess and change that context.

When Representative Diane Wilkerson spoke at a recent Massachusetts constitutional convention, she spoke of growing up in Arkansas after the Supreme Court decision in *Brown*. Fighting tears, she recalled how the public hospital had refused to admit her mother to deliver her children. She said, "I know the pain of being less than equal and I cannot and will not impose that status on anyone else.... I was but one generation removed from an existence in slavery. I could not in good conscience ever vote to send anyone to that place from which my family fled."[147]

About what pending issue was she speaking? She cast her vote against proposals to ban same-sex marriage in the Massachusetts Constitution. Proposals to create a separate civil union status would offer legal and social benefits to these couples, but excluding them from marriage would erect a "separate but equal" regime that would not grant real equality. This argument is one of many surprising legacies of *Brown*. References to

Brown have reverberated ever since the Massachusetts Supreme Judicial Court found that the marriage law excluding same-sex couples was in violation of the Massachusetts Constitution.[148] The analogy between *Brown* and same-sex marriage divided black clergy, with each side claiming the heritage of the pivotal civil rights case.[149] The debate has registered in the public imagination that the struggle for gay rights is indeed the civil rights struggle of our day. Crucial to continuing struggles for education equality and for racial justice, *Brown* is invoked in each new civil rights struggle. A key legacy of *Brown v. Board of Education* is that people now convinced of its rightness ask themselves what new struggle will be analogous a half century from now.

Notes

Introduction

1. The epigraph to this chapter is from Julian Bond, The Broken Promise of *Brown,* May 15, 2004, NAACP Commemoration of Brown v. Board of Education, Topeka Kansas, www.blackcommentator.com/91/91_j_bond.html (last visited Dec. 13, 2009). The Supreme Court decision in *Brown* appears at *Brown v. Board of Education,* 347 U.S. 483 (1954).

2. *See* Robert L. Hayman, Jr., and Leland Ware, *Introduction,* in Choosing Equality Essays and Narratives on the Desegregation Experience (Robert C. Hayman Jr. and Leland Ware, Eds.), 2–3 (2008).

3. Parents Involved in Community Schools v. Seattle School District No. 1, 551 U.S. 701 (2007).

Chapter 1

1. The epigraph to this chapter is from Rebecca Brown, *Common Interests and Integration,* 52 St. Louis U. L.J. 1131, 1137 (2008) (quoting Justice Thurgood Marshall, personal communication with Rebecca Brown, Washington, D.C., 1985).

2. Parents Involved in Community Schools v. Seattle School District No. 1, 551 U.S. 701 (2007). The plans at issue used students' racial classifications only as a tie-breaker for oversubscribed schools (Seattle) or as guidelines affecting allocation of student choices and transfers to preserve 15–50 percent African-American enrollment in a district with 30 percent African-American students.

3. *Brown at 50: King's Dream or Plessy's Nightmare?* Civil Rights Project, Jan. 17, 2004, www.civilrightsproject.ucla.edu/news/pressreleases/brown04.php.

4. *See Introduction: Brown at Fifty,* 117 Harv. L. Rev. 1302 (2004); *see also* Edward Lazarus, *Evaluating Brown v. Board: Were the Revisionists Right?* CNN, May 17, 2004, www.cnn.com/2004/LAW/05/17/lazarus.brown/index.html (listing

disappointments while emphasizing *Brown*'s victory in ending state-sponsored racial oppression).

5. *See* RISA L. GOLUBOFF, THE LOST PROMISE OF CIVIL RIGHTS (2007); MICHAEL J. KLARMAN, FROM JIM CROW TO CIVIL RIGHTS: THE SUPREME COURT AND THE STRUGGLE FOR RACIAL EQUALITY (2004); Regina Austin, *Back to Basics: Returning to the Matter of Black Inferiority and White Supremacy in the Post-Brown Era*, 6 J. APP. PRAC. & PROCESS 79 (2004).

6. *See* chapter 2.

7. A LEXIS search of law review articles produced 878 such references (Brown w/2 Board w/9 landmark).

8. *See* john a. powell, *A New Theory of Integrated Education*, *in* SCHOOL RESEGREGATION: MUST THE SOUTH TURN BACK? 281, 297 (John Charles Boger & Gary Orfield eds., 2005).

9. *Brown at 50, supra* note 3.

10. *Id.* at 4 (describing both selections of private schools and movement to white suburbs).

11. JENNIFER L. HOCHSCHILD & NATHAN SCOVRONICK, THE AMERICAN DREAM AND THE PUBLIC SCHOOLS 37 (2003).

12. *Id.* at 25.

13. For example, the University of Illinois announced its plans for celebration with two sharply contrasting sentences: "On May 17, 1954, America was changed forever when the United States Supreme Court ruled unanimously to outlaw racial segregation in the nation's public schools," and "[t]hat landmark decision in favor of simple social justice set the country on a course of debate, dissent, and change that continues today." University of Illinois at Urbana-Champaign, *Brown vs Board of Education* Jubilee Commemoration, Jan. 2004, www.eui.uiuc. edu/archives/ebc/brown/website/index.html.

14. *See* Lani Guinier, *From Racial Liberalism to Racial Literacy: Brown v. Board of Education and the Interest-divergence Dilemma*, 2004 J. AM. HIST. 92, 105–9 (2004) (causes and effects of housing segregation); JAMES E. RYAN & MICHAEL HEISE, *The Political Economy of School Choice*, 111 YALE L.J. 2043 (2002). For a probing argument that residential segregation operates like a "locked-in racial monopoly," *see* Daria Roithmayr, *Locked In Segregation*, 12 VA. J. SOC. POL'Y & L. 197 (2005).

15. Alan Duke, *"Prom Night in Mississippi" Reveals Racial Divides*, CNN, Jan. 21, 2009, www.cnn.com/2009/SHOWBIZ/Movies/01/21/mississippi.prom/ index.html.

16. E.g., Missouri v. Jenkins, 515 U.S. 70, 89 (1995); Board of Education v. Dowell, 498 U.S. 237, 248 (1991).

17. Kenneth L. Smith & Ira G. Zepp, Jr., *Martin Luther King's Vision of the Beloved Community*, CHRISTIAN CENTURY, Apr. 3, 1974, 361. *See* Martin Luther King, Jr., Sermon at Dexter Avenue Baptist Church: Birth of a New Nation (Apr. 7, 1957), in A Call to Conscience: The Landmark Speeches of Dr. Martin Luther King, Jr. (Clayborne Carson, Chris Shephard, and Andrew Young, eds.) 13 (2001). Available at the Martin Luther King, Jr. Research and Education Institute, http://mlk-kpp01.stanford.edu/index.php/kingpapers/article/the_ birth_of_a_new_nation_sermon_delivered_at_dexter. Desegregation even at its best would only eliminate invidious treatment against blacks in education, public accommodations, and employment, but would not achieve integration, which requires welcoming the participation of blacks in "the total range of human activities." Smith & Zepp, *supra*.

18. Smith & Zepp, *supra* note 17, at 361. Elaborated by the Southern Christian Leadership Conference with Dr. King as its first president, the "beloved community" would make "brotherhood a reality" and reject "black supremacy for this merely substitutes one kind of tyranny for another." Southern Christian Leadership Conference, *This is SCLC, in* CIVIL RIGHTS SINCE 1787: A READER ON THE BLACK STRUGGLE 461, 463 (Jonathan Birnbaum & Clarence Taylor eds., 2000). Segregation, in contrast, "does as much harm to the segregator *as it does to the* segregated. The *segregated* develops a false sense of inferiority and the *segregator* develops a false sense of superiority, both contrary to the American ideal of democracy." *Id.*

19. Kenneth Meeks, *The 75 Most Powerful African Americans in Corporate America*, BLACK ENTERPRISE, Feb. 2005. Parsons had been both CEO and chairman of the board. He is still chairman of the board but stepped down as CEO in 2007. *See* the biography of Richard Parsons at the web site of Time Warner, www.timewarner.com/corp/management/corp_executives/bio/parsons_richard.html.

20. *See* Sam Schechner, *Can't Get Enough Oprah?* WALL ST. J., Jan. 15, 2008, at B1.

21. William C. Rhoden, *Power Is Colorblind in the New N.B.A.*, N.Y. TIMES, Feb. 4, 2004, at D1.

22. Michael Klarman, UNFINISHED BUSINESS: RACIAL EQUALITY IN AMERICAN HISTORY 197 (2007).

23. *See* Michael Cooper & Aron Philhofer, *Democratic Candidates Keep Outraising Republicans*, N.Y. TIMES, Oct. 16, 2007, at A18.

24. Linda Darling-Hammond, *Educational Quality and Inequality: What Will It Take to Leave No Child Behind, in* ALL THINGS BEING EQUAL: INSTIGATING OPPORTUNITY IN AN INEQUITABLE TIME 39, 43 (Brian D. Smedley & Alan Jenkins eds., 2007) (using U.S. Department of Education statistics). Students of color are typically taught by teachers with lower qualifications than those teaching white students and have unequal access to advanced placement courses, science labs, and other components of quality educational programs. *Id.* at 43.

25. GARY ORFIELD & CHUNGMEI LEE, RACIAL TRANSFORMATION AND THE CHANGING NATURE OF SEGREGATION 8, 9 (2006).

26. GOLUBOFF, *supra* note 5, at 198–216.

27. Plessy v. Ferguson, 163 U.S. 537 (1896).

28. Lawrence Blum, *The Promise of Racial Integration in a Multicultural Age, in* MORAL AND POLITICAL EDUCATION 383, 393 (Nomos XLIII, Stephen Macedo & Yael Tami eds., 2001) (quoting Robert Carter, *The Unending Struggle for Equal Educational Opportunity*, 96 TCHRS. C. REC. 621 (1995)).

29. CHARLES OGLETREE, ALL DELIBERATE SPEED: REFLECTIONS ON THE FIRST HALF CENTURY OF *BROWN V. BOARD OF EDUCATION* 296–97 (2004).

30. ROY L. BROOKS, INTEGRATION OR SEPARATION? A STRATEGY FOR RACIAL EQUALITY (1996). *See also* DERRICK BELL, SILENT COVENANTS: *BROWN V. BOARD OF EDUCATION AND THE* UNFULFILLED HOPES FOR RACIAL REFORM 161 (2004); Derrick Bell, *Brown v. Board of Education and the Interest-Convergence Dilemma*, 93 HARV. L. REV. 518 (1980); Derrick Bell, *Integration Ideals and Client Interests in School Desegregation Litigation*, 85 YALE L.J. 470 (1976).

31. BELL, SILENT COVENANTS, *supra* note 30, at 49–68; MARY DUDZIAK, COLD WAR CIVIL RIGHTS: RACE AND THE IMAGE OF AMERICAN DEMOCRACY (2000).

32. Darling-Hammond, *supra* note 24, at 67–78.

33. SHERYLL CASHIN, THE FAILURE OF INTEGRATION: HOW RACE AND CLASS ARE UNDERMINING THE AMERICAN DREAM (2004).

34. HOCHSCHILD & SCOVRONICK, *supra* note 11, at 30 (quoting Thomas Payzant).

35. After the war and the enactment of the Civil Rights Amendments, Roberts recalled the legislative solution for his desegregation suit: "The man of yesterday, borne down by servile oppression, a stranger in the land of his nativity, his limbs galled by chains and fetters and naught but black despair settled upon his troubled mind... now wrested by the powerful arm of justice from his tormentors and placed on the moral platform untrammeled, free and supplied with all that is necessary to a fully developed member of the brotherhood of man.... Who among us can refrain from giving vent to highest exultation over these remarkable events?" George R. Price & James Brewer Stewart, *The Roberts Case, the Easton Family, and the Dynamics of the Abolitionist Movement in Massachusetts, 1776–1870*, 4 MASS. HIST. REV. 89, 93 (2002) (quoting Benjamin F. Roberts, *Our Progress in the Old Bay State*, NEW ERA (1870)). Roberts had first publicly resisted segregation by refusing in 1800 to sit in the section set aside for blacks in his church; he and his family were ejected from the church. *Id.* at 98–99.

36. James Oliver Horton & Michele Gates Moresi, *Roberts, Plessy, and Brown: The Long Hard Struggle against Segregation*, 15 ORG. AM. HIST. MAG. OF HIST. 14 (2001), www.oah.org/pubs/magazine/deseg/horton.html (quoting lawyers Charles Sumner and Robert Morris).

37. *Id.* at 15. David Herbert Donald's biography of Charles Sumner (Roberts's lawyer and a leading abolitionist) emphasizes that Sumner's commitment to equality in education, social relations, and politics for both black and white Americans was quite unusual for a white leader. DAVID HERBERT DONALD, CHARLES SUMNER (1996). On the response of the Massachusetts court, *see* LEONARD W. LEVY, THE LAW OF THE COMMONWEALTH AND CHIEF JUSTICE SHAW (1957).

38. Roberts v. City of Boston, 59 Mass. 198 (1850).

39. *See* CHARLES M. WOLLENBERG, ALL DELIBERATE SPEED: SEGREGATION AND EXCLUSION IN CALIFORNIA SCHOOLS, 1855–1975 19 (1976). California mandated that both children of African descent and Indian children be educated separately from other children, and later, the legislature alternately supported and rejected separate schools for Asian children. *Id.* at 20, 26, 33–34. The courts approved the separate schools for Chinese students and for Japanese students, including schools in the relocation camps for Japanese and Japanese Americans during World War II. *Id.* at 43–47, 73, 75–81.

40. *See id.* at 22–27.

41. *See* NANCY K. MACLEAN, BEHIND THE MASK OF CHIVALRY: THE MAKING OF THE SECOND KU KLUX KLAN (1994); DAVID M. OSHINSKY, WORSE THAN SLAVERY: PARCHMAN FARM AND THE ORDEAL OF JIM CROW JUSTICE (1997); IDA B. WELLS-BARNETT, SOUTHERN HORROR: LYNCH LAW IN ALL ITS PHASES (1894); RICHARD WORMSER, THE RISE AND FALL OF JIM CROW (2003); B. W. Arnett & J. A. Brown, *The Black Laws*, OHIO STATE JOURNAL (1886).

42. *See* DOUGLAS A. BLACKMON, SLAVERY BY ANOTHER NAME: THE RE-ENSLAVEMENT OF BLACK AMERICANS FROM THE CIVIL WAR TO WORLD WAR II (2008); WILLIAM A. LINK, JACKSON DAVIS, AND THE LOST WORLD OF JIM CROW EDUCATION (2000).

43. KLARMAN, *supra* note 22 at 78–79, 86.

44. An important feature of King's vision pointed to the ways the civil rights movement would benefit whites and everyone in the society, "an injection of the idealism, self-sacrifice and sense of public service which is the hallmark of our movement." MARTIN LUTHER KING, JR., WHY WE CAN'T WAIT 141 (Signet

Classics 2000) (1964). *See also* Martin Luther King, Jr., Speech before the Youth March for Integrated Schools (Apr. 18, 1959), www.peaceworkmagazine.org/ pwork/1298/declead4.htm: ("Thus, the Negro, in his struggle to secure his own rights is destined to enlarge democracy for all the people, in both a political and a social sense."). Even more pointed are the reflections of James Baldwin, who emphasized the distorting effects of racial oppression on whites and that whites can only liberate themselves when blacks are liberated. *See* JAMES BALDWIN, THE FIRE NEXT TIME (1975).

45. *See* LOUIS R. HARLAN, BOOKER T. WASHINGTON: THE WIZARD OF TUSKEGEE 1901–1915 174 (1983). In John Hope Franklin's magisterial history, first published in 1947 and revised in 1956, integration seldom appears in the account of the struggles to overturn slavery, pursue self-help, and survive lynching and race riots. JOHN HOPE FRANKLIN, FROM SLAVERY TO FREEDOM: A HISTORY OF AMERICAN NEGROES (Rev. 2d ed. 1956).

46. MANNING MARABLE & LEITH MULLINGS, LET NOBODY TURN US AROUND: VOICES OF RESISTANCE, REFORM, AND RENEWAL 227–29 (2009). The declaration of the Niagara Movement had this to say about schooling: "Education: Common school education should be free to all American children and compulsory. High school training should be adequately provided for all, and college training should be the monopoly of no class or race in any section of our common country. We believe that, in defense of our own institutions, the United States should aid common school education, particularly in the South, and we especially recommend concerted agitation to this end. We urge an increase in public high school facilities in the South, where the Negro-Americans are almost wholly without such provisions. We favor well-equipped trade and technical schools for the training of artisans, and the need of adequate and liberal endowment for a few institutions of higher education must be patent to sincere well-wishers of the race." *Id.*

47. *Id.* at 229.

48. *Id.* at 227.

49. *See id.* at 228 ("we regard as unjust, the exclusion of black boys from the military and naval training schools.").

50. *See* PETER IRONS, JIM CROW'S CHILDREN: THE BROKEN PROMISE OF THE BROWN DECISION 6–10 (2002); Theresa Perry, *Up from the Parched Earth: Toward a Theory of African-American Achievement, in* THERESA PERRY, CLAUDE STEELE, & ASA G. HILLIARD III, YOUNG, GIFTED, AND, BLACK: PROMOTING HIGH ACHIEVEMENT AMONG AFRICAN-AMERICAN STUDENTS 1, 11–51 (2003); WORMSER, *supra* note 41, at 27–28, 43–51.

51. W. E. B. DU BOIS, A SOLILOQUY ON VIEWING MY LIFE FROM THE LAST DECADE OF ITS FIRST CENTURY 251 (Herbert Aptheker ed., 1968).

52. *See* FRANKLIN, *supra* note 45, at 478, 484.

53. *See* GOLUBOFF, *supra* note 5.

54. *Id.* at 176.

55. *Id.* at 143.

56. *See* FRANKLIN, *supra* note 45, at 488–511, 516–28.

57. *See* RICHARD KLUGER, SIMPLE JUSTICE: THE HISTORY OF *BROWN V. BOARD OF EDUCATION* AND BLACK AMERICA'S STRUGGLE FOR EQUALITY 135–36 (2d ed. 2004).

58. *Id.* at 163–66.

59. *See* DAVID LEVERING LEWIS, W. E. B. DU BOIS: THE FIGHT FOR EQUALITY AND THE AMERICAN CENTURY 1919–1963 309–14 (2000).

60. *Id.* at 322 (quoting W. E. B. Du Bois).

61. *Id.* at 325.

62. *See* FRANKLIN, *supra* note 45, at 519–28. *See also* ROBERT MANN, WHEN FREEDOM WOULD TRIUMPH: THE CIVIL RIGHTS STRUGGLE IN CONGRESS, 1954–1968 9 (2007). Franklin D. Roosevelt did end the practice of segregation in the federal offices in the District of Columbia and appointed blacks to federal offices, though most were low-level or clerical posts.

63. *See* LEWIS, *supra* note 59, at 326–33.

64. *Id.* at 330 (describing W. E. B. Du Bois, *On Being Ashamed of Oneself: An Essay on Race Pride*, 40 CRISIS 199 (Sept. 1933), *See* HARVARD SITKOFF, A NEW DEAL FOR BLACKS: THE EMERGENCE OF CIVIL RIGHTS AS A NATIONAL ISSUE: THE DEPRESSION DECADE (1978).

65. W. E. B. Du Bois, *Segregation*, 41 CRISIS 20 (Jan. 1934).

66. W. E. B. Du Bois, *Does the Negro Need Separate Schools?* J. NEGRO EDUC. (July 1935), *reprinted in* EUGENE F. PROVENZO, DU BOIS ON EDUCATION 134, 143 (2002).

67. John W. Davis cited W. E. B. Du Bois in his defense before the Supreme Court of the "separate but equal" doctrine but in so doing misunderstood Du Bois's long-term hope for desegregation. *See* Yale Kamisar, *Foreword: The School Desegregation Cases in Retrospect—Some Reflections on Causes and Effects, in* ARGUMENT: THE COMPLETE ORAL ARGUMENT BEFORE THE SUPREME COURT IN BROWN V. BOARD OF TOPEKA, 1952–55 xiii, xxvi–xxix (Leon Friedman ed., 1969). Du Bois made clear in his autobiography, in the context of medical education, that integration remained his long-term goal but that because it would take so long, creating and supporting all-black institutions should be a priority. *See* LEWIS, *supra* note 59, at 291–92 (quoting W. E. B. Du Bois, *Dusk of Dawn: An Essay toward an Autobiography of a Race Concept* (1940)). The NAACP board debated and rejected Du Bois's argument for opposing enforced segregation while supporting "divergent development" through black institutions, and in 1934 Du Bois resigned his post as editor of the *Crisis*, the NAACP's "organ." *Id.* at 341–44. Demonstrating that the argument pertained to tactics rather than to ends, Du Bois wrote: "Use segregation.... Use every bit that comes your way and transmute it into power," and that power "someday will smash all race separation." *Id.* at 345.

68. Quoted in WORMSER, *supra* note 41, at 149.

69. "I favor integration on buses and in all areas of public accommodation and travel.... I am for equality. However, I think integration in our public schools is different. In that setting, you are dealing with one of the most important assets of an individual—the mind. White people view black people as inferior. A large percentage of them have a very low opinion of our race. People with such a low view of the black race cannot be given free rein and put in charge of the intellectual care and development of our boys and girls." Martin Luther King, Jr., *reprinted in* Samuel G. Freedman, *Still Separate, Still Unequal*, N.Y. TIMES, May 16, 2004, § 7, at 8.

70. *See* LEWIS, *supra* note 59, at 341–48; CARY D. WINTZ, AFRICAN AMERICAN POLITICAL THOUGHT, 1890–1930: WASHINGTON, DU BOIS, GARVEY, AND RANDOLPH 157 (1996).

71. *See* LEWIS, *supra* note 59, at 342.

72. *See* KLUGER, *supra* note 57, at 169.

73. *See* PETER M. ASCOLI, JULIUS ROSENWALD: THE MAN WHO BUILT SEARS, ROEBUCK AND ADVANCED THE CAUSE OF BLACK EDUCATION IN THE AMERICAN SOUTH (2006); Diane Granat, *Saving the Rosenwald Schools: Preserving African*

American History, 20 APF REPORTER 4 (2003), www.aliciapatterson.org/APF2004/ Granat/Granat.html.

74. Pearson v. Murray, 182 A. 590 (1936).

75. Missouri *ex rel.* Gaines v. Canada, 305 U.S. 337 (1938). States resisted complying with this ruling, however, with seventeen enacting out-of-state graduate scholarship programs *after* the Supreme Court rejected this scheme in *Gaines.* *See* KLARMAN, *supra* note 22, at 136.

76. *See* Sipuel v. Board of Regents, 332 U.S. 631 (1948); Sweatt v. Painter, 339 U.S. 629 (1950); McLaurin v. Oklahoma State Regents, 339 U.S. 637 (1950).

77. *See* MARK V. TUSHNET, THE NAACP'S LEGAL STRATEGY AGAINST SEGREGATED EDUCATION, 1925–1950 (2d ed. 2005).

78. *See* JUDITH KILPATRICK, THERE WHEN WE NEEDED HIM: WILEY AUSTIN BRANTON, CIVIL RIGHTS WARRIOR 38–44 (2007).

79. *See* TUSHNET, *supra* note 77; MARK V. TUSHNET, MAKING CIVIL RIGHTS LAW: THURGOOD MARSHALL AND THE SUPREME COURT, 1956–1961 116 (1996).

80. A. Philip Randolph, *Why Should We March?* (survey graphic), (Nov. 1942), *reprinted in* Birnbaum Taylor, *supra* note 18, at 488–89.

81. The 1963 March on Washington traces its roots to this effort. *See id.* (editors' note).

82. *See* ALDON D. MORRIS, THE ORIGINS OF THE CIVIL RIGHTS MOVEMENT: BLACK COMMUNITIES ORGANIZING FOR CHANGE 14–15 (1984).

83. *See* PATRICIA SULLIVAN, DAYS OF HOPE: RACE AND DEMOCRACY IN THE NEW DEAL ERA (1996).

84. *See* GARY GERSTLE, AMERICAN CRUCIBLE: RACE AND NATION IN THE TWENTIETH CENTURY 195 (2001).

85. *See* Bayard Rustin, *Nonviolence vs. Jim Crow*, FELLOWSHIP (July 1942), *reprinted in* REPORTING CIVIL RIGHTS—PART ONE: AMERICAN JOURNALISM 1941–1963 15 (Clayborne Carson et al. comps., 2003); Pauli Murray, *A Blueprint for First Class Citizenship*, CRISIS (Nov. 1944), *reprinted in* Carson et al., *supra*, at 62. *See also* PAULI MURRAY, SONG IN A WEARY THROAT: AN AMERICAN PILGRIMAGE (1987).

86. *See* Rustin, *supra* note 85.

87. Murray, *Blueprint*, *supra* note 85, at 62–63.

88. Thomas Sancton, *The Race Riots*, NEW REPUBLIC, July 5, 1943, *reprinted in* Carson et al., *supra* note 85, at 37.

89. *See* GERSTLE, *supra* note 84, at 215–16; KILPATRICK, *supra* note 78, at 16–17; Lucille B. Milner, *Jim Crow in the Army*, NEW REPUBLIC, Mar. 13, 1944 *reprinted in* Carson et al., *supra* note 85, at 60.

90. GERSTLE, *supra* note 84, at 218.

91. PRESIDENT'S COMMISSION ON CIVIL RIGHTS, TO SECURE THESE RIGHTS: THE REPORT OF THE PRESIDENT'S COMMITTEE ON CIVIL RIGHTS (1947).

92. Mendez v. Westminster, 64 F. Supp. 544 (C.D. Cal. 1946), *aff'd*, 161 F.2d 774 (9th Cir. 1947) (*en banc*); WOLLENBERG, *supra* note 39, at 108, 114. "Ironically, although Mexicans were by far the most segregated group in California public education by the end of the 1920s they were never specifically mentioned in the Education Code," which permitted segregation of Chinese, Japanese, Mongolians, and Indians until 1935. *Id.* at 118.

93. *Id.* at 132. His prior involvement in administering internment camps for Japanese Americans alerted him to the dangers of race-based public policies.

94. 334 U.S. 1 (1948).

95. Norman I. Silber, With All Deliberate Speed: The Life of Philip Elman—An Oral History Memoir 192–93 (2004).

96. *Id.* at 193 (recounting Elman's recollection).

97. *See id.* at 194–96 (discussing challenge to racial segregation in train dining cars resulting in a victory on statutory rather than constitutional grounds and challenges to racially separate graduate and law schools).

98. *See* Kluger, *supra* note 57, at 315–21, 362–64, 412–25, 492–500, 708–10. For an assessment that the Court used the social science material to help legitimize rather than to help reach its decision, *see* Sanjay Mody, *Brown Footnote Eleven in Historical Context: Social Science and the Supreme Court's Quest for Legitimacy*, 54 Stan. L. Rev. 793 (2002). Commissioning social science also represented an effort to counter the widespread use of eugenics and "scientific" claims undergirding racial hierarchy in America. *See* John P. Jackson, Jr., Science for Segregation: Race, Law, and the Case against Brown v. Board of Education (2005).

99. Chief Justice Earl Warren's clerk, Earl Pollack, explained: "The only reason to have included footnote #11 was as a rebuttal to the cheap psychology of *Plessy* that said inferiority was only in the mind of the Negro. The Chief Justice was saying in effect that we know a lot more now about how human beings work than they did back then and can therefore cast doubt on that preposterous line of argument." Quoted in Kluger, *supra* note 57, at 706. *See* Plessy v. Ferguson 163 U.S. 537 (1896). The *Plessy* Court without embarrassment presumed white superiority: "If one race be inferior to the other socially, the Constitution of the United States cannot put them upon the same plane." *Id.* at 552. Even Justice John Marshall Harlan, whose brave dissent rejected white superiority as a matter of law, assumed whites would remain dominant even without legal reinforcement: "The white race deems itself to be the dominant race in this country. And so it is in prestige, in achievements, in education, in wealth and in power. So, I doubt not, it will continue to be for all time if it remains true to its great heritage and holds fast to the principles of constitutional liberty. But in view of the Constitution, in the eye of the law, there is in this country no superior, dominant, ruling class of citizens." *Id.* at 559 (Harlan, J., dissenting).

100. *See* Yehuda Amir, *Contact Hypothesis in Ethnic Relations, in* The Handbook of Interethnic Coexistence 162–81 (Eugene Weiner ed., 1998). *See infra* chapter 6, text accompanying note 158.

101. *See* Kluger, *supra* note 57, at 291. *See also* Jack Greenberg, Crusaders in the Courts: How a Dedicated Band of Lawyers Fought for the Civil Rights Revolution (1994).

102. *See* James Poling, *Our Greatest Civil Liberties Lawyer*, Collier's, Feb. 23, 1952, *reprinted in* Carson et al., *supra* note 85, at 141, 145–46 (2003) (quoting Thurgood Marshall, "A lawsuit is an educational process in itself. It educates not only the defendant and his lawyers, it also enlightens the general public in the area. When we are fighting to get Heman Sweatt into the University of Texas, more than 200 white students set up an NAACP branch on the campus.... It's such suits that bring home to many people the fact that Negroes have rights as Americans which must be respected.") *See also id.* at 150 ("To hear some people talk, one would get the impression that the majority of Americans are lawless people who will not follow the law as interpreted by the Supreme Court. This is simply not true."); Woodrow Wilson International Center for Scholars, Civil Rights, Politics and the Law: Three Civil Rights Lawyers Reminisce (Phillippa Strum ed., Jan.

19, 2006) (quoting of William Taylor, "Of course I knew nothing about race relations but Thurgood and others knew how deeply entrenched racism was and still they thought people would come around. Then massive resistance set in and, as Harris Wofford says, the federal government was of no help.").

103. Kluger, *supra* note 57, at 293.

104. *Compare* GOLUBOFF, *supra* note 5, at 238–72, *with* KENNETH W. MACK, REPRESENTING THE RACE: CREATING THE CIVIL RIGHTS LAWYER, 1920–1955 (forthcoming). *See also* Kenneth W. Mack, *Which Side Is Brown v. Board On?* L.A. TIMES, July 4, 2007, www.latimes.com/news/opinion/la-oe-mack4jul04,0,4240344. story?coll=la-opinion-rightrail.

105. *See* Carl T. Rowan, *The Decisive Battle*, MINNEAPOLIS TRIB., Nov. 29–Dec. 8, 1953, *reprinted in* Carson et al., *supra* note 85, at 157. Rowan quotes David McClary, a white man in South Carolina, as *Brown v. Board of Education* was pending: "Segregation is our way of life. Both races want it. And if that court rules we got to mix 'em, we're gonna make every effort to avoid it." Rowan identified the state-mandated segregation in hospitals, transportation, chain gangs, public entertainment, and schools that would be altered if the NAACP won its challenge to school segregation. *Id.* at 161–62.

106. *Id.* (discussing strategy, assisted by William Coleman's insights after clerking for Justice Felix Frankfurter).

107. *See* KLUGER, *supra* note 57, at 290–542. On Thurgood Marshall's role, *see* Mallery Laing, *Woman Recalls Poor Treatment by White Students after Father's Lawsuit Integrated California Schools*, U. CENT. FLA. NEWSROOM, Oct. 21, 2004, http://news.ucf.edu/UCFnews/index?page=article&id=0024004I1cf2c03offac563ca9007e25.

108. *See* Briggs v. Elliott, 342 U.S. 350 (1952).

109. DUDZIAK, *supra* note 31, at 91; KLUGER, *supra* note 57, at 560–62.

110. DUDZIAK, *supra* note 31, at 91.

111. *See* KLUGER, *supra* note 57, at 555–57.

112. BENJAMIN F. HORNSBY, JR., STEPPING STONE TO THE SUPREME COURT: CLARENDON COUNTY 17 (1992). *See also* BROWN V. BOARD: THE LANDMARK ORAL ARGUMENT BEFORE THE SUPREME COURT (Leon Friedman ed., 2004).

113. KLUGER, *supra* note 57, at 574 (quoting Frankfurter).

114. *Id.* at 617–18.

115. *Id.* at 649 (quoting NAACP brief).

116. Brown v. Board of Education, 347 U.S. 483 (1954). Chief Justice Fred Vinson passed away just before reargument; given his lack of support for desegregation, Justice Frankfurter reportedly told a clerk: "This is the first indication I have ever had that there is a God." KLUGER, *supra* note 57, at 549.

117. Brown v. Board of Education, 347 U.S. 483, 493 (1954).

118. *Id.* at 494.

119. *Id.* at 495.

120. A typical contemporaneous journalistic description of the *Brown* decision noted the delay in implementation while asserting: "The ruling foreshadows the integration of white and Negro children in the same schools in communities which have known nothing but segregation in their entire histories." Robert J. Donovan, *Supreme Court, 9–0, Bans Segregation in Schools*, N.Y. HERALD-TRIB., May 13, 1954, *reprinted in* Carson et al., *supra* note 85, at 204–5.

121. Denise C. Morgan, *What is Left to Argue in Desegregation Law? The Right to Minimally Adequate Education*, 8 HARV. BLACKLETTER L.J. 99, 106 (1991).

122. *See* Morton J. Horwitz, The Warren Court and the Pursuit of Justice 29–30 (1999); Klarman, *supra* note 22, at 152–57; Silber, *supra* note 95, at 196–208.

123. *See* Kluger, *supra* note 57, at 720–30.

124. *See* Klarman, *supra* note 22, at 154.

125. *Brown v. Board of Education* (II), 349 U.S. 294, 300–301 (1955); Kluger, *supra* note 57, at 745–48.

126. *Brown (II)*, 349 U.S. at 301.

127. Robert J. Cottrol, Raymond T. Diamond, & Leland B. Ware, *Brown v. Board of Education*: Caste, Culture, and the Constitution 192–94 (2003).

128. *Id.* Michael Klarman argues that Brown exacerbated resistance and forestalled acceptance of integration, which Southern white moderates otherwise were moving to support. Klarman, *supra* note 5, at 348–61.

129. What actually happened remains a mystery. *See* Christopher Metress, *Introduction* to The Lynching of Emmett Till: A Documentary Narrative 1 (Christopher Metress ed., 2002).

130. *See id.* When the federal Department of Justice reopened an investigation into the murder, assistant attorney general for civil rights R. Alexander Acosta stated: "This brutal murder and grotesque miscarriage of justice outraged a nation and helped galvanize support for the modern American civil rights movement." U.S. Department of Justice, Justice Department to Investigate 1955 Emmett Till Murder (May 10, 2004), press release, www.usdoj.gov/opa/pr/2004/May/04_crt_311.htm. The investigation did not produce any new charges or sanctions. Jerry Mitchell, *Grand Jury Issues No Indictments in Till Killing*, Clarion Ledger, Feb. 27, 2007, at 1A.

131. *See* Alexander Bickel, *The Decade of School Desegregation: Progress and Prospects*, 64 Colum. L. Rev. 193 (1964). For a general account of resistance to implementation, *see* James T. Patterson, *Brown V. Board of Education*: A Civil Rights Milestone and Its Troubled Legacy (2001).

132. *See* James N. Rhea, *A Man Has to Take a Stand: We Went South*, Providence J. & Evening Bull., Oct. 20, 1957, *reprinted in* Carson et al., *supra* note 85, at 386; Dan Wakefield, *Respectable Racism*, Nation, Oct. 22, 1955, *reprinted in id.* at 222–23.

133. Briggs v. Elliott, 132 F. Supp. 776 (E.D.S.C. 1955).

134. *See* James v. Almond, 170 F. Supp. 331 (E.D. Va. 1959). The school closing law enacted in 1956 was rejected by the state supreme court in 1959; Virginia then repealed its compulsory school attendance laws, and Prince Edward County closed its schools to avoid desegregating them. *See* Matthew D. Lassiter & Andrew B. Lewis, The Moderates' Dilemma: Massive Resistance to School Desegregation in Virginia (1998); Benjamin Muse, Virginia's Massive Resistance (1961).

135. Harrison v. Day, 200 Va. 439 (1959); Allen v. County School Board, 198 F. Supp. 497 (1961).

136. J. Kenneth Moreland, The Tragedy of Closed Public Schools: Prince Edward County, Virginia: A Report for the Virginia Advisory Committee to the United States Commission on Civil Rights (1964), www.library.vcu.edu/jbc/speccoll/report1964.pdf.

137. The lawfulness of racial exclusion in private settings itself reflects a series of public policy choices. *See* Imani Perry, *Dismantling the House of Plessy: A*

Private Law Study of Race in Cultural and Legal History with Contemporary Resonances, 33 Stud. in L., Pol. & Soc'y 91 (2004).

138. Jill L. Ogline, Paper Presented at the Annual Meeting of the Association for the Study of African American Life and History: Challenging the Conventional Narrative: Prince Edward County, the NAACP, and the Role of Litigation in the Civil Rights Movement (Sept. 28, 2004).

139. *See* Griffin v. County School Board, 377 U.S. 218 (1964) ("closing the Prince Edward schools and meanwhile contributing to the support of the private segregated white schools that took their place denied petitioners the equal protection of the laws"). For details on the Prince Edward County story, *see* Oliver W. Hill, The Big Bang: *Brown V. Board of Education* and Beyond, The Autobiography of Oliver W. Hill, Sr. (2000); Lassiter & Lewis, *supra* note 134; Kluger, *supra* note 57; Klarman, *supra* note 5.

140. *See* Patterson, *supra* note 131, at 86–117.

141. *See* H. Harvie Wilkinson, From Brown to Bakke: The Supreme Court and School Integration: 1954–1978 80–82 (1981).

142. *Id.* at 78, 101–17.

143. *See* 102 Cong. Rec. 4255, 4459–60 (1956) ("The Southern Manifesto"); Anthony J. Badger, New Deal/New South: An Anthony J. Badger Reader (2007).

144. Cooper v. Aaron, 358 U.S. 1 (1958). *See* Dennis J. Hutchinson, *Unanimity and Desegregation: Decision-making in the Supreme Court, 1948–1958*, 68 Geo. L.J. 1 (1979).

145. *See* Klarman, *supra* note 22, at 155 (noting that Eisenhower authorized the National Guard to enforce desegregation in Little Rock).

146. *Id.* at 157.

147. Richard Bardolph, *State Legislation to Thwart School Desegregation*, in The Civil Rights Record: Black Americans and the Law, 1849–1970 378 (1970).

148. Ben H. Bagdikian, *You Can't Legislate Human Relations*, in Carson et al., *supra* note 85, at 394–95.

149. *See* Matthew Pratt Guterl, The Color of Race in America, 1900–1940 (2002). The labor movement, the New Deal, and World War II helped forge "whiteness" while subordinating blacks, just as an earlier generation of Irish immigrants became "white" by embracing racism against blacks. *See* David R. Roediger, Working toward Whiteness: The Strange Journey from Ellis Island to the Suburbs (2005); Noel Ignatiev, How the Irish Became White (1996).

150. Aldon D. Morris, The Origins of the Civil Rights Movement (1986). Some grassroots protests and politics preceded the struggles over implementing *Brown*. *See* Jeff Wiltse, Contested Waters: A Social History of Swimming Pools in America (2007); Sitkoff, *supra* note 64.

151. *See* Gary Orfield, Reconstruction of Southern Education: Schools and the 1964 Civil Rights Act 33–39 (1969). President Johnson urged Congress to enact the civil rights bill as the best memorial for the slain President John F. Kennedy. Klarman, *supra* note 22, at 176. *See also* Walter F. Murphy & Joseph Tanenhaus, The Study of Public Law 52 (1972). Johnson's personal commitment to the issue deserves as much attention as his political acumen. *See, e.g.,* Strum, *supra* note 102, at 20–21 (reporting Roy Wilkins's comments in 1960 that

Lyndon Johnson "'has the most fire in his belly on civil rights,'" "'he knows what racism is doing to the South, corrupting the politics of the South'").

152. From 1962 to 1967, Democratic presidents appointed Byron White, Arthur Goldberg, Abe Fortas, and Thurgood Marshall. In addition, William J. Brennan proved a forceful leader for racial desegregation, though he was appointed by a Republican president in 1956.

153. Green v. County School Board, 391 U.S. 430, 440 (1968).

154. George P. Shultz, *How a Republican Desegregated the South's Schools*, N.Y. TIMES, Jan. 8, 2003, at A27 (quoting TOM WICKER, ONE OF US: RICHARD NIXON AND THE AMERICAN DREAM (1991) ("the Nixon administration accomplished more in 1970 to desegregate Southern school systems than had been done in the 16 previous years").

155. Swann v. Charlotte-Mecklenburg Board of Education, 402 U.S. 1 (1971).

156. CHARLES T. CLOTFELTER, AFTER BROWN: THE RISE AND RETREAT OF SCHOOL DESEGREGATION 25-30, 179 (2004).

157. Keyes v. School District No. 1, 413 U.S. 189 (1973).

158. HOCHSCHILD & SCOVRONICK, *supra* note 11, at 38-40 (reviewing studies); Gary Orfield, *Introduction* to SCHOOL RESEGREGATION: MUST THE SOUTH TURN BACK? 20 (John Charles Boger & Gary Orfield eds., 2005).

159. HOCHSCHILD & SCOVRONICK, *supra* note 11, at 38.

160. JAMES S. COLEMAN ET AL., U.S. DEPARTMENT OF HEALTH, EDUCATION, AND WELFARE, EQUALITY OF EDUCATIONAL OPPORTUNITY 318-19 (1966). "The higher achievement of all racial and ethnic groups in schools with greater proportions of white students is largely, perhaps wholly, related to effects associated with the student body's educational background and aspirations. This means that the apparent beneficial effect of a student body with a high proportion of white students comes not from racial composition per se, but from the better educational background and higher educational aspirations that are, on the average, found among white students." *Id.* at 307.

161. KLARMAN, *supra* note 22, at 190.

162. RONALD P. FORMISANO, BOSTON AGAINST BUSING: RACE, CLASS AND ETHNICITY IN THE 1960s AND 1970s (1991).

163. CLOTFELTER, *supra* note 156, at 75-96.

164. San Antonio Independent School District v. Rodriguez, 411 U.S. 1 (1973). The Court also allowed private discrimination to proceed outside equal protection guarantees even when the private group received public support through a state liquor license. Moose Lodge No. 107 v. Irvis, 407 U.S. 163 (1972).

165. Milliken v. Bradley, 418 U.S. 717 (1974).

166. *See,* e.g., CASHIN, *supra* note 33, at 8, 32-38; KLARMAN, *supra* note 22, at 140-41.

167. WOLLENBERG, *supra* note 39, at 182-83.

168. HOCHSCHILD & SCOVRONICK, *supra* note 11, at 45.

169. Columbus Board of Education v. Penick, 443 U.S. 449, 479-81 (1979) (Powell, J., dissenting).

170. CLOTFELTER, *supra* note 156, at 90-95, 181-85.

171. *Id.* at 81-138, 181-85. From *Brown* on, the Court rejected official segregation. The question, then and now, is what about unofficial segregation?— What does it communicate when whites resist education with nonwhites? Racial separation of students within an ostensibly diverse school frequently occurs

through tracking that is based on academic talent and need but often reflects past opportunities as well. *See* Jeffrey Gettleman, *The Segregated Classrooms of a Proudly Diverse School*, N.Y. TIMES, Apr. 3, 2005, at A31. Studies indicate that students with the same test scores face different placement in academic tracks in racially correlated patterns. JEANNIE OAKES, KEEPING TRACK: HOW SCHOOLS STRUCTURE INEQUALITY 233 (2d ed. 2005).

172. *See* Calhoun v. Cook, 332 F. Supp. 804, 806 (N.D. Ga.), *vacated in part and remanded*, 451 F.2d 583 (5th Cir. 1971); Mapp v. Board of Education, 525 F.2d 169 (6th Cir. 1975), *cert. denied*, 427 U.S. 911 (1976). On debate over causes of white flight, *see* KEVIN M. KRUSE, WHITE FLIGHT: ATLANTA AND THE MAKING OF MODERN CONSERVATISM (2005); David Armor, *White Flight and the Future of School Desegregation*, *in* SCHOOL DESEGREGATION: PAST, PRESENT, AND FUTURE 187, 196 (Walter G. Stephan & Joe R. Feagin eds., 1980).

173. Robert A. Jordan, *School Committee Vote an Ending That May Only Invite Resegregation*, BOSTON GLOBE, July 18, 1999, at C4.

174. *See* Guinier, *supra* note 14, at 92; Dean M. Hashimoto, *Science as Mythology in Constitutional Law*, 76 OR. L. REV. 111 (1997). On *Brown*'s influence on the course of social science research on inequality, *see* Kenneth K. Wong & Anna C. Nicotera, *Brown v. Board of Education and the Coleman Report: Social Science Research and the Debate on Educational Equality*, 79 PEABODY J. EDUC. 122 (2004).

175. *Compare* Green v. County School Board, 391 U.S. 430, 438 (1968) ("root and branch"), *with* Board of Education v. Dowell, 498 U.S. 237, 250 (1991) ("to the extent practicable"), and H. L. POHLMAN, CONSTITUTIONAL DEBATE IN ACTION: CIVIL RIGHTS AND LIBERTIES 32 (2d ed. 2004).

176. HOCHSCHILD & SCOVRONICK, *supra* note 11, at 35. *See* Freeman v. Pitts, 503 U.S. 467 (1992) (permitting withdrawal of desegregation remedy in portions that achieved compliance). *See also* Missouri v. Jenkins, 515 U.S. 70 (1995) (rejecting remedy intended to improve Kansas City schools and attract white students).

177. *Brown at 50*, *supra* note 3, at 20 (finding that fifty years after *Brown*, desegregation has succeeded in many places but is also being abandoned).

178. *See* Board of Education v. Dowell, 498 U.S. at 248 (1991) (holding new assignment plan producing essentially single-race schools does not violate equal protection in a district previously subject to a school desegregation decree); Freeman v. Pitts, 503 U.S. 467, 487 (1992) (withdrawing judicial supervision of aspects of school system after finding those aspects had achieved unitary status after historical segregation).

179. *See* JONATHAN RIEDER, CANARSIE: THE JEWS AND ITALIANS OF BROOKLYN AGAINST LIBERALISM (1985).

180. President Bill Clinton successfully installed Ruth Bader Ginsburg in 1993 after ten justices were selected by Republican presidents. *See* KLUGER, *supra* note 57, at 759.

181. *See* Alexander v. Sandoval, 532 U.S. 275 (2001) (rejecting private right of action under civil rights statute and halting efforts to pursue educational equality without proof of intentional racial discrimination).

182. David L. Kirp, *Interring a Dream: The Quiet Death of School Integration*, AMERICAN PROSPECT, Aug. 12, 2002, at 17 (recounting that the Supreme Court denied a request by black parents to review resegregation in Charlotte-Mecklenburg, scene of the landmark 1971 *Swann* case); Sam Dillon, *Alabama*

School Rezoning Plan Brings Out Cry of Resegregation, N.Y. TIMES, Sept. 17, 2007, at A1.

183. *See* CAROLA SUÁREZ-OROZCO, MARCELO M. SUÁREZ-OROZCO, & IRINA TODOROVA, LEARNING A NEW LAND: IMMIGRANT STUDENTS IN AMERICAN SOCIETY (2008).

184. ERICA FRANKENBERG, CHUNGMEI LEE, & GARY ORFIELD, A MULTIRACIAL SOCIETY WITH SEGREGATED SCHOOLS: ARE WE LOSING THE DREAM? 24 (2003).

185. One detailed study of the Boston area explores the complex interaction among these factors. DAVID J. HARRIS AND NANCY MCARDLE, MORE THAN MONEY: THE SPATIAL MISMATCH BETWEEN WHERE HOMEOWNERS OF COLOR IN METRO BOSTON CAN AFFORD TO LIVE AND WHERE THEY ACTUALLY RESIDE (2004).

186. James Crawford, "Census 2000: A Guide for the Perplexed" (2002), James Crawford's Language Policy Web Site & Emporium www.languagepolicy. net/articles/census02.htm.

187. U.S. Census Bureau, "Census: Quick Facts," http://quickfacts.census. gov/qfd/states/06/0644000.html (Los Angeles); http://quickfacts.census.gov/ qfd/states/36/3651000.html (New York City); http://quickfacts.census.gov/qfd/ states/41/4159000.html) (Portland).

188. Marcelo Suárez- Orozco, Presentation, Harvard Law School (Jan. 22, 2008).

189. KLARMAN, *supra* note 22, at 203.

190. *See* Mary Ann Zher, *Un Da Nuevo for Schools*, EDUC. WEEK, Nov. 8, 2000, at 39; Kristi L. Bowman, *The New Face of School Desegregation*, 50 DUKE L.J. 1751, 1751 n. 1 (2001).

191. Consolidated Brief of Lt. Gen. Julius W. Becton, Jr., et al. as Amici Curiae in Support of Respondents at 29, Grutter v. Bollinger, 123 S. Ct. 2325 (2003) (Nos. 02–241 and 02–516), http://supreme.lp.findlaw.com/supreme_court/ briefs/02–241/02–241.mer.ami.military.pdf; Brief for Amici Curiae 65 Leading American Businesses in Support of Respondents *Grutter v. Bollinger*, 123 S. Ct. 2325 (2003) (Nos. 02–241 and 02–516), http://supreme.lp.findlaw.com/supreme_ court/briefs /02–241/02–241.mer.ami.sixtyfive.pdf.

192. Deborah Binder, *Benetton: A History of Company That Fights for a Better World* (Mar. 7, 2002), newterritoryfuerteventura.com/deborah/benetton.htm.

193. *See* Joe Klein, *The Benetton-ad Presidency*, NEWSWEEK, Dec. 19, 2004, at 73.

194. MICHAEL B. KATZ & MARK J. STERN, ONE NATION DIVISIBLE: WHAT AMERICA WAS AND WHAT IT IS BECOMING 211–16 (2006) (discussing the Office of Management and Budget's decision to compromise debate over proposal for a new category of "multiracial" instead allowing individuals the option of checking off more than one racial category); *see* David A. Hollinger, *Amalgamation and Hypodescent: The Question of Ethnoracial Mixture in the History of the United States*, 108 AM. HIST. REV. 1363 (2003).

195. CLOTFELTER, *supra* note 156, at 179–81; HOCHSCHILD & SCOVRONICK, *supra* note 11, at 136–42; Peter Irons, *Jim Crow's Children: The Broken Promise of the Brown Decision, in* DISMANTLING DESEGREGATION: THE QUIET REVERSAL OF BROWN V. BOARD OF EDUCATION 289–337 (Gary Orfield & Susan Eaton eds., 1996); PATTERSON, *supra* note 131, at 158–64, 191–205 (2001). *See also* WALTER STEPHAN, REDUCING PREJUDICE AND STEREOTYPING IN SCHOOLS (1999); Walter Stephan, *School Desegregation: An Evaluation of the Predictions Made in Brown v. Board of Education*, 85 PSYCHOL. BULL. 217 (1978).

196. *See* James E. Ryan & Thomas Saunders, *Emerging Trends or New Dead Ends?* 22 YALE L. & POL'Y REV. 463, 480 (2004) (citing James Bock, *Resegregated Schools Not All Bad, Some Say*, BALT. SUN, May 20, 1996, at 1A (64 percent of surveyed African Americans would prefer local schools to integrated schools outside their own communities)).

197. *See* Harold Berlak, *Race and the Achievement Gap*, 15 RETHINKING SCHOOL 10 (2001); Christopher Jencks & Meredith Phillips, *America's Next Achievement Test: Closing the Black-white Test Score Gap*, AMERICAN PROSPECT Sept.–Oct. 1998, at 44, 47; Pedro Noguera & Antwi Akom, *The Significance of Race in the Racial Gap in Academic Achievement*, IN MOTION, June 19, 2000, www. inmotionmagazine.com/pnaa.html; W. Jean Yeung & Dalton Conley, *Black-white Achievement Gap and Family Wealth*, 79 CHILD DEV. 303 (2008). *See also* KAREN L. MAPP, DAVID A. THOMAS, & TONIKA CHEEK CLAYTON, ACCOUNTABILITY AND THE ACHIEVEMENT GAP (A) AND (B) (Harvard Business School Case Series Nos. PEL043, PEL044, 2006).

198. CASHIN, *supra* note 33, at 222–36. The notably different results in schools run by the U.S. military are examined in chapter 6.

199. RICHARD D. KAHLENBERG, ALL TOGETHER NOW: CREATING MIDDLE-CLASS SCHOOLS THROUGH PUBLIC SCHOOL CHOICE 42 (2001).

200. *See supra* note 66 and accompanying text (discussing Du Bois); Cummings, *infra* note 214 (discussing Justice Thomas).

201. *See* William J. Glen, *Separate but Not Yet Equal: The Relation between School Finance Adequacy Litigation and African American Student Achievement*, 81 PEABODY J. EDUC. 63 (2006) (noting districts with adequacy remedies narrowed racial gap in student achievement); Michael Heise, EDUCATIONAL ADEQUACY AS LEGAL THEORY: IMPLICATIONS FROM EQUAL EDUCATIONAL OPPORTUNITY DOCTRINE (Cornell Legal Stud. Res. Paper 05-028, 2005). *See also* powell, *supra* note 8, at 281, 294.

202. *See* Missouri v. Jenkins, 515 U.S. 70, 114 (1995) (Thomas, J., concurring) (rejecting the remedial plan that turned to magnet schools to draw white students back to inner-city minority schools and concerned that "the courts are so willing to assume that anything that is predominantly black must be inferior").

203. *See* Grutter v. Bollinger, 539 U.S. 306 (2003); BEVERLY DANIEL TATUM, CAN WE TALK ABOUT RACE? AND OTHER CONVERSATIONS IN AN ERA OF SCHOOL RESEGREGATION (2007).

204. JOEL SPRING, DECULTURALIZATION AND THE STRUGGLE FOR EQUALITY: A BRIEF HISTORY OF THE EDUCATION OF DOMINATED CULTURES IN THE UNITED STATES (4th ed. 2003); WOLLENBERG, *supra* note 39, at 103–6.

205. *See* Kevin Gaines, *The Ambivalence of Citizenship: African-American Intellectuals in Search of Community*, in THE FRACTIOUS NATION? UNITY AND DIVISION IN CONTEMPORARY AMERICAN LIFE 170, 179–80 (John Rieder & Stephen Steinlight eds., 2003) (describing and criticizing this nostalgia for wrongly blaming integration for troubles of black communities, given that integration "has hardly been achieved in any meaningful sense.").

206. *See* BETH HARRY & JANETTE KLINGER, WHY ARE SO MANY MINORITY STUDENTS IN SPECIAL EDUCATION? UNDERSTANDING RACE AND DISABILITY IN SCHOOLS (2006); RACIAL INEQUITY IN SPECIAL EDUCATION (Daniel J. Losen & Gary Orfield eds., 2002).

207. *See* Dignity in Schools Campaign, "Push Out Factors," www.dignityin-schools.org/pushout-factors (last visited October 23, 2009). A lawsuit challenging the alternative school run by a for-profit company under contract alleges that the program

at issue includes little curricular or rehabilitation work and instead essentially represents "sentencing" the students to punishment and surveillance. *See* Verified Second Amended Complaint, Harris v. Atlanta Independent School System, No. 1:08-cv-1435-BBM (N.D. Ga. Mar. 31, 2009). Some schools use expulsions without providing any alternative instruction—and with racially disparate effects. E-mail from Deborah Gordon Klehr, staff attorney, Education Law Center, to Martha Minow, dean, Harvard Law School (May 13, 2008, 10:15 P.M.) (on file with author); others ship disruptive students to programs with little educational content. *See also WTAE Channel 4 Action News: Disruptive Students Get Easy Ride through High School,* ABC TV, May 12, 2008, *transcript available at www.thepittsburghchannel.com/news/16243497/ detail.html*; Melissa Stormont, Timothy J. Lewis, & Sandra Covington Smith, *Behavior Support Strategies in Early Childhood Settings: Teachers' Importance and Feasibility Ratings,* 7 JOURNAL OF POSITIVE BEHAVIOR INTERVENTIONS 131 (2005); Terrance M. Scott & Lucille Eber, *Functional Assessment and Wraparound as Systemic School Processes: Primary, Secondary, and Tertiary Systems Examples,* 5 JOURNAL OF POSITIVE BEHAVIOR INTERVENTIONS 131 (2003). After Congress held a hearing in 2009 on the use of seclusion and restraints in schools, secretary of education Arne Duncan sent a letter to chief state school officers noting the option of positive behavioral interventions, used by eight thousand schools, to reduce seclusion or restraints and urging review, and where needed, revision of state policies or guidelines to protect students from unnecessary and inappropriate use of restraint and seclusion. *See* Bazelon Center for Mental Health Law, *Use of Restraint and Seclusion in Schools Decried,* MENTAL HEALTH POLICY REPORTER, May 27, 2009, www.bazelon.org/newsroom/ reporter/2009/5-27-09reporter.htm#1 (describing the hearing).

208. *See* ADVANCEMENT PROJECT AND CIVIL RIGHTS PROJECT, OPPORTUNITIES SUSPENDED: THE DEVASTATING CONSEQUENCES OF ZERO TOLERANCE AND SCHOOL DISCIPLINE POLICIES (2000), www.civilrightsproject.ucla.edu/research/discipline/ opport_suspended.php.

209. *See* DIGNITY IN SCHOOLS CAMPAIGN, ALTERNATIVE SCHOOLS AND PUSHOUT: RESEARCH AND ADVOCACY GUIDE (2007), http://dignityinschools.org/DSC_ alternative_Schools_Guide.pdf.

210. JAMIE DYCUS, AMERICAN CIVIL LIBERTIES UNION, MISSING THE MARK: ALTERNATIVE SCHOOLS IN THE STATE OF MISSISSIPPI 26–29 (2009), www.aclu.org/ crimjustice/juv/38800pub20090224.html.

211. *See* Hazel Markus, *Identity Matters: Ethnicity, Race, and the American Dream, in* JUST SCHOOLS: PURSUING EQUALITY IN SOCIETIES OF DIFFERENCE 63 (Martha L. Minow et al. eds., 2008); Claude M. Steele, *A Threat in the Air: How Stereotypes Shape the Intellectual Identities and Performance of Women and African Americans,* 52 AM. PSYCHOL. 613 (1997).

212. JAMES D. ANDERSON, THE EDUCATION OF BLACKS IN THE SOUTH, 1860–1935 (1988); VANESSA SIDDLE WALKER, THEIR HIGHEST POTENTIAL: AN AFRICAN AMERICAN SCHOOL COMMUNITY IN THE SEGREGATED SOUTH (1996).

213. No Child Left Behind Act of 2001, 20 U.S.C. § 6301; *see* Caroline Rothert, *Achievement Gaps and No Child Left Behind,* 26 YOUTH L. NEWS 11, 11–12 (2005).

214. COTTROL, DIAMOND, & WARE, *supra* note 127.

215. Parents Involved in Community Schools v. Seattle School District No. 1, 551 U.S. 701, 802–5 (2007) (Breyer, J. dissenting) (citing the Court's own endorsement of *Brown*).

216. *Id.* at 787–88 (Kennedy, J.) (concurring in part and concurring in the judgment).

217. *Id.* at 708–48 (2007) (Roberts, C.J.) (plurality opinion). For a sympathetic reading of the opinion, *see* J. Harvie Wilkinson III, Comment, *The Seattle And Louisville School Cases: There Is No Other Way,* 121 HARV. L. REV. 158 (2007).

218. 551 U.S. at 747–48 (2007) (Roberts, C.J.) (plurality opinion).

219. *See BROWN V. BOARD OF EDUCATION:* A BRIEF HISTORY WITH DOCUMENTS, 142–51 (Waldo E. Martin, Jr., ed., 1998) (citing Brief of Appellant at X, Brown v. Board of Educ., 347 U.S. 483 (1955)); Martin Luther King, Jr., I Have a Dream Speech (Aug. 28, 1963) ("I have a dream that my four little children will one day live in a nation where they will not be judged by the color of their skin but by the content of their character.").

220. "The plurality's postulate that '[t]he way to stop discrimination on the basis of race is to stop discriminating on the basis of race,' is not sufficient to decide these cases. To the extent the plurality opinion suggests the Constitution mandates that state and local school authorities must accept the status quo of racial isolation in schools, it is, in my view, profoundly mistaken." Parents Involved in Community Schools v. Seattle School District No. 1, 551 U.S. at 788 (Kennedy, J.) (concurring in part and concurring in the judgment) (citation omitted). A federal district court recently permitted a state university to include race as a factor in university admissions in a plan because the policy provides a highly individualized, holistic review of every applicant, and the method is narrowly tailored to advance the university's goal of assembling a diverse student body. Fisher v. University of Texas, 2009 U.S. Dist. LEXIS 77968 (W.D. Tex. Aug. 17, 2009).

221. His opinion asserted the resemblance between the challenged plans and plans during the prior fifty years that "represent local efforts to bring about the kind of racially integrated education that *Brown* long ago promised—efforts that this Court has repeatedly required, permitted, and encouraged local authorities to undertake." Parents Involved in Community Schools v. Seattle School District No. 1, 551 U.S. at 803 (Breyer, J., dissenting, joined by Justices Stevens, Ginsburg, and Souter) (citation omitted). Justice Breyer argues that the plurality opinion "undermines *Brown*'s promise of integrated primary and secondary education that local communities have sought to make a reality." *Id.* at 803–4. He summarizes *Brown* this way: "The last half century has witnessed great strides toward racial equality, but we have not yet realized the promise of *Brown*. To invalidate the plans under review is to threaten the promise of *Brown*. The plurality's position, I fear, would break that promise." *Id.* at 868.

222. Parents Involved in Community Schools v. Seattle School District No. 1, 551 U.S. at 798–99 (Stevens, J., dissenting).

223. *Id.* at 803.

224. Missouri. v. Jenkins, 515 U.S. 70 (1995); Milliken v. Bradley, 418 U.S. 717 (1974). *See* Gary Orfield, *Conservative Activists and the Rush toward Resegregation, in* LAW AND SCHOOL REFORM: SIX STRATEGIES FOR PROMOTING EDUCATIONAL EQUITY 39 (Jay P. Heubert ed., 1999).

225. Owen Fiss, *Groups and the Equal Protection Clause,* 5 PHIL. & PUB. AFF. 107 (1975); Reva Siegel, *Equality Talk: Antisubordination and Anticlassification Values in Constitutional Struggles over Brown,* 117 HARV. L. REV. 1470 (2004); Jack Balkin & Reva Siegel, *The American Civil Rights Tradition: Anticlassification or*

Antisubordination? 58 U. MIAMI L. REV. 9 (2003). *See also* ARTHUR KINOY, *The Constitutional Right of Negro Freedom*, 21 RUTGERS L. REV. 387 (1967).

226. EDUARDO BONILLA-SILVA, RACISM WITHOUT RACISTS: COLOR-BLIND RACISM AND THE PERSISTENCE OF RACIAL INEQUALITY IN THE UNITED STATES (2003); MICHAEL K. BROWN, MARTIN CARNOY, ELLIOTT CURRIE, TROY DUSTER, & DAVID B. OPPENHEIMER, WHITEWASHING RACE: THE MYTH OF A COLOR-BLIND SOCIETY (2005); André Douglas & Pond Cummings, *Grutter v. Bollinger, Clarence Thomas, Affirmative Action, and the Treachery of Originalism: The Sun Don't Shine Here in This Part of Town*, 21 HARV. BLACKLETTER L.J. 1 (2005).

227. Grutter v. Bollinger, 539 U.S. 306, 322–23 (2003).

228. Sam Dillon, *Most States Fail Demands in Education Law*, N.Y. TIMES, July 25, 2006, at A14. *See* RICHARD D. KAHLENBERG, ENFORCING THE NO CHILD LEFT BEHIND ACT (July 25, 2006), Century Foundation, www.tcf.org/list. asp?type=NC&pubid=1362 (last visited October 26, 2009).

229. Michael Heise, *Equal Educational Opportunity by the Numbers: The Warren Court's Empirical Legacy*, 59 WASH. & LEE L. REV. 1309 (2002) (asserting *Brown* decision influenced uses of social science in school finance and choice litigation).

Chapter 2

1. The epigraph to this chapter is from BROWN V. BOARD: THE LANDMARK ORAL ARGUMENT BEFORE THE SUPREME COURT 51 (Leon Friedman ed., New Press 2004) (transcript).

2. *See* Juan F. Perea, *Ethnicity and the Constitution: Beyond the Black and White Binary Constitution*, 36 WM. & MARY L. REV. 571 (1995).

3. *See infra* chapter 4.

4. JOHN HIGHAM, STRANGERS IN THE LAND: PATTERNS OF AMERICAN NATIVISM, 1860–1925 (2002); THE IMMIGRANT EXPERIENCE: THE ANGUISH OF BECOMING AMERICAN (Thomas C. Wheeler ed., 1992). For treatment of national origin discrimination in employment, *see* R. BELTON, D. AVERY, M. ONTIVEROS, & R. CORRADA, EMPLOYMENT DISCRIMINATION LAW 628–63 (7th ed. 2004).

5. Leti Volpp, *Impossible Subjects: Illegal Aliens and Alien Citizens*, 103 MICH. L. REV. 1595, 1597 (2005) (reviewing MAE NGAI, IMPOSSIBLE SUBJECTS: ILLEGAL ALIENS AND THE MAKING OF MODERN AMERICA (2004)).

6. *See* Jennifer Gordon & R.A. Lenhardt, *Citizenship Talk: Bridging the Gap Between Immigration and Race Perspectives*, 75 FORDHAM L. REV. 2493 (2007).

7. LANGUAGE LOYALTIES: A SOURCE BOOK ON THE OFFICIAL ENGLISH CONTROVERSY (James Crawford ed., 1992).

8. *See* DAVID WALLACE ADAMS, EDUCATION FOR EXTINCTION, AMERICAN INDIANS AND THE BOARDING SCHOOL EXPERIENCE 1875–1928 (1997); AWAY FROM HOME: AMERICAN INDIAN BOARDING SCHOOLS (Margaret L. Archuleta et al. eds., 2d ed. 2000). *See* chapter 4 of this book for further discussion of education of American Indian children.

9. *See* Juan F. Perea, *Buscando America: Why Integration and Equal Protection Fail to Protect Latinos*, 117 HARV. L. REV. 1420, 1420–1422 (2004) (discussing Mendez v. Westminster School District, 64 F. Supp. 544 (S.D. Cal. 1946), *aff'd*, 161 F.2d 774 (9th Cir. 1947)).

10. *See* Najia Aarim-Heriot, Chinese Immigrants, African Americans, and Racial Anxiety in the United States, 1848–82 (2003).

11. James R. Barrett, *Americanization from the Bottom, Up: Immigration and the Remaking of the Working Class in the United States, 1880–1930*, 79 J. Am. Hist. 996 (1992).

12. On nativism, *see* Higham, *supra* note 4; Robin Dale Jacobson, The New Nativism: Proposition 187 and the Debate over Immigration (2008).

13. *See* Plyler v. Doe, 457 U.S. 202 (1982); League of United Latin American Citizens v. Wilson, 908 F. Supp. 755 (C.D. Cal. 1995).

14. *See* Just Schools: Pursuing Equality in Societies of Difference (Martha Minow et al. eds., 2008).

15. *See* Erica Frankenberg et al., Harvard University Civil Rights Project, *A Multiracial Society with Segregated Schools: Are We Losing the Dream?* 4 (2003); Perea, *supra* note 9 at 1423–25.

16. George J. Borjas, *Know the Flow: Economics of Immigration*, National Review, Apr. 17, 1995, http://findarticles.com/p/articles/mi_m1282/is_n7_v47/ai_16823452; Jeffrey S. Passel & Roberto Suro, Rise, Peak and Decline: Trends in U.S. Immigration 1992–2004 (Sept. 27, 2005), Pew Charitable Trusts http://pewhispanic.org/reports/report.php?ReportID=53; Portrait of the USA, United States Information Agency, Sept. 1997, http://usa.usembassy.de/etexts/factover/ homepage.htm.

17. A. Jamieson, A. Curry, & G. Martinez, *School Enrollment in the United States: Social and Economic Characteristics of Students*, Current Population Reports, 20–533 (2001); Nina Bernstein, *Study Finds Immigration in U.S. Peaked in 2000*, N.Y. Times, Sept. 28, 2005.

18. Carnegie Corp. of America, The House We All Live In: A Report on Immigrant Civic Integration (2003).

19. *See* Keyes v. School District No. 1, Denver, 413 U.S. 189, 195 (1973); Marcelo Suárez-Orozco, Peter D. Roos, & Carola Suárez-Orozco, *Cultural, Educational, and Legal Perspectives on Immigration: Implications for School Reform*, in Law and School Reform: Six Strategies for Promoting Educational Equity 160 (Jay Heubert & Martha Minow eds., Yale University Press 1999). The Supreme Court rejected exclusion of noncitizen children, Plyler v. Doe, 457 U.S. 202 (1982); decades earlier, the Court rejected an antiimmigrant measure forbidding instruction in German in the public schools. Meyer v. Nebraska, 262 U.S. 390 (1923).

20. Gonzales v. Sheely, 96 F. Supp. 1004 (D. Ariz. 1951); Mendez v. Westminster School District, 64 F. Supp. 544 (S.D. Cal. 1946). For histories of these and other early cases on behalf of Mexican-American students, *see* Robert R. Alvarez, Jr., *The Lemon Grove Incident: The Nation's First Successful Desegregation Court Case*, 32 J. San Diego Hist. 116 (1986), www.sandiegohistory.org/journal/86spring/lemongrove.htm. Robert Carter, working with Thurgood Marshall at the NAACP, contributed an amicus brief to the Mendez appeal.

21. Keyes v. School District No. 1, Denver, 413 U.S. 189 (1973).

22. Ruben Donato, The Other Struggle for Equal Schools: Mexican-Americans during the Civil Rights Movement 57–76, 104–5 (SUNY Press 1997).

23. *Id.* at 76–85.

24. *Hearings on S. 428 before the Senate Committee on Labor and Public Welfare, Special Subcommittee on Bilingual Education*, 90th Cong. 1–2 (1967) (comments of Sen. Yarborough).

25. James T. Lyons, *The Past and Future Directions of Federal Bilingual-education Policy*, 508 ANNALS OF THE AMERICAN ACADEMY OF POLITICAL AND SOCIAL SCIENCES 66 (1990). Educators later tried to reclaim bilingual education as a strategy for equality instruction. *See* MARIA ESTALA BRISK, BILINGUAL EDUCATION: FROM COMPENSATORY TO QUALITY SCHOOLING (2005).

26. *See* the MALDEF web site, www.maldef.org/about/ (last visited Nov. 13, 2009).Founded after the assassinations of Martin Luther King, Jr., and Robert F. Kennedy, MALDEF represented a reaffirmation of the civil rights movement despite the setbacks and a period of violent reaction. *See* Mexican-American Legal Defense Fund, "MALDEF's 40th Anniversary" (2009), www.maldef.org/about/40th_anniversary/ (last visited Nov. 13, 2009).

27. Immigration Act of 1924, STATUTES AT LARGE OF THE UNITED STATES OF AMERICA, vol. 42, pt. 1, 153–69 (1925).

28. *See* Equal Employment Opportunity Commission, *Celebrating the 40th Anniversary of Title VII, Panel II* (June 23, 2004), www.eeoc.gov/abouteeoc/40th/panel/expanding.html (citing Exec. Orders Nos. 9346, 11478).

29. Perea, *supra* note 9.

30. JAMES CRAWFORD, BILINGUAL EDUCATION: HISTORY, POLITICS, THEORY AND PRACTICE 43 (4th rev. ed. 1999) (quoting memo by J. Stanley Pottinger, director of federal Office for Civil Rights. Pottinger authored the amicus brief for the federal government in support of the plaintiffs in *Lau v. Nichols* before the Supreme Court.).

31. *Id.* at 44.

32. *See* L. Ling-Chi Wang, *Lau v. Nichols: History of a Struggle for Equal and Quality Education (An Excerpt)*, 1 ASIAN AM. BILINGUAL CTR. NEWSL. 3 (Supp. Oct. 1975).

33. Garance Burke, *Ambivalent in Any Language*, BOSTON GLOBE, July 22, 2002.

34. Steinman worked through a translator, and it actually may have produced some misunderstandings. Lau recalled that Steinman selected him as a plaintiff because he thought a child born in the United States and raised by a widow would elicit judicial sympathy, but in fact Lau was born in Hong Kong and his father joined him and his mother after they arrived first in San Francisco. Burke, *supra* note 33.

35. STEPHANIE SAMMARTINO MCPHERSON, LAU V. NICHOLS: BILINGUAL EDUCATION IN PUBLIC SCHOOLS 46 (Enslow Publishers 2000).

36. Charles Euchner, *Languages, Law, and San Francisco,* EDUC. WK., Jan. 25, 1984, www.euchner.us/bilingual.htm.

37. MCPHERSON, *supra* note 35, at 46.

38. Lau v. Nichols, 483 F.2d 791, 797 (9th Cir. 1973).

39. Lau v. Nichols, 414 U.S. 563 (1974).

40. *Id.* at 566.

41. *Id.* at 568.

42. *Id.* at 569.

43. *Id.* at 569.

44. *Id.* at 568.

45. Justice Douglas's opinion did so implicitly; Justice Stewart's opinion, concurring in the judgment, did so by approving the federal regulations that required affirmative steps to accommodate the needs of students lacking English proficiency as authorized by the Civil Rights Act of 1964. Lau v. Nichols, 414 U.S.

569, 570 (Stewart, J., joined by Chief Justice Burger and Justice Blackmun, concurring in the judgment). Whether or not governmental intention to discriminate is a requirement for remedial action, controversy persists over the use of racial or ethnic classifications in both constitutional and statutory analysis.

46. For my earlier treatment of this issue, *see* MARTHA MINOW, MAKING ALL THE DIFFERENCE: INCLUSION, EXCLUSION AND AMERICAN LAW (1990).

47. Euchner, *supra* note 36 (discussing responses to *Lau v. Nichols* by San Francisco school authorities and advocates).

48. *Id.*

49. CRAWFORD, *supra* note 30, at 46–47, 51.

50. 20 U.S.C. § 1703(f) (2007).

51. 20 U.S.C. § 880(b) (2007) (codifying Bilingual Education Act of 1968 and 1974). *See* CRAWFORD, *supra* note 30, at 41–42. Liberal Republicans, active federal courts, and competition between Republicans and Democrats for Hispanic votes contributed to the bilingual education expansion. *See* GARETH DAVIES, SEE GOVERNMENT GROW: EDUCATION POLITICS FROM JOHNSON TO REAGAN 153 (University Press of Kansas 2007).

52. DAVIES, *supra* note 51, at 153 (quoting Elliot Richardson, secretary of health, education and welfare, who indicated his department would push for "culturally sensitizing teachers" in order to increase "the development of positive self-conception" by Hispanic children).

53. *See* CRAWFORD, *supra* note 30, at 48–58.

54. Castañeda v. Pickard, 648 F.2d 989 (5th Cir. 1981).

55. *Id.* at 1015.

56. On remand, the district court found that the school district did not discriminate against Mexican Americans in its ability grouping of students and teacher hiring practices and that the district had implemented adequate bilingual education programs. The Court of Appeals affirmed. 781 F.2d 456 (5th Cir. 1986).

57. "We understand § 1703(f) to impose on educational agencies not only an obligation to overcome the direct obstacle to learning which the language barrier itself poses, but also a duty to provide limited English speaking ability students with assistance in other areas of the curriculum where their equal participation may be impaired because of deficits incurred during participation in an agency's language remediation program." Castañeda v. Pickard, 648 F.2d at 1011.

58. Castañeda v. Pickard, 648 F.2d 989 (directing that language programs be evaluated in terms of adoption and implementation of a pedagogically sound approach for meeting the needs of limited English proficiency students).

59. *Id.* at 1010.

60. "The court's second inquiry would be whether the programs and practices actually used by a school system are reasonably calculated to implement effectively the educational theory adopted by the school. [Adoption of a promising theory is inadequate if the] system fails to follow through with practices, resources and personnel necessary to transform the theory into reality." *Id.* at 1010.

61. *Id.* at 1011. Even when the federal government backed away from bilingual education, it affirmed the continued hold of the Castañeda inquiry into effective instruction and sufficient resources for students learning English. *See* UNITED STATES DEPARTMENT OF EDUCATION, MEMORANDUM: POLICY UPDATE ON SCHOOLS' OBLIGATIONS TOWARD NATIONAL ORIGIN MINORITY STUDENTS WITH LIMITED-ENGLISH PROFICIENCY (Sept. 27, 1991), www.ed.gov/about/offices/list/

ocr/docs/lau1991.html; U.S. DEPARTMENT OF EDUCATION, QUESTIONS THAT MIGHT BE RAISED UNDER PROPOSITION 227 (June 25, 2003), www.ed.gov/offices/OCR/archives/prop227q.html.

62. *See* DONATO, *supra* note 22, at 128–43.

63. *Id.* at 150–51.

64. CRAWFORD, *supra* note 30, at 264 (app. A).

65. *Id.* This is also sometimes called "developmental bilingual education."

66. *Id.* at 265. *See also* Maria G. López & Abbas Tashakkori, *Narrowing the Gap: Effects of a Two-way Bilingual Education Program on the Literacy Development of At-risk Primary Students*, 9 J. EDUC. FOR STUDENTS PLACED AT RISK 325 (2004) (finding benefits).

67. CRAWFORD, *supra* note 30, at 265–67.

68. *Id.* at 265.

69. *Id.* at 52–53.

70. *Id.* at 55–57; *see also* Gary Orfield, *The 1964 Civil Rights Act and American Education*, *in* LEGACIES OF THE 1964 CIVIL RIGHTS ACT 89, 118–19, 126 (Bernard Grofman ed., 2000).

71. *See* Barbara J. Brunner, *Bilingual Education under the No Child Left Behind Act of 2001*, 169 ED. LAW REP. 505, 518–20 (2002); Bethany Li, Note, *From Bilingual Education to OELALEAALEPS: How the No Child Left Behind Act Has Undermined English Language Learners' Access to a Meaningful Education*, 14 GEO. J. ON POVERTY L. & POL'Y 539, 559–60 (2007); Rosemary Salome, True American: Language, Identity, and the Education of Immigrant Children 157–159 (2010).

72. *See* Li, *supra* note 71, at 558–59.

73. No Child Left Behind Act, 20 U.S.C. § 6821 (2002); *see also id.* at §§ 6801, 6811–71, 6891–6983.

74. *See infra* chapter 6.

75. *See* Institute for Language and Education Policy: Research Based Advocacy for Schools and Communities (2009), www.elladvocates.org/index.html: "Has bilingual instruction become a taboo subject at the U.S. Department of Education? That would seem to explain the omission of the subject from three federally funded 'guidebooks' on educating English-language learners, released in late October. In advising practitioners on how to serve these students, the authors made no mention whatsoever of language of instruction."

76. *See* Lisa Ellhern, *Proposition 227: The Difficulty of Insuring English Language Learners' Rights*, 33 COLUM. J.L. & SOC. PROBS. 1 (1999); Christine H. Rossell & Keith Baker, *The Educational Effectiveness of Bilingual Education*, 30 RESEARCH IN THE TEACHING OF ENGLISH 7 (1996); Charu A. Chandrasekhar, Comment, *The Bay State Buries Bilingualism: Advocacy Lessons from Bilingual Education's Recent Defeat in Massachusetts*, 24 CHICANO-LATINO L. REV. 43 (2003). *See also* Suárez-Orozco et al., *supra* note 19, at 160, 190–91 (discussing debate over whether proficiency in English requires up to six years to acquire).

77. *See* Thomas F. Felton, comment, *Sink or Swim? The State of Bilingual Education in the Wake of California Proposition 227*, 48 CATH. U. L. REV. 843 (1999).

78. Chandrasekhar, *supra* note 76, at 43. California still allows parents to elect either bilingual education or immersion under certain circumstances.

79. William N. Myhill, *The State of Public Education and the Needs of English Language Learners in the Era of "No Child Left Behind,"* 8 J. GENDER RACE & JUST. 393, 425 (2004).

80. Cal. Educ. Code § 310; Ariz. Rev. Stat. Ann. § 15–753(A); Mass. Gen. Laws Ann. Ch. 71A § 5(a). *See also* Chandrasekhar, *supra* note 76, at 43.

81. Cal. Educ. Code § 311; Ariz. Rev. State. § 15–753(B)(2)(3); Mass. Gen. Laws ann. Ch. 71A § 5(b)(2)(3).

82. *Compare* Castañeda v. Pickard, 648 F.2d 989 (5th Cir. 1981), *with* Valeria G. v. Wilson, 12 F. Supp. 2d 1007 (N.D. Cal. 1998).

83. Horne v. Flores, 129 S. Ct. 2579 (2009).

84. Quotation from § 204(f), 88 Stat. 515; 20 U. S. C. § 1703(f).

85. "'Sheltered English immersion' or 'structured English immersion' means an English language acquisition process for young children in which nearly all classroom instruction is in English but with the curriculum and presentation designed for children who are learning the language.... Although teachers may use a minimal amount of the child's native language when necessary, no subject matter shall be taught in any language other than English, and children in this program learn to read and write solely in English." Ariz. Rev. Stat. Ann. § 15–751(5) (West 2009).

86. Horne v. Flores, 129 S. Ct. at 2597.

87. *Id.* at 2601 (citing Brief for American Unity Legal Defense Fund et al. as Amici Curiae 10–12).

88. *Id.* at 2623 (Breyer, J., dissenting).

89. *Id.* at 2601 (majority opinion).

90. *Id.* at 2607 (Breyer, J., dissenting). The dissent emphasized that the district court's findings concluded that "the State's method of paying for the additional costs associated with English learning education was 'arbitrary and capricious and [bore] no relation to the actual funding needed.'" *Id.* at 2611 (citing Flores v. Arizona, 172 F. Supp. 2d 1225, 1239 (D. Ariz. 2000)). The dissent also noted that "no one in this case suggests... that there are no extra costs associated with English-learning education irrespective of the teaching method used." *Id.* at 2614. Additional expenses include teacher training in the school's chosen method, tutoring, and special assessments.

91. *Id.* at 2631 (quoting Cristina M. Rodriguez, *Language and Participation*, 94 CAL. L. REV. 687, 693 (2006)).

92. Jonathan Simon, *Horne v. Flores: The Roberts Court Takes Aim at Institutional Reform Litigation* PrawfsBlog, Aug. 23, 2009, http://prawfsblawg.blogs.com/prawfsblawg/2009/08/horne-v-flores-the-roberts-court-takes-aim-at-institutional-reform-litigation.html. Some hope that the remand will allow further challenge to the defects of the state's approach. Michelle Chen, *Horne v. Flores: Lessons in Equality*, RACEWIRE, June 25, 2009, www.racewire.org/archives/2009/06/horne_v_flores_lessons_in_equa_1.html.

93. Larry Yudelson, *N.J. School May Get Hebrew Track*, JEWISH DAILY FORWARD, Feb. 27, 2009, www.forward.com/articles/103172/.

94. *See infra* chapter 5.

95. *See infra* chapter 3.

96. Peg Meier, *An Oasis for Learning*, MINNEAPOLIS STAR TRIB., Feb. 2, 2003, at 1E.

97. Twin Cities International Elementary School, www.tiesmn.org/ (last visited May 12, 2006). The middle school is no longer functioning. *See* www.twincitiesinternationalschool.org/ (last visited Oct. 28, 2009).

98. Press release, Human Dignity and Humiliation Studies, The Somali Documentary Project Goes to Dadaab (Nov. 23, 2005) www.humiliationstudies.org/news-old/archives/000851.html.

99. According to the 2000 census, the immigrant population in Minnesota included 125,000 Hispanics, 60,000 Hmong, 20,000 non-Hmong Southeast Asians, 11,151 Somalis, 6,000 Russians, 2,500 West Africans, 2,000 East Africans (not Somali), 1,600 Yugoslavians, and 500 Tibetans. *See* University of Minnesota, *International Directory*, www.international.umn.edu/directory/profile/tcmn.html.

100. Elizabeth Weiss Green, *Klein Relieves Some Critics' Concerns about Arab School*, N.Y. SUN, May 16, 2007, www.nysun.com/new-york/klein-relieves-some-critics-concerns-about-arab/54557/.

101. Thomas Zambito, *Ex-principal of Arab School Loses Round in Court*, N.Y. DAILY NEWS, Dec. 6, 2007, at 10 ("[I]n tearful testimony this week, Almontaser said she was trying to make a teaching point about the meaning of intifadeh when she explained to the reporter that its root translation was 'shaking off oppression.'").

102. *See* Perea, *supra* note 9, for a defense of cultural particularity rather than coerced assimilation as the proper focus of equality efforts in schools.

103. Plyler v. Doe, 457 U.S. 202 (1982).

104. Proposition 187, *reprinted in* MARK G. YUDOF, DAVID L. KIRP, BETSY LEVIN, & RACHEL MORAN, EDUCATIONAL POLICY AND THE LAW 691 (4th ed. 2002).

105. League of United Latin American Citizens v. Wilson, 908 F. Supp. 755 (C.D. Cal. 1995).

106. *See* Terry McDermott, *Some Are Embittered by Fate of Prop. 187*, L.A. TIMES, Aug. 2, 1999, at A1.

107. BEVERLY A. BOYSON & DEBORAH J. SHORT, SECONDARY SCHOOL NEWCOMER PROGRAMS IN THE UNITED STATES (2003). Nine New York schools and one California school participate in a network of schools for new immigrants. *See* Internationals: Network for Public Schools, www.internationalsnps.org/ (last visited Nov. 13, 2009). Other schools and programs developed independently; these include Newcomer in San Francisco, http://portal.sfusd.edu/template/default.cfm?page=hs.newcomer, and International Academy-LEAP in St. Paul, Minnesota, www.spps.org/Inernational_Academy-LEAP.html. *See* Note, *Federal Funding for Newcomer Schools: A Bipartisan Immigrant Education Initiative*, 120 HARV. L. REV. 799 (2007). From their start, these schools prompted questions about potential civil rights violations due to segregation. Pam Belluck, *Newcomer Schools Raise Old Questions*, N.Y. TIMES, Mar. 26, 1995, at A39. But the Office for Civil Rights in the U.S. Department of Education dismissed an early complaint. Pam Belluck, *Complaint against Newcomer School*, N.Y. TIMES, Nov. 14, 1995, at B4. The Office for Civil Rights also has in the past treated newcomer schools as compatible with Title VI of the 1964 Civil Rights Act, which prohibits discrimination in programs receiving federal funding. *See* Note, *Federal Funding for Newcomer Schools*, *supra*, at 810–11 (citing Michael Williams, assistant secretary for civil rights, Department of Education, memorandum to Senior Staff, Office for Civil Rights, at n. 8 (Sept. 27, 1991), www.ed.gov/about/offices/list/ocr/docs/lau1991.html).

108. Deirdre Fernandes, *Schools to Open Special Program: Newcomer's Academy Will Help Hispanics with Language Barrier*, WINSTON-SALEM JOURNAL, Apr. 22, 2003, at A1. *See* Center for Applied Linguistics, www.cal.org/resources/digest/lucas001.html ("Newcomer schools are special schools for recent immigrant students. A major purpose of these schools is to support the adjustment of recent immigrants into their new society and school. This includes, but is not limited

to, English language development and, in some cases, continued native language development. In many newcomer schools, students attend classes for half a day and then a regular middle or high school for the other half; in others, students attend all day for 6 months before they are enrolled in mainstream schools." (internal citations omitted)).

109. Note, *Federal Funding for Newcomer Schools, supra* note 107, at 802 (citing Richard Frey, *Hispanic Youth Dropping Out of U.S. Schools*, PEW HISPANIC CENTER 8, 10 fig. 6 (2003)).

110. CENTER FOR RESEARCH ON EDUCATION, DIVERSITY AND EXCELLENCE, UNIVERSITY OF CALIFORNIA, SANTA CRUZ, PROGRAM ALTERNATIVES FOR LINGUISTICALLY DIVERSE STUDENTS 18 (Fred Genesee ed., 1999).

111. Lucy Hood, *Educating Immigrant Students*, 4 CARNEGIE REPORTER 2, 5 (spring 2007). In a survey of new American adolescents in Massachusetts, 59.7 percent reported that their families provide support to relatives in their home country, and 20 percent reported major trauma experienced by their families since coming to the United States—with major trauma including serious illness, death, robberies, and involvement of child protection services. LISA H. THURAU-GRAY, RESPONSES OF YOUTH TO THE NEW YOUNG AMERICANS PROJECT SURVEY 16 (Juvenile Justice Law Center, Suffolk University Law School 2003), available at New England Juvenile Defender's Center, www.nejdc.net/downloads/nyap_report_021304.pdf.

112. Hood, *supra* note 111. *See also* Inside Schools, www.insideschools.org/fs/school_profile.php?id=1176.

113. *See* Note, *Federal Funding for Newcomer Schools, supra* note 107, at 811 (discussing Haywood, California, Language Center).

114. Deborah J. Short, *Newcomer Programs: An Educational Alternative for Secondary Immigrant Students*, 34 EDUC. & URB. SOC'Y 173, 181 (2002).

115. *Id.* at 177.

116. *Compare* Cal. Educ. Code § 311 (West 2002 & Supp. 2006), *with* Mass. Gen. Laws Ann. Ch. 71A § 109 (West. Supp. 2005).

117. *See* Note, *Federal Funding for Newcomer Schools, supra* note 107, at 815–20 (proposing federal funding).

118. *See* Robert A. Frahm, *Big Test, No Hope: No Child Left Behind Offers No Break for Language Barrier*, HARTFORD COURANT, Oct. 19, 2003, at A1.

119. Erin Archerd, Recent Development, *Spanish-language Test Accommodations: Recommended or Required by NCLB?* 9 HARV. LATINO L. REV. 163 (2006).

120. Jared Stearns & Suzanne Sataline, *New Immigrants Get Break on MCAS Test*, BOSTON GLOBE, Feb. 21, 2004, at B1. *See* Press Release, U.S. Department of Education, *Secretary Paige Announces New Policies to Help English-language Learners* (Feb. 19, 2004), press release, www.ed.gov/news/pressreleases/2004/02/02092004.html.

121. *Id.*

122. Stearns & Sataline, *supra* note 120.

123. *Id.* at B4 (quoting Steven Mills, deputy school superintendent in Worcester).

124. Virginia opted out; Utah House of Representatives voted to prioritize Utah's educational goals above federal educational goals.

125. *See* Li, *supra* note 71, at 565.

126. LEARNING IN THE GLOBAL ERA: INTERNATIONAL PERSPECTIVES ON GLOBALIZATION AND EDUCATION (Marcelo M. Suárez-Orozco ed., 2007).

127. *See* Kimberly J. Jenkins, *Constitutional Lessons for the Next Generation of Public Single-sex Elementary and Secondary Schools*, 47 WM. & MARY L. REV. 1953 (2006); Nancy Levit, *Embracing Segregation: The Jurisprudence of Choice and Diversity in Race and Sex Separatism in Schools*, 2005 U. ILL. L. REV. 455; Denise C. Morgan, *Anti-subordination Analysis after United States v. Virginia: Evaluating the Constitutionality of K–12 Single-sex Public Schools*, 1999 U. CHI. LEGAL. F. 381.

128. *See, e.g.*, NANCY F. COTT, THE GROUNDING OF MODERN FEMINISM (1987); Barbara Welter, *The Cult of True Womanhood: 1820–1860*, 18 AM. QUARTERLY 151 (summer 1966); Martha Minow, *"Forming underneath Everything That Grows": Toward a New History of Family Law*, 1985 WIS. L. REV. 819. The notion of "true womanhood" did not extend to African-American women. *See* Vera L. Williams, *Reform or Retrenchment? Single Sex Education and the Construction of Race and Gender*, 2004 WIS. L. REV. 15, 38, 55–57.

129. A. Brown et al., *The Equal Rights Amendment: A Constitutional Basis for Equal Rights for Women*, 80 YALE L.J. 871, 876 (1971); Martha Minow, *Rights of One's Own*, 98 HARV. L. REV. 1084 (1985) (reviewing ELISABETH GRIFFITH, IN HER OWN RIGHT: THE LIFE OF ELIZABETH CADY STANTON (1984)).

130. Debates continue, as I have explored elsewhere, over the meaning of equality. *See* Martha Minow, *Differences among Difference*, 1 UCLA WOMEN'S L. J. 165 (1991); Martha Minow, *Adjudicating Differences: Conflicts among Feminist Lawyers*, *in* CONFLICTS IN FEMINISM 149 (M. Hirsh & E. Keller eds., 1990); Martha Minow, *Feminist Reason: Getting It and Losing It,* 38 J. Legal Educ. 47 (1988).

131. ILANA DEBARE, WHERE GIRLS COME FIRST: THE RISE, FALL, AND SURPRISING REVIVAL OF GIRLS' SCHOOLS (2005); Julia F. Mead, *Single-gender "Innovations": Can Publicly Funded Single-gender School Choice Options Be Constitutionally Justified?* 39 EEDUC. ADMIN. Q. 164, 177 (2003); Peter Meyer, *Learning Separately: The Case for Single-sex Schools*, 8 EDUC. NEXT 10 (winter 2008).

132. DEBARE, *supra* note 131, at 17; ROSEMARY C. SALOMONE, SAME, DIFFERENT, EQUAL: RETHINKING SINGLE-SEX SCHOOLING (2003); JANICE STREITMATTER, FOR GIRLS ONLY: MAKING A CASE FOR SINGLE-SEX SCHOOLING (1999); DAVID TYACK & ELIZABETH HANSOT, LEARNING TOGETHER: A HISTORY OF COEDUCATION IN AMERICAN PUBLIC SCHOOLS (1992).

133. DEBARE, *supra* note 131, at 30–40; TYACK & HANSOT, *supra* note 132.

134. *See* Bray v. Lee, 337 F. Supp. 934 (D. Mass. 1972); Berkelman v. San Francisco Unified School District, 501 F.2d 1264 (9th Cir. 1974).

135. DEBARE, *supra* note 131, at 49.

136. TYACK & HANSOT, *supra* note 132; Sally Schwager, *A Familiar Mingling: Review of Learning Together*, 252 SCIENCE 1324 (1991).

137. DEBARE, *supra* note 131, at 51–52, 67; TYACK & HANSOT, *supra* note 132.

138. TYACK & HANSOT, *supra* note 132, at 109–24.

139. DEBORAH L. RHODE, JUSTICE AND GENDER 292 (1989).

140. The first wave women's rights movement grew from the movement to abolish slavery; the second wave women's rights movement drew from the movement for racial equality but also reflected independent sources. President Kennedy created a commission on women's equality in 1961, before he became engaged in the debates over racial justice, and Congress enacted the Equal Pay Act in 1963, before the 1964 Civil Rights Act. The National Organization for Women was not founded until 1966.

141. Paul Burstein, *The Impact of EEO Law: A Social Movement Perspective, in* LEGACIES OF THE 1964 CIVIL RIGHTS ACT 129, 142 (Bernard Grofman ed., 2000).

142. HISTORY OF THE 1964 CIVIL RIGHTS ACT 234 (1985); *see also* 110 Cong. Rec. 2581 (1964) (statement of Congresswoman Edith Green) (suggesting that Rep. Howard W. Smith proposed to insert "sex" to prevent the passage of Title VII); Jo Freeman, *How "Sex" Got into Title VII: Persistent Opportunism as a Maker of Public Policy*, 9 L. & INEQUALITY 163, 165 (1991); Robert C. Bird, *More Than a Congressional Joke: A Fresh Look at the Legislative History of Sex Discrimination of the 1964 Civil Rights Act*, 3 WM. & MARY J. WOMEN & L. 137, 137 (1997).

143. Title IX was renamed in 2002 for its lead drafter, Representative Patsy Mink.

144. *See* Julia Lamber, *Intercollegiate Athletics: The Program Expansion Standard under Title IX's Policy Interpretation*, 12 S. CAL. REV. L. & WOMEN'S STUD. 31 (2002).

145. *See* 20 U.S.C. § 1681(a)(1).

146. 20 U.S.C. § 1681(a)(5).

147. For thoughtful treatments, *see* Robert L. Hayman, Jr., & Nancy Levit, *Un-natural Things: Constructions of Race, Gender, and Disability, in* CROSSROADS, DIRECTIONS, AND A NEW CRITICAL RACE THEORY 173–75 (Francisco Valdes et al. eds., 2002); Christine A. Littleton, *Reconstructing Sexual Equality*, 75 CAL. L. REV. 1279 (1987).

148. *E.g.,* Michael M. v. Superior Court, 450 U.S. 464 (1981); Geduldig v. Aiello, 417 U.S. 484 (1974).

149. SALOMONE, *supra* note 132, at 185.

150. EILEEN MCDONAGH & LAURA PAPPANO, PLAYING WITH THE BOYS: WHY SEPARATE IS NOT EQUAL IN SPORTS (2007).

151. *See* Denise C. Morgan, *Finding a Constitutionally Permissible Path to Sex Equality: The Young Women's Leadership School of East Harlem*, 14 N.Y.L. SCH. J. HUM. RTS. 95, 112 (1997).

152. *See* Ruth Bader Ginsburg, *Gender and the Constitution*, 44 U. CINN. L. REV. 1 (1975). Ginsburg also recognized that in some instances, the institutions themselves would need to change rather than expecting women to assimilate to institutions designed without them in mind. *See* JOAN WILLIAMS, UNBENDING GENDER: WHY FAMILY AND WORK CONFLICT AND WHAT TO DO ABOUT IT 219 (2000). See Cary Franklin, Sex Roles and the Foundations of Constitutional Sex Discrimination Law (unpublished paper, on file with Author).

153. WILLIAMS, *supra* note 152, at 81–107; American Civil Liberties Union, *Tribute: The Legacy of Ruth Bader Ginsburg and WRP Staff* (Mar. 7, 2006), www.aclu. org/womensrights/gen/24412pub20060307.html; Susan Moke, *Gender*, www.indiana.edu/rcapub/v18n2/p17.html; SALOMONE, *supra* note 312, at 50–53. The Supreme Court struck down a statute preferring men over women as administrators of estates without identifying a standard of review. Reed v. Reed, 404 U.S. 71 (1971). Again without a clear standard, the Court then rejected differential treatment of male and female spouses of members of the armed forces for purposes of dependency benefits. Frontiero v. Richardson, 411 U.S. 677 (1973). The Court applied intermediate scrutiny in a 1976 case rejecting a statute prohibiting the sale of "nonintoxicating" beer to males under the age of twenty-one and females under the age of eighteen. Craig v. Boren, 429 U.S. 190 (1976); United States v. Virginia, 518 U.S. 515 (1996).

154. Frontiero v. Richardson, 411 U.S. at 690–91 (rejecting requirement of proof of dependency for husbands of armed services members, given the

automatic dependency allowance for wives of armed forces members); Reed v. Reed, 404 U.S. at 73–74 (rejecting state preference for men rather than women as administrators of estates); Weinberger v. Wisenfeld, 420 U.S. 636, 652–53 (1975) (rejecting exclusion of widowers from social security program supporting widows).

155. Mississippi University for Women v. Hogan, 458 U.S. 718 (1982).

156. United States v. Virginia, 518 U.S. at 557–58.

157. Vorchheimer v. School District of Philadelphia, 532 F.2d 880 (3d Cir. 1976), aff'd, 430 U.S. 703 (1977) (by an equally divided Court).

158. Id. at 881–83 (summarizing trial court findings).

159. Vorchheimer v. School District of Philadelphia, 400 F. Supp. 326 (E.D. Pa. 1975), rev'd, 532 F.2d 880 (3d Cir. 1976).

160. 20 U.S.C. § 1702(a)(1) (2007).

161. 20 U.S.C. § 1703(a) (2007).

162. Vorchheimer v. School District of Philadelphia, 532 F.2d at 887–88.

163. Id., at 889 (Gibbons, J., dissenting and referring to Plessy); id. (discussing 20 U.S.C. § 1703(c)).

164. NANCY LEVIT & ROBERT R. M. VERCHICK, FEMINIST LEGAL THEORY: A PRIMER 95 (2006).

165. Petition for Writ of Certiorari, Vorchheimer v. School District of Philadelphia, 430 U.S. 703 (No. 76–37).

166. Mississippi University for Women v. Hogan, 458 U.S. 718 (1982) (requiring an "exceedingly persuasive justification" for sex-based distinctions).

167. Newberg v. Board of Public Education, 26 Pa. D. & C. 3d 682 (Ct. Com. Pl., Phila. 1983).

168. SALOMONE, supra note 132, at 126.

169. Philadelphia High School for Girls, webgui.phila.k12.pa.us/schools/g/girlshigh/about-us; SALOMONE, supra note 132, at 26–32. Salomone reports that its admissions policy does not exclude boys, and people at the school respond to the occasional inquiry from a boy applicant with help finding an appropriate alternative. Id. at 32.

170. Mead, supra note 131, at 171, 177.

171. See Jill Elaine Hasday, The Principle and Practice of Women's "Full Citizenship": A Case Study of Sex-segregated Public Education, 101 MICH. L. REV. 755 (2002).

172. Subsequent developments address whether the options must be "comparable" rather than "equal." See Kay Bailey Hutchinson, Foreword, The Lesson of Single-sex Public Education: Both Successful and Constitutional, 50 AM. U. L. REV. 1075 (2001) (discussing United States v. Virginia, 518 U.S. 515 (1996), and H.R. 4577, 106th Cong. (2d. Sess. 2000), signed into law and effective through Sept. 30, 2001). "Comparable" public school programs may signal similar quality while "equal" programs suggests identical offerings; hence a comparable girls' school might not include the same opportunities for computer science as the boys' school and still on some views satisfy the equal protection clause. Id. at 1080 (quoting United States v. Virginia, 518 U.S. at 565 (Rehnquist, C.J., concurring)).

173. Garrett v. Board of Education Detroit, 775 F. Supp. 1004 (E.D. Mich. 1991). The court also pointed to indications that the Office of Civil Rights in the Department of Education construed Title IX to forbid sex-based admissions in public elementary schools. See id. at n. 9 (presenting the view that subsequent agency staff have changed).

174. For a description of Spencer Holland's views and a discussion of his subsequent work in mentoring programs, *see* Rhonda Wells-Wilbon & Spencer Holland, *Social Learning Theory and the Influence of Male Role Models on African-American Children in PROJECT 2000*, 6 QUALITATIVE REPORT (Dec. 4, 2001), www.nova.edu/ssss/QR/QR6-4/wellswilbon.html.

175. SALOMONE, *supra* note 132, at 130-32.

176. *See* Charles Vergon, *Male Academies for At-risk Urban Youth: Legal and Policy Lessons from the Detroit Experience*, 79 ED. LAW REP. 351, 352 (1993); Gregory Huskisson, *Preserving Manhood: Civic, Political Leaders Unite to Rescue Young Black Males at Risk*, DET. FREE PRESS, Jan. 29, 1991, at 1B. For these references and other insights about the situation, I learned from reading Jia Michelle Cobb, *Resurrecting Civil Rights Litigation as a "Problem-solving" Tool: The Lawyers' Role in Garrett v. Board of Education* (spring 2005) (unpublished paper, on file with author).

177. *See* Brief of Amici Curiae States in Support of the Commonwealth of Virginia at 8-11 (Nos. 94-1941, 94-2107), at 18 (cited in William Henry Hurd, *Gone with the Wind? VMI's Loss and the Future of Single-sex Public Education*, 4 DUKE J. GENDER L. & POL'Y 27, 39 n. 99 (1997)).

178. *U.S. Judge Blocks Plan for All-male Public Schools in Detroit*, N.Y. TIMES, Aug. 16, 1991; *All-male School Gets Green Light in Detroit*, N.Y. TIMES, Mar. 1, 1991; Brenda Gilchrist, *Leaders Start Organizing Protest for Male Schools*, DET. FREE PRESS, Aug. 19, 1991, at 1B; Michael John Weber, *Immersed in an Educational Crisis: Alternative Programs for African-American Males*, 45 STAN. L. REV. 1099 (1993); Note, *Inner-City Single-Sex Schools: Educational Reform or Invidious Discrimination?*, 105 HARV. L. REV. 1741 (1992).

179. As one scholar commented, "[t]he practice of sex-segregated public education...has historically been entangled in both racial and class stratification." Hasday, *supra* note 171, at 757.

180. Rosemary Salomone, *The Legality of Single-sex Education in the United States*, *in* GENDER IN POLICY AND PRACTICE: PERSPECTIVES ON SINGLE SEX AND COEDUCATIONAL SCHOOLING 53 (Amanda Datnow & Lea Hubbard eds., Routledge Falmer 2002).

181. *Id.* at 1006-7.

182. *See* Linda McClain, *"Irresponsible" Reproduction*, 47 HASTINGS L.J. 339, 446 (1996) ("Particularly when differences such as race, ethnicity, and class exist, there are risks of incomprehension and misinterpretation, as well as solipsistic use of one's own experience as a measure or norm.").

183. Salomone, *supra* note 180, at 136. On local support for the all-male academies, *see All-male Schools; McGriff's Inflammatory Remarks Don't Aid Her Cause*, DET. FREE PRESS, Aug. 15, 1991, at 12A (superintendent of schools describing ACLU and NOW as "outsiders"); Brenda J. Gilchrist, *Leaders Start Organizing Protest for Male Schools*, DET. FREE PRESS, Aug. 19, 1991, at 1B.

184. Mary B. W. Tabor, *Planners of a New Public School for Girls Look to Two Cities*, N.Y. TIMES, July 22, 1996, at B1-2.

185. *See, e.g.,* Inesse Baram-Blackwell, *Separating Dick and Jane: Single-sex Public Education under the Washington State Equal Rights Amendment*, 81 WASH. L. REV. 337, 361 (2006).

186. United States v. Virginia, 518 U.S. 515 (2009); Jacques Steinberg, *All-girls Public School to Open Despite Objections*, N.Y. TIMES, Aug. 14, 1996 at B1. This juxtaposition provides the opening for Rosemary Salomone's 2003 book, which

suggests that the links between the two events expose assumptions not only about sex and schooling but also about race and poverty. *See* SALOMONE, *supra* note 132; Michael Heise, *Survey of Book: Are Single-sex Schools Inherently Unequal?* 102 MICH. L. REV. 1219 (2004) (reviewing ROSEMARY C. SALOMONE, SAME, DIFFERENT, EQUAL: RETHINKING SINGLE-SEX SCHOOLING (2003)).

187. Danielle Burton, *10 Things You Didn't Know about Ruth Bader Ginsburg*, U.S. NEWS & WORLD REPORT, Oct. 1, 2007, www.usnews.com/articles/news/national/2007/10/01/10-things-you-didnt-know-about-ruth-bader-ginsburg.html.

188. *See* Cornelia T. L. Pillard, *United States v. Virginia: The Virginia Military Institute, Where the Men are Men and So Are the Women*, in CIVIL RIGHTS STORIES 265 (Myriam Gilles & Risa Goluboff eds., 2007) ("Given the other problems facing American women, like entrenched economic inequality and rampant sexual exploitation and violence, admission to VMI might seem low on the list of priorities for the United States government's civil rights enforcers and the big guns of the women's rights bar").

189. *Id.* at 270.

190. SALOMONE, *supra* note 132, at 165 (quoting Justice Ginsburg). *See also* Carol Pressman, *The House That Ruth Built: Justice Ruth Bader Ginsburg, Gender, and Justice*, 14 N.Y.L. SCH. J. HUM. RTS. 311 (1997).

191. *See* Cass R. Sunstein, *The Supreme Court, 1995 Term, Foreword: Leaving Things Undecided*, 110 HARV. L. REV. 4, 75 (1996).

192. Pillard, *supra* note 188, at 277.

193. United States v. Virginia, 518 U.S. at 555–56.

194. *Id.* at 534; William Henry Hurd, who represented Virginia, later argued that the state's problem was not the exclusion of women from VMI but the failure to provide a separate but equal alternative. Hurd, *supra* note 177. Similarly, Linda Peter argued that Justice Scalia was wrong to worry that the VMI decision signaled the end of single-sex education because the decision was limited to a situation lacking a remotely equivalent alternative education for the excluded group. Linda L. Peter, Note, *What Remains of Public Choice and Parental Rights: Does the VMI Decision Preclude Exclusive Schools or Classes Based on Gender?*, 33 CAL. W. L. REV. 249 (1997).

195. United States v. Virginia, 518 U.S. at 565 (Rehnquist, C.J., concurring).

196. Heise, *supra* note 186, at 1229.

197. United States v. Virginia, 518 U.S. at 534 n. 7.

198. United States v. Virginia, 518 U.S. at 535.

199. Pillard, *supra* note 188, at 290 (footnote omitted).

200. DEBARE, *supra* note 131, at 250 (quoting Ann Rubenstein Tisch). *See also* Joe Dolce, *The Power of One*, O THE OPRAH MAGAZINE, Oct. 2001, www.oprah.com/article/omagazine/uyl_omag_200110_tisch.

201. Elizabeth Weil, *Teaching Boys and Girls Separately*, N.Y. TIMES, Mar. 2, 2008, at MM38.

202. *See, e.g.*, Young Women's Leadership Network, Our Schools, The Young Women's Leadership Network School of East Harlem, www.ywlfoundation.org/network_schl_harl.htm (last visited Oct. 15, 2009).

203. Private support contributes about $1,000 per student in addition to the public funds, and Ann Rubenstein Tisch has also helped to secure links with artistic, corporate, and postsecondary partners, opening opportunities for the students. SALOMONE, *supra* note 132, at 21–22. Tisch founded the Young Women's Leadership Foundation, which supports this and other similar schools and lobbies

for them. Young Women's Leadership Foundation, web site, www.ywlfounda-tion.org/about_what2.htm#5 (last visited Oct. 15, 2009) (reporting influence on No Child Left Behind funding of single-sex instruction, and reporting that by the 2004–5 school year, thirty-three single-sex public schools would be in opera-tion and roughly ninety other coeducational public schools would offer single-gender classrooms). *See also* Ann Richards School for Young Women Leaders, annrichardsschool.org/about/index.php (citing influence of the model of the Harlem school, copied in New York, Chicago, and Texas) (last visited Oct. 15, 2009).

204. Young Women's Leadership Foundation, *supra* note 203. The school also reports that 87 percent of its alumnae are still enrolled in college or have gradu-ated; student enrollment is 59 percent Hispanic; 34 percent African-American; 3 percent Asian; and 3 percent other. *Id.*

205. National Association of Secondary School Principals, *2005 Breakthrough High Schools*, www. principals.org/s_nassp, at 9 (follow "Awards and Recogni-tion"; then follow "Breakthrough Schools"; then follow "Breakthrough Schools Past and Present") (last visited Oct. 15 2009).

206. Morgan, *supra* note 127 (supporter); Wendy Kaminer, *The Trouble with Single-sex Schools*, Atlantic Monthly, Apr. 1998, at 22; Fred Kaplan, *Storm Gathers over School in Flower*, Boston Globe, Feb. 23, 1998, at A1 (describing lawsuit by National Organization for Women and New York Civil Liberties Union claiming the school violates Title IX). For a thoughtful treatment of the suit and underlying issues, *see* Salomone, *supra* note 132, at 1–25, 61–63. For detailed discussion of the splintering of civil rights and women's groups, *see* Nancy Levit, The Gender Line: Men, Women, and the Law 153–66 (1998).

207. Rosemary C. Salomone, *Feminist Voices in the Debate over Single-sex Schooling: Finding Common Ground*, 11 Mich. J. Gender & L. 63, 70 (2004).

208. *See* Salomone, *supra* note 132; Kaminer, *supra* note 206.

209. Interview with Professor Vicki Jackson, Georgetown Law Center, depu-ty assistant attorney general, Office of Legal Counsel, U.S. Department of Jus-tice, 2000–2001 (Apr. 9, 2008); interview with Dean Elena Kagan, Harvard Law School, who served in the White House domestic policy and legal staffs during the Clinton administration (July 12, 2007).

210. Salomone, *supra* note 132, at 17; Rachel P. Kovner, *Education Dept. Readies Rules to Support Single-sex Schools*, N.Y. Sun, May 1, 2002, at 1.

211. Salomone, *supra* 132, at 18.

212. *See* Weil, *supra* note 201.

213. Salome, *supra* note 132, at 150.

214. For discussion of the racial dimension of conflicts over single-sex educa-tion, *see* Galen Sherwin, *Single-sex Schools and the Antisegregation Principle*, 30 N.Y.U. Rev. L. & Soc. Change 35, 38 (2005).

215. Shortchanging Girls, Shortchanging America: A Nationwide Poll to Assess Self-Esteem, Educational Experiences, Interest in Math and Science, and Career Aspirations of Girls and Boys Ages 9–15 (American Association of University Women 1991) (describing how girls' self-esteem falls during puberty and how girls are subtly discouraged from careers in math and science). Popular books on the subject came out in the early 1990s. *See* Myra Sadker & David Sadker, Failing at Fairness: How America's Schools Cheat Girls 1 (1995); Mary Bray Pipher, Reviving Ophelia; Saving the Selves of Adolescent Girls (1994); Judy Mann, The Difference: Discovering the

HIDDEN WAYS WE SILENCE GIRLS—FINDING ALTERNATIVES THAT CAN GIVE THEM A VOICE (1996). In 1993, Harvard University Press reissued the landmark work CAROL GILLIGAN, IN A DIFFERENT VOICE: PSYCHOLOGICAL THEORY AND WOMEN'S DEVELOPMENT (1982). *See* Jenkins, *supra* note 127, at 1963–64.

216. *See, e.g.*, Catherine G. Krupnick, *Women and Men in the Classroom: Inequality and Its Remedies*, ON TEACHING AND LEARNING 1–6 (1985).

217. On sexual harassment, *see* Campbell Leaper & Christa Spears Brown, *Perceived Experiences with Sexism among Adolescent Girls*, 79 CHILD DEVELOPMENT 685–704 (2008); AAUW EDUCATIONAL FOUNDATION, HOSTILE HALLWAYS: BULLYING, TEASING, AND SEXUAL HARASSMENT IN SCHOOL (2001), www.aauw.org/research/upload/hostilehallways.pdf; Nan Stein, Deborah L. Tolman, Michelle V. Porche, & Renee Spencer, *Gender Safety: A New Concept for Safer and More Equitable Schools*, 1 J. SCHOOL VIOLENCE 35, 35–49 (2002). Although one AAUW report indicates that coeducation shortchanges girls, *see* SHORTCHANGING GIRLS, SHORTCHANGING AMERICA, *supra* note 215, another presses that improving coeducation rather than providing single-sex education should be the remedy, *see* BEYOND THE GENDER WARS: A CONVERSATION ABOUT GIRLS, BOYS, AND EDUCATION (AMERICAN ASSOCIATION OF UNIVERSITY WOMEN 2001), www.aauw.org/research/upload/BeyondGenderWar.pdf. The American Association of University Women (AAUW) sees itself as an organization having a "position" on the legal question. *See AAUW's Position on Single-sex Education* (2009), http://www.aauw.org/advocacy/issue_advocacy/actionpages/singlesex.cfm (last visited Oct. 15, 2009),

218. Commentators cast more doubt on the constitutional basis for all-male schools, given the historical advantage of males in education; *see* Levit, *supra* note 127; Sharon K. Mollman, *The Gender Gap: Separating the Sexes in Public Education*, 68 IND. L.J. 149 (1992). *See also* Jody S. Cohen, *Women Outpacing Men on U.S. College Campuses*, CHI. TRIB., July 12, 2006, at C3.

219. Weil, *supra* note 201. *See* Nancy Levit, *Separating Equals: Educational Research and Long-term Consequences of Sex Segregation*, 67 GEO. WASH. L. REV. 451, 469–72 (1999).

220. *Id.* at 469–72; Weil, *supra* note 201.

221. *See* SALOMONE, *supra* note 132, at 80–81 (discussing WILLIAM POLLACK, REAL BOYS: RESCUING OUR SONS FROM THE MYTH OF BOYHOOD (1998)); DAN KINDLON & MICHAEL THOMPSON, RAISING CAIN: PROTECTING THE EMOTIONAL LIFE OF BOYS (2000).

222. *See, e.g.*, Brian R. Ballou, *State's Eighth-graders Score Well in Writing Test, Despite Gender Gap*, BOSTON GLOBE, Apr. 4, 2008, at B3 (60 percent of girls in Massachusetts scored at or above proficient in the eighth-grade writing assessment compared with 32 percent of the boys; nationwide, 41 percent of the girls scored proficient or above contrasted with 20 percent of the boys).

223. On underachievement by boys and men, *see* Judith Warner, *What Girls Ought to Learn from Boys in "Crisis,"* N.Y. TIMES, July 12, 2006, at A1 (gender gap shows disadvantage for low-income males across most races); WILLIAM S. POLLACK, REAL BOYS; VOICES (2000); CHRISTINA HOFF SOMMERS, THE WAR AGAINST BOYS: HOW MISGUIDED FEMINISM IS HARMING OUR YOUNG MEN (2000). Although special concerns are rightly raised about black boys' academic risks, the data suggest problems across the color line. Cynthia Tucker, *Pushy Parents Are the Best Boost for Black Boys*, ATLANTA JOURNAL-CONSTITUTION, May 25, 2003, at 10C. *But see* Caryl Rivers & Rosalind Chait Barnett, Opinion, *The Myth of "The Boy Crisis,"* WASH. POST, Apr. 9, 2006, at B1; Tamar Lewin, *A More Nuanced Look at*

Men, Women and College, N.Y. TIMES, July 12, 2006, at B1 (study by American Council on Education based on 2003–4 data finds men of all races more likely than women to be in college).

224. No Child Left Behind Act of 2001, 20 U.S.C.A. § 7215(a)(23) (2002).

225. Nondiscrimination on the Basis of Sex in Education Programs or Activities Receiving Federal Financial Assistance, 67 Fed. Reg. 31,098 (May 8, 2002) (to be codified at 34 C.F.R. pt. 106).

226. Bill McAuliffe, *Feds May Clear Way for Single-sex Classes*, Minneapolis STAR TRIB., June 14, 2004, at 3B; Nora Kizer Bell, Opinion, *Single-gender Ed: Not Just an Alternative*, CHRISTIAN SCIENCE MONITOR, Dec. 30, 2002, at 21.

227. Nondiscrimination on the Basis of Sex in Education Programs or Activities Receiving Federal Financial Assistance, 69 Fed. Reg. 11,276, 11,277 (Mar. 9, 2004) (to be codified at 34 C.F.R. pt. 106). At the same time, the congressional reauthorization of Title I spending for schools serving poor children made single-sex schools eligible for funding. Press release, U.S. Department of Education, *Department to Provide More Educational Options for Parents* (Mar. 3, 2004), www.ed.gov/news/pressreleases/2004/03/03032004.html.

228. *See* Office for Civil Rights, Department of Education, Guidelines Regarding Single Sex Classes and Schools (May 3, 2002), www.ed.gov/about/offices/list/ocr/t9-guidelines-ss.html, for the Bush administration's interpretation of the law.

229. Nondiscrimination on the Basis of Sex in Education Programs or Activities Receiving Federal Financial Assistance, 69 Fed. Reg. at 11276; 10:11 National Association of State Boards of Education, Policy Update, Single Sex Schools, www.nasbe.org/Educational_Issues/Policy_Updates/10_11.html(last visited June 19, 2006); Kelley Beaucar Vlahos, *Single-sex Schools Score Big Victory*, FOX NEWS.COM, Mar. 23, 2004, www.foxnews.com/story/0,2933,114899,00.html.

230. *See supra* note 227.

231. Nondiscrimination on the Basis of Sex in Education Programs or Activities Receiving Federal Financial Assistance, 71 Fed. Reg. 62,530, 62,532 (Oct. 25, 2006) (to be codified at 34 C.F.R. pt. 106).

232. *Id.* at 62,533.

233. *Id.* at 62,535.

234. *Id.* at 62,537.

235. *Id.* at 62,540.

236. *Id.* at 62,532. The school system might be able, therefore, to establish a single-sex school for boys while providing the same coursework and opportunities for girls in only a coeducational setting.

237. Diana Jean Schemo, *Federal Rules Back Single-sex Public Education*, N.Y. TIMES, Oct. 25, 2006, at A1.

238. 69 Fed. Reg. 11,276.

239. 71 Fed. Reg. 62,534.

240. *Id.* at 62,533.

241. *See id.* at 62,534–35.

242. Schemo, *supra* 237.

243. *Id.*

244. Mead, *supra* note 131, at 182.

245. A.N.A v. U. S. Department of Education, Civil Action No. 3:08-cv-00004-CRS (W.D. Ky., May 19, 2008).

246. The complaint argues that that the 2006 federal regulations apparently permitting the Kentucky school's practices were promulgated in an arbitrary and capricious manner, as they were issued despite being criticized in 96 percent of the public comments and because they lack empirical support for claimed benefits. It also argues that the regulations violate Title IX by permitting exclusion on the basis of sex from public educational programs. *Id.*

247. *Id.*

248. On debates over the uses of social science in educational reform, *see* chapter 6. Advocates increasingly call attention to boys' learning needs and educational difficulties while using the language of equal opportunity. Such arguments might reduce the chances of success for court challenges to the final rule. Depending on the variations in the design of schools—and different interpretations of these decisions—single-sex education could be constitutional or it could be unconstitutional, which in turn may depend on whether these schools are apparently effective in remedying educational disadvantage.

249. *See* Susan S. Klein et al., *Continuing the Journey toward Gender Equity*, 23 EDUC. RESEARCHER 13 (1994) (research on gender relations in the classroom is inconclusive); Michael Kimmel, *Saving the Males: The Sociological Implications of the Virginia Military Institute and the Citadel*, 14 GENDER & SOC'Y 494 (2000) (possible benefits for females in single-sex education but limited data especially on elementary schools); Diane S. Pollard, *Single-sex Education*, EDUC. DEV. CENTER, INC. (Oct. 1999) (insufficient evidence but initial indications suggest benefits for adolescent girls from single-sex settings offering an opportunity to consider gender identity issues); Kusum Singh, Claire Vaught, & Ethel W. Mitchell, *Single-sex Classes and Academic Achievement in Two Inner-city Schools*, 67 J. NEGRO EDUC. 157 (1998) (class grades better in the single-sex classes but test scores better in coed groups); Shirley Yates, *Boys' Goal Orientations, Self-concept and Achievement in the Transition from Single Sex to Coeducation*, REFEREED PROCEEDINGS OF THE 4TH INTERNATIONAL SELF CONFERENCE; Pamela Haag, *K–12 Single-sex Education: What Does the Research Say?* in AMERICAN ASSOCIATION OF UNIVERSITY WOMEN EDUCATIONAL FOUNDATION, SEPARATED BY SEX: A CRITICAL LOOK AT SINGLE-SEX EDUCATION FOR GIRLS (1998).

250. *See* Weil, *supra* note 201: "In 2005, the United States Department of Education, along with the American Institute for Research, tried to weigh in, publishing a meta-analysis comparing single-sex and coed schooling. The authors started out with 2,221 citations on the subject that they then whittled down to 40 usable studies. Yet even those 40 studies did not yield strong results: 41 percent favored single-sex schools, 45 percent found no positive or negative effects for either single-sex or coed schools, 6 percent were mixed (meaning they found positive results for one gender but not the other) and 8 percent favored coed schools. This meta-analysis is part of a larger project by the Department of Education being led by Cornelius Riordan, professor of Sociology at Providence College. He explained to me that such muddled findings are the norm for education research on school effects."

251. *See Separating Girls and Boys*, TEACHER, Jan. 1, 2007 (comparing views of Rosemary Salomone and Rosalind Chait Barnett).

252. *See* Joan Bertin, *Educational and Social Scientific Perspectives on All-female Education*, 14 N.Y. L. SCH. J. HUM. RTS. 175 (1998) (discussing VMI's brief).

253. *See* Fred A. Mael, *Single Sex and Coeducational Schooling: Relationships to Socioemotional and Academic Development*, 68 REV. OF EDUC. RES. 101, 117 (1998).

254. *See* Patricia B. Campbell & Ellen Wahl, *Of Two Minds: Single-sex Education, Coeducation, and the Search for Gender Equity in K–12 Public Schooling*, 14 N.Y.L. SCH. J. HUM. RTS. 289 (1998); Peter Daly & Neil Defty, *Extension of Single-sex Public School Provision: Evidential Concerns*, 18 EVALUATION & RES. IN EDUC. 129 (2004); Cynthia Fuchs Epstein, *Multiple Myths and Outcomes of Sex Segregation*, 14 N.Y.L. SCH. J. HUM. RTS. 185 (1998); Lea Hubbard & Amanda Datnow, *Do Single-sex Schools Improve the Education of Low-income and Minority Students? An Investigation of California's Public Single-gender Academies*, 36 ANTHROPOLOGY & EDUC. Q. 115, 117 (2005).

255. Valerie E. Lee & Anthony S. Bryk, *Effects of Single-sex Secondary Schools on Student Achievement and Attitudes*, 78 J. OF EDUC. PSYCHOL. 381 (1986); C. Riordan, *Single Gender Schools: Outcomes for African and Hispanic Americans*, 10 RESEARCH IN SOC. OF EDUC. AND SOCIALIZATION 177, 177–205 (1994); *See also* ANTHONY S. BRYK, VALERIE E. LEE, & PETER B. HOLLAND, CATHOLIC SCHOOLS AND THE COMMON GOOD (1993).

256. Riordan, *supra* note 255.

257. Herbert W. Marsh, *Effects of Attending Single-sex and Coeducational High Schools on Achievement, Attitudes, Behaviors, and Sex Differences*, 81 J. EDUC. PSYCHOL. 70 (1989).

258. Carolyn Jackson, *Can Single-sex Classes in Co-educational Schools Enhance the Learning Experiences of Girls and/or Boys? An Exploration of Pupils' Perceptions*, 28 BRIT. EDUC. RES. J. 37, 38–39 (2005) (discussing the reanalysis).

259. Hubbard & Datnow, *supra* 254, at 122–23.

260. *See, e.g.*, Thomas Spielhofer et al., *The Impact of School Size and Single-sex Education on Performance*, NATIONAL FOUNDATION FOR EDUCATION RESEARCH (2002), www.singlesexschools.org/NFER.pdf; MOLLY WARRINGTON ET AL., RAISING BOYS' ACHIEVEMENT IN PRIMARY SCHOOLS (2006).

261. *See* Valorie K. Vojdik, *Girls' Schools after VMI: Do They Make the Grade?* 4 DUKE J. GENDER L. & POL'Y 69 (1997).

262. *See* INTERPRETIVE SOCIAL SCIENCE: A SECOND LOOK (Paul Rabinow & William M. Sullivan eds., 1987); FIONA E. RAITT & M. SUZANNE ZEEDYK, THE IMPLICIT RELATION OF PSYCHOLOGY AND LAW: WOMEN AND SYNDROME EVIDENCE (2000); STEPHANIE RIGER, TRANSFORMING PSYCHOLOGY: GENDER IN THEORY AND PRACTICE (2000).

263. Haag, *supra* note 249.

264. Rivers & Barnett, *supra* note 223.

265. Critics of single-sex education charge that much assessment research is funded by think tanks with a particular political viewpoint and therefore is affected by such viewpoints. *See* Anne Connors, *East Harlem Girls School*, 14 N.Y.L. SCH. J. HUM. RTS. 33 (1998) (president of NYC NOW, opposing Young Women's Leadership School, suggests that most studies showing girls learn better in single-sex settings are funded by single-sex school proponents); Vojdik, *supra* note 261, at 95 (noting that research on the Young Women's Leadership School was sponsored by a "well-funded, conservative thinktank," the Manhattan Institute for Policy Research).

266. Morgan, *supra* note 151, at n. 81 (discussing studies).

267. Schemo, *supra* note 237 (quoting Stephanie Monroe).

268. *See* Laura Fortney, *Public Single-sex Elementary Schools: "Separate but Equal" in Gender Fifty Years Following Brown v. Board of Education*, 35 U. TOL. L. REV. 857, 886 (2004).

269. SALOMONE, *supra* note 132, at 114–15; GENDER GAPS: WHERE SCHOOLS STILL FAIL OUR CHILDREN (American Association of University Women, 1998), www.aauw.org/research/upload/gges.pdf.

270. An account of these developments hit the *New York Times*. Weil, *supra* note 201 (this account relies heavily on mass-market books). *See* LEONARD SAX, WHY GENDER MATTERS: WHAT PARENTS AND TEACHERS NEED TO KNOW ABOUT THE EMERGING SCIENCE OF SEX DIFFERENCES (2005); LEONARD SAX, BOYS ADRIFT: THE FIVE FACTORS DRIVING THE GROWING EPIDEMIC OF UNMOTIVATED BOYS AND UNDERACHIEVING YOUNG MEN (2007); MICHAEL GURIAN, BOYS AND GIRLS LEARN DIFFERENTLY: A GUIDE FOR TEACHERS AND PARENTS (2001). *See also* ABIGAIL NORFLEET JAMES, TEACHING THE MALE BRAIN: HOW BOYS THINK, FEEL, AND LEARN IN SCHOOL (2007).

271. *See* Weil, *supra* note 201.

272. *See* Caryl Rivers & Rosalind C. Barnett, *The Difference Myth*, BOSTON GLOBE, Oct. 28, 2007, at F1.

273. Marcella Bombardieri, *Summers' Remarks on Women Draw Fire*, BOSTON GLOBE, Jan. 17, 2005, at A1. Made at a small academic conference, Summers's remarks and the reaction to them provoked international news coverage, and the university posted a copy of Summers' remarks. Lawrence H. Summers, *Remarks at NBER Conference on Diversifying the Science and Engineering Workforce* (Jan. 14, 2005), www.president.harvard.edu/speeches/2005/nber.html. The issue was one of several cited by observers when Summers announced his resignation the next year. Daniel J. T. Schuker, *Summers Named Eliot Univ. Prof*, HARVARD CRIMSON, July 7, 2006.

274. *See* Mael, *supra* note 253; Sherwin, *supra* note 214. On the long-standing debate over cultural versus biological dimensions of gender differences, *see* Jerome Kagan, *Sex Roles: Biology and Culture*, 156 SCIENCE 371 (1967) (reviewing ELEANOR E. MACOBY, THE DEVELOPMENT OF SEX DIFFERENCES); Laura Severin & Mary Wyer, *The Science and Politics of the Search for Sex Differences*, editorial, 12 NWSA J. vii (fall 2000); ELEANOR MACOBY & CAROL N. JACKLIN, THE PSYCHOLOGY OF SEX DIFFERENCES (1974).

275. Weil, *supra* note 201 (quoting Salomone).

276. Hubbard & Datnow, *supra* note 254.

277. Caryl Rivers & Rosalind C. Barnett, *We Can All Learn Together*, L.A. TIMES, Oct. 2, 2006, at 13.

278. *See* Jackson, *supra* note 258.

279. *Id.*; Hubbard & Datnow, *supra* note 254.

280. Gary J. Simson, *Separate but Equal and Single-sex Schools*, 90 CORNELL L. REV. 443, 449–50 (2005).

281. Valerie E. Lee, Helen M. Marks, & Tina Byrd, *Sexism in Single-sex and Coeducational Independent Secondary School Classrooms*, 67 SOC. OF EDUC. 92 (1994).

282. Connors, *supra* note 265.

283. *See supra* chapter 1 (discussing DuBois; discussing Clarence Thomas).

284. Teresa Mendez, *Separating the Sexes: A New Direction for Public Education*, CHRISTIAN SCIENCE MONITOR, May 25, 2004, at 11.

285. Stephanie Wellen Levine, letter to the editor, N.Y. TIMES MAGAZINE, Mar. 16, 2008, at 12.

286. *See supra* note 188.

287. *See* Clark v. Arizona Interscholastic Association, 695 F.2d 1126 (9th Cir. 1982).

288. Weil, *supra* note 201, puts the current number of single-sex public high schools at forty-nine, while Carla Rivera of the *Los Angeles Times* estimates single-sex elementary and high schools: "Today, the National Association for Single Sex Public Education boasts of 253 schools available." Barbara Pytel, *Single Sex Classrooms: All Boys and All Girls in Classrooms—Do They Make a Difference?* (Dec. 5, 2006), Educational Issues http://educationalissues.suite101.com/article. cfm/single_sex_classrooms.

289. Jennifer Medina, *Boys and Girls Together, Taught Separately in Public School*, N.Y. TIMES, Mar. 11, 2009, at A24 (citing the National Association for Single-sex Public Education).

290. *See* Jenkins, *supra* note 127, at 63 (discussing difficulties in ensuring truly voluntary choice in that educators may press parents and students toward single-sex options).

291. *See* SALOMONE, *supra* note 132, at 239 (arguing there is no evidence that single-sex education is harmful and there is evidence that it can help some students).

292. United States v. Virginia, 518 U.S. 515 at 535.

293. *See* Sherwin, *supra* note 214 (single-sex schools are contrary to diversity as a value within schools).

294. The "coeducation" entry was moved to the "mixed-sex education" entry on May 9, 2008. *See* Wikipedia, *Mixed-sex Education*, http://en.wikipedia.org/ wiki/Mixed-sex_education (last visited Oct. 15, 2009).

295. *But see* JUDITH BUTLER, GENDER TROUBLE: FEMINISM AND THE SUBVERSION OF IDENTITY (1999); MICHEL FOUCAULT, HERCULINE BARBIN: BEING THE RECENTLY DISCOVERED MEMOIRS OF A NINETEENTH-CENTURY FRENCH HERMAPHRODITE (Richard McDougall trans., 1980).

296. "If you don't do it thoughtfully, you run the risk of reinforcing stereotypes and playing to students' weaknesses." Medina, *supra* note 289 (quoting Rosemary Salomone).

297. Hubbard & Datnow, *supra* note 254, at 122.

298. *Id.* at 123.

Chapter 3

1. Thomas Hehir & Sue Gamm, *Special Education: From Legalism to Collaboration, in* LAW AND SCHOOL REFORM: SIX STRATEGIES FOR PROMOTING EDUCATIONAL EQUITY 205 (Jay P. Heubert ed., 1999).

2. *E.g.*, Watson v. City of Cambridge, 32 N.E. 864 (Mass. 1893) (upholding exclusion of a disabled child "because he was too weak-minded to derive profit from instruction"); State *ex rel.* Beattie v. Board of Education, 172 N.W. 153 (Wis. 1919) (approving the exclusion of the child with disabilities "when its presence therein is harmful to the best interests of the school").

3. Board of Education v. State *ex rel.* Goldman, 191 N.E. 914 (Ohio Ct. App. 1934).

4. LINDA A. REDDY, INCLUSION OF DISABLED CHILDREN AND SCHOOL REFORM: A HISTORICAL PERSPECTIVE 5 (1999).

5. SEYMOUR B. SARASON & JOHN DORIS, EDUCATION HANDICAP, PUBLIC POL-ICY AND SOCIAL HISTORY: A BROADENED PERSPECTIVE ON MENTAL RETARDATION (1979).

6. *See id.*; ANN TURNBULL, RUD TURNBULL & MICHAEL L. WEHMEYER, EXCEP-TIONAL LIVES: SPECIAL EDUCATION IN TODAY'S SCHOOLS (5th ed. 2006).

7. *See* BURTON BLATT, IN AND OUT OF MENTAL RETARDATION: ESSAYS ON EDUCABILITY, DISABILITY, AND HUMAN POLICY (1981); Stephen Jay Gould, *Carrie Buck's Daughter*, 93 NAT. HIST. 14 (July 1984). *See also* BURTON BLATT & FRED KAPLAN, CHRISTMAS IN PURGATORY: A PHOTOGRAPHIC ESSAY ON MENTAL RETAR-DATION (1966).

8. *See* MARGRET A. WINZER, THE HISTORY OF SPECIAL EDUCATION: FROM ISOLATION TO INTEGRATION (1993). "The history of special education in the U.S. began after World War II, when a number of parent-organized advocacy groups surfaced. One of the first organizations was the American Association on Mental Deficiency, which held its first convention in 1947. By the early 1950s, fueled by the Civil Rights Movement, a number of other parent organizations were formed, including the United Cerebral Palsy Association, the Muscular Dystrophy Association, and John F. Kennedy's Panel on Mental Retardation. During the 1960s, an increasing level of school access was established for children with disabilities at the state and local levels." Learning Rx, History of Special Education, www.learningrx.com/history-of-special-education.htm (last visited Oct. 31, 2009).

9. Robert L. Hughes & Michael A. Rebell, *Special Educational Inclusion and the Courts: A Proposal for a New Remedial Approach*, 25 J.L. & EDUC. 523 (1996).

10. Anne Smith & Elizabeth B. Kozleski, *Witnessing Brown: Pursuit of an Equity Agenda in American Education,* 26 REMEDIAL & SPECIAL EDUC. 270 (2005).

11. Hobson had worked "at the Library of Congress as an economic researcher and then later as an social science statistical analyst with the Social Security Administration." *Guide to the Papers of Julius Hobson,* at the website of DC Public Library, http://dcpl.dc.gov/dcpl/cwp/view.asp?A=1264&Q=567171; (last visited Oct. 29, 2009); Harvard Library Biography Resource Center, Julius W(ilson) Hobson, www.galenet.com/servlet/BioRC (last visited Oct. 29, 2009).

12. *William Kunstler,* Obituary, NATION (Sept. 1995), http://findarticles.com/p/articles/ mi_hb1367/is_199509/ai_n6387555.

13. Tulane University, A Tradition of Discrimination, www.tulanelink.com/tulanelink/racist_legacy_01a.htm (last visited Nov. 7, 2009). His decision directing Tulane University to desegregate was reversed by the court of appeals on the grounds that the university had become private and hence outside the bounds of the Fourteenth Amendment. *See* Guillory v. Administrators of Tulane University, 203 F. Supp. 855 (D.C. La. 1962), *aff'd*, 306 F.2d 489 (5th Cir. 1962).

14. Plater Robinson, *A House Divided: A Study Guide on the History of Civil Rights in Louisiana* (1996), Southern Institute for Education and Research, www.southerninstitute.info/civil_rights_education/divided8.html.

15. *Id.* (quoting Judge Wright).

16. *Id.* (quoting Elie). *See also* A HOUSE DIVIDED (Xavier University Drexel Center 1987) (documentary film).

17. ADAM FAIRCLOUGH, RACE AND DEMOCRACY: THE CIVIL RIGHTS STRUGGLE IN LOUISIANA, 1915–1972, at 263 (1995).

18. M. Wood, *D.C. Circuit Has Special History among Appeals Courts, Roberts Says*, Apr. 26, 2005, Virginia Law School, www.law.virginia.edu/html/news/2005_spr/roberts.htm (last visited Nov. 9, 2009).

19. Hobson v. Hanson, 269 F. Supp. 401, 517-18 (D.D.C. 1967), *aff'd sub nom.*, Smuck v. Hobson, 408 F.2d 175 (D.C. Cir 1969). The three tracks were honors, general, and special education.

20. *Id.* The decision also criticized the segregation of class, due to the use of neighborhood school assignments.

21. *Id.* at 513.

22. Wolf v. Legislature of Utah, No. 182, 646 (3d Jud. Dist. Utah 1969), quoted in Hehir & Gamm, *supra* note 1, at 211 (citing Robert Burgdorf, *The Doctrine of the Least Restrictive Alternative*, *in* THE LEGAL RIGHTS OF HANDICAPPED PERSONS: CASES, MATERIALS, AND TEST 71-72 n. 80 (Robert Burgdorf ed., 1980)). *See* David L. Kirp, *Schools as Sorters: The Constitutional and Policy Implications of Student Classification*, 121 U. PA. L. REV. 705 (1973).

23. "Today, education is perhaps the most important function of state and local governments. Compulsory school attendance laws and the great expenditures for education both demonstrate our recognition of the importance of education to our democratic society. It is required in the performance of our most basic public responsibilities, even service in the armed forces. It is the very foundation of good citizenship. Today it is a principal instrument in awakening the child to cultural values, in preparing him for later professional training, and in helping him to adjust normally to his environment. In these days, it is doubtful that any child may reasonably be expected to succeed in life if he is denied the opportunity of an education. Such an opportunity, where the state has undertaken to provide it, is a right which must be made available to all on equal terms." Brown v. Board of Education, 347 U.S. 483, 493 (1954).

24. Wolf v. Legislature of Utah, No. 182, 646, quoted in Hehir & Gamm, *supra* note 1, at 276.

25. Jeffrey J. Zettel & Joseph Ballard, *The Education for All Handicapped Children Act of 1975, P.L. 94-142: Its History, Origins, and Concepts*, *in* SPECIAL EDUCATION IN AMERICA: ITS LEGAL AND GOVERNMENTAL FOUNDATIONS 12 (Joseph Ballard et al. eds., 1982).

26. Edwin W. Martin, Reed Martin, & Donna L. Terman, *The Legislative and Litigation History of Special Education*, 6 FUTURE OF CHILDREN 25, 27 (1996).

27. Gilhool worked for Philadelphia Community Legal Services and, after 1975, for Philadelphia's Public Interest Law Center; he later served as Pennsylvania's secretary of education.

28. *The Law: Rights for the Retarded*, TIME, Oct. 25, 1971, www.time.com/time/magazine/article/0,9171,877328,00.html.

29. FRED PELKA, THE ABC-CLIO COMPANION TO: THE DISABILITY RIGHTS MOVEMENT 137 (1997). Gilhool also devised initiatives to strengthen community services available for persons with disabilities. Pelka's authoritative history also describes Tom Gilhool as "the attorney most responsible for the rise of community services for people with developmental disabilities, allowing for their deinstitutionalization beginning in the 1970s." *Id.* at 137.

30. *Id.*

31. Pennsylvania Association of Retarded Children v. Commonwealth, 343 F. Supp. 279, 291 (E.D. Pa. 1972).

32. *Id.*; 334 F. Supp. 1257 (E.D. Pa. 1971).

33. 334 F. Supp. 1257–60; 343 F. Supp. 279 (order, injunction, and consent decree), www.faculty.piercelaw.edu/redfield/library/Pdf/case-parc.pennsylvania. pdf.

34. The court identified the problem: "(1) in the failure of the District of Columbia to provide publicly supported education and training to plaintiffs and other 'exceptional' children, members of their class, and (2) the excluding, suspending, expelling, reassigning and transferring of 'exceptional' children from regular public school classes without affording them due process of law." 348 F. Supp. 866, 868 (D.D.C. 1972).

35. *Id.* at 871.

36. *Id.* at 871.

37. *Id.* at 870.

38. *Id.* at 876.

39. Patricia M. Wald, *Frank M. Coffin Lecture on Law and Public Service: Whose Public Interest Is It Anyway? Advice for Altruistic Young Lawyers*, 47 ME. L. REV. 3, 11 (1995).

40. H.R. REP. NO. 332 (1974).

41. Martin et al., *supra* note 26, at 28.

42. *Id.* at 27–28.

43. Rehabilitation Act Amendments of 1974, Pub. L. No. 93–112 (codified as amended at 29 U.S.C. § 794).

44. Laura F. Rothstein, *Reflections on Disability Discrimination Policy—25 Years*, 22 U. ARK. LITTLE ROCK L. REV. 147 (2000).

45. Hairston v. Drosick, 423 F. Supp. 180 (S.D. W.Va. 1976).

46. *Id.* at 183.

47. Founded in 1950, the organization was first named the National Association for Retarded Children (1953–73), renamed the National Association for Retarded Citizens (1973–81), renamed the Association for Retarded Citizens of the United States (1981–92), and renamed "the Arc" in 1992. *The Arc's Name Changes throughout Its History*, www.thearc.org/NetCommunity/Page. aspx?&pid=403&srcid=270.

48. At the federal level, Congress enacted the Training of Professional Personnel Act of 1959, Pub. L. No. 86–158 (to train people to educate children with mental retardation); the Captioned Films Acts of 1958, Pub. L. No. 85–905 (training provisions for teachers of students with mental retardation), Pub. L. No. 85–926, and Pub. L. No. 87–715, which all supported the production and distribution of accessible films; and the Teachers of the Deaf Act of 1961, Pub. L. No. 87–276. Pub. L. No. 88–164 expanded previous specific training programs to include training across all disability areas. In addition, in 1965, the Elementary and Secondary Education Act, Pub. L. No. 89–10; the State Schools Act, Pub. L. No. 89–313 (providing states with direct grant assistance to help educate children with disabilities); the Handicapped Children's Early Education Assistance Act of 1968, Pub. L. No. 90–538; and the Economic Opportunities Amendments of 1972, Pub. L. No. 92–424 (authorizing support for early childhood programs and increasing Head Start enrollment for young children with disabilities). U.S. Department of Education, Special Education and Rehabilitation Services, Archived: A 25 Year History of the IDEA, http://www.ed.gov/policy/speced/leg/idea/history.pdf.

49. JOSEPH P. SHAPIRO, NO PITY: PEOPLE WITH DISABILITIES FORGING A NEW CIVIL RIGHTS MOVEMENT 165–66 (1993); CHILDREN'S DEFENSE FUND, CHILDREN

OUT OF SCHOOL IN AMERICA: A REPORT (1974) (two million children not enrolled in school, including hundreds of thousands of disabled children).

50. SHAPIRO, *supra* note 49, at 166. Edelman's work followed the pathbreaking Massachusetts study, *The Way We Go to School* (1967). Initiated by Hubie Jones, this study led to the nation's first special education law requiring integration and accommodation of students with disabilities in public schools.

51. *Vocational Rehabilitation Services: Oversight Hearing before the Select Subcommittee on Education on Future Directions of the Rehabilitation Services*, 93rd Cong. (1973).

52. The Act passed by a vote of 404 to 7 in the House and 87 to 7 in the Senate. Hehir & Gamm, *supra* note 1, at 213.

53. 20 U.S.C. §§ 1400–1490 (2007).

54. 20 U.S.C. § 1412(a)(5) (2007). For a history of the concept and analysis of its uses, *see* JEAN B. CROCKETT & JAMES M. KAUFFMAN, THE LEAST RESTRICTIVE ENVIRONMENT: ITS ORIGINS AND INTERPRETATIONS IN SPECIAL EDUCATION (1999).

55. *See* § 1412(a)(5); 34 C.F.R. § 104.33(b)(1)(i); 34 C.F.R. § 300.116.

56. Millions of students are currently identified as having a disability—and there has been a 30 percent increase in such identifications over the past ten years. National Education Association, Special Education and the Individuals With Disabilities Education Act, www.nea.org/specialed (last visited Oct. 31, 2009).

57. 20 U.S.C. §§ 1401, 1414, 1415 (2007).

58. 121 Cong. Rec. 25540 (1975).

59. Hehir & Gamm, *supra* note 1, at 213 (quoting Congressman C. D. Daniel).

60. PATRICK SCHWARZ, FROM DISABILITY TO POSSIBILITY: THE POWER OF INCLUSIVE CLASSROOMS 33–42 (2006).

61. Martin et al., *supra* note 26, at 30.

62. Hughes & Rebell, *supra* note 9, at 524.

63. *Id.* (As of 1996, 34.9 percent of disabled children were placed in regular classrooms full-time, 36.3 percent in part-time programs, 23.5 percent in separate classrooms, 3.9 percent in separate schools, 0.9 percent in residential facilities, and 0.5 percent in hospitals or visiting programs in the students' homes).

64. In 1998–99, the states reported that 47 percent of these students spent at least 80 percent of the school day in regular classrooms, which is a notable increase over the 31 percent of such students who did so in 1978. National Center for Education Statistics, Inclusion of Students with Disabilities in Regular Classrooms, http://nces.ed.gov/programs/coe/2002/section4/indicator28.asp (last visited Feb. 17, 2004).

65. 20 U.S.C. § 1412(5)(A) (2007).

66. Oberti v. Board of Education, 995 F.2d 1204 (3d Cir. 1993).

67. *See* Hartmann v. Loudoun County Board of Education, 118 F.3d 996 (4th Cir. 1997) (mainstreaming should be tried, but an autistic child was placed with aids in general classroom until disruptions proved excessive, and child received no benefits in the class); Sacramento City Unified School District v. Rachel H., 14 F.3d 1398 (9th Cir. 1994) (affirming placement of child with moderate retardation in regular classroom with supplemental support); Oberti v. Board of Education, 995 F.2d 1204 (district's duty to consider inclusion in regular class before exploring alternatives); Greer v. Rome City School District 950 F.2d 688 (11th Cir. 1991) (using a cost-benefit analysis, child with Down's syndrome appropriately mainstreamed); Daniel R. R. v. State Board of Education, 874 F.2d 1036 (5th Cir.

1989) (where possible, child to be mainstreamed with appropriate services). *See also* Martha M. McCarthy, *Inclusion of Children with Disabilities: Is it Required?* 95 EDUC. L. REP. 823 (1995) (discerning trend toward inclusion). For proposals to refine the trend toward inclusion with exceptions for students who are disruptive or not capable of benefiting academically from placement in the regular class-room, *see* Kathryn E. Crossley, Note, *Inclusion: A New Addition to Remedy a History of Inadequate Conditions and Terms*, 4 WASH. U. J.L. & POL'Y 239 (2000).

68. Oberti v. Board of Education, 995 F.2d at 1216–17; Daniel R. R. v. State Board of Education, 874 F.2d at 1047–48.

69. Daniel H. Melvin II, Comment, *The Desegregation of Children with Disabilities*, 44 DEPAUL L. REV. 599 (1995).

70. *See* SCHWARZ, *supra* note 60.

71. *See, e.g.*, G. Cartledge, *Restrictiveness and Race in Special Education: The Failure to Prevent or Return*, 3 LEARNING DISABILITIES 27 (2005).

72. *See* Marissa L. Antoinette, Comment, *Examining How the Inclusion of Disabled Students into the General Classroom May Affect Non-disabled Classmates*, 30 FORDHAM URB. L. J. 2039 (2003) (proposing a "three strikes" removal policy for a student who disrupts the regular classroom); Anne Proffitt Dupre, *A Study in Double Standards, Discipline, and the Disabled Student*, 75 WASH. L. REV. 1 (2000) (examining how the treatment of disruption and discipline poses problems for disabled students). For a general discussion of the question whether students with learning disabilities specifically benefit more from extra resources than do other students, *see* MARK KELMAN & GILLIAN LESTER, JUMPING THE QUEUE: AN INQUIRY INTO THE LEGAL TREATMENT OF STUDENTS WITH LEARNING DISABILITIES (1997).

73. These disagreements reflect in part an underlying dilemma about how to deal with differences. *See* MARTHA MINOW, MAKING ALL THE DIFFERENCE: INCLUSION, EXCLUSION AND AMERICAN LAW (1990).

74. MARA SAPON-SHEVIN, WIDENING THE CIRCLE: THE POWER OF INCLUSIVE CLASSROOMS 102–7 (2007).

75. *Id.* at 86–87. *See also* VIVIAN PALEY, YOU CAN'T SAY YOU CAN'T PLAY (1992).

76. SAPON-SHEVIN, *supra* note 74, at 93 (citing L. Saint-Laurent et al., *Academic Achievement Effects of an In-class Service Model on Students with and without Disabilities*, 64 EXCEPTIONAL CHILDREN 239 (1998); M. N. Sharpe et al., *Effects of Inclusion on the Academic Performance of Classmates without Disabilities*, 15 REMEDIAL AND SPECIAL EDUC. 281 (1994)).

77. SAPON-SHEVIN, *supra* note 74 (citing T. M. Hollowood et al., *Use of Instructional Time in Classrooms Serving Students with and without Severe Disabilities*, 61 EXCEPTIONAL CHILDREN 242 (1995)).

78. The federal Department of Education has assisted the development and assessment of positive behavioral intervention and supports. *See* TA Center on Positive Behavioral Interventions and Supports, www.pbis.org/ (last visited November 9, 2009).

79. Ruth Colker, *The Disability Integration Presumption: Thirty Years Later*, 154 U. PENN. L. REV. 789 (2006); Therese Craparo, Note, *Remembering the "Individuals" of the Individuals with Disabilities Education Act*, 6 N.Y.U. J. LEGIS. & PUB. POL'Y 467, 524 (2002–3).

80. Craparo, *supra* note 79, at 523. *See also* Theresa Bryant, *Drowning in the Mainstream: Integration of Children with Disabilities after Oberti v. Clementon*

School District, 22 OHIO N.U. L. REV. 83 (1995) (urging consideration of costs and whether the child with disabilities can benefit from the mainstream classroom and disrupts that classroom).

81. "It is not enough for a district to simply claim that a segregated program is superior: In a case where the segregated facility is considered superior, the court should determine whether the services which make the placement superior could be feasibly provided in a non-segregated setting (i.e. regular class). If they can, the placement in the segregated school would be inappropriate under the act (I.D.E.A.)." Roncker v. Walter, 700 F.2d 1058, 1063 (6th Cir. 1983), *cert. denied,* 464 U.S. 864 (1983).

82. Bryant, *supra* note 80, at 117 n. 283 (citing cases). *See also* KELMAN & LESTER, *supra* note 72. *See* MINOW, MAKING ALL THE DIFFERENCE, *supra* note 73.

83. *See id.*

84. *See* Samuel R. Bagenstos, Response, *Abolish the Integration Presumption? Not Yet,* 156 U. PA. L. REV. 157 (2007); Mark C. Weber, Response, *A Nuanced Approach to the Disability Integration Presumption,* 156 U. PA. L. REV. 174 (2007).

85. *See* Carl R. Smith, *Advocacy for Students with Emotional and Behavioral Disorders: One Call for Redirected Efforts,* 22 BEHAVIORAL DISORDERS 96–105 (1997); *See also* S. H. McConaughy & D. R. Ritter, *Best Practices in Multidimensional Assessment of Emotional or Behavioral Disorders, in* BEST PRACTICES IN SCHOOL PSYCHOLOGY IV, at 1303–20 (A. Thomas & J. Grimes eds., 2002).

86. *See* Honig v. Doe, 484 U.S. 305 (1988); 20 USC § 1415(k); CHARLES J. RUSSO & ALLAN G. OSBORNE, JR., ESSENTIAL CONCEPTS AND SCHOOL-BASED CASES IN SPECIAL EDUCATION LAW 155–75 (2007); Mark C. Weber, *Chapter 13, in* SPECIAL EDUCATION LAW AND LITIGATION TREATISE (3rd ed. 2008).

87. *See* BAZELON CENTER FOR MENTAL HEALTH LAW, WAY TO GO: SCHOOL SUCCESS FOR CHILDREN WITH MENTAL HEALTH NEEDS (2006); Minnesota School-wide Positive Behavior Interventions and Supports Overview, Pacer Center, www.pacer.org/pbis/index.asp. (last visited Nov. 9, 2009). Some note that isolation actually exacerbates behavioral and emotional problems. See SAPON-SHEVIN, *supra* note 74, at 113.

88. Colker, *supra* note 79, at 828–29 (reviewing studies).

89. *See* Wald, *supra* note 39, at 12. *See also* Stephen Nathanson, *Are Special Education Programs Unjust to Nondisabled Children?* 180 JOURNAL OF EDUCATION 17 (1998).

90. Martin et al., *supra* note 26, at 34.

91. Cedar Rapids Community School District v. Garret, F. 526 U.S. 66 (1999).

92. The Court described the student: "Garret F. is a friendly, creative, and intelligent young man. When Garret was four years old, his spinal column was severed in a motorcycle accident. Though paralyzed from the neck down, his mental capacities were unaffected. He is able to speak, to control his motorized wheelchair through use of a puff and suck straw, and to operate a computer with a device that responds to head movements. Garret is currently a student in the Cedar Rapids Community School District, he attends regular classes in a typical school program, and his academic performance has been a success. Garret is, however, ventilator dependent, and therefore requires a responsible individual nearby to attend to certain physical needs while he is in school." *Id.* at 69.

93. *Id.* at 67 (referencing Board of Education v. Rowley, 458 U.S. 176, 192, 202 (1982)).

94. Board of Education v. Rowley, 458 U.S. at 181 n. 4 (giving deference to educators while recognizing congressional preference for mainstreaming); Oberti v. Board of Education, 995 F.2d 1204.

95. Craparo, *supra* note 79, at 503–5.

96. *See* Jane K. Babin, Comment, *Adequate Special Education: Do California Schools Meet the Test?* 37 SAN DIEGO L. REV. 211 (2000).

97. DISABILITY RIGHTS ADVOCATES, DO NO HARM: HIGH STAKES TESTING AND STUDENTS WITH LEARNING DISABILITIES (2001); Pamela Wright, *High-stakes Lawsuit in Massachusetts: How High Are the Stakes?* Wrights Law, www.wrightslaw.com/info/test.highstakes.mass.htm (last visited Nov. 9, 2009).

98. Variable instruction within special education is also a serious problem, with inadequate teacher quality more likely a problem in low-income, high-minority schools and districts. *See* BETH HARRY & JANETTE KLINGNER, WHY ARE SO MANY MINORITY STUDENTS IN SPECIAL EDUCATION? UNDERSTANDING RACE & DISABILITY IN SCHOOLS (2005).

99. *Id.* at 210.

100. SCHWARZ, *supra* note 60, at 37–39.

101. *See* RACIAL INEQUITY IN SPECIAL EDUCATION (Daniel J. Losen & Gary Orfield eds., 2002); HARRY & KLINGNER, *supra* note 98; A. J. Artiles & S. Trent, *Overrepresentation of Minority Students in Special Education: A Continuing Debate*, 27 J. SPECIAL EDUC. 410 (1994); Robert A. Garda, Jr., *The New IDEA: Shifting Educational Paradigms to Achieve Racial Equality in Special Education*, 56 ALA. L. REV. 1071 (2005); Alan Gartner & Dorothy Kerzner Lipsky, *Over-representation of Black Students in Special Education: Problem or Symptom?* 7 POVERTY & RACE 3 (1998), www.prrac.org/news.php; Theresa Glennon, *Race, Education, and the Construction of a Disabled Class*, 1995 WIS. L. REV. 1237 (1995). *See also* Martha L. Thurlow, J. Ruth Nelson, Ellen Teelucksingh, & Ingrid L. Draper, *Multiculturalism and Disability in a Results-based Educational System: Hazards and Hopes for Today's Schools*, *in* SPECIAL EDUCATION, MULTICULTURAL EDUCATION, AND SCHOOL REFORM: COMPONENTS OF QUALITY EDUCATION FOR LEARNERS WITH MILD DISABILITIES (Cheryl A. Utley & Festus E. Obiakor eds., 2001).

102. *See supra*, 70–76 section "Disability," subsection "From Litigation to Legislation" (discussing *Hobson v. Hanson*).

103. Daniel J. Losen & Kevin G. Welner, *Disabling Discrimination in Our Public Schools: Comprehensive Legal Challenges to Inappropriate and Inadequate Special Education Services for Minority Children*, 36 HARV. C.R.-C.L. L. REV. 407, 434 (2001).

104. Daniel J. Losen & Gary Orfield, *Introduction* to Losen & Orfield, *supra* note 101, at xix; Joel McNally, *Black Over-representation in Special Education Not Confined to Segregation States*, 17 RETHINKING SCHOOLS (2003), www.rethinkingschools.org/archive/17_03/ over173.shtml.

105. MINORITY STUDENTS IN SPECIAL AND GIFTED EDUCATION (M. Suzanne Donovan & Christopher T. Cross eds., 2002), www.nap.edu/openbook.php?record_id=10128&page=R1.

106. Garda, *supra* note 101, at 1073.

107. *See* Larry P. v. Riles, 495 F. Supp. 926, 955 (N.D. Cal. 1979), *aff'd in part and rev'd in part*, 793 F.2d 969 (9th Cir. 1984); Hobson v. Hanson, 269 F. Supp. at 443, 514.

108. Garda, *supra* note 101, at 1086.

109. *Id.* at 1078.

110. Losen & Orfield, *supra* note 104, at xvi (citing OFFICE FOR CIVIL RIGHTS, U.S. DEPARTMENT OF EDUCATION, ELEMENTARY AND SECONDARY SCHOOL, CIVIL RIGHTS COMPLIANCE REPORTS (2000)). In 2004, Congress found that studies placed African Americans at 15 percent of the student population and 20 percent of those referred for special education eligibility. Pub. L. No. 108–446, § 101.

111. MINORITY STUDENTS IN SPECIAL AND GIFTED EDUCATION 44. (M. Suzanne Donovan & Christopher T. Cross, eds., 2002).

112. HARRY & KLINGNER, *supra* note 98, at 4.

113. Losen & Orfield, *supra* note 104, at xxi.

114. SAPON-SHEVIN, *supra* note 74, at 69 n. 10 (citing studies).

115. HARRY & KLINGNER, *supra* note 98; Glennon, *supra* note 101, at 1317. *See also* LISA DELPIT, OTHER PEOPLE'S CHILDREN: CULTURAL CONFLICT IN THE CLASSROOM (1996).

116. Glennon, *supra* note 101; John L. Hosp & Daniel J. Reschly, *Referral Rates for Intervention or Assessment: A Meta-analysis of Racial Differences*, 37 J. SPECIAL EDUC. 67, 67 (2003); Donald P. Oswold et al., *Community and School Predictors of Overrepresentation of Minority Children in Special Education, in* Losen & Orfield, *supra* note 101, at 106.

117. HARRY & KLINGNER, *supra* note 98, at 173; Glennon, *supra* note 101, at 1285.

118. A. A. Ortiz, *Learning Disabilities Occurring Concomitantly with Linguistic Differences*, 30 J. LEARNING DISABILITIES 321 (1997); A. A. Ortiz, *Prevention of School Failure and Early Intervention for English Language Learners, in* ENGLISH LANGUAGE LEARNERS WITH SPECIAL EDUCATION NEEDS: IDENTIFICATION, ASSESSMENT, AND INSTRUCTION 31 (A. J. Artiles & A. A. Ortiz eds., 2002).

119. KELMAN & LESTER, *supra* note 72, at 68.

120. Garda, *supra* note 101, at 1084–85 (citing studies).

121. *See id.* at 1072 (citing reports and journalists' accounts).

122. Individuals with Disabilities Education Improvement Act of 2004, 20 U.S.C. § 1418 (2005).

123. Losen & Orfield, *supra* note 101; Glennon, *supra* note 101. *See also* Patrick Linehan, *Guarding the Dumping Ground: Equal Protection, Title VII and Justifying the Use of Race in the Hiring of Special Educators*, 2001 BYU EDUC. & L.J. 179, 180 (recommending hiring special educators of color to reduce the overidentification of students of color).

124. Gartner & Lipsky, *supra* note 101, at 3 (underrepresentation); HARRY & KLINGNER, *supra* note 98, at 19 (indicating Hispanic overrepresentation in learning disability category).

125. Colker, *supra* note 79.

126. Garda, *supra* note 101. *See also* SAPON-SHEVIN, *supra* note 74, at 172, 180–84 (arguing for treating disability as one of many kinds of diversity to be valued in classrooms).

127. Concluding that wealth discrimination does not warrant heightened scrutiny under the equal protection clause, the Supreme Court rejected a constitutional challenge to state reliance on property taxes to fund schools that resulted in higher expenditures for students in districts with valuable property and for students in districts with less valuable property. San Antonio Independent School District v. Rodriguez, 411 U.S. 1 (1973). Ironically, as a result, socioeconomic

status classifications can be used by public schools to govern school assignments and produce socioeconomic integration, which has been pursued in a few districts as a form of integration and has found a few national champions. *See* RICHARD KAHLENBERG, ALL TOGETHER NOW: CREATING MIDDLE-CLASS SCHOOLS THROUGH PUBLIC SCHOOL CHOICE (2001).

128. It may also be a haven for students who are transgendered and others who are perceived to be gay or lesbian. The school developed with the guidance of the Institute for the Protection of Lesbian and Gay Youth, later renamed the Hetrick-Martin Institute, which Emery Hetrick and Damien Martin founded in 1979 after hearing about a homeless fifteen-year-old boy who had been beaten up and kicked out of his emergency shelter because he was gay. Hetrick-Martin Institute, *Our History,* ww.hmi.org/Page.aspx?pid=229 (last visited Nov. 3, 2009).

129. *See* Katherine Zoepf, *Protests Mark Opening of Expanded Harvey Milk School,* N.Y. TIMES, Sept. 9, 2003, at B3.

130. For a look at the rising number of referrals nationwide for children displaying transgender behaviors and identities, *see* Patricia Leigh Brown, *Supporting Boys or Girls When the Line Isn't Clear,* N.Y. TIMES, Dec. 2, 2006, at A1.

131. *See* David S. Doty, *Finding a Third Way: The Use of Public Engagement and ADR to Bring School Communities Together for the Safety of Gay Students,* 12 HASTINGS WOMEN'S L.J. 39, 42 (2001) ("at least one lower federal court has ruled that Title IX does encompass same-sex, student-on-student harassment, and it seems likely that other courts will follow"). Federal courts have construed the federal regulation to bar harassment of one student by another student with regard to sexual orientation. Theno v. Tonganoxie Unified School District, 404 F. Supp. 2d 1281, 1302 (D. Kan. 2005); Montgomery v. Independent School District No. 709, 109 F. Supp. 2d 1081, 1092–93 (D. Minn. 2000). *See also* Ray v. Antioch Unified School District, 107 F. Supp. 2d 1165, 1170 (N.D. Cal. 2000) (regulation governs sexual harassment of one student by another of the same sex).

132. Janet E. Halley, *"Like Race" Arguments, in* WHAT'S LEFT OF THEORY? NEW WORK ON THE POLITICS OF LITERARY THEORY 41 (Judith Butler et al. eds., 2000). Halley argues that analogies to race may secure legal advances but rest on inaccuracies, especially in imagining an immutable and coherent sexual identity, displacing bisexuals, and undermining the element of choice in sexual identification. *Id.* at 52–53.

133. Lawrence v. Texas, 539 U.S. 558 (2003).

134. *Id.* at 578.

135. Brief of Professors of History George Chauncy, Nancy F. Cott, John D'Emilio, Estelle B. Freedman, Thomas C. Holt, John Howard, Lynn Hunt, Mark D. Jordan, Elizabeth Lapovsky Kennedy, and Linda P. Kerber as Amici Curiae in Support of Petitioners at 15–20, Lawrence v. Texas, 539 U.S. 558 (2003) (No. 02-102). Drafted by George Chauncey, professor of history at the University of Chicago, the brief is echoed in the majority opinion's statement that "[f]ar from possessing 'ancient roots'... American laws targeting same sex-couples did not develop until the last third of the 20th century." Lawrence v. Texas, 539 U.S. at 559. Chauncey's father was a southern minister who lost his post after supporting *Brown* and received death threats in 1957 for helping the desegregation effort in Little Rock. Rick Perlstein, *Moment of Decision,* UNIV. OF CHICAGO MAGAZINE, Aug. 2003, at 26, 28.

136. Rose Arce, *Classes Open at Gay High School,* CNN, Sept. 8, 2003, www.cnn.com/2003/ EDUCATION/09/08/gay.school/index.html.

137. *Id.* (quoting Long).

138. *See* Tania Branigan, *Responding to a Need, Or to Fear? Criticism Greets School for Gay Youth*, WASH. POST, Sept. 9. 2003, at A3.

139. *Id.* (quoting Bill Dobbs).

140. *Gay School Not Right Solution*, Editorial, BATTLE CREEK ENQUIRER, Aug. 4, 2003, at 6A.

141. Branigan, *supra* note 138 (quoting students and advocates).

142. *See* James Quinn, *Reactions to a "Gay School,"* NEWSDAY, Dec. 3, 2003, www.newsday.com/news/student-briefing-page-on-the-news-1.281037.

143. Thanks to Susan Steinway for this observation.

144. *See* Harper v. Poway Unified School District, 485 F.3d 1052 (9th Cir. 2007) (student claiming free speech and free exercise rights to wear an anti homosexual t-shirt to school). *See also Suspensions, Furor over "Anti-Gay" Shirts: Parents, Students, Church Leaders Press Board for Free-speech Rights*, WORLDNET-DAILY, May 23, 2007, www.wnd.com/index.php?fa=PAGE.view&pageId=41725 (reporting efforts by Christian group to defend students suspended from San Juan High School in Citrus Heights, California, after wearing t-shirts and distributing literature quoting biblical injunctions against homosexuality and sodomy); *School Supports Sodomy*, CALIFORNIA CATHOLIC DAILY, Apr. 24, 2007, www.calcatholic.com/news/newsArticle.aspx?id=c7fe38ae-b03c-4cd5-b916–79680b90a44e; Doty, *supra* note 131, at 41.

145. Schroeder v. Maumee Board of Education, 296 F. Supp. 2d 869 (N.D. Ohio 2003).

146. Benoit Denizet-Lewis, *Coming Out in Middle School*, N.Y. TIMES MAG. (Sept. 23, 2009), www.nytimes.com/2009/09/27/magazine/27out-t.html.

147. Sarah Barringer Gordon, *"Free" Religious and "Captive" Schools: Protestants, Catholics, and Education, 1945–1965*, 56 DEPAUL L. REV. 1177 (2006).

148. *Id.* at 1201–9.

149. *Id.* at 1210–18.

150. *See* Skoros v. City of New York, 437 F.3d 1 (2d Cir. 2006). This decision reflects the Supreme Court's recent opinions concerning County of Allegheny v. ACLU Greater Pittsburgh, 492 U.S. 573 (1989). For further discussion, see chapter 5.

151. *See* Zelman v. Simmons-Harris, 536 U.S. 639 (2002); Rosenberger v. University of Virginia, 515 U.S. 819 (1995); Widmar v. Vincent, 454 U.S. 263 (1981).

152. *See* Michael W. McConnell, *The Problem of Singling Out Religion*, 50 DEPAUL L. REV. 1 (2000); Michael W. McConnell, *Religious Participation in Public Programs: Religious Freedom at a Crossroads*, 59 U. CHI. L. REV. 115 (1992); Michael W. McConnell, *The Selective Funding Problem: Abortions and Religious Schools*, 104 HARV. L. REV. 989 (1991); Michael W. McConnell, *The Origins and Historical Understanding of the Free Exercise of Religion*, 103 HARV. L. REV. 1410 (1990). This view should be distinguished from the conception that religion should never be treated differently from other personal views or commitments. Christopher Eisgruber and Lawrence Sager argue that equality would forbid the government from treating religion differently from any other category even if that difference takes the form of a preference or accommodation. *See* Christopher L. Eisgruber & Lawrence G. Sager, *The Vulnerability of Conscience: The Constitutional Basis for Protecting Religious Conduct*, 61 U. CHI. L. REV. 1245 (1994).

153. Michael McConnell, *Originalism and the Desegregation of Decisions*, 81 VA. L. REV. 947 (1995); Michael W. McConnell, *The Originalist Case for Brown v. Board of Education,* 19 HARV. J. L. & PUB. POL'Y 457 (1996).

154. *See* Rosenberger v. University of Virginia, 515 U.S. at 819. *See also* Transcript of Oral Arguments, Rosenberger v. University of Virginia, 515 U.S. 819 (1995) (No. 94–329).

155. *See* Noah Feldman, *From Liberty to Equality: The Transformation of the Establishment Clause*, 90 CAL. L. REV 673 (2002) for a thoughtful analysis of the emerging judicial opinions.

156. Rosenberger v. University of Virginia, 515 U.S. at 820.

157. Good News Club v. Milford Central School, 533 U.S. 98, 107 (2001).

158. Michael McConnell, *Neutrality under the Religion Clauses*, 81 Nw. U. L. REV. 146 (1986); Michael McConnell, *Accommodation of Religion*, 1985 SUP. CT. REV. 1 (1985).

159. Widmar v. Vincent, 454 U.S. at 263. Jeffrey Rosen has suggested that while McConnell was working as a law clerk for the Court, he persuaded Justice William Brennan to write an opinion for the Court ruling unconstitutional a public university's policy of excluding religious worship activities from its spaces, arguing that a public university campus religious organization can not be denied the right of access to facilities equivalent to those that the university grants to other organizations. *See* Jeffrey Rosen, *Is Nothing Secular?* N.Y. TIMES MAG., Jan 30, 2000, at 40, 43. As McConnell completed his clerkship before the case was argued, direct influence does not seem clear.

160. *See* Douglas Laycock, *Equal Access and Moments of Silence: The Equal Status of Religious Speech by Private Speakers*, 81 Nw. U. L. REV. 1 (1986).

161. Board of Education of Westside Community Schools v. Mergens, 496 U.S. 226 (1990).

162. *Id.* The Equal Access Act is codified at 20 U.S.C. §§ 4071–74.

163. Lamb's Chapel v. Center Moriches Union Free School District, 508 U.S. 384 (1993). *See also* Good News Club v. Milford Central School, 533 U.S. 98 (2001).

164. *Religious Freedom: Hearings before the Senate Judiciary Comm.*, 104th Cong. (1995) (statement of Michael W. McConnell, professor, University of Chicago Law School).

165. *Id.* (referring to Settle v. Dickson County School Board, 53 F.3d 152 (6th Cir. 1995)).

166. *See Religious Freedom, supra* note 164.

167. McConnell, *Selective Funding Problem, supra* note 152, at 1043–44. At a more abstract level, McConnell also proposed comparable treatment of the constitutional analysis regarding government funding of religious schools and government funding of abortions. *Id.* at 989–94.

168. *See* Derek H. Davis, *A Commentary on the Supreme Court's "Equal Treatment" Doctrine as the New Constitutional Paradigm for Protecting Religious Liberty*, 46 J. CHURCH & ST. 717 (2004).

169. Zelman v. Simmons-Harris, 536 U.S. 639 (2002).

170. Mitchell v. Helms, 530 U.S. 793 (2000) (plurality opinion) (rejecting establishment clause challenge because the program was generally available).

171. Zelman v. Simmons-Harris, 536 U.S. at 676 (Thomas, J., concurring).

172. *Id.* at 682.

173. Mitchell v. Helms, 530 U.S. at 835 n. 19. The Court permitted the exclusion of pastoral ministry studies from a state higher education scholarship, however, as part of the breathing room needed to enforce both the establishment and free exercise clauses. *See* Locke v. Davey, 540 U.S. 712 (2004).

174. *See* Christopher P. Coval, *Good News for Religious Schools and the Freedom of Speech*, 83 B.U. L. Rev. 705 (2003). For a strong statement of the contrary view, *see* Noah Feldman, Divided by God: America's Church-state Problem—And What We Should Do about It (2005) (urging a ban on government financial aid to religion in order to prevent divisiveness while supporting evenhanded public displays of religious symbols).

175. Arnold H. Loewy, *The Positive Reality and Normative Virtues of a "Neutral" Establishment Clause*, 41 Brandeis L.J. 533, 542–43 (2003).

176. Zelman v. Simmons-Harris, 536 U.S. at 643. *See infra* chapter 5 (discussing Clint Bolick's legal strategy behind the school choice case).

177. Zelman v. Simmons-Harris, 536 U.S. at 676–77 (Thomas, J. concurring).

178. *Id. See also* Harry G. Hutchison, *Liberal Hegemony? School Vouchers and the Future of the Race*, 68 Mo. L. Rev. 559 (2003) (arguing that the traditional left-wing view opposing school vouchers would be contrary to the interests of impoverished students of color).

179. *See* Camille Wilson Cooper, *School Choice and the Standpoint of African American Mothers: Considering the Power of Positionality*, 74 J. Negro Educ. 174 (2005) ("In 2000, a national public opinion poll conducted by the Joint Center for Political and Economic Studies (JCPE) found that 57% of African Americans favor public voucher programs, including 74% of African Americans with children in their households. Moreover, market advocates have estimated that African American parents participate in at least 42 privately funded voucher programs throughout the country that target inner-city children (Moe, 1999)." (citing Joint Center for Political and Economic Studies 2000 National Opinion Poll, www.jointcenter.org)). *See also* Terry M. Moe, *School Vouchers: The Public Revolution Private Money Might Bring*, Wash. Post, May 9, 1999, at B3.

180. Thomas C. Pedroni, Market Movements: African American Involvement in School Voucher Reform (2007). Self-selection of parents pursuing school choice complicates efforts to compare their children's achievement with the achievement of those remaining in public schools unless a comparison can be drawn between families who pursued but did not secure school choice. In addition, the religious orientation of the student may affect achievement. *See* William H. Jeynes, *The Effects of Religious Commitment on the Academic Achievement of Black and Hispanic Children*, 34 Urban Educ. 458 (1999) (suggesting that more devout minority students performed better academically than less devout minority students in parochial schools).

181. Frank Macchiarola, *Why the Decision in Zelman Makes So Much Sense*, 59 N.Y.U. Ann. Survey Am. L. 459, 467 (2003). *See also* Mark Tushnet, *Vouchers after Zelman*, 2002 Sup. Ct. Rev. 1.

182. *Compare* Chang-Ho C. Ji & Joo Hyun Kim, Paper Presented at the Annual Meeting of the Western Political Science Association: Going Parochial: Race, Religion, and School Vouchers in Urban Parochial Schools(March 17, 2005), www.allacademic.com/meta/ p87518_index.html (arguing that Protestant parochial schools in greater Los Angeles area more segregated than public schools in the same area), *with* Jay P. Greene, Education Myths: What Special Interest Groups Want You to Believe about Our Schools and Why It Isn't So (2005); Timothy J. Ilg, Joseph D. Massucci, & Geral M. Cattaro, *Brown at 50: The Dream Is Still Alive in Urban Catholic Schools*, 36 Educ. and Urban Soc'y 355 (2004).

183. *See* Lisa M. Stulberg, Race, Schools, and Hope: African Americans and School Choice after Brown (2008) (considering vouchers and charter

schools); Hayes Mizell, *School Choice Not Best Option for Black Kids*, TIMES AND DEMOCRAT, Aug. 30, 2007.

184. *See infra* chapter 5.

185. Dan D. Goldhaber & Eric R. Eide, *What Do We Know (and Need to Know) about the Impact of School Choice Reforms on Disadvantaged Students?* 72 HARV. EDUC. REV. 157 (2002). *See also* WILLIAM G. HOWELL & PAUL E. PETERSON WITH PATRICK J. WOLF & DAVID E. CAMPBELL, THE EDUCATION GAP: VOUCHERS AND URBAN SCHOOLS (rev. ed. 2006).

186. *See* Zelman v. Simmons-Harris, 536 U.S. 639; MARTHA MINOW, PART-NERS, NOT RIVALS: PRIVATIZATION AND THE PUBLIC GOOD 93 (2002).

187. After the *Zelman* decision, lower courts addressed programs funding religious provision of social services and demanded protection of individual choices both in the assurance of secular options and in scrutiny of any pressures placed on individuals. *See* IRA C. LUPU & ROBERT W. TUTTLE, THE STATE OF THE LAW—2007: LEGAL DEVELOPMENTS AFFECTING GOVERNMENT PARTNERSHIPS WITH FAITH-BASED ORGANIZATIONS (2007); Ira C. Lupu & Robert W. Tuttle, *The Faith-based Initiative and the Constitution*, 55 DEPAUL L. REV. 1 (2005); THE ROUNDTABLE ON RELIGION AND SOCIAL WELFARE POLICY, INDIRECT FINANCING OF FAITH-BASED SOCIAL SERVICES (2008), www.religionandsocialpolicy.org/ resources/vouchers.cfm.

188. *See* Ira C. Lupu & Robert Tuttle, *Sites of Redemption: A Wide-angle Look at Government Vouchers and Sectarian Service Providers*, 18 J. L. & POL. 539 (2002). While sympathetic to opening educational oppertunities for disadvantaged students, I have in the past worried that vouchers will undermine the vision of the "common school" where children of different backgrounds learn together, a vision predating *Brown* but invigorated by it. *See, e.g.*, Martha Minow, Commentary, *Contemporary Challenges Facing the First Amendment's Religion Clauses*, 43 N.Y.L. SCH. L. REV. 101, 123–24 (1999).

189. *See* Thomas C. Berg, *Why a State Exclusion of Religious Schools from School Choice Programs Is Unconstitutional*, 2 FIRST AMENDMENT L. REV. 23 (2004); Joseph P. Viteritti, *Blaine's Wake: School Choice, the First Amendment, and State Constitutional Law*, 21 HARV. J.L. & PUB. POL'Y 657, 666–68 (1998); Becket Fund for Religious Liberty, Schools, http://www.becketfund.org/index.php/topic/7.html?PHPSESSID=62ba0f6636265319fc0e41e12d94a852. The federal government might do well to preserve state and local decisions on this issue. Martha Minow, *The Government Can't, May, or Must Fund Religious Schools: Three Riddles of Constitutional Change for Laurence Tribe*, 42 TULSA L. REV. 911 (2007).

190. *See* Martha Minow, *On Being a Religious Professional: The Religious Turn in Professional Ethics*, 150 U. PA. L. REV. 661 (2001); Rosen, *supra* note 159.

191. Douglas NeJaime, *Inclusion, Accommodation, and Recognition: Accounting for Differences Based on Religion and Sexual Orientation*, 32 HARV. J. L. & GENDER 303 (2009).

192. Rosen, *supra* note 159.

193. The developments have a variety of critics. *See* FELDMAN, *supra* note 174; Davis, *supra* note 168.

194. *See* MINOW, *supra* note 186, at 89–93, 116–18.

195. *See* ANTHONY S. BRYK ET AL., CATHOLIC SCHOOLS AND THE COMMON GOOD (1993).

196. *See* JOHN BOWEN, WHY THE FRENCH DON'T LIKE HEADSCARVES: ISLAM, THE STATE, AND PUBLIC SPACE (2007).

197. *See* WILLIAM JULIUS WILSON, THE TRULY DISADVANTAGED: THE INNER CITY, THE UNDERCLASS, AND PUBLIC POLICY 125–32 (1987).

198. Pub. L. No. 89–10, 79 Stat. 27 (codified as amended at 20 U.S.C. §§ 6301–7941 (2002)).

199. SANDRA J. STEIN, THE CULTURE OF EDUCATION POLICY 26–27 (2004).

200. *See* MARK G. YUDOF, DAVID L. KIRP, BETSY LEVIN, & RACHEL F. MORAN, EDUCATIONAL POLICY AND THE LAW 743 (4th ed. 2002).

201. Thomas W. Payzant & Jessica Levin, *Improving America's Schools for Children in Greater Need, in* NATIONAL ISSUES IN EDUCATION: ELEMENTARY AND SECONDARY EDUCATION ACT 55–75 (John F. Jennings ed., 1995).

202. *Id.* Working out the details for using the funds can be complicated. *See, e.g., No Child Left Behind Consolidated Application Update, 2007–8: Title I Application Supplement—General Instructions,* www.forms.nysed.gov/emsc/titlei/supp0708/instructions.htm (last visited Nov. 5, 2009).

203. *See* CYNTHIA M. DUNCAN, WORLDS APART: WHY POVERTY PERSISTS IN RURAL AMERICA (1999); CHAIM I. WAXMAN, THE STIGMA OF POVERTY: A CRITIQUE OF POVERTY THEORIES AND POLICIES (2d ed. 1983); Michael A. Rebell, *Poverty, "Meaningful" Educational Opportunity, and the Necessary Role of the Courts,* 85 N.C. L. REV. 1467, 1471–76 (2007).

204. *See* PAUL A. SRACIC, *SAN ANTONIO V. RODRIGUEZ* AND THE PURSUIT OF EQUAL EDUCATION: THE DEBATE OVER DISCRIMINATION AND SCHOOL FUNDING (2006). Some trace the turn to equalizing resources to the Supreme Court's approval of financial remedies for Detroit after its rejection of an interdistrict desegregation plan. *See, e.g.,* Alfred A. Lindseth, *Educational Adequacy Lawsuits: The Rest of the Story* (Apr. 23, 2004) (discussing Milliken v. Bradley, 418 U.S. 717 (1974) ("Milliken I") and Milliken v. Bradley, 433 U.S. 267 (1997) ("Milliken II")) (unpublished paper on file with the author).

205. *See* Quentin A. Palfrey, *The State Judiciary's Role in Fulfilling Brown's Promise,* 8 MICH. J. RACE & L. 1, 7–8 (2002) ("To get the property tax rate to be used to fund local schools, one must divide the amount to be raised by local property taxes by the assessed valuation of the property in the district. This is sometimes known as the district's 'willingness' or 'effort' to support its schools. The standard way of comparing the ability of school districts to raise revenues is to divide the total value of the district's assessed property by the number of pupils in the district.... Even at high tax rates, districts with low property values cannot adequately fund their schools, whereas wealthy districts can raise large amounts of funding even at lower tax rates.") (notes omitted).

206. The presence of commercial and industrial properties near where poor families live can in contrast produce a more substantial tax base. Still, impoverished families tend to have diminished access to public schooling resources drawn from local taxes.

207. *See* Roosevelt Elementary School District v. Bishop, 877 P.2d 806, 809 (Ariz. 1994) (Ruth Fisher Elementary School District assessed property valuation of $5.8 million per pupil, and San Carlos Unified School District assessed property valuation of $749 per pupil).

208. KEVIN CAREY & THE EDUCATION TRUST, THE FUNDING GAP 2 (2003).

209. *See* San Antonio Independent School District v. Rodigruez, 411 U.S. 1 (1973).

210. *Id. See also* Robert Berne & Leanna Stiefel, *School Finance Litigation in the Name of Educational Equity: Its Evolution, Impact, and Future, in* EQUITY AND

ADEQUACY IN EDUCATION FINANCE: ISSUES AND PERSPECTIVES 2–24 (Helen F. Ladd et al. eds., 1999).

211. San Antonio Independent School District v. Rodriguez, 411 U.S. at 8.

212. *See* Serrano v. Priest, 487 P.2d. 1241, 1250 (Cal. 1971). Because the California court relied both on the state and federal constitution, its decision could stand after the Supreme Court's rejection of a similar argument, as noted by the trial judge on remand and later affirmed by the California Supreme Court. Serrano v. Priest II, 557 P.2d 929 (Cal. 1976). The state legislature responded with a law capping how quickly districts could increase revenues through taxation, which was intended to allow low-spending districts to close the gap with high-spending districts. In practice, though, many communities exercised the option of overriding the ceiling, and subsequent reforms altered the California system yet again. *See* William A. Fischel, *Did Serrano Cause Proposition 13?* 42 NAT'L TAX J. 465 (1989). For contrasting assessments, *see* Isaac Martin, *Does School Finance Litigation Cause Taxpayer Revolt? Serrano and Proposition 13*, 40 LAW & SOC'Y REV. 525 (2006); Kirk J. Stark & Jonathan Zasloff, *Tiebout and Tax Revolts: Did Serrano Really Cause Proposition 13?*, 50 UCLA L. REV. 801 (2003).

213. *See* Martin R. West & Paul E. Peterson, *The Adequacy Lawsuit: A Critical Appraisal, in* SCHOOL MONEY TRIALS: THE LEGAL PURSUIT OF EDUCATIONAL ADEQUACY 1, 4 (Martin R. West & Paul E. Peterson eds., 2007).

214. San Antonio Independent School District v. Rodriguez, 411 U.S. at 28. Declining to find education a fundamental right, the Court also rejected an equal protection challenge to disparities in educational opportunities if they fell short of fully depriving one group of any educational opportunity at all. *Id.* at 55.

215. *Id.* at 72, 82–83 (Marshall, J., dissenting).

216. *Id.* at 90, 110.

217. Richard Kahlenberg, *Middle-class Schools for All*, 8 DEMOCRACY 29 (2008); Ledyard King, *Schools Turning to Wealth, Not Race, to Integrate Schools*, USA TODAY, Jan. 11, 2007, www.usatoday.com/ news/education/2007–01–11-schools-income_x.htm.

218. KAHLENBERG, *supra* note 127. *See supra* chapter 1 for a discussion of this proposal in relation to racial desegregation and *infra* chapter 6 for further analysis of socio-economic integration efforts.

219. *See* KAHLENBERG, *supra* note 127, at 228–57 (discussing La Cross, Wisconsin; Wake County, North Carolina; Manchester, Connecticut). *See also* CAMBRIDGE PUBLIC SCHOOLS, CONTROLLED CHOICE PLAN 7 (2001), www.cpsd.us/Web/PubInfo/ControlledChoice.pdf. Although drafted in 2001, this policy is linked to the kindergarten registration web site for 2010–11. Cambridge Public Schools, *FRC: School Registration*, www.cpsd.us/frc/k_reg.cfm (last visited Nov. 5, 2009).

220. *See* DOUGLAS S. REED, ON EQUAL TERMS: THE CONSTITUTIONAL POLITICS OF EDUCATIONAL OPPORTUNITY (2001).

221. *See* West & Peterson, *in* West & Peterson, *supra* note 213, at 2–8, 12–16; Palfrey, *supra* note 205, at 21 (noting failures of equity suits after 1980 in Georgia, New York, Colorado, Maryland, Oklahoma, North Carolina, and South Carolina, and plaintiff success only in Wyoming and Arkansas). Renewed efforts in New York produced a court victory in 2003, with disputes over implementation remaining unresolved. *See* JONATHAN KOZOL, THE SHAME OF THE NATION: THE RESTORATION OF APARTHEID SCHOOLING IN AMERICA 255 (2005).

222. Peter Enrich, *Leaving Equity Behind: New Directions in School Finance Reform*, 48 VAND. L. REV. 101, 158 (1995).

223. *See* Robinson v. Cahill, 303 A.2d 273 (N.J. 1973).

224. *See National Access Network Litigation New Jersey,* www.schoolfunding. info/states/nj/lit_nj.php3 (last visited Nov. 5, 2009).

225. KOZOL, *supra* note 221, at 50.

226. *See* Enrich, *supra* note 222, at 154.

227. *See* Molly McUsic, *The Law's Role in the Distribution of Education: The Promises and Pitfalls of School Finance Litigation, in* LAW AND SCHOOL REFORM: SIX STRATEGIES FOR PROMOTING EDUCATIONAL EQUITY 88 (Jay P. Heubert ed., 1999). *See also* Eric A. Hanushek, *Good Intentions Captured: School Funding Adequacy and the Courts, in* COURTING FAILURE: HOW SCHOOL FINANCE LAWSUITS EXPLOIT JUDGES' GOOD INTENTIONS AND HARM OUR CHILDREN xiii, xv (Eric A. Hanushek ed., 2006).

228. Betsy Levin, *Current Trends in School Finance Reform Litigation: A Commentary,* 1977 DUKE L.J. 1099 (1978).

229. *See* Michael A. Rebell, *Adequacy Litigations: A New Path to Equity? in* BRINGING EQUITY BACK: RESEARCH FOR A NEW ERA IN AMERICAN EDUCATIONAL POLICY 291 (Janice Petrovich & Amy Stuart Wells eds., 2005). *See also* Paul L. Tractenberg, *The Evolution and Implementation of Educational Rights under the New Jersey Constitution of 1947,* 29 RUTGERS L.J. 827 (1998).

230. *See* Rachel Wainer Apter, *Institutional Constraints, Politics, and Good Faith: A Case Study of School Finance Reform in Massachusetts,* 17 CORNELL J.L. & PUB. POL'Y 621 (2008).

231. Frederick M. Hess, *Adequacy Judgments and School Reform, in* West & Peterson, *supra* note 213, at 159–94 (reviewing efforts in Kentucky, New Jersey, Maryland, and Ohio). *See also* Michael Heise, *Adequacy Litigation in an Era of Accountability, in* West & Peterson, *supra* note 213, at 262–77 (suggesting that states lower their proficiency standards in order to avoid exposure to adequacy suits); David J. Hoff, *Movement Afoot to Reframe Finance-adequacy Suits,* EDUC. WK., Oct. 26, 2005, at 25; Lindseth, *supra* note 204.

232. *See* GARY BURTLESS, DOES MONEY MATTER? THE EFFECT OF SCHOOL RESOURCES ON STUDENT ACHIEVEMENT AND ADULT SUCCESS (1996); COMMITTEE ON EDUCATION FINANCE, MAKING MONEY MATTER: FINANCING AMERICA'S SCHOOLS (Helen F. Ladd & Janet S. Hansen eds., 1999); *Investing in Our Children's Future: School Finance Reform in the 90s,* Symposium, 28 HARV. J. ON LEGIS. 293 (1991); Rebell, *supra* note 203, at 1479–67 (reviewing critiques of research by Eric Hanushek for failure to consider variations in teacher salaries, proportion of students with special needs, and misidentifying appropriate studies for metaanalysis). ERIC A. HANUSHEK & ALFRED A. LINDSETH, SCHOOLHOUSES, COURTHOUSES, AND STATEHOUSES: SOLVING THE FUNDING-ACHIEVEMENT PUZZLE IN AMERICA'S PUBLIC SCHOOLS (2009).

233. Some scholars claim to show that there is no relationship between finance arrangements after school equity suits and academic achievement of disadvantaged students. *See, e.g.,* Williamson M. Evers & Paul Clopton, *High Spending, Low Performing School Districts, in* Hanushek, *supra* note 227, at 103; Eric A. Hanushek, *Science Violated: Spending Projections and the "Costing Out" of an Adequate Education, in* Hanushek, *supra* note 227, at 257. Others claim to find positive effects. *See, e.g.,* Willam J. Glen, *Separate but Not Yet Equal: The Relation between School Finance Adequacy Litigation and African-American Student Achievement,* 81 PEABODY J. EDUC. 63–93 (2006). Hanushek's recent work emphasizes that a well-educated workforce is a priority but challenges assertions that

resources can turn students at risk of academic failure into academic successes. HANUSHEK & LINDSETH, *supra* note 232, at 1311–70.

234. Matthew G. Springer & James W. Guthrie, *The Politicization of the School Finance Legal Process, in* West & Peterson, *supra* note 213, at 102–24. School finance research has been supported by organizations identified as conservative (e.g., the Hoover Institute). *See* Paul E. Peterson, Hoover Institution, *Reforming Education in Florida: A Study Prepared by the Koret Task Force on K–12 Education* (2006), www.hoover.org/publications/blook/online/395672.html. Participants in school finance litigation also write law review articles about it. *See, e.g.,* Rebell, *supra* note 203.

235. *See* Palfrey, *supra* note 205, at 40, 52–61. *See also* KOZOL, *supra* note 221, at 9, 17.

236. GARY ORFIELD & CHUNGMEI LEE, HARVARD CIVIL RIGHTS PROJECT, *BROWN* AT 50: KING'S DREAM OR *PLESSY*'S NIGHTMARE? (2004).

237. Press Release, ACLU of Northern California, Landmark Education Case Will Hold State Responsible for Pervasive Substandard Conditions in Public Schools (May 17, 2000), www.aclunc.org/news/press_releases/landmark_education_case_will_hold_state_responsible_for_pervasive_substandard_conditions_in_public_schools.shtml; KOZOL, *supra* note 221, at 171.

238. California Department of Education, *The Williams Case: An Explanation,* www.cde.ca.gov/eo/ce/wc/wmslawsuit.asp (last visited Nov. 5, 2009); Sacramento County Office of Education, *Williams v. State of California Education Lawsuit Settlement,* www.scoe.net/williams/index.html (last visited Nov. 5, 2009).

239. Peter Schrag, *Williams Deal: Better California Schools by Inches,* SACRAMENTO BEE, Aug. 18, 2004, at B7; Schoolwise Press, *The Spirit of the Williams Adequacy Lawsuit Has Been Lost* (2004), web site of Schoolwise Press, www.schoolwisepress.com/smart/news/rotation_news/williams.html. Michael Kirst observed that the settlement moved students in the low-funded schools "from the basement to the first floor, but there are two more floors to go." KOZOL, *supra* note 221, at 256 (quoting Michael Kirst, former president of California Board of Education).

Chapter 4

1. The epigraph to this chapter is from Mike Cole, *Introduction: Human Rights, Education, and Equality, in* EDUCATION, EQUALITY, AND HUMAN RIGHTS: A HANDBOOK FOR STUDENTS 1, 4 (Mike Cole ed., 2000).

2. *See* Mary Noden Lochner, *Alaska Native Civil Rights History Shaped State,* NORTHERN LIGHT (Feb. 27, 2007), www.thenorthernlight.org/2007/02/27/alaskanativecivilrightshistoryshapedstate/. Before statehood, the territorial government approved segregated schooling for Native Alaskans, managed by the Bureau of Indian Affairs. *See id.*; Alaska Native Education, *Report of the Education Task Force,* www.alaskool.org/resources/anc2/ ANC2_Sec4.html.

3. Interdisciplinary essays examine equality for groups versus for individuals in the context of schooling, in JUST SCHOOLS: PURSUING EQUALITY IN SOCIETIES OF DIFFERENCE (Martha Minow et al. eds., 2008).

4. 268 U.S. 510 (1925).

5. 406 U.S. 205 (1972).

6. Jessica Calefati, *A Third High School for Gay Students*, U.S. NEWS & WORLD REPORT (Oct. 24, 2008), www.usnews.com/blogs/on-education/2008/10/24/a-third-high-school-for-gay-students.html.

7. This is the mission of multicultural arts schools in Chicago and Milwaukee. *See* the web site of Multicultural Arts High School, http://ma.lvlhs.org (last visited Oct. 31, 2009); the web site of Sherman Multicultural Arts School, www2.milwaukee.k12.wi.us/Sherman (last visited Oct. 31, 2009).

8. *See* Jon Reyhner, *American Indian/Alaska Native Education: An Overview* (2006), American Indian Education http://jan.ucc.nau.edu/jar/AIE/Ind_Ed.html (last visited Oct. 25, 2009).

9. *Id.*

10. *See, e.g.*, DAVID WALLACE ADAMS, EDUCATION FOR EXTINCTION: AMERICAN INDIANS AND THE BOARDING SCHOOL EXPERIENCE, 1875–1928, at 6–10 (1995); JON REYHNER & JEANNE EDER, AMERICAN INDIAN EDUCATION: A HISTORY 48–51, 59–78 (2004).

11. *Id.* at 14–39, 112–67.

12. Richard H. Pratt, *The Advantages of Mingling Indians with Whites* (extract from Official Report of the Nineteenth Annual Conference of Charities and Correction, 1892), *in* AMERICANIZING THE AMERICAN INDIANS: WRITINGS BY THE "FRIENDS OF THE INDIAN" 1880–1990, at 260, 261 (Francies Paul Prucha ed., 1973).

13. Daniel E. Witte & Paul T. Mero, *Removing Classrooms from the Battlefield: Liberty, Paternalism, and the Redemptive Promise of Educational Choice*, 2008 BYU L. REV. 377.

14. *See* COHEN'S HANDBOOK OF FEDERAL INDIAN LAW 6–113 (2005) (§ 1); HELEN HUNT JACKSON, A CENTURY OF DISHONOR: A SKETCH OF THE UNITED STATES GOVERNMENT'S DEALINGS WITH SOME OF THE INDIAN TRIBES (1881).

15. ADAMS, *supra* note 10, at 9, 12–21; TSIANINA LOMAWAIMA, AWAY FROM HOME: AMERICAN INDIAN BOARDING SCHOOL EXPERIENCES, 1879–2000 (2000); REYHNER & EDER, *supra* note 10, at 4–5. *See* COHEN'S HANDBOOK, *supra* note 14, at 1355–75 (§ 22.02).

16. REYHNER & EDER, *supra* note 10, at 308–20; LOMAWAIMA, *supra* note 15, at 1879–2000.

17. COHEN'S HANDBOOK, *supra* note 14, at 82 (§ 1.04).

18. *See* Wheeler Howard Act (Indian Reorganization Act), 48 Stat. 984–88 (1934) (codified as amended at 25 U.S.C. § 461 et seq.).

19. COHEN'S HANDBOOK, *supra* note 14, at 89–113 (§§ 1.06–1.07).

20. ADAMS, *supra* note 10, at 251–54.

21. *See* GEORGE PIERRE CASTILE, TO SHOW HEART: NATIVE AMERICAN SELF-DETERMINATION AND FEDERAL INDIAN POLICY, 1960–1975 (1999).

22. REYHNER & EDER, *supra* note 10, at 250–54.

23. *Indian Education: A National Tragedy—A National Challenge*, S. Rep. No. 91–501, xi (1969), www.tedna.org/pubs/Kennedy/toc.htm.

24. *Id.* at 105–17.

25. *Id.* at 98–100 (§ 1.07).

26. "[T]he story of the Indian in America is something more than the record of the white man's frequent aggression, broken agreements, intermittent remorse and prolonged failure. It is a record also of endurance, of survival, of adaptation and creativity in the face of overwhelming obstacles. It is a record of enormous contributions to this country—to its art and culture, to its strength and spirit, to

its sense of history and its sense of purpose." *President's Special Message to the Congress on Indian Affairs,* 1970 Pub. Papers 565 (July 8, 1970), www.residency. ucsb.edu/ws/index.php?pid=2573&st=&st. *See* Reyhner & Eder, *supra* note 10.

27. Adams, *supra* note 10, at 258–59.

28. *Id.* at 325–26.

29. Pub. L. No. 93–638, 88 Stat. 2203 (1975) (codified as amended at 25 U.S.C. § 450 et. seq.).

30. Pub. L. No. 100–297 (1988).

31. 25 U.S.C. §§ 2901–6.

32. 25 U.S.C. §§ 452–57.

33. *See* Jonathan B. Taylor & Joseph P. Kalt, *American Indians on Reservations: A Databook of Socioeconomic Change between the 1990 and 2000 Censuses* 2 (Jan. 2005), http:// www.hks.harvard.edu/hpaied/pubs/documents/AmericanIndiansonReservationsADatabookofSocioeconomicChange.pdf. "In 2000, 511,000 people living on reservations in the lower forty-eight states identified themselves as single-race American Indians or Alaska Natives, up 25% from a decade earlier. An additional 97,000 single-race Indians lived in Alaska, 3,000 in Hawaii, and 229,000 in designated Indian statistical areas. The remaining 1.6 million lived outside Indian areas in the lower forty-eight states, for an off-reservation total of 1.9 million and a U.S. total of 2.4 million." *Id.*

34. Institute of Education Sciences, National Center for Education Statistics, *Status and Trends in Elementary and Secondary Education of American Indians and Alaskan Natives: 2008,* http://nces.ed.gov/pubs2008/nativetrends/ind (last visited Oct. 31, 2009).

35. Adams, *supra* note 10, at 52–59.

36. *See* Vine Deloria, Jr., & Daniel R. Wildcat, Power and Place: Indian Education in America (2001).

37. Adams, *supra* note 10, at 30–50.

38. Lomawaima, *supra* note 15, at 26.

39. Adams, *supra* note 10, at 336–37; Rhyner & Eder, *supra* note 10, at 199–200.

40. Charla Bear, *American Indian School a Far Cry from the Past,* National Public Radio, www.npr.org/templates/story/story.php?storyId=17645287 (last visited Oct. 31, 2009).

41. Native American Languages Act, Pub. L. No. 101–477, §§ 102–7, 104 Stat. 1153 (1990) (codified at 25 U.S.C. §§ 2901–6).

42. *Id.* Analogously, an initiative in Vancouver authorized greater control by native leaders over the curriculum in native schools, acknowledging cultural grounding as a potential response to the high dropout rate. Petti Fong & Bill Curry, *Native Schools Get Own Curriculum,* Globe & Mail (Toronto), July 6, 2006, at A7.

43. *See* Kirk Johnson, *On the Reservation and Off, Schools See a Changing Tide,* N.Y. Times, May 25, 2008, at A12.

44. *Id.*

45. *Id.* (describing unwritten code at the Hardin High School, in Hardin, Montana, marking a "white side of the parking lot" and an "Indian side").

46. Ed.gov, *Strengthening Academic Competitiveness for Tribal Colleges and Universities: Technical Assistance Workshop,* www.ed.gov/about/inits/list/whtc/edlite-index.html (last visited Oct. 25, 2009); American Indian College Fund, Tribal Colleges, http://www.collegefund.org/colleges/main.html (last visited Oct.

25, 2009). The Tribally Controlled College or University Assistance Act, Pub. L. No. 105-244, § 902 (1998), enabled some shift of resources to higher education programs controlled by tribes, increasing the number of tribally controlled colleges from a few to twenty-six in 2002. OFFICE OF INDIAN EDUCATION PROGRAMS, FINGERTIP FACTS 3 (2002). *See also* James A. Larmore & George S. McClellan, *Native American Student Retention in U.S. Post-secondary Education*, 109 NEW DIRECTIONS FOR STUDENT SERVICES 17 (2005).

47. American Indian College Fund, *2007–2008 Annual Report and Audited Financials* 7, www.collegefund.org/news/publications.html. With now up to thirty-two tribal colleges and universities, educating 16,900 students, these schools over the past twenty-five years have doubled the number of American Indians receiving postsecondary degrees. *Id.*

48. ARTHUR M. COHEN & FLORENCE B. BROWN, THE AMERICAN COMMUNITY COLLEGE 56 (5th ed. 2008).

49. THE RENAISSANCE OF AMERICAN INDIAN HIGHER EDUCATION: CAPTURING THE DREAM (Maenette K. P. A. Benham & Wayne J. Stein eds., 2002).

50. COHEN'S HANDBOOK, *supra* note 14, at 1365 (§ 22.03(2)(b)).

51. RONALD H. HECK & MAENETTE KAPE'AHIOKALANI PADEKEN AH NEE BENHAM, CULTURE & EDUCATIONAL POLICY IN HAWAI'I: THE SILENCING OF NATIVE VOICES 13 (Erlbaum 1998).

52. There are multiple definitions of Native Hawai'ian. In Hawai'i Revised Statutes, § 10-2, "Hawai'ians" are defined as "any descendant of the aboriginal peoples inhabiting the Hawai'ian Islands which exercised sovereignty and subsisted in the Hawai'ian Islands in 1778, and which peoples thereafter have continued to reside in Hawaii." HAW. REV. STAT. § 10-2 (2009). The Office of Hawai'ian Affairs using "native Hawai'ian" to refer to someone with at least 50 percent "blood quantum" of Native Hawai'ian ancestry. Office of Hawai'ian Affairs, *Office of Hawai'ian Affairs Vision and Mission* (2008), www.oha.org/ (follow "About OHA"; then follow "Vision and Mission") (last visited Oct. 25, 2009). The Kamehameha Schools require proof that at least one ancestor of the applicant born before 1959 was Native Hawaiian. Web site of Kamehameha Schools, Data Center, www.ksbe.edu/datacenter/hooulu-faq.php (last visited Oct. 25, 2009). A robust tradition of adoption by Native Hawai'ians has further complicated the definition, and at least one litigant argued that an adoptee can be identified as Native Hawai'ian if his or her adoptive parents would be so identified. *See* Rick Daysog, *School Lets Non-Hawai'ian Stay; In Exchange, the Student Will Drop His Suit against Kamehameha Schools*, HONOLULU STAR BULL., Nov. 29, 2003, http://starbulletin.com/2003/11/29/news/story3.html. The Office of Hawai'ian Affairs rejects that view, however, and requires proof in terms of the biological parents. Office of Hawai'ian Affairs, *supra.*

53. *Kamehameha Continuing to Serve More Hawa'iians*, JULY 1, 2006–JUNE 30, 2007, KAMEHAMEHA SCHOOLS ANNUAL REPORT 3 at 1, 5, www.ksbe.edu/index. php?topic=annualreports. Quite apart from the admissions policies, serious questions about the management of the charity have arisen and produced reforms in recent years. *See* SAMUEL P. KING & RANDALL W. ROTH, BROKEN TRUST: GREED, MISMANAGEMENT, AND POLITICAL MANIPULATION AT AMERICA'S LARGEST CHARITABLE TRUST (2006).

54. Kamehameha Schools, Campuses, web site of www.ksbe.edu/campuses. php (last visited Oct. 29, 2009).

55. Doe v. Kamehameha Schools, 470 F.3d 827 (9th Cir. 2006) (*en banc*). For a discussion of the panel decision, *see* Recent Case, *Civil Rights—Section*

1981—Ninth Circuit Holds That Private School's Remedial Admissions Policy Violates § 1981—Doe v. Kamehameha Schools, 416 F.3d 1025, 119 HARV. L. REV. 661 (2005).

56. *See* Doe v. Kamehameha Schools, 470 F.3d at 848 (citing the Augustus F. Hawkins–Robert T. Stafford Elementary and Secondary School Improvement Amendments of 1988, 20 U.S.C. §§ 4901–9 (1988) (repealed 1994) ("Special efforts in education recognizing the unique cultural and historical circumstances of Native Hawai'ians."), the Native Hawai'ian Education Act of 1994, 20 U.S.C. §§ 7901–41, and a congressional committee report for the No Child Left Behind Act of 2001, H.R. REP. No. 107–63(I), at 333). The majority en banc opinion concluded: "it is clear that a manifest imbalance exists in the K–12 educational arena in the state of Hawai'i, with Native Hawai'ians falling at the bottom of the spectrum in almost all areas of educational progress and success. Furthermore, it is precisely this manifest imbalance that the Kamehameha Schools' admissions policy seeks to address. The goal is to bring Native Hawai'ian students into educational parity with other ethnic groups in Hawai'i." *Id.* at 843. It continued: "[N]othing in the record suggests that educational opportunities in Hawai'i are deficient for students, like Plaintiff, who lack any Native Hawai'ian ancestry. To the contrary, the same statistical data that portray the difficulties of Native Hawai'ian children generally portray much greater educational achievement, in both public and private primary and secondary schools, for children of all other racial and ethnic groups in Hawai'i. Those students denied admission by Kamehameha Schools have ample and adequate alternative educational options." *Id.* at 844.

57. Judge Willie Fletcher's concurring opinion for four judges reasoned that "Congress has invariably treated 'Native Hawai'ian' as a political classification [rather than a racial one] for purposes of providing exclusive educational and other benefits. Under the special relationship doctrine, Congress has the power to do so. I see nothing in § 1981 to indicate that Congress intended to impose upon private institutions a more restrictive standard for the provision of benefits to Native Hawai'ians than it has imposed upon itself." 470 F.2d 849, 856–87 (9th Cir. 2006) (concurring opinion). The will establishing the trust and the schools themselves were created before the overthrow of the Hawai'ian government. A Timeline of the Kamehameha Schools, Kapālama, Kamehameha School Archives, http://kapalama.ksbe.edu/archives/Timelines/Schools/KSHistory.php (last visited Oct. 31, 2009). Hawaii's Senator Daniel Akaka introduced legislation, passed by the House of Representatives in 2007, by which Congress would recognize Native Hawai'ians as a political group analogous to American Indians and Alaska natives. *See* http://akaka.senate.gov/akakabill-b.html (discussing S. 147, The Native Hawai'ian Government Reorganization Act of 2005).

58. For a historical defense of the idea, *see* ANDREW KRULL, THE COLOR-BLIND CONSTITUTION (1998). For critiques of color blindness as an approach to equality, *see* Barbara J. Flagg, *"Was Blind, But Now I See": White Race Consciousness and the Requirement of Discriminatory Intent,* 91 U. MICH. L. REV. 953 (1993); Neil Gotanda, *A Critique of "Our Constitution Is Color-Blind,"* 44 STAN. L. REV. 1 (1991); Glenn C. Loury, *America's Moral Dilemma: Will It Be Color Blindness or Racial Equality?* 27 J. OF BLACKS IN HIGHER EDUC. 90 (2000).

59. Lisey Doi, web post (July 17, 2006, 2:43 EST), Hawaiian Cultural Preservation, http://hawaiianculturalpreservation.blogspot.com/2006/07/kamehameha-schools-article.html.

60. *Compare* Grutter v. Bollinger, 539 U.S. 306 (2003), *with* Parents Involved in Community Schools v. Seattle Public School District No. 1, 551 U.S. 701 (2007).

61. Eric Yamamoto, Susan Kiyomi Serrano, & Eva Paterson, *Kamehameha Admissions Don't Offend Our Civil Rights* (Vernellia R. Randall ed.), http://academic.udayton.edu/race/02rights/Hawaii07.htm (last visited Oct. 26, 2009).

62. Georgia Ka'apuni McMillen, *A School of One's Own*, N.Y. Times, Aug. 29, 2005, http://query.nytimes.com/gst/fullpage.html?res=9901EEDF1631F93A A1575BC0A9639C8B63&sec=&spon=&pagewanted=all.

63. *See* Ken Kobayashi, *$7M: An Attorney Involved in a Challenge to Kamehameha Schools' Hawaiians-only Policy Reveals the Amount of a Settlement*, Honolulu Star Bull. (Feb. 9, 2008), http://archives. starbulletin.com/2008/02/09/news/story02.html.

64. Jim Dooley, *School's $7M Deal Raises Ire, Eyebrows*, Honolulu Advertiser, Feb. 8, 2008, at 1B.

65. Web site of Kamehameha Schools, www.ksbe.edu/campus/schools.html (last visited Oct. 27, 2009).

66. Kamehameha Schools, Financial Aid and Scholarship Services, web site of Kamehameha Schools, www.ksbe.edu/finaid/ (last visited Oct. 27, 2009).

67. King & Roth, *supra* note 53, at 40–42.

68. *Id.* at 47–51.

69. Kamehameha Schools, Admissions Office, web site of Kamehameha Schools, www.ksbe.edu/admissions/admissions.php (last visited Oct. 27, 2009).

70. King & Roth, *supra* note 53, at 55–59, 76–77.

71. Kamehameha Schools, Community Education,web site of Kamehameha Schools, http://extension.ksbe.edu/content/index.php?option=com_content&task=blogcategory&id=31&Itemid=54 (last visited Oct. 27, 2009).

72. Gordon Y. K. Pang, *Native Hawaiian Students Bloom in Charter Schools*, Honolulu Advertiser, Nov. 15, 2006, at 1A.

73. *Id.*

74. Maintaining traditions could be separated from the identity or ancestry of those who maintain them, as explored by novelist Marge Piercy, Woman on the Edge of Time (1976). *See also* Peg Tittle, *Rational Bases of Identity: Toward Cultural Anarchy*, 29 Humanist of Canada 3 (Autumn 96), http://tittle.humanists. net/rational_bases_of_identity.htm.

75. *See* David Strauss, Do It but Don't Tell Me (Feb. 2008) (unpublished manuscript on file with author).

76. U.S. Government Accountability Office, Report to Congressional Requesters, Native Hawaiian education Act: Greater Oversight Would Increase Accountability and Enable Targeting of Funds to Areas with Greatest Need, GAO-08–422, at 1 (Mar. 25, 2008), www.gao.gov/new.items/d08422.pdf.

77. On the Japanese internment and schooling, *see* Yoon Park, Wherever I Go, I Will Always Be a Loyal American: Seattle's Japanese American Schoolchildren during World War II: Studies in the History of Education (2001).

78. Brown v. Board of Education, 347 U.S. 483, 493 (1954).

79. *Id.* at 495.

80. Thanks to Adam Szubin for this point.

81. Board of Education of Kiryas Joel Village School District v. Grumet, 512 U.S. 687 (1994).

82. The versions in place at the time of the litigation were 28 U.S.C. §§ 1400–1402, 1404, 1409, 1411–14 (Supp. V. 1993); N.Y. Educ. Law §§ 4004–5 (McKinney 1995).

83. *See* Aguilar v. Felton, 473 U.S. 402 (1985): Wolman v. Walter, 433 U.S. 229 (1977). The Supreme Court later overturned these restrictions as it moved toward a neutral, equal treatment approach to religion. Agostini v. Felton, 521 U.S. 203 (1997). *See supra* ch. 3 (discussing religion cases).

84. Board of Education of Kiryas Joel Village School District v. Grumet, 512 U.S. 687 (1994).

85. JEROME R. MINTZ, HASIDIC PEOPLE: A PLACE IN THE NEW WORLD (1992); ISRAEL R. RUBIN, SATMAR: AN ISLAND IN THE CITY (1972).

86. WILLIAM M. KEPHART & WILLIAM W. ZELLNER, EXTRAORDINARY GROUPS 161–75 (4th ed. 1991).

87. *See* Allan L. Nadler, *Piety and Politics: The Case of the Satmar Rebbe*, 31 JUDAISM 135 (1982). *See also* AMY GUTMAN, IDENTITY IN DEMOCRACY 189 (2003).

88. Suzanne Fields, *Public School District for Sect Denied*, ATLANTA J. & CONST., June 30, 1994, at A2.

89. Parents' Association of P.S. 16 v. Quinones, 803 F.2d 1235, 1238 (2d cir. 1986) (recounting quotation from media coverage).

90. Mintz, *supra* note 85, at 162. The Satmar's brief indicated a preference for living together to facilitate religious observance and values but rejected the suggestion that separatism was a religious tenet.

91. Nathan Lewin, counsel for Kiryas Joel, telephone interview by the author (Nov. 4, 1994); Affidavit of Steven M. Bernardo, app. J. at 115–17a, Board of Education of Kiryas Joel Village School District v. Grumet, 512 U.S. 687 (1994).

92. Nomi Maya Stolzenberg, Board of Education of Kiryas Joel Village School District v. Grumet: *A Religious Group's Quest for Its Own Public School*, in LAW AND RELIGION; CASES IN CONTEXT (Gregory Alexander & Eduardo Penalver eds., 2010), USC Law Legal Studies Paper No. 09–30, at 13, http://ssrn.com/abstract=1441413.

93. Justice Souter wrote for a majority that the legislature wrongly allowed public authority to be used for religious benefit, giving too much authority over a secular social function to a religious body, given the pivotal governance role played by the community's religious figures; Justice Kennedy analogized the problem to impermissible apportionment of voting districts along racial lines. Justice O'Connor disapproved of the legislature appearing to favor one religious group over other groups; and Justice Stevens objected that the Satmar should not be allowed to use a public school to shield their children from secular influences. Board of Education of Kiryas Joel Village School District v. Grumet, 512 U.S. 687 (1994). For a spirited academic debate about the case, *see The Church-state Game: A Symposium on Kiryas Joel*, 47 FIRST THINGS 36 (Nov. 1994), www.leaderu.com/ftissues/ft9411/articles/kiryas.html (last visited Oct. 31, 2009).

94. Stolzenberg, *supra* note 92, at 56–57.

95. Milliken v. Bradley, 418 U.S. 717, 744–45 (1974).

96. Board of Education of Kiryas Joel Village School District v. Grumet, 512 U.S., at 711 (Stevens, J., concurring).

97. *Id.*

Chapter 5

1. Frederick M. Hess, *Fulfilling the Promise of School Choice* (Sept. 2008), AM. ENTER. INST. ONLINE, www.aei.org/outlook/28679.

2. *See* Green v. County School Board, 391 U.S. 430 (1968) (challenging the constitutionality of a freedom of choice plan); CHARLES T. CLOTFELTER, AFTER BROWN: THE RISE AND RETREAT OF SCHOOL DESEGREGATION 100-123 (2004).

3. *See* Martha Minow, *Reforming School Reform,* 68 FORDHAM L. REV. 257 (1999).

4. The publication of *A Nation at Risk* by the National Commission on Excellence in Education in 1983 stimulated the movement for accountability in education. NATIONAL COMMISSION ON EXCELLENCE IN EDUCATION, A NATION AT RISK: THE IMPERATIVE FOR EDUCATIONAL REFORM (1983), www.ed.gov/pubs/NatAtRisk/index.html. At a meeting of governors in 1989, President George H. W. Bush joined the governors in articulating a set of broad performance goals for American schools, and in 1991, President Bush proposed voluntary national testing tied to standards. In 1994, President Clinton signed into law the Goals 2000: Educate America Act, which provided grants to help states develop academic standards. President George W. Bush pursued mandatory testing tied to state standards and secured the No Child Left Behind Act as a response to the perceived failures of public schooling. For a discussion of the No Child Left Behind Act, *see infra* text accompanying notes 19-23.

5. Even strong advocates of public schooling describe school choice as a "jolt to the system" that could prompt school improvement. DAVID TYACK, SEEKING COMMON GROUND: PUBLIC SCHOOLS IN A DIVERSE SOCIETY 178 (2003). Perhaps the most extreme version of parental choice appears in the burgeoning homeschooling movement. Still small as a percentage of schooling in the entire population, homeschooling nonetheless is among the fastest growing sectors of K–12 education in the United States. *See* DANIEL PRINCIOTTA & STACEY BIELICK, U.S. DEPARTMENT OF Education, NCES 2006–042, HOMESCHOOLING IN THE UNITED STATES: 2003 (2006), http://nces.ed.gov/pubs2006/2006042.pdf.

6. Innovations may pursue pedogogical alternatives or missions related to curricular focus or identity-based theme.

7. The Massachusetts Department of Elementary and Secondary Education explains: "Charter schools are independent public schools designed to encourage innovative educational practices. Charter schools are funded by tuition charges assessed against the school districts where the students reside. The state provides partial reimbursement to the sending districts for the tuition costs incurred." Mass. Department of Elementary and Secondary Education, *School Finance: Charter Schools,* http://finance1.doe.mass.edu/pdf/-charter-Default.html(1).pdf (last visited Oct. 18, 2009). Utah similarly describes its funding method for charter schools: "Charter schools are funded on the principle that state funds follow the student. Charter schools also receive appropriate portions of local money from the school districts in which the charter school students reside. Charter schools may also apply for state and federal start-up funds. A charter school may not charge tuition or require students or parents to make donations, and it is subject to the same rules regarding school fees as other public schools." Utah State Office of Education, *Utah Charter Schools Funding,* www.usoe.k12.ut.us/charterschools/funding.htm (last visited Oct. 16, 2009). Some states fund charter

schools at a lower level than conventional public schools. Thus, "Minnesota charter schools only receive the state portion (about 75% of a district school's total per pupil allocation); in New Jersey and Colorado [charters] also receive less than 100 per cent of the per pupil funding. In other states, charters must negotiate their funding in their charter contract, often below the level of funding of their district counterparts. In Arizona, charter students are funded at about 80 per cent of their district peers." Igor Kitaev, *Charter Schools in the USA—A Fast-growing Phenomenon*, INT'L INST. EDUC. PLAN. NEWSL., Jan.–Mar. 2001, at 7, www.iiep.unesco.org/fileadmin/user_upload/pdf/jane01.pdf.

8. Pierce v. Society of Sisters, 268 U.S. 510 (1925).

9. States vary in their degree of requirements applicable to private schools. *See* OFFICE OF NON-PUBLIC EDUC., U.S. DEPARTMENT OF EDUC., STATE REGULATION OF PRIVATE SCHOOLS (2000), www.ed.gov/pubs/RegPrivSchl/.

10. Wisconsin v. Yoder, 406 U.S. 205 (1972).

11. *Id.* at 224.

12. *See* NATIONAL CENTER FOR EDUCATION STATISTICS, U.S. DEPARTMENT OF EDUCATION, NCES 2009–030, ISSUE BRIEF: 1.5 MILLION HOMESCHOOLED STUDENTS IN THE UNITED STATES IN 2007 (2008), http://nces.ed.gov/pubs2009/2009030.pdf.

13. *Id.*

14. *See, e.g.*, Parents Involved in Community Schools v. Seattle School District No. 1, 551 U.S. 701, 802–05 (2007).

15. On magnet schools, *see* Grace Chen, *What Is a Magnet School?* PUB. SCH. REV. (Dec. 4, 2007), www.publicschoolreview.com/articles/2. An example of district-wide choice is Cambridge, Massachusetts. Its district-wide choice plan initially emerged as a racial desegregation effort, but starting in 2000, public officials altered the plan to eliminate concerns with race and turned instead to promote socioeconomic integration in the schools. *See* OFFICE OF INNOVATION AND IMPROVEMENT, U.S. DEPARTMENT OF EDUCATION, INNOVATIONS IN EDUCATION: CREATING STRONG DISTRICT SCHOOL CHOICE PROGRAMS (2004), www.ed.gov/admins/comm/choice/choiceprograms/report.pdf.

16. *See* LAURI STEEL & ROGER LEVINE, EDUCATIONAL INNOVATION IN MULTIRACIAL CONTEXTS: THE GROWTH OF MAGNET SCHOOLS IN AMERICAN EDUCATION (1994) (contract research with the U.S. Department of Education) (reporting on distinctive curriculum and instructional methods in 2,433 magnet schools nationwide that attract students from outside neighborhood zones and seek racial desegregation); WHO CHOOSES? WHO LOSES? CULTURE, INSTITUTIONS, AND THE UNEQUAL EFFECTS OF SCHOOL CHOICE 26 (Bruce Fuller et al. eds., 1996) (discussing the Magnet School Assistance Act, 20 U.S.C. § 7231 (2002)).

17. Parents Involved in Community Schools v. Seattle School District No. 1, 551 U.S. 701 (2007). On recent efforts to use magnet schools to promote racial diversity, *see* Tim Pugmire, *New Magnet Schools Are Key to Suburban Desegregation Plan*, Minnesota Public Radio, Sept. 21, 2005, http://news.minnesota.publicradio.org/features/2005/08/09_pugmiret_deseg/.

18. Alexander Russo, *When School Choice Isn't*, WASH. MONTHLY, Sept. 2002, at 15.

19. George W. Bush campaigned for the presidency in no small measure on a proposal to enact school reform premised on testing in relation to national standards, and his major domestic accomplishment was the enactment of the No Child Left Behind Act in 2001. *See* Andrew Rudalevige, *The Politics of "No Child Left Behind,"* EDUC. NEXT, fall 2003, at 63.

20. *E.g.*, Sara S. Davis, letter to the editor, WASH. POST, Aug. 29, 2006, at A14; No Child Left Page, http://nochildleft.com/ (last visited July 10, 2009).

21. *See Court Hears NEA Appeal in NCLB Unfunded Mandates Lawsuit*, DEL. STATE EDUC. ASS'N ACTION! Dec. 2006, at 21, www.dsea.org/Publications/PDF/actionnovdec06.pdf.

22. *See* Staci Hupp, *Ranking Confusion: Schools Can Pass and Fail*, INDIANAPOLIS STAR, Aug. 10, 2006, at A1.

23. In addition, the inclusion of school choice mechanisms through transfers has not produced noticeable options for students in failing schools. By the fifth year of implementation, only 1 percent of students in schools identified for improvement took opportunities to transfer to better performing schools, perhaps due to operational issues, lack of provision of information to parents about transfer options, or parents' preferences for convenience or deferring to the child's preference. Lynn A. Karoly, Gail L. Zellman, Brian M. Stecher, Georges Vernez, Laura S. Hamilton, Susan J. Bodilly, & Jennifer Li, *Lessons Learned: Education Priorities for the Obama Administration*, RAND REV., summer 2009, at 14, 16.

24. U.S. Charter Schools, *What Is a Charter School?* www.uscharterschools.org/pub/uscs_docs/o/faq.html#2 (last visited Oct. 16, 2009). Nationwide, a total of 4,578 charter schools were operating in 2009, with a total of 1,407,421 students enrolled. CENTER FOR EDUCATION REFORM, THE ACCOUNTABILITY REPORT 2009: CHARTER SCHOOLS (2009), www.edreform.com/accountability/. *See also* Sam Dillon, *Ohio Goes after Charter Schools That Are Failing*, N.Y. TIMES, Nov. 8, 2007, at A1 (noting four thousand charter schools); Center for Education Reform, *Number of Charter Schools Up 11 Percent Nationwide: More Than Half of Charter Students Are Low-income or Minority* (May 10, 2007), press release, www.edreform.com/Archive/?Number_of_Charter_Schools_Up_11_Percent_NationwideMore_than_Half_of_Charter_Students_Are_LowIncome_or_Minority. On the chartering process and the need to protect public values, *see* Stephen D. Sugarman & Emelei M. Kuboyama, *Approving Charter Schools: The Gatekeeper Function*, 53 ADMINISTRATIVE L. REV. 869 (2001).

25. NATIONAL CENTER FOR EDUCATION STATISTICS, U.S. DEPARTMENT OF EDUCATION, DIGEST OF EDUCATION STATISTICS (2005) (providing national charter school data).

26. James Forman, Jr., *The Secret History of School Choice: How Progressives Got There First*, 93 GEO. L.J. 1287, 1295–1309 (2005).

27. Robert C. Bulman & David L. Kirp, *The Shifting Politics of School Choice*, *in* SCHOOL CHOICE AND SOCIAL CONTROVERSY: POLITICS, POLICY, AND LAW 36, 52–53 (Stephen D. Sugarman & Frank R. Kemerer eds., 1999); *see also* KELAN J. KELLY, NEVADA LEGISLATIVE COUNSEL BUREAU, CHARTER SCHOOLS: BACKGROUND PAPER 97–1 (1997).

28. Bob Perlman, *Smarter Charters? Creating Boston's Pilot Schools*, *in* CREATING NEW SCHOOLS: HOW SMALL SCHOOLS ARE CHANGING AMERICA 38 (Evans Clinchy ed., 2000), www.bobpearlman.org/Articles/SmarterCharters.htm. The choice of state, district, or school-level control could affect the degree of programmatic and budgetary autonomy and also the source and scope of funding for these new schools. *See* Editorial, *Clipped Wings for Pilot Schools*, BOSTON GLOBE, Dec. 5, 2007, at A22.

29. *See* Jonathan P. Krisbergh, Comment, *Marginalizing Organized Educators: The Effect of School Choice and "No Child Left Behind" on Teacher Unions*, 8 U. PA. J. LAB. & EMP. L. 1025 (2006); Sarah Mead & Andrew Rotherham, *A Sum*

Greater Than Its Parts: What States Can Teach Each Other about Charter Schooling, EDUC. SECTOR REP., Sept. 1997, at 10, www.educationsector.org/research/research_show.htm?doc_id=521913. *See generally* Martin H. Malin & Charles Taylor Kerchner, *Charter Schools and Collective Bargaining: Compatible Marriage or Illegitimate Relationship?* 30 HARV. J.L. & PUB. POL'Y 885 (2007); Arne Duncan, U.S. secretary of education, *Partners in Reform,* remarks to the National Education Association (July 2, 2009) (transcript available at www.ed.gov/news/speeches/2009/07/07022009.pdf).

30. *See* National School Boards Association, *Cleveland Voucher Program,* www.nsba.org/MainMenu/Advocacy/FederalLaws/SchoolVouchers/VoucherStrategyCenter/ClevelandVoucherProgram.aspx (last visited Oct. 24, 2009). The District of Columbia program was not renewed by Congress. *See* Elizabeth Hillgrove, *Senate Kills GOP's Voucher Bid,* WASH. TIMES, Mar. 11, 2009, at A13, www.washingtontimes.com/news/2009/mar/11/senate-kills-gops-dc-vouchers-bid/; Amanda Paulson, *Milwaukee's Lessons on School Vouchers,* CHRISTIAN SCI. MONITOR, May 23, 2006, at 1, www.csmonitor.com/2006/0523/p01s03-usgn.html. A plan that would have made Georgia the first state to have universal school vouchers failed in the legislature. *Georgia School Voucher Bill Dies in Session,* Associated press, Mar. 12, 2009, www.onlineathens.com/stories/031209/gen_408394651.shtml. The state supreme court voided a school voucher initiative in Florida as a violation of the state constitutional guarantee of "uniformity in public education," prompting an initiative to alter the state constitution. *See* Pete Chagnon, *Florida School Vouchers Put to Vote,* ONE NEWS NOW, May 2, 2008, www.onenewsnow.com/Education/Default.aspx?id=83438. On special needs vouchers, see *infra* (text at notes 170–171).

31. The actual latitude of choice in programs enabling students to transfer to other schools in their own or other districts depends on working out the mechanism to ensure public funding follows the child. Difficulties obtaining the funds apparently curbs the effect of such a program in Michigan, according to critics. PATRICK L. ANDERSON, RICHARD MCLELLAN, JOSEPH P. OVERTON, & GARY WOLFRAM, MACKINAC CENTER FOR PUBLIC POLICY, THE UNIVERSAL TUITION TAX CREDIT: A PROPOSAL TO ADVANCE PARENTAL CHOICE IN EDUCATION 26, 26–27 (1997), www.mackinac.org/archives/1997/s1997–04.pdf.

32. *See Pro Choice*, ECONOMIST, June 9, 2007, at 38.

33. METCO's web site notes: "[A] suburban METCO district receives less than $3,380 to educate, transport and provide special services for METCO students. Unfortunately, an average METCO district spends in excess of $6,000 to $10,000 to educate, transport, and provide special services for its resident students." Metropolitan Council for Educational Opportunity, *Fact about the Success of the METCO program*, www.metcoinc.org/success.htm (last visited Oct. 16, 2009). The viability of METCO is also put in jeopardy by the Supreme Court's decision restricting the use of race in school assignments. Parents Involved in Community Schools v. Seattle School District No. 1, 551 U.S. 701 (2007). Rochester, New York, pioneered a similar urban-suburban transfer program designed to reduce racial isolation; its rule that white students were not allowed to transfer from Rochester's city schools to "better" suburban schools except where the white student's enrollment would not "upset the racial balance of the school" faced a protracted challenge in federal court that ended with a financial settlement to the white student challenger and suspension of the program's eligibility rules. *See* Brewer v. West Irondequoit Central School District, 212 F.3d 738 (2d Cir. 2000);

Adversity.Net, *Case 32: Jessica Haak v. Rochester Schools* (Mar. 14, 2003), www.adversity.net/c32_jessica_haak.htm.

34. LEONARD S. RABINOWITZ & JAMES E. ROSENBAUM, CROSSING THE CLASS AND COLOR LINES: FROM PUBLIC HOUSING TO WHITE SUBURBS 49–72 (2002).

35. *Id.* at 174–92.

36. Pierce v. Society of Sisters, 268 U.S. 510 (1925). For a discussion of the case, *see supra* text accompanying note 6.

37. R. FREEMAN BUTTS, PUBLIC EDUCATION IN THE UNITED STATES: FROM REVOLUTION TO REFORM (1978); CARL F. KAESTLE, PILLARS OF THE REPUBLIC: COMMON SCHOOLS AND AMERICAN SOCIETY, 1780–1860 (1983); JONATHAN MESSERLI, HORACE MANN: A BIOGRAPHY (1972); DAVID TYACK, THE ONE BEST SYSTEM: A HISTORY OF AMERICAN URBAN EDUCATION (1973).

38. MICHAEL B. KATZ, THE IRONY OF EARLY SCHOOL REFORM: EDUCATIONAL INNOVATION IN MID-NINETEENTH-CENTURY MASSACHUSETTS (1968); DAVID TYACK, SEEKING COMMON GROUND: PUBLIC SCHOOLS IN A DIVERSE SOCIETY 12–13 (2003).

39. TYACK, *supra* note 37, at 76–77.

40. In a 1909 poll of five hundred fourteen- to sixteen-year-olds, 80 percent said that they preferred factory work over attending school. TYACK, *supra* note 37, at 99 (discussing Helen Todd, *Why Children Work: The Children's Answer*, 40 MCCLURE'S MAG. 68 (1913)).

41. *Id.* at 27.

42. *Id.* at 45, 137.

43. Universal Declaration of Human Rights, G.A. Res. 217A, at 71, U.N. GAOR, 3d Sess., 1st plen. mtg., U.N. Doc. A/810 (Dec. 12, 1948), www.un.org/Overview/rights.html.l.

44. Zelman v. Simmons-Harris, 536 U.S. 639 (2002). See chapter 3 *supra* and text at note 85, this chapter.

45. *E.g.*, Cato Institute, *Education and Child Policy: School Choice,* www.cato.org/subtopic_display_new.php?topic_id=64&ra_id=3 (last visited Oct. 16, 2009) (listing books, articles, and chapters sponsored by the Cato Institute on school choice); Press Release, Heritage Foundation, School-choice Movement Continues to Grow, Report Says (Apr. 26, 2005), www.heritage.org/press/newsreleases/nr042605a.cfm (summarizing Heritage Foundation study reporting that more than one million families homeschool their children and more than 624,000 use vouchers, tax credits, or tax deductions to elect schools). *See generally* LIBERTY & LEARNING: MILTON FRIEDMAN'S VOUCHER IDEA AT FIFTY (Robert C. Enlow & Lenore T. Ealy eds., 2006).

46. Milton Friedman, *The Role of Government in Education, in* ECONOMICS AND THE PUBLIC INTEREST 123 (Robert A. Solo ed., 1955); MILTON FRIEDMAN, CAPITALISM AND FREEDOM (1962). *See* Friedman Foundation for Educational Choice, Home Page, www.friedmanfoundation.org/friedman/Welcome.do (last visited Oct. 16, 2009).

47. Friedman, *Role of Government in Education, supra* note 46, at 124–35.

48. Nick Gillespie, *The Father of Modern School Reform*, REASON, Dec. 2005, at 44–47, www.reason.com/news/show/36333.html.

49. Friedman, *Role of Government in Education, supra* note 46, at 123 n. 2.

50. *Id.* at 144.

51. Milton Friedman endorsed gradual integration through vouchers: "The appropriate activity for those who oppose segregation and racial prejudice is to try to persuade others of their views; if and as they succeed, the mixed schools

will grow at the expense of the nonmixed, and a gradual transition will take place." *Id.*

52. Griffin v. County School Board of Prince Edward County, 377 U.S. 218 (1964). On the legal treatment of racial exclusion in private settings, *see* Imani Perry, *Dismantling the House of Plessy: A Private Law Study of Race in Cultural and Legal History With Contemporary Resonances*, 33 STUD. IN L., POL. & SOC'Y 91 (2004); Joseph William Singer, *No Right to Exclude: Public Accommodations and Private Property*, 90 NW. U. L. REV. 1283, 1286–88 (1996). *See also* Robert Cover, *Foreword: Nomos and Narrative*, 97 HARV. L. REV. 4 (1983).

53. Gerard Robinson, *Freedom of Choice: From Brown To School Vouchers*, SCH. REFORM NEWS, June 1, 2004, www.heartland.org/Article.cfm?artId=15065.

54. Green v. County School Board of New Kent County, 391 U.S. 430 (1968).

55. *See* Christopher Jencks, *Private Schools for Black Children*, N.Y. TIMES MAGAZINE, Nov. 3, 1968, at 30; Theodore Sizer & Phillip Whitten, *A Proposal for a Poor Children's Bill of Rights*, PSYCHOL. TODAY, Apr. 1968, at 62; Forman, *supra* note 26, at 1309.

56. PETER W. COOKSON, JR., SCHOOL CHOICE: THE STRUGGLE FOR THE SOUL OF AMERICAN EDUCATION 75 (1995).

57. *See* Forman, *supra* note 26, at 1312; ELIOT LEVINSON, THE ALUM ROCK VOUCHER DEMONSTRATION: THREE YEARS OF IMPLEMENTATION (1976), www.rand.org/pubs/papers/P5631/. Initial reports of declines in reading achievement seem to reflect methodological difficulties rather than a genuine effect. Paul M. Workman, Charles S. Reichardt, & Robert G. St. Pierre, *A Secondary Analysis of Student Achievement Test Scores*, 2 EVALUATION Q. 193–214 (1978).

58. COOKSON, *supra* note 56, at 76.

59. Scott Gelber, *"The Crux and the Magic": The Political History of Boston Magnet Schools, 1968–1989*, 41 EQUITY & EXCELLENCE IN EDUC. 453 (2008); Christine H. Rossell, *Magnet Schools: No Longer Famous but Still Intact*, EDUC. NEXT, spring 2005, http://findarticles.com/p/articles/mi_moMJG/is_2_5/ai_n13487200.

60. JOHN CHUBB & TERRY MOE, POLITICS, MARKETS, AND AMERICA'S SCHOOLS (1990).

61. *See, e.g.,* EDWARD B. FISKE & HELEN F. LADD, WHEN SCHOOLS COMPETE: A CAUTIONARY TALE (2000); SHARON GEWIRTZ, STEPHEN BALL, & RICHARD BOWE, MARKETS, CHOICE AND EQUITY IN EDUCATION (1995); Laura F. Rothstein, *School Choice and Students with Disabilities, in* SCHOOL CHOICE AND SOCIAL CONTROVERSY (Stephen D. Sugerman & Frank R. Kemere eds., 1999).

62. *See* Martha Minow, *Reforming School Reform*, 68 FORDHAM L. REV. 257, 263 (1999); Jeffrey R. Henig, *The Case against School Choice: Politics, Markets, and Fools by Kevin B. Smith & Kenneth J. Meier*, 89 AM. POL. SCI. REV. 1039 (1995) (book review).

63. STEVEN M. TELES, THE RISE OF THE CONSERVATIVE LEGAL MOVEMENT: THE BATTLE FOR CONTROL OF THE LAW 80 (2008).

64. *Id.* at 245 (quoting interview with Clint Bolick).

65. The book was published in 1991 by the Pacific Research Institute for Public Policy, a nonprofit organization founded in 1979 to advance "a free economy, private initiative, and limited government." Pacific Research Institute, Home Page, http://liberty.pacificresearch.org/. (last visited Oct. 17, 2009).

66. CLINT BOLICK, UNFINISHED BUSINESS: A CIVIL RIGHT'S STRATEGY FOR AMERICA'S THIRD CENTURY 136, 141 (1990). *See* TELES, *supra* note 63, at 86.

67. *See* TELES, *supra* note 63, at 238 (quoting letter from Institute for Justice to redacted party regarding grant application (Feb. 10, 1992)).

68. CLINT BOLICK, VOUCHER WARS 218–19 (2003).

69. Clint Bolick & Laura Underkuffler, *Debate Club: Are School Vouchers the Next Great Civil Rights Issue?* LEGAL AFFAIRS, June 13, 2005, www.legalaffairs. org/webexclusive/debateclub_vouchers0605.msp.

70. Lemon v. Kurtzman, 403 U.S. 602 (1971).

71. Aguilar v. Felton, 473 U.S. 401 (1985).

72. Comm. for Public Education v. Nyquist, 413 U.S. 756 (1973). Similarly, in *Sloan v. Lemon*, 413 U.S. 825 (1973), the Court rejected a statute reimbursing parents for $150 or $75 paid as tuition to nonpublic schools.

73. Wolman v. Walter, 433 U.S. 229 (1977).

74. *E.g.*, Comm. for Pub. Education & Religious Liberty v. Regan, 444 U.S. 646 (1980) (allowing reimbursement to nonpublic schools, including parochial schools, for the expenses involved in maintaining records and administered tests required by the state); Board of Education v. Allen, 392 U.S. 236 (1968) (permitting the government to loan secular textbooks to students in nonpublic schools).

75. Mueller v. Allen, 463 U.S. 388 (1983).

76. *See supra* chapter 3 (discussing legal changes affecting religious schools).

77. In Jenkins v. Leininger, 659 N.E.2d 1366 (Ill. App. Ct. 1995), a 1992 suit in Chicago on behalf of a group of parents and schoolchildren to create a court-ordered voucher system, Bolick argued that because the Illinois state constitution guaranteed children access to an "efficient" and "high-quality" education, students attending inadequate public schools should receive government vouchers equal to the cost the state spent on each student, roughly $2,100–$2,900 a year. The Cook County Circuit Court dismissed the case in March 1993, and the court of appeals affirmed it on grounds that the issue raised a question properly left to the legislature. Bolick also filed Arviso v. Honig (The case was filed in Los Angeles County Superior Court, on June 11, 1992. *See* www.ij.org/ index.php?option=com_content&task=view&id=1196&Itemid=165), seeking similar relief based on a 1971 California Supreme Court decision that ruled that education is a "fundamental right" but lost in Los Angeles Superior Court and again before the California Court of Appeals.

78. Bagley v. Raymond, 728 A.2d 127 (Me. 1999), *cert. denied*, 528 U.S. 947 (1999). A second effort also failed to dislodge Maine's policy. Anderson v. Town of Durham, 895 A.2d 944 (Me. 2006), *cert. denied*, 549 U.S. 1051 (2006).

79. *See* Chittenden Town School District v. Department of Education, 738 A.2d 539 (Vt. 1999), *cert. denied*, 528 U.S. 1066 (1999).

80. TELES, *supra* note 63, at 241 (quoting Olin Grant Report (June 16, 1992)).

81. Jackson v. Benson, 578 N.W.2d 602 (Wis. 1998); Kotterman v. Killian, 972 P.2d 606 (Ariz. 1999); Simmons-Harris v. Goff, 711 N.E.2d 203, 216 (Ohio 1999). After the Ohio Supreme Court approved the Cleveland school choice plan, critics filed suit in the U.S. District Court for the Northern District of Ohio, which ruled that the program unconstitutionally "advances religion" because the "overwhelming majority of schools from which a student may choose are sectarian and . . . no adjacent public school has chosen to participate in the Program." The U.S. Court of Appeals for the Sixth Circuit affirmed. This case went up to the Supreme Court, which reversed and approved the program. Zelman v. Simmons-Harris,

536 U.S. 639 (2002). *See generally* George Will, *School Choice Tide Is Turning*, WASH. POST, Feb. 1, 2007, at A15 and chapter 3 *supra*.

82. Aguilar v. Felton, 473 U.S. 402 (1985), *overruled by* Agostini v. Felton, 521 U.S. 203 (1997). *Aguilar v. Felton* was the case that prompted the Satmar Hasidic Community in the Village of Kiryas Joel to seek authorization to create a public school for their disabled children. *See supra* chapter 4.

83. Zelman v. Simmons-Harris, 536 U.S. 639.

84. Zelman v. Simmons-Harris, 536 U.S. at 650–53 (private parental choice); *see also id.* at 655–60 (all types of schools).

85. *See id.* at 645. *See also* Stephen Macedo, *Constituting Civil Society: School Vouchers, Religious Nonprofit Organizations, and Liberal Public Values*, 75 CHI.-KENT L. REV. 417 (2000) (emphasizing importance of nondiscrimination requirement so that private schools receiving public vouchers become "more attuned to public values").

86. *See* Michael W. McConnell, *Neutrality under the Religion Clauses*, 81 NW. U. L. REV. 146 (1986); Michael W. McConnell, *The Problem of Singling Out Religion*, 50 DEPAUL L. REV. 1 (2000). *See* Noah Feldman, *From Liberty to Equality: The Transformation of the Establishment Clause*, 90 CAL. L. REV. 673 (2002). *See generally supra* chapter 3 (discussing equality and religion).

87. Good News Club v. Milford Central School, 533 U.S. 98 (2001); Mitchell v. Helms, 530 U.S. 793 (2000) (plurality opinion); Rosenberger v. University of Virginia, 515 U.S. 819 (1995).

88. Good News Club v. Milford Central School, 533 U.S. 98; Rosenberger v. University of Virginia, 515 U.S. 819. Continuing advocacy along these lines has produced decisions and settlements. *See, e.g.*, Press Release, Liberty Counsel, *Court Approves School District's Settlement of Lawsuit by Christian Group* (Feb. 5, 2009), www.lc.org/index.cfm?PID=14100&PRID=775 (discussing the approval by federal court of a settlement of a lawsuit filed by Liberty Counsel on behalf of Child Evangelism Fellowship of Georgia challenging a policy that charged higher fees to a religious group than to other groups in using the school facility).

89. *Good News Club*, 533 U.S. 98; Rosenberger v. University of Virginia, 515 U.S. 819.

90. Zelman v. Simmons-Harris, 536 U.S. 639 (2002) (majority opinion). In her concurring opinion, Justice O'Connor stressed the variety of choices available to parents that included secular private schools and options within the public system as well. This opinion thus sought to stress the free choice of parents and also sought to view the program as having a smaller effect of directing funds to religious schools. Hence, if only private schools were counted, 96 percent of participating students enrolled in religious schools, but "[w]hen one considers the option to attend community schools, the percentage of students enrolled in religious schools falls to 62.1 percent. If magnet schools are included in the mix, this percentage falls to 16.5 percent." *Id.* at 664 (O'Connor, J., concurring). Justice Stevens in dissent challenged this analysis. *Id.* at 685 (Stevens, J., dissenting).

91. *See id.* at 676–84 (Thomas, J., concurring) (discussing freedom-of-choice plans). Similarly, Justice Souter in dissent criticized consideration of the public magnet and community schools as irrelevant to the whole justification for considering private parental choices as a circuit breaker, insulating public dollars from direct aid to religious schools. *Id.* at 699 (Souter, J. dissenting). Justice Breyer in dissent went even further by rejecting evidence of parental choice as insufficient to overcome the establishment clause's commitment to guard against the kinds of

religious-based social divisions that could come with contests over public dollars. *Id.* at 728 (Breyer, J., dissenting).

92. *Id.* at 681 (Thomas, J., concurring).

93. *Id.* at 682 ("While the romanticized ideal of universal public education resonates with the cognoscenti who oppose vouchers, poor urban families just want the best education for their children, who will certainly need it to function in our high-tech and advanced society.")

94. Bolick & Underkuffler, *supra* note 69.

95. MORRIS P. FIORINA ET AL., THE NEW AMERICAN DEMOCRACY 488–89 (5th ed. 2007).

96. Alveda C. King, *Fighting for School Choice: It's a Civil Right*, WALL ST. J., Sept. 11, 1997, at A14. *See also* William G. Howell, Martin R. West, & Paul E. Peterson, *What Americans Think about Their Schools*, EDUC. NEXT, fall 2007, www.hoover.org/publications/ednext/8769517.html (showing 68 percent of African Americans surveyed in favor of vouchers, as opposed to 38 percent of whites, and 47 percent of African Americans surveyed in favor of charter schools, as opposed to 42 percent of whites); web site of Black Alliance for Educational Options, www.baeo.org/programs?program_id=7 (last visited Oct. 17, 2009) ("BAEO is committed to expanding the educational options available to all families—regardless of income—but our focus is on helping low income and working class black families").

97. PEOPLE FOR THE AMERICAN WAY, PARENTAL RIGHTS: THE TROJAN HORSE OF THE RELIGIOUS RIGHT ATTACK ON PUBLIC EDUCATION (1996), http://site.pfaw.org/ site/PageServer?pagename=report_parental_rights; Anti-Defamation League, *School Vouchers: The Wrong Choice for Public Education*, www.adl.org/vouchers/ print.asp. (last visited Oct. 17, 2009).

98. *See* Pat Kossan, *Arizona's High Court Bans School Vouchers*, ARIZ. REPUBLIC, Mar. 26, 2009, at A1 (Arizona Supreme Court rejects use of state money to pay private tuition for private or religious schools as a violation of the state constitution).

99. *See* COOKSON, *supra* note 56, at 90–94.

100. Bolick & Underkuffler, *supra* note 69.

101. *Id.*

102. *Id.*

103. *See* PEOPLE FOR THE AMERICAN WAY, *supra* note 93. The Cato Institute, devoted to "limited government, individual liberty, free markets and peace," published two of his books: CLINT BOLICK, VOUCHER WARS: WAGING THE LEGAL BATTLE OVER SCHOOL CHOICE (2003), and THE AFFIRMATIVE ACTION FRAUD: CAN WE RESTORE THE AMERICAN CIVIL RIGHTS VISION? (1996). *See also* CLINT BOLICK, LEVIATHAN: THE GROWTH OF LOCAL GOVERNMENT AND THE EROSION OF LIBERTY (2004); CLINT BOLICK, DAVID'S HAMMER: THE CASE FOR AN ACTIVIST JUDICIARY (2006).

104. His editorial dubbing law professor Lani Guinier a "quota queen" triggered so much controversy that President Clinton withdrew his nomination after he had selected her to head the Department of Justice Civil Rights Division. William Powers, *The Dynamics of Personal Destruction*, NAT'L J., Jan. 20, 2001, www.theatlantic.com/politics/nj/powers2001-01-25.htm. *See* Clint Bolick, *Clinton's Quota Queens*, WALL ST. J., Apr. 30, 1993, at A12. Guinier's actual positions endorsed cumulative voting and multimember districts, not racial quotas. *See* LANI GUINIER, THE TYRANNY OF THE MAJORITY (1994); Laurel Leff, *From Legal*

Scholar to Quota Queen: What Happens When Politics Pulls the Press into the Groves of Academe, 32 COLUM. JOURNALISM REV. 36 (1993). After President Clinton withdrew Guinier's nomination, Bolick proceeded with less success to attack each of the subsequent Democratic nominees to the civil rights post. TELES, *supra* note 63, at 258.

105. MATTHEW J. BROUILLETE, MACKINAC CENTER FOR PUBLIC POLICY, SCHOOL CHOICE IN MICHIGAN: A PRIMER FOR FREEDOM IN EDUCATION (1999), www.mackinac.org/archives/1999/s1999-06.pdf.

106. KENNETH J. SALTMAN, THE EDISON SCHOOLS: CORPORATE SCHOOLING AND THE ASSAULT ON PUBLIC EDUCATION (2005).

107. Greg Anrig, *An Idea Whose Time Has Gone: Conservatives Abandon Their Support for School Vouchers*, WASH. MONTHLY, Apr. 1, 2008, at 29.

108. Sol Stern, *School Choice Isn't Enough: Instructional Reform Is the Key to Better Schools*, CITY J., winter 2008, at 53. But see William McGurin, In Post-Obama Illinois, Hope and Change Wall St. J., April 27, 2010, at A15.

109. NATIONAL CENTER FOR EDUCATION EVALUATION AND REGIONAL ASSISTANCE, U.S. DEPARTMENT OF EDUCATION, NCEE 2007-4009, EVALUATION OF THE DC OPPORTUNITY SCHOLARSHIP PROGRAM: IMPACTS AFTER ONE YEAR (2007), http://ies.ed.gov/ncee/pdf/20074009.pdf.

110. James Oliphant, *Spending Plan Kills Funding for Washington School Vouchers*, L.A. TIMES, Mar. 11, 2009, at A13. One commentator charged the Obama administration with failing to bring forward a more recent evaluation showing successes in the program. *See* Deroy Murdock, *Obama Admin. Stifles Favorable DC Voucher Study*, REAL CLEAR POLITICS, Apr. 10, 2009, www.realclearpolitics.com/articles/2009/04/obama_admin_stifles_favorable.html.

111. *Topic A: Obama's Compromise on D.C.'s School Vouchers Program*, WASH. POST, May 10, 2009, at A17.

112. Anrig, *supra* note 107 (noting lack of cross-district choice initiatives); Hess, *supra* note 1 (reporting how even staunch defenders of school choice concede disappointing academic results). Public aid to private school education is not over. In 2008, Georgia joined five other states by enacting a $50 million scholarship tax credit offering 100 percent tax credits for donations by corporations to pay for scholarships to enable low-income students to attend private schools. Alliance for School Choice, *Georgia Gov. Sonny Perdue Approves $50 Million School Choice Program*, PR Newswire, May 14, 2008, Westlaw, 5/14/08 PRWIRE 19:13:00.

113. For a sample of the debate, *see* Martin R. West et al., *School Choice in Dayton, Ohio after Two Years: An Evaluation of the Parents Advancing Choice in Education Scholarship Program* (Harvard Kennedy School John F. Kennedy School of Government, Working Paper No. RWP02-021, 2001), http://ssrn.com/abstract=320253; William G. Howell et al., *The Effect of School Vouchers on Student Achievement: A Response to Critics* (Taubman Center on State and Local Government, Program on Education Policy and Governance, Working Paper, 2000), www.hks.harvard.edu/taubmancenter/pdfs/working_papers/peterson_01_response.pdf. Some advocacy organizations direct research explicitly on the increase in numbers of students able to use school choice mechanisms, rated along degrees of freedom from regulation. *See* Robert C. Enlow, The Foundation for Educational Choice, *Grading School Choice: Evaluating School Choice Programs by the Friedman Gold Standard*, SCHOOL CHOICE ISSUES IN DEPTH, Feb. 2008, www.friedmanfoundation.org/downloadFile.do?id=268.

114. *See* Henry M. Levin, *Foreword* to SCHOOL CHOICE AND DIVERSITY: WHAT THE EVIDENCE SAYS, at vii–viii (Janelle T. Scott ed., 2005).

115. *See* Nancy Rosenblum, *Separating the Siamese Twins: "Pluralism" and "School Choice," in* SCHOOL CHOICE: THE MORAL DEBATE 79, 81–83 (Alan Wolfe ed., 2003).

116. *See, e.g.*, MARK SCHNEIDER, PAUL TESKE, & MELISSA MARSCHALL, CHOOSING SCHOOLS: CONSUMER CHOICE AND THE QUALITY OF AMERICAN SCHOOLS 185–203 (2000) (discussing District 4 in New York City); LISA M. STULBERG, RACE, SCHOOLS, AND HOPE: AFRICAN AMERICANS AND SCHOOL CHOICE AFTER BROWN 114–56 (2008) (discussing the West Oakland Community School).

117. One study seeking to control for self-selection effects found that students who have won a New York City lottery to enroll in charter schools have outperformed other students who lost the lottery and attended regular public schools. *See* John Hecinger & Ianthe Jeanne Dugan, *Charter Schools Pass Key Test in Study*, WALL ST. J., Sept. 22, 2009, at A2 (reporting study by Caroline Hoxby, professor of economics at Stanford University).

118. NATIONAL CENTER FOR EDUCATION STATISTICS, U.S. DEPARTMENT OF EDUCATION, NCES 2005–456, AMERICA'S CHARTER SCHOOLS: RESULTS FROM THE NAEP 2003 PILOT STUDY 4 (2004), http://nces.ed.gov/nationsreportcard/pdf/studies/2005456.pdf.

119. *See, e.g.*, JOHN F. WITTE, THE MARKET APPROACH TO EDUCATION: AN ANALYSIS OF AMERICA'S FIRST VOUCHER PROGRAM 112–56 (2000); HERBERT J. WALBERG, SCHOOL CHOICE: THE FINDINGS 21–28, 80–81, 106–8 (2007) (citing studies). Debates over findings in the Milwaukee system arise over whether parents actually choose the schools their students attend and whether educational rather than other goals affect their choice. *See* Martin West, *No Choice in Milwaukee!?! Remarkable Finding by an Un-credible Study*, EDUC. NEXT, spring 2008, at 80–81 (reviewing DAVID DODENHOFF, WISCONSIN POLICY RESEARCH INSTITUTE REPORT, FIXING THE MILWAUKEE PUBLIC SCHOOLS: THE LIMITS OF PARENT-DRIVEN REFORM (2007), www.wpri.org/Reports/Volume%2020/Vol20no8/vol20no8.pdf).

120. CHARTER SCHOOL OUTCOMES (Mark Berends et al. eds., 2007); EDWARD B. FISKE & HELEN F. LADD, WHEN SCHOOLS COMPETE: A CAUTIONARY TALE 277 (2000) (based on study of New Zealand choice experiment).

121. *See* NEL NODDINGS, WHEN SCHOOL REFORM GOES WRONG (2007). *See also* KEVIN K. KUMASHIRO, THE SEDUCTION OF COMMON SENSE: HOW THE RIGHT HAS FRAMED THE DEBATE ON AMERICA'S SCHOOLS (2008); KEVIN B. SMITH & KENNETH J. MEIER, THE CASE AGAINST SCHOOL CHOICE: POLITICS, MARKETS, AND FOOLS (1995).

122. *See* Stern, *supra* note 108, at 59 (acknowledging lack of evidence that vouchers improve student achievement and evidence of improvement based on instructional changes in Massachusetts system, without school choice); Anrig, *supra* note 107. *See also* CHESTER E. FINN, TROUBLEMAKER: A PERSONAL HISTORY OF SCHOOL REFORM SINCE SPUTNIK (2008).

123. *See* Susan Saulny, *U.S. Gives Charter Schools a Big Push in New Orleans*, N.Y. TIMES, June 13, 2006, at A17.

124. Jay Mathews, *Charter Schools Take Hold in Post-Katrina New Orleans*, WASH. POST, June 9, 2008, at A1. For caution that the New Orleans experiment jeopardizes accountability by loosening state and federal requirements, *see* Danielle Holley-Walker, *The Accountability Cycle: The Recovery School District Act and New Orleans' Charter Schools*, 40 CONN. L. REV. 125 (2007).

125. Parents Involved in Community Schools v. Seattle School District No. 1, 551 U.S. 701 (2007).

126. *See* Howard L. Fuller & Deborah Greiveldinger, *The Impact of School Choice on Racial Integration in Milwaukee Private Schools* (Aug. 2002), www.friedmanfoundation.org/downloadFile.do?id=27.

127. *See* Jay P. Greene, *Choosing Integration, in* Scott, *supra* note 114, at 27, 34–39; JAY P. GREENE, MANHATTAN INSTITUTE FOR POLICY RESEARCH, A SURVEY OF RESULTS FROM VOUCHER EXPERIMENTS: WHERE WE ARE AND WHAT WE KNOW 9 (2000), www.manhattan-institute.org/pdf/cr_11.pdf (sponsored by a group supportive of school choice).

128. *See* Michael J. Avlies & Charles V. Willie, *Controlled Choice Assignments: A New and More Effective Approach to School Desegregation*, 19 URB. REV. 1573 (1987); Amy Stuart Wells & Robert L. Crain, *Where School Desegregation and School Choice Policies Collide: Voluntary Transfer Plans and Controlled Choice, in* Scott, *supra* note 114, at 59; ROBERT L. CRAIN ET AL., FINDING NICHES: DESEGREGATED STUDENTS SIXTEEN YEARS LATER (1989).

129. Parents Involved in Community Schools v. Seattle School District No. 1, 551 U.S. 701. Cambridge, Massachusetts, the site of a model controlled choice plan, replaced attention to racial balance with attention to socioeconomic balance in 2001. *See* Edward B. Fiske, *Controlled Choice in Cambridge, Massachusetts, in* DIVIDED WE FAIL: COMING TOGETHER THROUGH PUBLIC SCHOOL CHOICE (2002). Controlled choice plans can avoid the exacerbation of segregation by race and class. *See* Richard D. Kahlenberg, *Equitable Public School Choice: Student Achievement, Integration, Democracy, and Public Support, in* PUBLIC SCHOOL CHOICE VS. PRIVATE SCHOOL VOUCHERS 137 (Richard D. Kahlenberg ed., 2003).

130. Parents Involved in Community Schools v. Seattle School District No. 1, 551 U.S. at 798.

131. *Id.* at 706.

132. *Id.*

133. American Civil Rights Foundation v. Berkeley Unified School District, 172 Cal. App. 4th 207 (Ct. App. 2009). Less clear is the legal status of provisions in state charter legislation directing that the charter school enrollments should not stray from the racial composition of the district. Seventeen states in 2003 had statutes specifying that charter schools had to comply with desegregation decrees or reflect the racial balances of their districts or communities, while twelve states did not have provisions addressing racial composition in their charter statutes. *See* Kelly E. Rapp & Suzanne E. Eckes, *Dispelling the Myth of "White Flight": An Examination of Minority Enrollment in Charter Schools*, 21 EDUC. POL'Y 615 (2007).

134. NAACP LEGAL DEFENSE FUND & CIVIL RIGHTS PROJECT, STILL LOOKING TO THE FUTURE: VOLUNTARY K–12 SCHOOL INTEGRATION 37–41 (2008), www.naacpldf.org/content/pdf/voluntary/Still_Looking_to_the_Future_Voluntary_K-12_School_Integration;_A_Manual_for_Parents,_Educators_and_Advocates.pdf.

135. Sean F. Reardon, John T. Yun, & Michal Kurlander, *Implications of Income-based School Assignment Policies for Racial School Segregation*, 28 EDUC. EVALUATION & POL'Y ANALYSIS 49–75 (2006). States that included racial provisos in their charter school legislation, requiring charter schools to approximate district-wide demographic averages, increased the percent of black students enrolled in the charter schools. Linda A. Renzulli, *District Segregation, Race Legislation, and Black Enrollment in Charter Schools*, 87 SOC. SCI. Q. 618 (2006).

136. Tracy Jan, *An Imbalance Grows in Cambridge Schools*, BOSTON GLOBE, July 23, 2007, at A1.

137. Gordon MacInnes, *Choosing Segregation, in* Kahlenberg, *supra* note 129, at 89.

138. HOPES, FEARS, AND REALITY: A BALANCED LOOK AT AMERICAN CHARTER SCHOOLS IN 2008 10-11 (Robin J. Lake ed., 2008), www.crpe.org/cs/crpe/download/csr_files/pub_ncsrp_hfro8_deco8.pdf (comparing data from different states); *see also* Gregory R. Weiher & Kent L. Tedin, *Does Choice Lead to Racially Distinctive Schools? Charter Schools and Household Preferences*, 21 J. OF POL'Y ANALYSIS & MGMT. 79 (2002) (students entering Texas charter schools joined schools with higher concentrations of students of their own racial-ethnic background than they would find in traditional public schools).

139. In Arizona, white students attend charter elementary schools that have higher percentages of white students than the schools they exited and black students attend charter elementary schools that enroll higher percentage of blacks than the district schools they exited. ERICA FRANKENBERG & CHUNGMEI LEE, HARV. CIVIL RIGHTS PROJECT, CHARTER SCHOOLS AND RACE: A LOST OPPORTUNITY FOR INTEGRATED EDUCATION (2003), www.eric.ed.gov/ERICDocs/data/ericdocs2sql/content_storage_01/0000019b/80/1b/36/18.pdf; Casey D. Cobb & Gene V. Glass, Paper Presented at the Annual Meeting of the American Educational Research Association: Arizona Charter Schools: Resegregating Public Education? (Apr., 2003) (unpublished manuscript, on file at www.eric.ed.gov/ERICDocs/data/ericdocs2sql/content_storage_01/0000019b/80/1b/2e/b6.pdf)); David R. Garcia, *The Impact of School Choice on Racial Segregation in Charter Schools*, 22 EDUC. POL'Y 805 (2007). In South Carolina, though, the racial composition of charter schools closely matches that of traditional public schools, perhaps reflecting the experience with a lawsuit challenging the charter school statute. And one study found that choice programs (magnet, open enrollment schools, and charter schools) in San Diego, California, produced greater ethnic and racial mixing than the districts' schools. JULIAN R. BETTS, DOES SCHOOL CHOICE WORK? EFFECTS ON STUDENT INTEGRATION AND ACHIEVEMENT (2006).

140. NATIONAL CENTER FOR EDUCATION STATISTICS, U.S. DEPARTMENT OF EDUCATION, *School Choice: Charter Schools, in* THE CONDITION OF EDUCATION 2007 69 (2007), http://nces.ed.gov/pubs2007/2007064.pdf.

141. *See* James Forman, Jr., *Do Charter Schools Threaten Public Education? Emerging Evidence from Fifteen Years of a Quasi-market for Schooling*, 2007 U. ILL. L. REV. 839-80 (2007).

142. *See* Lake, *supra* note 138.

143. *Id.* at 11.

144. *See, e.g.*, Weiher & Tedin, *supra* note 138, at 79; Linda A. Renzulli & Lorraine Evans, *School Choice, Charter Schools, and White Flight*, 52 SOC. PROBS. 398 (2005) (where white and nonwhite students are distributed equally among schools, whites turn to charter schools in higher rates; where schools are significantly racially separated, whites use charter schools less).

145. Garcia, *supra* note 139, at 823.

146. Thomas S. Dee & Helen Fu, *Do Charter Schools Skim Students or Drain Resources?* 23 ECON. OF EDUC. REV. 259 (2004).

147. Nancy Mitchell, *Charters More Diverse*, ROCKY MTN. NEWS, Dec. 20, 2005, at 6A.

148. Katherine Kersten, *Black Flight: The Exodus to Charter Schools*, WALL ST. J., Mar. 2, 2006, at A15 (describing study of Center for School Change, University of Minnesota).

149. *See, e.g.*, Joe Robertson, *Kansas City Considers Extending African-Centered Schools*, KAN. CITY STAR, Feb. 6, 2006, at A1. "Advocates describe [African-centered education] as an academic and character-building program guided by African and African-American cultural and intellectual traditions. Students who otherwise might think the culture is inferior are immersed in it and presented with role models. They don't have to overcome anything, but can expect to excel as who they are." *Id.*

150. *See* Rosalind Rossi, *School Board Approves Plans for Final 2 Charter Schools*, CHI. SUN-TIMES, Apr. 30, 1998, at 20; Regina Jennings, *Institute of Positive Education*, *in* ENCYCLOPEDIA OF BLACK STUDIES 272–74 (Mambo Ama Mazama & Molefi Kete Asante eds., 2004).

151. Judy Putnam, *Michigan Has More Segregated Schools: Charters That Draw Students from Mostly Black Schools Drive up Numbers*, GRAND RAPIDS PRESS, Feb. 15, 2006, at 1; Katherine Kersten, *Black Flight: The Exodus to Charter Schools*, WALL ST. J., Mar. 2, 2006, at A15.

152. Steve Brandt, *Minority Students Continue Minneapolis School Exodus*, MINNEAPOLIS STAR TRIB., Feb. 22, 2006, at 3B.

153. Renzulli, *supra* note 135, at 620–22.

154. Weiher & Tedin, *supra* note 138, at 90.

155. Lynn Schnaiberg, *Charter Schools: Choice, Diversity May Be at Odds*, EDUC. WEEK, May 10, 2000, at 1.

156. Alexandra O'Rourke, *Rethinking Race and Education: Ethnocentric Charter Schools and the Law* (May 19, 2006) (unpublished paper on file with the author).

157. Amy Stuart Wells, Jennifer Jellison Holme, Alejandra Lopez, & Camille Wilson Cooper, *Charter Schools and Racial and Social Class Segregation*, *in* Kahlenberg, *supra* note 129, at 81.

158. William A. Fischel, *The Congruence of American School Districts and Other Local Government Boundaries: A Google-Earth Exploration* 14–22 (Dartmouth Coll. Econ. Department, Working Paper, 2007).

159. Taryn Williams, *Outside the Lines: The Case for Socioeconomic Integration in Urban School Districts*, 2010 BYU EDUC. & L.J. (forthcoming).

160. *Id.* at 29.

161. Macedo, *supra* note 85, at 436. Ohio ultimately changed the plan to include a larger region. OHIO REV. CODE ANN. §§ 3313.974–79 (West 1999).

162. *See* Carol Ascher & Nathalie Wamba, *Charter Schools: An Emerging Market*, paper presented at Conference on School Choice and Racial Diversity, Teachers College, Columbia University, New York (May 22, 2000).

163. 34 C.F.R. § 106 (2006); Charter School Policy Institute, *Single-sex Charter Schools*, www.charterschoolpolicy.org/yes/files/FS5_Single_Sex_Charters.pdf (last visited Oct. 24, 2009). Section 504 of the Rehabilitation Act also requires reasonable accommodation for students who fit its disability terms. *See* Lauren Morando Rhim, Eileen M. Ahearn, & Cheryl M. Lange, *Charter School Statutes and Special Education: Policy Answers or Policy Ambiguity?* 41 J. SPECIAL EDUC. 50 (2007).

164. *See* web site of National Association for Single Sex Public Education, www.singlesexschools.org/schools-schools.htm (last visited Oct. 17, 2009).

165. Thanks to Jennifer Siegel for this insight and the research summarized in the text.

166. Peter Sherman, *Gender-based Schools Could Open in Fall*, St. J.-Reg., Apr. 21, 2009, at 15, www.sj-r.com/homepage/x297231657/Gender-based-schools-could-open-in-fall.

167. *See Ga. County Going to All Single-sex Public Schools*, Associated Press, Feb. 14, 2008, www.ajc.com/metro/content/metro/storeies/2008/02/14/gaschools_0215.html.

168. *See* Mary Bailey Estes, *Zero Reject and School Choice: Students with Disabilities in Texas' Charter Schools*, 2 Leadership and Pol'y in Schools 213, 215 (2003).

169. William G. Howell & Paul E. Peterson, The Education Gap: Vouchers and Urban Schools 73–74 (rev. ed. 2002). *See also* Walberg, *supra* note 119, at 47 (reporting study of Florida's McKay Scholarship Program, a special needs voucher program allowing parents to choose among private schools for students with special learning needs; 90 percent of participating parents were satisfied with the chosen school compared with one-third of parents of special needs students in public schools).

170. *See* Jay P. Greene & Marcus A. Winters, *The Politics of Special Ed Vouchers: What You Can Expect from the Presidential Candidates*, Wash. Times, May 1, 2008, at A15.

171. *See* Lauren Morando Rhim et al., Project Intersect Report No. 5: Access and Accountability for Students with Disabilities in California Charter Schools 19 (2006) (in 2003–4, California charter schools on average enrolled 7.4 percent students with disabilities while regular public schools enrolled 10.2 percent); Estes, *supra* note 168, at 223 (in 1999–2000, Texas charter school enrollments included 8.6 percent students with identified disabilities compared with 12.3 percent in the traditional public schools).

172. Steven Goldsmith, *Charter Schools Serving More Urban and Disadvantaged Students, Study Finds* (Nov. 21, 2005), University of Washington News, http://uwnews.org/article.asp?articleid=13490.

173. Lake, *supra* note 138, at 33–42.

174. Julia F. Mead, Charter Schools Designed for Children with Disabilities: An Initial Examination of Issues and Questions Raised 11, 32 (2008), www.uscharterschools.org/specialedprimers/download/special_report_mead.pdf (special report prepared as part of web site created for Primers on Special Education in Charter Schools).

175. *See id.* at 11.

176. Rhim et al., *supra* note 163, at 56.

177. Several states have enacted special needs vouchers. For example, Georgia enacted the Special Needs Scholarship Act and a school choice tax program to assist parents of children with disabilities. *See* Ga. Code Ann. § 20-2-2A-1 (2007). Florida adopted a voucher program for students with disabilities. *See* John M. McKay Scholarship for Students with Disabilities, Fla. Stat. Ann § 1002.39 (West 2007). The Florida Supreme Court rejected the program as a violation of the state constitution's guarantee of a uniform system of public schools. Bush v. Holmes, 2004 Fla. App. LEXIS 12479 (2004). Other state voucher programs aiming at students with disabilities may also face legal challenges and ongoing policy disputes. *See* Wendy F. Hensel, *Vouchers for Students with Disabilities? The Future of Special Education?* (2009) (unpublished manuscript on file with the author).

178. National Center for Education Statistics, U.S. Department of Education, NCES 2005–456, America's Charter Schools: Results from the NAEP 2003 Pilot Study 2 (2004), http://nces.ed.gov/nationsreportcard/pdf/studies/2005456.

179. *Id.*

180. Mead, *supra* note 176, at 10.

181. Florida directed the commission charged with approving charter school applications to examine the feasibility of charter schools specifically for students with disabilities, including autism. *See* Fla. Stat. § 1002.335(4)(b)(13) (2007).

182. Mead, *supra* note 176, at 10.

183. Edward Garcia Fierros & Neil A. Blomberg, *Restrictiveness and Race in Special Education Placements in For-profit and Non-profit Charter Schools in California*, 3 Learning Disabilities 1, 3 (2005).

184. Mead, *supra* note 176, at 11.

185. *See* Renzulli & Evans, *supra* note 144, at 412.

186. *See* Rhim et al., *supra* note 173, at 25.

187. *See generally* Jay Heubert, *Schools without Rules? Charter Schools, Federal Disability Law, and the Paradoxes of Deregulation*, 32 Harv. C.R.-C.L. L. Rev. 301 (1997).

188. One such school triggered national controversy. *See* Anthony DiMaggio, *The Right-wing's War on the Gibran Academy: Arabic as a Terrorist Language*, Counterpunch, Aug. 30, 2007, www.counterpunch.org/dimaggio08302007.html.

189. *See* Luis A. Huerta, *Losing Public Accountability: A Home Schooling Charter, in* Inside Charter Schools: The Paradox of Radical Decentralization 177 (Bruce Fuller ed., 2000).

190. Peg Meier, *An Oasis for Learning*, Minneapolis Star Trib., Feb. 2, 2003, at 1E.

191. Twin Cities International Elementary School, home page, www.twincitiesinternationalschool.org/ (last visited July 12, 2009).

192. According to the 2000 census, the immigrant population in Minnesota included 125,000 Hispanics, 60,000 Hmong, 20,000 non-Hmong Southeast Asians, 11,151 Somalis, 6,000 Russians, 2,500 West Africans, 2,000 East Africans (not Somali), 1,600 Yugoslavians, and 500 Tibetans. *See* University of Minnesota, International Directory, www.international.umn.edu/directory/profile/tcmn.html (last visited Oct. 23, 2009).

193. Dan Lips, *School Choice: Right for America,* www.cato.org/research/education/articles/schoice.html (last visited Oct. 24, 2009).

194. Note, *Church, Choice, and Charters: A New Wrinkle for Public Education?*, 122 Harv. L. Rev. 1750, 1757–69 (2009); *Debate Rages over NYC Hebrew Charter School*, Associated Press, Feb. 3, 2009; Abby Goodnough, *Hebrew Charter School Spurs Debate in Florida*, N.Y. Times, Aug. 24, 2007, at A1. New York City's approval of a Hebrew-language charter school provoked controversy for focusing on celebrating one among all cultures. *See* Anthony Weiss, *New York Approves Plan for First Public School with Hebrew Focus,* Haaretz (Jan. 18, 2009), www.haaretz.com/hasen/spages/1056528.html; *Debate Rages over Hebrew Charter School in New York City,* U.S. News/Associated Press, (Feb. 3, 2009), www.districtadministration.com/newssummary.aspx?news=yes&postid=5186. New York also has a charter school devoted to Greek and Latin languages and cultural studies, and other schools offering dual-language study in Chinese, Russian, Korean,

and Haitian Creole. Elissa Gootman, *State Weighs Approval of Brooklyn School Dedicated to Hebrew*, N.Y. TIMES, Jan. 12, 2009, at A17.

195. *See* U.S. DEPARTMENT OF EDUCATION, PRESERVING A CRITICAL NATIONAL ASSET: AMERICA'S DISADVANTAGED STUDENTS AND THE CRISIS IN FAITH-BASED URBAN SCHOOLS (2008), www.ed.gov/admins/comm/choice/faithbased/report.pdf (reporting that administration of President George W. Bush endorses the use of charter schools to permit greater religious expression within public school settings).

196. Zelman v. Simmons-Harris, 536 U.S. 639 (2002).

197. One commentator questions how a charter system that approves a particular school endorsing a given faith differs significantly from public financial support of parochial education through a tuition voucher. *Church, Choice, and Charters, supra* note 194, at 1766, 1771.

198. *See id.* at 1757.

199. *E.g.*, N.Y. EDUC. § 2852.3 (2007).

200. *See* Jaweed Kaleem, *Catholic Schools May Get a New Life as Charters*, MIAMI HERALD, Mar. 19, 2009, at 1A.

201. *See* Gail Robinson, *New Debates over Church, State, School and Charters*, GOTHAM GAZETTE, Mar. 16, 2009, www.gothamgazette.com/article/issueoftheweek /20090316/200/2856.

202. *See* Eva Ruth Moravec, *Catholic Schools Studying Charter Status*, SAN ANTONIO EXPRESS, Nov. 26, 2008, at 6B; Eric W. Robelen, *Former D.C. Catholic Schools Start New Life as Charters*, EDUC. WEEK, Sept. 10, 2008, at 7.

203. Bill Johnson, *Escuela de Guadalupe Finds Funds to Stay Open*, ROCKY MTN. NEWS, Dec. 5, 2007.

204. Pierce v. Society of Sisters, 268 U.S. 510 (1925).

205. Griffin v. County School Board, 377 U.S. 218 (1964).

206. Green v. County School Board, 391 U.S. 430 (1968).

207. *Missouri v. Jenkins*, 515 U.S. 70 (1995).

208. Zelman v. Simmons-Harris, 536 U.S. 639 (2002).

209. Heather K. Gerken, *Second-order Diversity*, 118 HARV. L. REV. 1099 (2005).

210. *See* Richard A. Shweder, *After Just Schools: The Equality-difference Paradox and Varieties of Liberal Hope*, *in* JUST SCHOOLS: PURSUING EQUALITY IN SOCIETIES OF DIFFERENCE 254 (Martha Minow et al. eds., 2008).

211. ANTHONY BRYK ET AL., CATHOLIC SCHOOLS AND THE COMMON GOOD 11 (1993); David E. Campbell, *Bowling Together*, EDUC. NEXT, fall 2001, at 55; WALBERG, *supra* note 119, at 72 (citing Daniel A. McFarland & Carolos Starmanns, *Student Government and Political Socialization* (unpublished manuscript)).

212. *See* EDUCATING CITIZENS: INTERNATIONAL PERSPECTIVES ON CIVIC VALUES AND SCHOOL CHOICE (Patrick J. Wolf & Stephen Macedo eds., 2004).

213. Jay P. Greene, *Civil Values in Public and Private Schools*, *in* LEARNING FROM SCHOOL CHOICE 83 (Paul E. Peterson & Bryan C. Hassel eds., 1998).

Chapter 6

1. JOHN DEWEY, HUMAN NATURE AND CONDUCT 323 (1922).

2. *See* LANI GUINIER & GERALD TORRES, THE MINER'S CANARY (2002); Michelle Fine, *The Power of the Brown v. Board of Education Decision: Theorizing Threats to Sustainability*, 59 AM. PSYCHOL. 502 (2004).

3. RALPH ELLISON, *An American Dilemma: A Review, in* SHADOW AND ACT 303, 304–5 (Vintage International 1995) (1964).

4. *See* ANGELO N. ANCHETA, SCIENTIFIC EVIDENCE AND EQUAL PROTECTION OF THE LAW 28–37 (2006) (citing Kentucky's brief in Berea College v. Kentucky and the Supreme Court's opinions in Muller v. Oregon, Ozawa v. United States, and Buck v. Bell); DAVID L. FAIGMAN, LABORATORY OF JUSTICE: THE SUPREME COURT'S 200-YEAR STRUGGLE TO INTEGRATE SCIENCE AND THE LAW 170–204 (2004): Herbert Hovenkamp, *Social Science and Segregation before* Brown, 1985 DUKE L.J. 624, 627–37. Pioneering social science evidence in legal argument in 1907, Louis D. Brandeis produced a landmark brief containing statistics relevant to health and labor. NANCY WOLLOCH, MULLER V. OREGON: A BRIEF HISTORY WITH DOCUMENTS (1996).

5. GUNNAR MYRDAL, AN AMERICAN DILEMMA: THE NEGRO PROBLEM AND MODERN DEMOCRACY (1944).

6. Stephen Smith & Kate Ellis, *Decision of the Century: Brown vs. Board of Education* (American Radio Works) (transcript available at http://americanradio-works.publicradio.org/features/marshall/brown.html) (quoting Marshall).

7. Kenneth Clark, *The Social Scientist as an Expert Witness in Civil Rights Legislation,* 1 SOCIAL PROBLEMS 5, 5–10 (1953).

8. *Id.*, at 7.

9. *Id.*

10. *See* LAWRENCE S. WRIGHTSMAN, JUDICIAL DECISIONMAKING: IS PSYCHOLOGY RELEVANT? 137–40 (Perspectives In Law and Psychology Series Vol. 11, 1999).

11. *Id.* Decades later, a replicated study showed African-American children still picking a dark-skinned doll as the "bad doll" in response to researchers' questions. Hazel Trice Edney, *New "Doll Test" Produces Ugly Results,* FINAL CALL, Sept. 14, 2006.

12. ANCHETA, *supra* note 4, at 48–51; Smith & Ellis, *supra* note 6 (quoting Clark). *See* Transcript of Record at 86–90, quoted in Edmond Cahn, *Jurisprudence,* 30 N.Y.U. L. REV. 150, 162–63 (1955) (quoting Clark's testimony in Briggs v. Elliott, 98 F.Supp. 529 (E.D. S.C. 1951) (case consolidated with *Brown*)).

13. FAIGMAN, *supra* note 4, at 176 (quoting JUAN WILLIAMS, THURGOOD MARSHALL: AMERICAN REVOLUTIONARY 197 (1998)); *id.* at 177 (quoting RICHARD KLUGER, SIMPLE JUSTICE: THE HISTORY OF *BROWN V. BOARD OF EDUCATION* AND BLACK AMERICA'S STRUGGLE FOR EQUALITY 328 (1977) (quoting Coleman)).

14. Faigman, *supra* note 4, at 184.

15. Note, *Grade School Segregation: The Last Attack on Racial Discrimination,* 61 YALE L.J. 730 (1952).

16. FAIGMAN, *supra* note 4, at 198. The absence of any controls troubled many critics. See, e.g., ERNEST VAN DEN HAAG & RALPH ROSS, THE FABRIC OF SOCIETY 165–66 (1957).

17. Subsequent commentators have pointed out that the Clarks obtained findings that black students in integrated schools also preferred the white dolls; some suggest that these findings contradicted their support of integrated schooling. *See* Herbert Garfinkel, *Social Science Evidence and the School Segregation Cases,* 21 J. POL. 37 (1959) (showing that the findings may have captured the large social influences on a sense of racial inferiority—including the legal endorsement of racial segregation before *Brown*). Lani Guinier notes that the Clarks' studies neglected the degree to which black children with high degrees of contact with whites may have experienced greater distress over their racial stigma than

did black children in segregated communities and that the Clark studies implied that black children were "damaged goods." Lani Guinier, *From Racial Liberalism to Racial Literacy: Brown v. Board of Education and the Interest-divergence Dilemma,* 2004 J. Am. Hist. 92, 110–12. Michael Heise emphasizes methodological limitations from the small sample size, lack of a control group, confusion about causation, as well as criticisms of judicial reliance on social science evidence for a constitutional judgment. Michael Heise, *Judicial Decision-making, Social Science Evidence, and Equal Educational Opportunity: Uneasy Relations and Uncertain Futures,* 31 Seattle L. Rev. 863 (2008).

18. A. S. Winston, *Science in the Service of the Far Right: Henry E. Garrett, the IAAEE, and the Liberty Lobby,* 54:1 Journal of Social Issues 179 (1998). On the reliance on social science by segregationists, *see* Sanjay Mody, Note, *Brown Footnote Eleven in Historical Context: Social Science and the Supreme Court's Quest for Legitimacy,* 54 Stan. L. Rev. 793, 825 n. 139 (2002).

19. Winston, *supra.*

20. Guinier, *supra* note 17. *See* Regina Austin, *Back to Basics: Returning to the Matter of Black Inferiority and White Supremacy in the Post-Brown Era,* 6 J. of Appellate Practice And Process 79 (2004).

21. Clark, *supra* note 7, at 7.

22. *Id.,* at 7–8.

23. *Id.,* at 8–9 (quoting testimony of Professor Henry E. Garrett; Mr. Buck; and Dr. Kelly).

24. *Id.* at 9.

25. *Id.*

26. *Id.*

27. *Id.* at 10.

28. Wrightsman, *supra* note 10, at 138–39.

29. Sweatt v. Painter, 339 U.S. 629 (1950).

30. McLaurin v. Oklahoma State Regents, 339 U.S. 637 (1950).

31. 163 U.S. 537 (1896).

32. *Id.*

33. Kluger, *supra* note 13, at 685.

34. *Id.* at 683.

35. *Id.* at 687 (citing Justice Frankfurter's unpublished memorandum).

36. Kluger, *supra* note 13, at 708.

37. See Mody, *supra* note 18. *See* also Michael J. Klarman, *Brown vs. Board of Education: Law or Politics?* (Univ. Va. School of Law, Pub. Law Research Paper No. 02-11, 2002), http://ssrn.com/abstract=353361; Michael J. Klarman, From Jim Crow to Civil Rights: The Supreme Court and the Struggle for Racial Equality (2004).

38. Scott Brewer, *Scientific Expert Testimony and Intellectual Due Process,* 107 Yale L.J. 1535, 1553 (1998).

39. *See* Brown v. Board of Education, 347 U.S. 483, 494 n. 11 (1954); Michael Heise, *Brown v. Board of Education, Footnote 11 and Multidisciplinarity,* 90 Cornell L. Rev. 279 (2005); Mody, *supra* note 18, at 793 (2002) (arguing that the justices did not rely on the social science evidence but hoped to increase the legitimacy of their decision by citing the research).

40. Ancheta, *supra* note 4, at 52–58; Wrightsman, *supra* note 10. Before the Supreme Court, John W. Davis criticized Clark's studies as "fragmentary expertise based on an examined presupposition." *See* Mark V. Tushnet, Making

CIVIL RIGHTS LAW: THURGOOD MARSHALL AND THE SUPREME COURT, 1936–1961 179 (1994). Later critics argued that the research results were ambiguous and could have shown damage from unsegregated environments, not from segregation; some objected that the conclusions reflected political precommitments of the researchers. Debate over the validity of the research submitted in *Brown* continues among social scientists. *Id.* at 140 (citing S. W. Cook, *Social Science and School Desegregation: Did We Mislead the Supreme Court?* 5 PERSONALITY AND SCH. PSYCHOL. BULL. 420 (1979); and Harold B. Gerard, *School Desegregation: The Social Science Role*, 38 AM. PSYCHOLOGIST 869 (1983)).

41. James Reston, *A Sociological Decision: Court Founded Its Segregation Ruling on Hearts and Minds Rather Than Laws*, N.Y. TIMES, May 18, 1954, at 14, *quoted in* Mody, *supra* note 18, at 804 n. 42.

42. MORTON HORWITZ, THE WARREN COURT 27–28 (1998).

43. See Gordon J. Beggs, *Novel Expert Evidence in Federal Civil Rights Litigation*, 45 AM. U. L. REV. 1, 9–16 (1995): Michael Heise, *supra* note 39, at 294–95, 298–308 (2005). The Supreme Court plurality cited disputes among parties and amici over the impact of racial diversity on student test scores and socialization when it recently rejected voluntary racial integration plans. *See* Parents Involved in Community Schools v. Seattle School District No. 1, 551 U.S. 701 (2007). For a discussion of this development, *see* Michael Heise, *supra* note 17.

44. *See* HORWITZ, *supra* note 42, at 131 (discussing John Dewey).

45. For defenses of an interpretive approach to social science, *see* CLIFFORD GEERTZ, *Thick Description: Toward an Interpretive Theory of Culture*, *in* THE INTERPRETATION OF CULTURES 3 (1973); CHARLES TAYLOR, *Interpretation and the Sciences of Man*, *in* PHILOSOPHY AND THE HUMAN SCIENCES: PHILOSOPHICAL PAPERS VOL. 2 15 (1985); Peter Winch, THE IDEA OF SOCIAL SCIENCE AND ITS RELATION TO PHILOSOPHY 24–62 (2d ed. 1994); *see also* SCHOOLS OF THOUGHT: TWENTY-FIVE YEARS OF INTERPRETIVE SOCIAL SCIENCE (Joan Wallach Scott and Debra Keates eds., 2001).

46. *See* ANCHETA, *supra* note 4, at 150.

47. *See* Heise, *supra* note 39.

48. *See* discussions of social science debates, *supra* chapters 2–5.

49. KLUGER, *supra* note 13, at 336.

50. *Id.* at 559.

51. IAN A. M. NICHOLSON, INVENTING PERSONALITY: GORDON ALLPORT AND THE SCIENCE OF SELFHOOD 194 (2003).

52. *Id.* at 213–16.

53. GORDON W. ALLPORT, THE NATURE OF PREJUDICE (1954).

54. *See* RUPERT BROWN, PREJUDICE: ITS SOCIAL PSYCHOLOGY 2–15 (1995).

55. NICHOLSON, *supra* note 51. *See generally* Thomas F. Pettigrew & Linda R. Tropp, *Allport's Intergroup Contact Hypothesis: Its History and Influence*, *in* ON THE NATURE OF PREJUDICE: FIFTY YEARS AFTER ALLPORT 262, 263 (John F. Dovidio et al. eds., 2005) (citing Verner M. Sims and James R. Patrick, *Attitude toward the Negro of Northern and Southern College Students*, 7 J. SOC. PSYCHOL. 192 (1936)).

56. *See* ALLPORT, *supra* note 53, at xv–xvi.

57. *Id.* at 281.

58. Thomas Pettigrew, *Foreword* to GORDON W. ALLPORT, THE NATURE OF PREJUDICE V (Basic Books 1979) (1954).

59. RUPERT BROWN, GROUP PROCESSES: DYNAMICS WITHIN AND BETWEEN GROUPS 343 (2d ed. 2000).

60. Walter G. Stephan, *Improving Intergroup Relations in the Schools, in* SCHOOL DESEGREGATION IN THE 21ST CENTURY 267 (Christine H. Rossell et al. eds., 2002).

61. *Id.* at 269.

62. *See* James A. Banks, *Diversity, Transformative Citizenship Education, and School Reform, in* JUST SCHOOLS: PURSUING EQUALITY IN SOCIETIES OF DIFFERENCE 227 (Martha Minow et al. eds., 2008) (citing studies). Integration efforts need to ensure equal status and guard against stereotyping for positive effects to ensue. *Id.* at 240; *see also* SHERYLL CASHIN, THE FAILURES OF INTEGRATION: HOW RACE AND CLASS ARE UNDERMINING THE AMERICAN DREAM 39–82 (2004).

63. In their preface to a volume commemorating the fiftieth anniversary of the book, the editors note how it foreshadowed new developments in the field, laid the foundation for generations of work, and continues to stimulate work that supports, extends, and at times modifies his analysis. Preface to Dovidio et al., *supra* note 55, at xiii–xv. The editors' opening chapter describes Allport's book as "the foundational work for the social psychology of prejudice" and "the most widely cited work on prejudice." John F. Dovidio et al., *Introduction: Reflecting on "The Nature of Prejudice": Fifty Years after Allport, in* Dovidio et al., *id.* at 1, 1.

64. Dovidio et al., *supra* note 63, at 3–10.

65. Alice H. Eagly & Amanda B. Diekman, *What Is the Problem? Prejudice as an Attitude-in-Context, in* Dovidio et al., *supra* note 55, at 19, 23–28.

66. Victoria M. Esses et al., *Instrumental Relations among Groups: Group Competition, Conflict, and Prejudice, in* Dovidio et al., *supra* note 55, at 227, 238–39.

67. Dovidio et al., *supra* note 63, at 10–14.

68. BROWN, *supra* note 54, at 346–54; Samuel L. Gaertner & John F. Dovidio, *Categorization, Recategorization, and Intergroup Bias, in* Dovidio et al., *supra* note 55, at 71, 76–81. *See also* Martha Minow, *Fragments or Ties? The Defense of Difference, in* THE FRACTIOUS NATION? UNITY AND DIVISION IN CONTEMPORARY AMERICAN LIFE (Jonathan Rieder & Stephen Steinlight eds., 2003).

69. Walter G. Stephan & Cookie White Stephan, *Intergroup Relations Program Evaluation, in* Dovidio et al., *supra* note 55, at 431.

70. MICHAEL B. KATZ & MARK J. STERN, ONE NATION DIVISIBLE: WHAT AMERICA WAS AND WHAT IT IS BECOMING 89 (2006). The "color line" can also be seen in racial disparities in income, incarceration, and college graduation. In 2002, the median household income was 54 percent higher for white households than for African-American households. *See* CARMEN DeNAVAS-WALT ET AL., U.S. CENSUS BUREAU, INCOME IN THE UNITED STATES: 2002, at 3 (2003). In 2004, the rate of incarceration was 6.4 times higher for African Americans than for whites. *See* Prison Policy Initiative, *Incarceration Is Not an Equal Opportunity Punishment,* www.prisonpolicy.org/articles/not_equal_opportunity.pdf (last visited Oct. 29, 2009). In 2005, the nationwide college graduation rate was 62 percent for white students but only 42 percent for African-American students. *See Black Student College Graduation Rates Remain Low, but Modest Progress Begins to Show,* 50 J. BLACKS HIGHER EDUC. 88 (winter 2005–6).

71. KATZ & STERN, *supra* note 70, at 114–17.

72. *Id.* at 224.

73. *See* Banks, *supra* note 62, at 235 (on average, white students attend schools that are 80 percent white although minority enrollment nationwide approaches 40 percent).

74. *See supra* chapters 2, 3, and 4.

75. *See supra* chapter 5.

76. *See supra* chapters 1 and 5.

77. San Antonio Independent School District v. Rodriguez, 411 U.S. 1 (1973).

78. Plyler v. Doe, 457 U.S. 202 (1982); *see* 42 U.S.C. § 2000 (2000); Larry P. v. Riles, 793 F.2d 969 (9th Cir. 1984); Rose v. Council for Better Education, Inc., 790 S.W.2d 186 (Ky. 1989); Abott v. Burke 575 A.2d 359 (N.J. 1990).

79. By using the phrase, President George W. Bush appropriated the concept but not the commitments of the Children's Defense Fund, founded by Marian Wright Edelman. When asked about President Bush's use of the phrase, Edelman replied: "the Bush Administration's single-issue No Child Left Behind Education Act...seems to be a smokescreen to dismantle all of the gains we have made for children. His policy can be interpreted as 'leave no millionaire behind.'" *5 Questions For: Marian Wright Edelman,* EBONY, Jan. 2004, at 20, 20.

80. For instance, the rate of college graduation is 46 percent for black women but only 35 percent for black men. *See, e.g., Black Women Now Hold a Large Lead over Black Men in Enrollments at the Nation's Highest-Ranked Law Schools,* 50 J. BLACKS HIGHER EDUC. 42 (winter 2005–6).

81. Judges have resisted implementing the American Disabilities Act (ADA) to its full potential; numerous decisions have had a detrimental impact on the ADA's ability to protect the rights of the disabled. There have been recent efforts to restore the ADA to its full and intended potency. *See* Robert L. Burgdorf, Jr., *Restoring the ADA and Beyond: Disability in the 21st Century,* 13 TEX. J. C.L. & C.R. 241, 255–56, 268–71 (2008); *see also* Michelle A. Travis, *Lashing Back at the ADA Backlash: How the Americans with Disabilities Act Benefits Americans without Disabilities,* 76 TENN. L. REV. 311, 315–20 (2009) (describing forms of social backlash to the ADA). Like the ADA, the IDEA has been treated with skepticism by courts and the public. Courts have narrowed the eligibility criteria required to be found disabled under the statute, and this could potentially restigmatize disability in education. Wendy F. Hensel, *Sharing the Short Bus: Eligibility and Identity under the IDEA,* 58 HASTINGS L.J. 1147, 1162–79, 1198–201 (2007); *see also* Mark C. Weber, *The IDEA Eligibility Mess,* 57 BUFF. L. REV. 83, 87–151 (2009) (characterizing the IDEA eligibility requirement as confusing, given unclear court decisions, recent challenges to learning disability diagnostic techniques, and the problem of overrepresentation of African Americans in some disability categories).

82. Neeraj Kaushal et al., *Immigrants and the Economy, in* THE NEW AMERICANS: A GUIDE TO IMMIGRATION SINCE 1965 176, 176–88 (Mary C. Waters et al. eds., 2007); Carola Suárez-Orozco & Marcelo Suárez-Orozco, *Education, in id.*; Mary C. Waters, *America's Immigration Success Story,* online op-ed, FORBES, May 29, 2007, www.forbes.com/2007/05/21/outsourcing-waters-harvard-oped-cx_mcw_0529harvard.html (noting that immigrants are more successfully integrated in the United States than they are in European countries, including France, Britain, and Germany).

83. *See* Guadalupe San Miguel, Jr., CONTESTED POLICY: THE RISE AND FALL OF FEDERAL BILINGUAL EDUCATION IN THE UNITED STATES, 1960–2001, at 80–82

(2004) (describing the scene in the 1990s that spawned a movement opposed to bilingual education that saw action at the federal level and in several states, including California, Arizona, Oregon, New York, and others); James Crawford, *What Now for Bilingual Education?* 13 RETHINKING SCH. (fall 1998–99), www.rethinkingschools.org/archive/13_02/bimain.shtml (reviewing the battle over the English-only instructional approach that was at the center of California's Proposition 227 debate); Maria T. Padilla, *Bilingual Class Must Focus on English Skills*, ORLANDO SENTINEL, July 18, 2001, at D1 (critiquing the bilingual education debate in central Florida); John Tierney, *The Big City; Polyglot City Raises a Cry for English*, N.Y. TIMES, Aug. 16, 1999, at B1 (noting that successful leaders of the bilingual education revolt in California contemplated a similar plan in New York City).

84. About 20 percent of current students enrolled in Catholic schools are not Catholic; these schools attract poor and minority students in search of alternatives to struggling urban public schools. Paul Vitello and Winnie Hu, *Catholic Schools, under the Threat of Extinction, Are Being Reinvented*, N.Y. TIMES, Jan. 18, 2009, A25. The Archdiocese of Washington, D.C., converted its parochial schools into city charter schools. *Id.* The financial troubles and declining enrollments at Catholic schools stem from many factors, including the need to pay salaries and pensions for teachers, given the shrinking numbers of nuns and priests who taught at no extra expense; shifts in the ethnic identities and financial resources of Catholics in America; inadequate business and managerial expertise; and changing messages from the Vatican about the place of Catholic schools in parents' religious obligations. *Id.*

85. *Id.* In 1965, about half of all Catholic children in the country were enrolled in Catholic elementary schools, according to the National Catholic Educational Association, whereas in 2009, only 15 percent are. *Id.* Proposals within the Catholic community include recasting Catholic schools to serve specific populations, such as the poor or children with disabilities. *Id.* (summarizing research from Catholic universities).

86. Robert D. Putnam, *E Pluribus Unum: Diversity and Community in the Twenty-first Century*, 30 SCANDINAVIAN POL. STUD. 137 (2007).

87. Susan Eaton and Gina Chirichigno, *Charters Must Commit to Diversity*, BOSTON GLOBE, July 19, 2009, at C9. *See supra* chapter 5, discussing varying degrees of racial integration among charter schools in different school districts. *Compare, e.g.*, Linda A. Renzulli & Lorraine Evans, *School Choice, Charter Schools, and White Flight*, 52 SOC. PROBS. 398 (2005) (charter schools chosen more by whites when regular schools are more racially integrated), Gregory R. Weiher & Kent L. Tedin, *Does Choice Lead to Racially Distinctive Schools? Charter Schools and Household Preferences*, 21 J. POL'Y ANALYSIS & MGMT. 79 (2002) (charter school selections of white, African-American, and Latino families all indicate a preference for student bodies with a larger proportion of the household's own racial group), *and* Kelly E. Rapp & Suzanne E. Eckes, *Dispelling the Myth of "White Flight": An Examination of Minority Enrollment in Charter Schools*, 21 EDUC. POL'Y 615, 621 (2007) ("One explanation for the high percentage of minority students attending charter schools could be the existence of ethnocentric schools.") *with* JULIAN R. BETTS ET AL., DOES SCHOOL CHOICE WORK? EFFECTS ON STUDENT INTEGRATION AND ACHIEVEMENT 31–34 (2006) (three California choice programs produced greater integration than the traditional district schools), *and* David R. Garcia, *The Impact of School Choice on Racial Segregation in Charter Schools*, 22 EDUC. POL'Y 805, 805 (2007) ("Charter elementary school choosers enter charter

schools that are more racially segregated than the district schools they exited, although on entrance to high school, choosers enter charter schools that are as racially segregated or more integrated than the district schools they exited.").

88. *See* JULIE F. MEAD, CHARTER SCHOOLS DESIGNED FOR CHILDREN WITH DISABILITIES 11 (2008), www.uscharterschools.org/specialedprimers/download/special_report_mead.pdf; LAUREN MORANDO RHIM ET AL., PROJECT INTERSECT, ACCESS AND ACCOUNTABILITY FOR STUDENTS WITH DISABILITIES IN CALIFORNIA CHARTER SCHOOLS 19–26 (2006), www.education.umd.edu/EDSP/ProjectIntersect/docs/IRR5Revimar07.pdf. Two researchers note the interaction between disability and race: parents of white students with special needs may be particularly likely to send their children to charter schools, "because special education classrooms in public schools tend to have higher proportions of nonwhites than the schools in which they are located." Renzulli & Evans, *supra* note 87, at 412.

89. *See, e.g.*, Jeremy Meyer, *Kunsmiller Selective or Inclusive?* web post to Colorado Classroom Blog, web site of *Denver Post,* http://blogs.denverpost.com/coloradoclassroom/ (Feb. 3, 2009).

90. See an especially thoughtful recent comment: Ashley's Mom, *The Illusion of Inclusion,* web post to Physical and Mental Disabilities Community, June 13, 2009, 12:24 PST, http://stanford.wellsphere.com/physical-mental-disabilities-article/the-illusion-of-inclusion/715688.

91. James Vaznis, *Charter Schools Lag in Serving the Neediest,* BOSTON GLOBE, Aug. 12, 2009, at A1 (in Boston, English-language learners represented less than 4 percent of students in all but one charter school in 2008–9, with many charter schools enrolling none, while they represent nearly one-fifth of students in the system overall).

92. Stephanie Simon, *Hard-hit Schools Try Public-relations Push,* WALL ST. J., Aug. 17, 2009, at A3.

93. Jennifer L. Hochschild & Nathan Scovronick, THE AMERICAN DREAM AND THE PUBLIC SCHOOLS 201 (2003).

94. Pierce v. Society of Sisters, 268 U.S. 510 (1925).

95. Specialized programs could produce some kinds of integration. Single-sex schools and schools for students with disabilities, for example, can produce racially and ethnically diverse student bodies. So can an Arabic-language school. Yet, in practice, diversity in many such schools is constrained due to the composition of the school district or the preferences of parents and students. Hence, the East Harlem Women's Leadership School in New York City is 34 percent students of color and 61 percent students of Hispanic origin; *see* InsideSchools.org, Young Women's Leadership School, http://insideschools.org/index12.php?fso=1138 (last visited Oct. 29, 2009). In Minneapolis, the Twin Cities International Elementary School, founded by educational leaders in the East African community and prominently featuring classes in Arabic, is mainly composed of students of East African heritage. *See* Twin Cities International Elementary School, www.twincitiesinternationalschool.org/ (last visited Oct. 29, 2009).

96. Encouraging social integration through postsecondary education is another vehicle, although it involves at best only half the population and does so in the segmented markets of elite colleges, community colleges, and universities and colleges in between these levels.

97. Preparation for equal citizenship may have declined as a goal of American schooling when compared with social mobility. *See, e.g.*, David F. Labaree, *Public Goods, Private Goods: The American Struggle over Educational Goals*, 34 AM.

EDUC. RES. J. 39 (1997). Social integration actually is a crucial dimension of both preparation for citizenship and social mobility.

98. *See, e.g.*, Claude M. Steele, University Lecture at Columbia University, Identity and Stereotype Threat: Their Nature and What to Do about Them at School and Work (Sept. 29, 2009), recording available at www.universityprograms. columbia.edu/university-lecture-provost-claude-m-steele; Esther Rebecca Cohn-Vargas, Nurturing Identity Safety in Elementary Classrooms (2007) (unpublished Ph.D. dissertation, Fielding Graduate University).

99. *See, e.g.*, ANNE T. HENDERSON & KAREN L. MAPP, A NEW WAVE OF EVIDENCE: THE IMPACT OF SCHOOL, FAMILY, AND COMMUNITY CONNECTIONS UPON STUDENT ACHIEVEMENT (2002), www.sedl.org/connections/resources/evidence.pdf.

100. See Robert L. Crain & Rita E. Mahard, *The Effect of Research Methodology on Desegregation-Achievement Studies: A Meta-Analysis*, 88 AM. J. SOC. 839 (1983); GARY ORFIELD, MUST WE BUS? SEGREGATED SCHOOLS AND NATIONAL POLICY 121–24 (1978).

101. *See* JAMES S. COLEMAN ET AL., EQUALITY OF EDUCATIONAL OPPORTUNITY 20–23 (1966); PETER SCHRAG, FINAL TEST: THE BATTLE FOR ADEQUACY IN AMERICA'S SCHOOLS 208 (2003). *See* Banks, *supra* note 62, at 236 (quoting RACE-CONSCIOUS POLICIES FOR ASSIGNING STUDENTS TO SCHOOLS: SOCIAL SCIENCE RESEARCH AND THE SUPREME COURT CASES, NATIONAL ACAD. EDUCATION (2007)).

102. RICHARD D. KAHLENBERG, ALL TOGETHER NOW: CREATING MIDDLE-CLASS SCHOOLS THROUGH PUBLIC SCHOOL CHOICE 8, 23–46 (2001). *See supra* chapter 3.

103. KAHLENBERG, *supra* note 102, at 47–66, 72–76.

104. *Id.* at 171, 340 n. 93 (discussing San Antonio Independent School District v. Rodriguez, 411 U.S. 1 (1973)).

105. *See* Tom Wicker, Tragic Failure: Racial Integration in America (1996); Todd Gitlin, The Twilight of Common Dreams: Why America Is Wracked by Culture Wars (1995). Racial divisions affect political decisions about school finance—*see* JEFFREY R. HENIG ET AL., THE COLOR OF SCHOOL REFORM: RACE, POLITICS, AND THE CHALLENGE OF URBAN EDUCATION (1999); James E. Ryan, *The Influence of Race in School Finance Reform*, 98 MICH. L. REV. 480 (1999)—but it is not clear that class differences would be less divisive politically.

106. KAHLENBERG, *supra* note 102, at 110–14.

107. *Id.* at 116–17.

108. *Id.* at 228–57.

109. *Id.* at 43–45.

110. However, as Kahlenberg reminds us, "[h]igh school may ... be too late to integrate some children because many low-income children drop out of school entirely after completing the eighth grade." *Id.* at 115.

111. *See* MICHAEL J. KLARMAN, UNFINISHED BUSINESS: RACIAL EQUALITY IN AMERICAN HISTORY 202 (2007) (percentage of blacks living below the poverty level were three times that of whites in 2004).

112. Amanda Lepof, *Empirical Study Finds Socio-economic Status Not a Likely Substitute for Race in CA College Admissions*, DIVERSITY DIG. (fall/winter 2002), www.diversityweb.org/Digest/fw02/studyrace.html; Robert Bruce Slater, *Why Socioeconomic Affirmative Action in College Admissions Works against African Americans*, 8 J. BLACKS HIGHER EDUC. 57 (1995); *see also* STEPHEN J. ROSE & ANTHONY P. CARNEVALE, CENTURY FOUNDATION, SOCIOECONOMIC STATUS, RACE/ETHNICITY, AND SELECTIVE COLLEGE ADMISSIONS (2003). For a discussion of the similar failure to produce racial diversity of the "Texas Plan," under which

top-ranking students in each high school are guaranteed admission to elite state universities, *see* B. Forest, *Hidden Segregation? The Limits of Geographically Based Affirmative Action*, 21 POL. GEOGRAPHY 855 (2002).

113. Minow, *supra* note 68, at 638 (citing CASHIN, *supra* note 62, at 176–77 (2004)).

114. Richard D. Kahlenberg, *Socioeconomic School Integration: A Reply to the Responses*, EQUALITY & EDUC., Dec. 1, 2001, www.equaleducation.org/commentary.asp?opedid=901.

115. The effect of peers on student achievement is well-documented. *See, e.g., Weili Ding & Steven F. Lehrer, Do Peers Affect Student Achievement in China's Secondary Schools?* (National Bureau of Economic Research, Working Paper No. 12305, 2006), www.nber.org/papers/w12305; Caroline Hoxby, *Peer Effects in the Classroom: Learning From Gender and Race Variation* (National Bureau of Economic Research, Working Paper No. 7867, 2000), www.nber.org/papers/w7867. But such studies have not disentangled the benefit of being with higher performing peers from potential harm to students' performance due to teachers' low expectations or other environmental factors.

116. *See* Harold Berlak, *Race and the Achievement Gap*, 15 RETHINKING SCH. ONLINE (summer 2001), www.rethinkingschools.org/archive/15_04/Race154.shtml; Pedro Naguera & Antwi Akom, *The Significance of Race in the Racial Gap in Academic Achievement*, IN MOTION MAG., June 19, 2000, www.inmotion-magazine.com/pnaa.html; Christopher Jencks & Meredith Phillips, *America's Next Achievement Test: Closing the Black-white Test Score Gap*, AMERICAN PROSPECT, Sept.–Oct. 1998, at 44, 47; GARY R. HOWARD, WE CAN'T TEACH WHAT WE DON'T KNOW: WHITE TEACHERS, MULTIRACIAL SCHOOLS 2–9 (2d ed. 2006); Karen L. Mapp et al., *Race, Accountability and the Achievement Gap* (Public Education Leadership Project at Harvard University, Case Study PEL-044, 2006).

117. Martha Minow, *After Brown: What Would Martin Luther King Say?* 12 LEWIS & CLARK L. REV. 599, 624–25, 637 (2008).

118. PEDRO NOGUERA, CITY SCHOOLS AND THE AMERICAN DREAM 25 (2003). See also KENNETH B. CLARK, DARK GHETTO: DILEMMAS OF SOCIAL POWER, 121–125, 134 (1965) (urging teachers to hold children of color to high expectations).

119. Sabrina Zirkel, *Ongoing Issues of Racial and Ethnic Stigma in Education 50 Years after Brown v. Board,* 37 URB. REV. 107, 114–15 (2005).

120. *See* LISA DELPIT, OTHER PEOPLE'S CHILDREN: CULTURAL CONFLICT IN THE CLASSROOM (1995); GENEVA GAY, CULTURALLY RESPONSIVE TEACHING: THEORY, RESEARCH, AND PRACTICE (2000); Tyrone C. Howard, *Culturally Relevant Pedagogy: Ingredients for Critical Teacher Reflection*, 42 THEORY INTO PRAC. 195 (2003); GLORIA LADSON-BILLINGS, THE DREAMKEEPERS: SUCCESSFUL TEACHERS OF AFRICAN AMERICAN CHILDREN (1994); Claude M. Steele et al., *Contending with Group Image: The Psychology of Stereotype and Social Identity Threat, in* ADVANCES IN EXPERIMENTAL SOC. PSYCHOL. 379 (Mark P. Zanna ed., 34th ed. 2002).

121. BEVERLY DANIEL TATUM, "WHY ARE ALL THE BLACK KIDS SITTING TOGETHER IN THE CAFETERIA?" AND OTHER CONVERSATIONS ABOUT RACE 94 (1997).

122. See JOHN U. OGBU, BLACK AMERICAN STUDENTS IN AN AFFLUENT SUBURB: A STUDY OF ACADEMIC DISENGAGEMENT (2003), for the initial controversial claim of peer pressure to avoid academic achievement in order to avoid "acting white"; recently, no cost to social popularity has been found among students with average performance but did appear among high-performing students. *See* David

Austen-Smith & Roland G. Fryer, Jr., *An Economic Analysis of "Acting White,"* 120 Q.J. ECON. 357 (2005).

123. Exempt from No Child Left Behind, these schools nonetheless have significantly better results in closing the racial gap in achievement when compared with schools covered by the Act, as explored below. For general information, *see* U.S. Department of Defense, Education Activity, Domestic Dependent Elementary and Secondary Schools Home Page, www.am.dodea.edu/ddessasc/ (last visited Oct. 28, 2009).

124. *See* National Center for Education Statistics, DoDEA State Profile, http://nces.ed.gov/nationsreportcard/states/profile.asp (last visited Aug. 7, 2009).

125. *Id.*

126. *Id.*

127. ALAN VANNEMAN ET AL., NATIONAL CENTER FOR EDUCATION STATISTICS, ACHIEVEMENT GAPS 13 (2009). The study relies on performance on the NAEP test, and the national average is based on the forty-four states reporting their results.

128. *Id.*

129. CLAIRE SMREKAR ET AL., MARCH TOWARD EXCELLENCE: SCHOOL SUCCESS AND MINORITY STUDENT ACHIEVEMENT IN DEPARTMENT OF DEFENSE SCHOOLS viii (2001).

130. *Id.*, at vii–ix.

131. See Leslie R. Hinkson, Schools of the Nation: Department of Defense Schools and the Black-White Test Score Gap (Sept. 2007) (unpublished Ph.D. dissertation, Princeton University) (on file with Mudd Library, Princeton University).

132. SMREKAR ET AL., *supra* note 129, at ix–xi.

133. *Id.* at 28.

134. *Id.*

135. *Id. See also* Collyn Bray Swanson, A Comparison of Achievement between African American Military Dependent High School Students in the Department of Defense Schools and a Public School System (Aug. 2004) (unpublished Ph.D. dissertation, University of Denver) (on file with Penrose Library, University of Denver) (noting concept of "mastery learning" presented to teachers in Department of Defense schools, reflecting the understanding that all students can learn, though they may do so in different ways).

136. *See* SMREKAR ET AL., *supra* note 129, at 18. Comparing expenditures here is difficult; the Department of Defense schools do not receive federal or state grants or private donations, unlike many other schools, and these additional funds are not included in the national per-pupil school district calculations. *Id.*

137. *Id.* at x.

138. *Id.* at 41.

139. Claire E. Smrekar & Debra E. Owens, *"It's a Way of Life for Us": High Mobility and High Achievement in Department of Defense Schools*, 72 J. NEGRO EDUC. 165, 167 (2003). In one fifth-grade classroom at Fort Knox's Walker Intermediate School, eight of the twenty-five fifth graders joined the class after the start of the year and four left, but the students stay in touch as pen pals, and the teachers incorporate the pen-pal postcards into class geography and math lessons. Daniel Golden, *Making the Grade: Pentagon-run Schools Excel in Academics, Defying Demographics*, WALL ST. J., Dec, 22, 1999, at A1.

140. Smekar & Owens, *supra* note 139, at 173.

141. SMREKAR ET AL., *supra* note 129, at 31–33; Smrekar & Owens, *supra* note 139, at 173. On parental participation, *see* News Release, Department of Defense Education Activity, www.dodea.edu/communications/news/negp/factsheet.pdf.

142. *Id.*

143. *See* SMREKAR ET AL., *supra* note 129, at 31–37, 43–44. Although approximately two-thirds of military families qualify for subsidized school lunch, the percentage of single-parent households is only 6.2 percent, compared with a national rate of 27 percent; yet the deployment patterns mean that many military households are run for long periods as single-parent families. *See* Hinkson, *supra* note 131. In addition, spouses of military personnel have higher educational levels than their civilian counterparts. *Id.*

144. Charles Brown, Relatively Equal Opportunity in the Armed Forces: Impacts on Children of Military Families (2000) (unpublished manuscript). On average, African-American students in U.S. public schools attend schools where 35 percent of the students are white or Asian American, while 52 percent of African-American students in Department of Defense schools attend schools with that kind of student mix. *Id.*

145. *See* MOSKOS & JOHN SIBLEY BUTLER, ALL THAT WE CAN BE: BLACK LEADERSHIP AND RACIAL INTEGRATION THE ARMY WAY (1996).

146. SMREKAR ET AL., *supra* note 129, at 46.

147. Golden, *supra* note 139; Smreker & Owens, *supra* note 139. *See also* BEATRICE L. BRIDGLALL & EDMUND W. GORDON, ERIC CLEARINGHOUSE ON URBAN EDUCATION, RAISING MINORITY ACADEMIC ACHIEVEMENT: THE DEPARTMENT OF DEFENSE MODEL (2003), www.ericdigests.org/2004–2/minority.html.

148. *See* DAVID & MYRA SADKER & KAREN R. ZITTLEMAN, STILL FAILING AT FAIRNESS: HOW GENDER BIAS CHEATS GIRLS AND BOYS IN SCHOOL AND WHAT WE CAN DO ABOUT IT (2009); Judith Mulholland et al., *Do Single-gender Classrooms in Coeducational Settings Address Boys' Underachievement? An Australian Study*, 30 EDUC. STUD. 19 (2004). *See also* Catherine G. Krupnick, *Women and Men in the Classroom: Inequality and Its Remedies*, 1 ON TEACHING & LEARNING 18 (1985).

149. *See* ROSEMARY C. SALOMONE, SAME, DIFFERENT, EQUAL: RETHINKING SINGLE-SEX SCHOOLING 202–6 (2003).

150. *See* MARA SAPON-SHEVIN, WIDENING THE CIRCLE: THE POWER OF INCLUSIVE CLASSROOMS 90 (2007). *See also* L. Florian, *Inclusive Practice: What, Why and How? in* THE ROUTLEDGEFALMER READER IN INCLUSIVE EDUCATION 29 (Keith Topping & Sheelagh Maloney eds., 2005).

151. Tom Hehir, *Changing the Way We Think About Kids with Disabilities, in* INCLUSIVE EDUCATION: READINGS AND REFLECTIONS 101, 106 (Gary Thomas & Mark Vaughan eds., 2004) (summarizing National Longitudinal Transition Study, examining progress of eight thousand students in high schools in the 1980s).

152. DOROTHY KERZNER LIPSKY & ALAN GARTNER, INCLUSION AND SCHOOL REFORM: TRANSFORMING AMERICA'S CLASSROOMS 187–90 (1997).

153. *See* Elizabeth Englander, *Is Bullying a Junior Hate Crime? Implications for Interventions*, 51 AM. BEHAV. SCIENTIST 205 (2007); KEVIN J. STROM, BUREAU OF JUSTICE STATISTICS, HATE CRIMES REPORTED IN CIBRS, 1997–1999 (2001), www.ojp.usdoj.gov/bjs/pub/pdf/hcrn99.pdf; Kurt Naumann, School Violence Resource Center, Briefing Paper: Bullying (2001), www.arsafeschools.com/Files/Bullying.doc.

154. *See* JENNIFER L. HOCHSCHILLD & NATHAN SCOVRONICK, THE AMERICAN DREAM AND THE PUBLIC SCHOOLS 194 (2003).

155. *See* SUSAN EATON, THE CHILDREN IN ROOM E4: AMERICAN EDUCATION ON TRIAL 128-29 (2007).

156. Nathan Glazer, *Some Problems in Acknowledging Diversity, in* MAKING GOOD CITIZENS 168, 178 (Diane Ravitch & Joseph Viteritti eds., 2001).

157. BROWN, *supra* note 54, at 355-56; Janet W. Schofield & Rebecca Eurich-Fulcer, *When and How School Desegregation Improves Intergroup Relations, in* BLACKWELL HANDBOOK OF SOCIAL PSYCHOLOGY: INTERGROUP PROCESS 475 (Rupert Brown & Samuel L. Gaertner eds., 2001) (summarizing the literature). *See also* Rupert Brown & Miles Hewstone, *An Integrative Theory of Intergroup Contact,* 37 ADVANCES IN EXPERIMENTAL SOC. PSYCHOL. 255 (2005) (summarizing research on decategorization, redrawing group boundaries, reducing the salience of group identities—so that members of different groups experience shared affiliations on an equal basis).

158. *See* Yehuda Amir, *Contact Hypothesis in Ethnic Relations, in* THE HANDBOOK OF INTERETHNIC COEXISTENCE 162 (Eugene Weiner ed., 1998); Thomas F. Pettigrew & Linda R. Tropp, *A Meta-analytic Test of Intergroup Contact Theory,* 90 J. PERSONALITY & SOC. PSYCHOL. 751 (2006); Thomas F. Pettigrew & Linda R. Tropp, *Does Intergroup Contact Reduce Prejudice? Recent Meta-analytic Findings, in* REDUCING PREJUDICE AND DISCRIMINATION: SOCIAL PSCYHOLOGICAL PERSPECTIVES 93 (S. Oskamp ed., 2000).

159. CLAIRE SELLTIZ ET AL., RESEARCH METHODS IN SOCIAL RELATIONS 119-20 (3d ed. 1976); HUGH DONALD FORBES, ETHNIC CONFLICT: COMMERCE, CULTURE, AND THE CONTACT HYPOTHESIS 26-28 (1997). *See also* Jill V. Hamm, Bradford B. Brown, & Daniel J. Hect, *Bridging the Ethnic Divide: Student and School Characteristics in African American, Asian-descent, Latino, and White Adolescents' Cross-ethnic Friend Nominations,* 15 J. RES. ON ADOLESCENCE 21 (2005).

160. Stephan, *supra* note 60, at 272 (citing studies).

161. Thomas F. Pettigrew & Linda R. Tropp, *How does Intergroup Contact Reduce Prejudice? Meta-analytic Tests of Three Mediators,* 38 EUR. J. SOC. PSYCHOL. 922 (2008).

162. Stephan, *supra* note 60, at 279.

163. Pettigrew & Tropp, *A Meta-analytic Test of Intergroup Contact Theory, supra* note 158; Lincoln Quillian & Mary E. Campbell, *Beyond Black and White: The Present and Future of Multiracial Friendship Segregation,* 68 AM. SOC. REV. 540 (2003); Kara Joyner & Grace Kao, *School Racial Composition and Adolescent Racial Homophily,* 8 SOC. SCI. Q. 810 (2000). *See also* Pettigrew & Tropp, *Allport's Intergroup Contact Hypothesis, supra* note 55; Michal Kurlaender & John T. Yun, *Measuring School Composition and Student Outcomes in a Multiracial Society,* 113 AM. J. EDUC. 213 (2007).

164. Sandra Bowman Damico, Afesa Bell-Nathaniel, & Charles Green, *Effects of School Organizational Structure on Interracial Friendships in Middle School,* 74 J. EDUC. RES. 391 (1981).

165. *See, e.g.,* Christopher L. Aberson & Christina Tomolillo, *Implicit Bias and Contact: The Role of Interethnic Friendships,* 144 J. SOC. PSYCHOL. 335 (2004); Christopher Bratt, *Contact and Attitudes between Ethnic Groups: Survey-based Study of Adolescents in Norway,* 45 ACTA SOCIOLOGICA 107 (2002); Lindsey Cameron, Adam Rutland, Rupert Brown, & Rebecca Douch, *Changing Children's Intergroup Attitudes toward Refugees: Testing Different Models of Extended*

Contact, 77 CHILD DEV. 1208 (2006); Xavier Escandell & Alin M. Ceobanu, *When Contact with Immigrants Matters: Threat, Interethnic Attitudes and Foreigner Exclusionism in Spain's Comunidades Autonomas*, 32 ETHNIC & RACIAL STUD. 44 (2009); Orit Ichilov & Shira Even-Dar, *Interethnic Contacts in an Alternative Educational Environment: The Israeli Shelef Project*, 13 J. YOUTH & ADOLESCENCE 145 (1984); Lauren M. McLaren, *Anti-immigrant Prejudice in Europe: Contact, Threat Perception, and Preferences for the Exclusion of Migrants*, 81 SOC. FORCES 909 (2003).

166. Anja Eller & Dominic Abrams, *"Gringos" in Mexico: Cross-sectional and Longitudinal Effects of Language School Promoted Contact on Intergroup Bias*, 6 GROUP PROCESSES & INTERGROUP REL. 55 (2003).

167. Jay Gottlieb, *Improving Attitudes toward Retarded Children by Using Group Discussion*, 47 EXCEPTIONAL CHILD 106 (1980) (noting that one study showed that simply discussing the situation of individuals with disabilities shifted students with negative attitudes to report positive attitudes toward students with disabilities). *See* Douglas Fuchs & Lynn S. Fuchs, *Sometimes Separate Is Better*, 52 EDUC. LEADERSHIP 22 (1995) (noting that most of the literature on effects of intergroup contact involving individuals with disabilities focuses not on improving the attitudes of students without disabilities but on how intergroup contact helps to prepare disabled children for mainstream life); D. C. Harper & D. P. Wacker, *Children's Attitudes toward Disabled Peers and the Effects of Mainstreaming*, 7 ACAD. PSYCHOL. BULL. 87 (1985) (discussing another study, which found that interacting with disabled peers helped facilitate more positive—and more nuanced—attitudes toward disabled students). *See also* László Dorogi, Szabo Tova Mos, & József Bognár, *Goal Orientation and Perceived Motivational Climate in Hungarian Athletes with Physical and Visual Disabilities and in Able-bodied Athletes*, 40 KINESIOLOGY 162 (2008); Tova Most & Amatzia Weisel, *Contact with Students with Hearing Impairments and the Evaluation of Speech Intelligibility and Personal Qualities*, 33 J. SPECIAL EDUC. 103 (1999); David Slininger, Claudine Sherrill, & Catherine M. Jankowski, *Children's Attitudes toward Peers with Severe Disabilities: Revisiting Contact Theory*, 17 ADAPTED PHYSICAL ACTIVITY Q. 176 (2000).

168. Norman Anderssen, *Does Contact with Lesbians and Gays Lead to Friendlier Attitudes? A Two Year Longitudinal Study*, 12 J. COMMUNITY & APPLIED SOC. PSYCHOL. 124 (2002); Justin E. Heinze & Stacey S. Horn, *Intergroup Contact and Beliefs about Homosexuality in Adolescence*, 38 J. YOUTH & ADOLESCENCE 937 (2009); Christopher T.H. Liang & Craig Alimo, *The Impact of White Heterosexual Students' Interactions on Attitudes toward Lesbian, Gay and Bi-sexual People: A Longitudinal Study*, 46 J. C. STUDENT DEV. 237 (2005); Gregory M. Herek & Eric K. Glunt, *Interpersonal Contact and Heterosexuals' Attitudes toward Gay Men: Results from a National Survey*, 30 J. SEX. RES. 239 (1993) (demonstrating that those who have interpersonal contact with gay men in their lives are more likely to have positive attitudes toward gay men than those who have no such regular interpersonal contact); *see* also Gregory M. Herek & J. P. Capitanio, *"Some of My Best Friends": Intergroup Contact, Concealable Stigma, and Heterosexuals' Attitudes toward Gay Men and Lesbians*, 22 SOC. PSYCHOL. BULL. 412 (1996) (corroborating the findings made by Herek and Glunt concerning lesbians). *See also* Edward Schiappa, Peter Gregg, & Dean Hewes, *The Parasocial Contact Hypothesis*, 72 COMM. MONOGRAPHS 92 (2005); Edward Schiappa, Peter B. Gregg, & Dean E. Hewes, *Can One TV Show Make a Difference? Will & Grace and the Parasocial Contact Thesis*, 51

J. HOMOSEXUALITY 15 (2006) (developing what the authors call "the parasocial contact hypothesis," which concerns the "relationships" people have with television and film stars with whom they are "in contact" on a regular basis).

169. P. J. Henry & Curtis D. Hardin, *The Contact Hypothesis Revisited: Status Bias in the Reduction of Implicit Prejudice in the United States and Lebanon,* 17 PSYCHOL. SCI. 862 (2006); Miles Hewstone, Ed Cairns, Alberto Voci, Juergen Hamberger, & Ulrike Niens, *Intergroup Contact, Forgiveness, and Experience of "The Troubles" in Northern Ireland,* 62 J. SOC. ISSUES 99 (2006).

170. *See* Joanne Hughes, *Mediating and Moderating Effects of Inter-group Contact: Case Studies from Bilingual/Bi-national Schools in Israel,* 33 J. ETHNIC & MIGRATION STUD. 419 (2007); Christopher A. Cooper, Moshe Haspel, & H. Gibbs Knotts, Paper Presented at the American Political Science Association: The Impact of Diverse Contexts on Racial Attitudes: Evaluating Threat and Contact among Whites, Blacks and Hispanics (Aug. 30, 2007), www.allacademic.com//meta/p_mla_apa_research_citation/2/0/9/0/7/pages209077/p209077-1.php.

171. *See* Renee Edwards, You Need to Understand My Gender Role: Empirical Test of Tannen's Model of Gender and Communication, 50 SEX ROLES 491, 491–505 (2004).

172. *See* SALOMONE, *supra* note 149, at 223–24 (reporting study of single-sex education experiment in Australia that apparently did not alter math and science achievement for girls or boys but resulted in a more relaxed and comfortable feeling for boys and for girls in single-sex classes with more participation and less harassment from other students and more benefits for low-achieving students). See *supra* chapter 2 on research about single-sex classrooms.

173. *Id.* at 200–201. *See also* ANCHETA, *supra* note 4 at 113–19; NORMAN BLAIKIE, APPROACHES TO SOCIAL ENQUIRY: ADVANCING KNOWLEDGE 165 (2007); HANDBOOK OF THE PSYCHOLOGY OF WOMEN AND GENDER (Rhoda K. Unger ed., 2004) (discussing uses of social science in dealing with gender classifications).

174. Pettigrew & Tropp, *A Meta-analytic Test of Intergroup Contact Theory,* *supra* note 158, at 751–83.

175. Milton Bennett, *Towards Ethnorelativism: A Developmental Model of Intercultural Sensitivity,* in EDUCATION FOR THE INTERCULTURAL EXPERIENCE 22 (R. Michael Paige ed., 1993); Thomas Pettigrew, *Intergroup Contact Theory,* 49 ANN. REV. PSYCHOL. 65 (1998).

176. Daniel C. Batson et al., *Empathy and Attitudes: Can Feeling for a Member of a Stigmatized Group Improve Feelings toward the Group?* 72 J. PERSONALITY & SOC. PSYCHOL. 105 (1997); Pettigrew & Tropp, *How Does Intergroup Contact Reduce Prejudice? supra* note 161; Theresa K. Vescio, Gretchen B. Sechrist, & Matthew P. Paolucci, *Perspective Taking and Prejudice Reductions: The Meditational Role of Empathy Arousal and Situational Attributions,* 33 EUR. J. SOC. PSYCHOL. 455 (2003).

177. *See* ROBERT L. SELMAN, THE PROMOTION OF SOCIAL AWARENESS: POWERFUL LESSONS FROM THE PARTNERSHIP OF DEVELOPMENTAL THEORY AND CLASSROOM PRACTICE 29–45 (2003); C. Daniel Batons, Shannon Early, & Giovanni Salvarani, *Perspective Taking: Imagining How Another Feels versus Imaging How You Would Feel,* 23 PERSONALITY & SOC. PSYCHOL. BULL. 751–58 (1997).

178. SAPON-SHEVIN, *supra* note 150 at 24–27, 37–47 (2007). *See also* VIVIAN PALEY, YOU CAN'T SAY YOU CAN'T PLAY 3–134 (1993).

179. PATRICK SCHWARZ, FROM DISABILITY TO POSSIBILITY: THE POWER OF INCLUSIVE CLASSROOMS 41 (2006).

180. HOCHSCHILD & SCOVRONICK, *supra* note 93, at 145 (2003) (quoting Poll); *see also* Ruth Colker, *The Disability Integration Presumption: Thirty Years Later*, 154 U. PENN. L. REV. 789 (2006).

181. Patricia Gurin, *The Compelling Need for Diversity in Higher Education: Expert Testimony in Gratz et al. v. Bollinger et al.*, 5 MICH. J. RACE & L. 363 (1999) (observational); Mitchell J. Chang, Nida Denson, Victor Sáenz, & Kimberly Misa, *The Educational Benefits of Sustaining Cross-racial Interaction among Undergraduates*, 77 J. HIGHER EDUC. 430 (2006) (observational); Deborah H. Gruenfeld, Melissa C. Thomas-Hunt, & Peter H. Kim, *Cognitive Flexibility, Communication Strategy, and Integrative Complexity in Groups: Public versus Private Reactions to Majority and Minority Status*, 34 J. EXPERIMENTAL SOC. PSYCHOL. 202 (1998) (experimental); Anthony Lising Antonio et al., *Effects of Racial Diversity on Complex Thinking in College Students*, 15 PSYCHOL. SCI. 507, 507–10 (2004) (experimental).

182. Emily Buss, *The Adolescent's Stake in the Allocation of Educational Control between Parent and State Author* 67 U. CHI. L. REV. 1233, 1233–89 (2000).

183. *Id.* at 1263–64.

184. Jaana Juvonen, Adrienne Nishina, & Sandra Graham, *Ethnic Diversity and Perceptions of Safety in Urban Middle Schools*, 17 PSYCHOL. SCI. 393 (2006). *See also* Jochen Thijs, *Racist Victimization among Children in the Netherlands: The Effect of Ethnic Group and School*, 25 ETHNIC & RACIAL STUD. 310 (2002) (greater ethnic heterogeneity in Dutch schools is associated with lower racist victimization); Sandra Graham, Amy Bellmore, Adrienne Nishina, & Jaana Juvonen, *It Must Be Me: Ethnic Diversity and Attributions for Peer Victimization in Middle School*, 38 J. YOUTH & ADOLESCENCE 487, 497 (2009) (students who are members of ethnic or racial minorities within a classroom are more likely to attribute harassment to their minority status than are students who are in a majority within the classroom and nonetheless experience harassment).

185. Jennifer Jellison Holme, Amy Stuart Wells, & Anita Tijerina Revilla, *Learning Through Experience: What Graduates Gained by Attending Desegregated High Schools*, 38 EQUITY & EXCELLENCE IN EDUC. 14 (2005). *See also* SUSAN E. EATON, THE OTHER BOSTON BUSING STORY: WHAT'S WON AND LOST ACROSS THE BOUNDARY LINE (2001) (urban minority students participating in a program giving them entrance to suburban schools reported far greater comfort in racially diverse or predominantly white environments than did their friends and family members who lacked such desegregated experiences).

186. HOCHSCHILD & SCOVRONICK, *supra* note 93, at 148.

187. *E.g.*, T. COX, JR., CULTURAL DIVERSITY IN ORGANIZATIONS: THEORY, RESEARCH, AND PRACTICE (1993); Antonio et al., *supra* note 181; Patricia M. King & Bettina C. Shuford, *A Multicultural View Is a More Cognitively Complex View*, 40 AM. BEHAV. SCI. 153 (1996); Jeffrey F. Milem & Kenji Hakuta, *The Benefits of Racial and Ethnic Diversity in Higher Education, in* MINORITIES IN HIGHER EDUCATION: SEVENTEENTH ANNUAL STATUS REPORT 36–67 (Deborah J. Wilds ed., 2000); Poppy Lauretta McLeod, Sharon Alisa Lobel, & Taylor H. Cox, Jr., *Ethnic Diversity and Creativity in Small Groups*, 27 SMALL GROUP RES. 248 (1996); Margaret Ormiston & Charlan J. Nemeth, *Creative Idea Generation: Harmony versus Stimulation*, 37 EUR. J. SOC. PSYCHOL. 524 (2007).

188. SCOTT E. PAGE, THE DIFFERENCE: HOW THE POWER OF DIVERSITY CREATES BETTER GROUPS, FIRMS, SCHOOLS, AND SOCIETIES 4–10, 13, 43 (2007).

189. *Id.* at 328.

190. *Id.* at 308.

191. *Id.* at 331–33 (citing the work of Jane Jacobs, Richard Florida, et al.).

192. Michael Kurlaender & John Yun, *Is Diversity a Compelling Educational Interest? Evidence from Metropolitan Louisville, in* DIVERSITY CHALLENGED: EVIDENCE ON THE IMPACT OF AFFIRMATIVE ACTION (Gary Orfield ed., 2001).

193. *See* WILLIAM JULIUS WILSON, THE TRULY DISADVANTAGED: THE INNER CITY, THE UNDERCLASS, AND PUBLIC POLICY (1990) (discussing subsequent follow-up research).

194. On school retention, *see* Ryan Wells, *Social and Cultural Capital, Race and Ethnicity, and College Student Retention*, 10 J. C. STUDENT RETENTION: RES., THEORY & PRAC. 103 (2008–9); Shaun R. Harper, *Realizing the Intended Outcomes of* Brown: *High-achieving African American Male Undergraduates and Social Capital*, 51 AM. BEHAV. SCI. 1030 (2008). On workplace diversity, *see* CYNTHIA ESTLUND, WORKING TOGETHER: HOW WORKPLACE BONDS STRENGTHEN A DIVERSE SOCIETY 74–83, 89–94, 179 (2003) (summarizing research on workplaces); Anthony Kwame Harrison, *Multiracial Youth Scenes and the Dynamics of Race: New Approaches to Racialization within the Bay Area Hip Hop Underground, in* TWENTY-FIRST CENTURY COLOR LINES: MULTIRACIAL CHANGE IN CONTEMPORARY AMERICA 201 (Andrew Grant-Thomas & Gary Orfield eds., 2009); Maria Rosario Jackson, *Toward Diversity That Works: Building Communities through Arts and Culture, in* GRANT-THOMAS & ORFIELD, *supra,* at 220.

195. ROBERT D. PUTNAM, BOWLING ALONE: THE COLLAPSE AND REVIVAL OF AMERICAN COMMUNITY 66 (2000).

196. *Id.*

197. PEGGY LEVITT, GOD NEEDS NO PASSPORT: IMMIGRANTS AND THE CHANGING AMERICAN RELIGIOUS LANDSCAPE 151–52 (2000).

198. *Id.* at 17–18.

199. *Id.* at 174.

200. DAVID TYACK, SEEKING COMMON GROUND 9 (2003).

201. *Id.* at 10–12, 20; LAWRENCE A. CREMIN, AMERICAN EDUCATION: THE NATIONAL EXPERIENCE 1783–1876 154–57, 170–81 (1980); JONATHAN MESSERLI, HORACE MANN: A BIOGRAPHY 400, 440–46, 498 (1971). *See generally* RICHARD PRATTE, THE PUBLIC SCHOOL MOVEMENT 44–53 (1973); DAVID TYACK & ELISABETH HANSOT, MANAGERS OF VIRTUE: PUBLIC SCHOOL LEADERSHIP IN AMERICA 1820–1980 (1982).

202. *See* DIANE RAVITCH, THE GREAT SCHOOL WARS: NEW YORK CITY 1805–1873 27–78 (1974).

203. *See* JORGE RUIZ-DE-VELASCO, MICHAEL E. FIX, & BEATRIZ CHU CLEWELL, URBAN INSTITUTE, OVERLOOKED AND UNDERSERVED: IMMIGRANT STUDENTS IN U.S. SECONDARY SCHOOLS, (Dec. 1, 2000), www.urban.org/url.cfm?ID=310022; ROSEMARY C. SALOME, TRUE AMERICAN: LANGUAGE, IDENTITY, AND THE EDUCATION OF IMMIGRANT CHILDREN, 190–193 (2010)

204. TYACK, *supra* note 200, at 3.

205. JONATHAN KOZOL, THE SHAME OF THE NATION: THE RESTORATION OF APARTHEID SCHOOLING IN AMERICA 273–82 (2005).

206. *Id.* at 279 (quoting David Engle).

207. Richard Bernstein, *The Fetish of Difference, in* Rieder & Steinlight, *supra* note 68, at 57.

208. *See* SAPON-SHEVIN, *supra* note 150, at 70 (quoting Steve Taylor, *Caught in the Continuum: A Critical Analysis of the Principle of the Least Restrictive*

Environment, 13 J. Ass'n for the Severely Handicapped 41 (1988), *reprinted in* 29 Res. & Practices for Persons with Severe Disabilities 218, 218–30 (2004)).

209. Minow, *supra* note 68, at 75.

210. Danielle s. Allen, Talking to Strangers; Anxieties of Citizenship Since *Brown v. Board of Education* (2004).

211. *Id.* at xxi.

212. *Id.* at 67–68, 75.

213. Levitt, *supra* note 197, at 17–18.

214. Patricia Gurin, Biren A. Nagda, & Gretchen E. Lopez, *The Benefits of Diversity in Education for Democratic Citizenship,* 60 J. Soc. Issues 17 (2004). *See also* Stephanie Morris, Seeds of Peace camp Plants Seed of Hope, available at http://archives.cnn.com/2002/us/07/18/seeds.of.peace (last visited Feb. 18, 2010)

215. *See* Rhoda Ann Kanaaneh, Surrounded: Palestinian Soldiers in the Israeli Military 40–41 (2009).

216. *See* Margaret C. Harrell et al., The Status of Gender Integration in the Military: Analysis of Selected Occupations 1–6 (2002). Women present in the military—up to 20 percent of those stationed in Iraq under the Bush administration—are engaged in challenging and valued work but find difficulties gaining respect. *See* Kirsten Holmstedt, Band of Sisters: American Women at War in Iraq xvii (2007); Erin Solaro, Women in the Line of Fire: What You Should Know about Women in the Military 291–92 (2006). Debate over the official policy of discharging gays and lesbians when discovered in the U.S. military includes concerns about depriving the military of talent as well as about resulting harassment and discrimination. *See* Nathaniel Frank, Unfriendly Fire: How the Gay Ban Undermines the Military and Weakens America 288, 294 (2009); Randy Shilts, Conduct Unbecoming: Gays and Lesbians in the U.S. Military 4–5 (St. Martin's Griffin 2005) (1993). The Israeli military has also confronted and dealt with issues of gender and homosexual identity within its ranks. *See* Aaron Belkin & Melissa Levitt, *Homosexuality and the Israel Defense Forces: Did Lifting the Gay Ban Undermine Military Performance?* 27 Armed Forces & Soc'y 541 (2001) (arguing integration of homosexuals into Israeli military did not influence military performance); Orna Sasson-Levy & Sarit Amram-Katz, *Gender Integration in Israeli Officer Training: Degendering and Regendering the Military,* 33 Signs 105 (2007) (arguing that the integration of women in male-dominant officer training course reinforced the military's pro-male gender regime).

217. Butler, *supra* note 145, at 29–30.

218. *Id.* at 29–36.

219. *Id.* at 5 (citing 1 Westat, Inc., The 1985 Army Experience Survey, Tabular Descriptions of Mid-career Separatees 64 (1986)).

220. *See id.* at 9.

221. *Id.* at 54–55.

222. *Id.* at 13, 73–93.

223. *Id.* at 71. The authors draw a parallel between army values and Catholic high schools in their shared emphasis on "communal organization over individual development and self-choice." *Id.* at 123.

224. *Id.* at 118, 140–41.

225. *Id.*

226. *See id.* at 118, 140–41; Joseph Schwarzwald et al., *Long-term Effects of School Desegregation Experiences on Interpersonal Relations in the Israeli Defense Forces,* 18 Personality & Soc. Psychol. Bull. 357, 20 (1992).

227. Jane L. Bays, Exploring Military Options for Students with Disabilities, www.education/com/print/military-options-disability-students/ (last visited Nov. 11, 2009).

228. *Id.*

229. *Id.*

230. *See supra* text accompanying notes 135–47 (discussing schools run by the U.S. military).

231. *See* BUTLER, *supra* note 145, at 143–69.

232. *See id.* at 147–60 (tracing history from the New Deal Civilian Conservation Corps to AmeriCorps); Will Marshall & Marc Magee, *Thinking Bigger about Citizenship, in* UNITED WE SERVE: NATIONAL SERVICE AND THE FUTURE OF CITIZENSHIP 72, 74–77 (E. J. Dionne, Jr., et al. eds., 2003) (tracing the concept to a 1910 essay by William James); Harris Wofford, *The Politics of Service, in* Dionne, *supra* (discussing efforts since the 1970s).

233. OLEN COLE, JR., THE AFRICAN-AMERICAN EXPERIENCE IN THE CIVILIAN CONSERVATION CORPS 48 (1999) (in 1940 there were 153 all-black companies in the Corps). Despite initial exclusion from the Corps, over eighty-five thousand American Indians participated in the program before its termination in 1942. Donald L. Parman, *The Indian and the Civilian Conservation Corps*, 40 PAC. HIST. REV. 39, 54 (1971).

234. Marshall & Magee, *supra* note 232, at 75.

235. Richard Just, *What Ever Happened to National Service? How a Bush Policy Pledge Quietly Disappeared*, WASH. MONTHLY, Mar. 2003, at 9.

236. *Id.; see also* AMERICAN YOUTH POLICY FORUM, REAUTHORIZATION OF THE NATIONAL AND COMMUNITY SERVICE TRUST ACT: A FORUM (2002), www.aypf.org/forumbriefs/2002/fb062002.htm (describing legislative efforts to expand national service).

237. *McCain, Obama Find Common Ground on National Service*, CNN, Sept. 12, 2008, www.cnn.com/2008/POLITICS/09/11/candidates.sept11/index.html.

238. *See* 42 U.S.C. § 12653(s)(1) (2006); James L. Perry et al., *Inside a Swiss Army Knife: An Assessment of AmeriCorps*, 9 J. PUB ADMIN. RES. & THEORY 225, 229 (1999). Service programs can emphasize individual virtue, social responsibility, or a personal stake in public justice; they can be cast in terms of patriotism, charity, community organizing, or democratic engagement. *See* E. J. Dionne, Jr., & Kayla Meltzer Drogosz, *United We Serve? The Promise of National Service, in* Dionne et al., *supra* note 232. The differences among volunteerism, national duty, and democratic participation could affect the appeal and design of the program, and different leaders have stressed different dimensions. *See* Marshall & Magee, *supra* note 232, at 77–78. Michael Lind argues that ambiguities in purpose indicate confusion among claims that national service would meet unmet social needs, help individual moral development, or advance democratic self-government. Michael Lind, *A Solution in Search of a Problem, in* Dionne et al., *supra* note 232, at 121, 126–30.

239. *See* Peter Frumkin & Brendan Miller, *Visions of National Service*, 45 SOC. SCI. & PUB. POL'Y 436, 439–40 (2008).

240. Leslie Lenkowsky, *Can Government Build Community? Lessons from the National Service Program, in* GIFTS OF TIME AND MONEY: THE ROLE OF CHARITY IN AMERICA'S COMMUNITIES 11, 21 (Arthur C. Brooks ed., 2005).

241. *See, e.g.*, Robert E. Litan, *The Obligations of September 11, 2001: The Case for Universal Service, in* Dionne et al., *supra* note 232 at 101, 103–4; *see also*

Charles Moskos, *A New Kind of Draft for the 21st Century*, Boston Globe, Feb. 9, 2003, at D12. The claim that national service can promote social integration emphasizes mutual reliance as well as mixing with different people, Stephen Hess, *Military Service and the Middle Class: A Letter to My Sons*, in Dionne et al., *supra* note 232, at 144, 145–46. William Galston, *Can Civic Knowledge Motivate the Next Generation?* in Dionne et al., *supra* note 232, at 175, 178. Public officials who called for exploring the possibility of a mandatory service program, include Representative James McDermott, who introduced legislation to establish a congressional commission to make recommendations on the subject. Congressional Commission on Civic Service Act, H.R. 1444, 111th Cong. (2009). *See* Bruce Chapman, *A Bad Idea Whose Time Has Passed: The Case against Universal Service*, in Dionne et al., *supra* note 232, at 108, 108–15, for a critique of mandatory service.

242. *See* Charles B. Rangel, Op-ed, *Bring Back the Draft*, N.Y. Times, Dec. 31, 2002, at A19; Charles B. Rangel, Letter to the Editor, *Race of Front-line Troops Isn't Real Issue*, USA Today, Jan. 27, 2003, at 16A (urging shared sacrifice).

243. *See* Chapman, *supra* note 241, at 108; John McCain, *Patriotism Means Reaching beyond Our Self-Interest*, in Dionne et al., *supra* note 232, at 60, 65–67; Richard Stengel, *A Time to Serve*, Time, Sept. 10, 2007, at 48. *See also* Charles Moskos, *Patriostism-lite Meets the Citizen Soldier*, in Dionne et al., *supra* note 232, at 33, 42 (linking military enlistment for overseas and homeland defense to educational benefits).

244. South Africa's government started the National Youth Service program in 2004; it focuses on out-of-school youth between the ages of eighteen and thirty-five. *See* Innovations in Civic Participation, South Africa and the National Youth Service Policy, www.icicp.org/ht/d/sp/i/1667/pid/1667 (last visited Oct. 26, 2009).

245. Robert Winnett, *Every Youngster to Carry Out 50 Hours Community Service by Age 19*, Daily Telegraph, Apr. 24, 2009, www.telegraph.co.uk/news/newstopics/politics/5209342/Every-youngster-to-carry-out-50-hours-community-service-by-age-19.html.

246. Richard Stengel has suggested a scholarship incentive program that parents and grandparents who volunteer could pass on to their children or grandchildren. Moskos, *supra* note 243.

247. *See* Corporation for National and Community Service, Still Serving: Measuring the Eight-year Impact of Americorps on Alumni 11 (2008), www.americorps.gov/pdf/08_0513_longstudy_report.pdf (small impact); Miranda Yates & James Youniss, *Community Service and Political-moral Identity in Adolescents*, 6 J. Res. on Adolescence 271, 274–75 (1996) (sizeable impact). While some studies have not shown a significant impact of participation in AmeriCorps on appreciation of ethnic or cultural diversity, *see* Perry et al., *supra* note 238, at 234; Corporation for National and Community Service, *supra*, at 11, another study found that service experience helped young people undo stereotypes and increase accommodation and social trust. *See* Constance Flanagan et al., *Social Participation and Social Trust in Adolescence: The Importance of Heterogeneous Encounters*, in Processes of Community Change and Soc. Action 149, 151–52 (Allen M. Omoto ed., 2005).

248. Danielle M. Vogenbeck, Social Network Analysis for Policy Design: Collaborative Discourse between Non-profit/Government Organizations and the Resulting Effect on Community Level Social Capital (Aug. 3, 2005)

(unpublished Ph.D. dissertation, University of Colorado at Denver) (on file with Auraria Library, University of Colorado at Denver).

249. *See* Alan Solomont & Steve Goldsmith, Editorial, *With Voluntarism on Rise Comes a Chance to Seize the Day*, BOSTON GLOBE, Aug. 22, 2009, at 9 (citing data from the Corporation for National and Community Service).

250. BUTLER, *supra* note 145, at 71.

251. ESTLUND, *supra* note 194, at 10–11, 60–69.

252. *Id.* at 76–83.

253. *Id.* at 84–89.

254. *Id.* at 92–94.

255. Gerben van der Vegt & Andreas Flache, *Understanding the Joint Effects of Interdependence and Diversity on Solidarity in Work Teams*, *in* SOLIDARITY AND PROSOCIAL BEHAVIOR: AN INTEGRATION OF SOCIOLOGICAL AND PSYCHOLOGICAL PERSPECTIVES 125, 126–34 (Detlef Fetchenhauer et al. eds., 2006) (reviewing studies).

256. *Id.* at 133 (indicating the power of cognitive frames); *see also* Karen van der Zee, *Ethnic Identity and Solidarity with Functional Groups*, *in* SOLIDARITY AND PROSOCIAL BEHAVIOR, *supra* note 255, at 175, 182–86 (showing influence of cultural frames, perceived threats, and functional interdependencies on perceived solidarity within diverse work teams).

257. *See* Paul Ongtooguk & Claudia S. Dybdahl, *Teaching Facts, Not Myths, about Native Americans*, *in* EVERYDAY ANTIRACISM: GETTING REAL ABOUT RACE IN SCHOOL 204, 204–7 (Mica Pollock ed., 2008); Mara Tieken, *Making Race Relevant in All-white Classrooms: Using Local History*, *in* Pollock, *supra*, at 200, 201–2. *See generally* EDUCATING DEMOCRATIC CITIZENS IN TROUBLED TIMES: QUALITATIVE STUDIES OF CURRENT EFFORTS (Janet S. Bixby & Judith L. Pace eds., 2008) (compilation of teacher- and student-written studies on different citizenship education programs).

258. *See* Willis D. Hawley, *Designing Schools That Use Student Diversity to Enhance Learning of All Students*, *in* LESSONS IN INTEGRATION: REALIZING THE PROMISE OF RACIAL DIVERSITY IN AMERICAN SCHOOLS 31, 34–36 (Erica Frankenberg & Gary Orfield eds., 2007).

259. Eaton & Chirichigno, *supra* note 87, at 9.

260. *See* Cambridge Public Schools, The Haggerty School, www.cps.ci.cambridge.ma.us/haggerty/ (last visited Oct. 26, 2009); Atlantis Charter School, www.atlantiscs.org/ (last visited Oct. 26, 2009).

261. *See* TYACK, *supra* note 200, at 2 (describing Horace Mann's idea of common school as "a place for both young and adult citizens to discover common civic ground, and, when they did not agree, to seek principled compromise."); *see also* RICHARD D. KAHLENBERG, *supra* note 102, at 23 (discussing Horace Mann's First Annual Report of 1837); AMY GUTMANN, IDENTITY IN DEMOCRACY 33 (2003) ("An alternative view—the identification view—suggests that *all individuals*, regardless of their ascriptive identities, can live morally better lives by identifying with disadvantaged people and contributing to just causes out of that identification.").

262. ROGERS M. SMITH, STORIES OF PEOPLEHOOD: THE POLITICS AND MORALS OF POLITICAL MEMBERSHIP 43–45, 69–77, 129 (2003).

263. *Id.* at 152, 199–200.

264. *See* Martha Minow, *We're All for Equality in U.S. School Reforms: But What Does It Mean?*, *in* Minow, *supra* note 62, at 21, 44.

265. Peggy Levitt, God Needs No Passport: Immigrants and the Changing American Religious Landscape 17–18 (2007).

266. *See id.* at 133–34, 147–50, 168, 174. See Robert Laurence Moore, Religious Outsiders and the Making of America (1987).

267. *See* Interpretive Social Science: A Second Look (Paul Rabinow & William M. Sullivan eds., 1988).

Chapter 7

1. Steve Adams, Remarks Given at the "The Great American Post Office" Ceremony: Oliver L. Brown et al. v. Board of Education of Topeka, Kansas, et al. (May 17, 2001), http://brownvboard.org/coalition/ marching/adamsremarks. htm.

2. Brown v. Board of Education, 347 U.S. 483, 494 n. 11 (1954); *see* Gunnar Myrdal, An American Dilemma (1944); Walter A. Jackson, Gunnar Myrdal and America's Conscience: Social Engineering and Racial Liberalism, 1938–1987 (1994).

3. *See* Carol Anderson, Eyes off the Prize: The United Nations and the African American Struggle for Human Rights, 1944–1955 (2003). Anderson argues that anticommunism contributed to the narrowing of the civil rights agenda.

4. *See* Mary L. Dudziak, Cold War Civil Rights: Race and the Image of American Democracy (2000); *supra* chapter 1. *See also* Anthony Lester, *Brown v. Board of Education Overseas,* 148 Proc. Am. Phil. Soc'y 455, 457–59 (2004) (noting Department of Justice briefs in pre-*Brown* civil rights cases indicating how the nation's foreign relations were embarrassed by its domestic acts of discrimination).

5. *Black/White and Brown: Brown versus the Board of Education of Topeka* (KTWU/Channel 11 broadcast, May 3, 2004) (transcript available at http://brownvboard.org/video/blackwhitebrown) (statement of Roger Wilkins).

6. Notable contributions include Gerald N. Rosenberg, The Hollow Hope: Can Courts Bring About Social Change? (2d ed. 2008); Michael J. Klarman, *How Brown Changed Race Relations: The Backlash Thesis,* 81 J. Am. Hist. 81 (1994).

7. *See supra* chapter 1.

8. On influences in other social movements, *see* David S. Meyer & Steven A. Boutcher, *Signals and Spillover: Brown v. Board of Education and other Social Movements,* 5 Persp. on Pol. 81 (2007).

9. See, e.g., Jeff Wiltse, Contested Waters: A Social History of Swimming Pools in America (2007); Richard C. Cortner, Civil Rights and Public Accommodations: The Heart of Atlanta Motel and McClung Cases (2001). *See generally* Gary Gerstle, American Crucible: Race and Nation in the Twentieth Century (2001); Michael J. Klarman, Unfinished Business: Racial Equality in American History 160–203 (2007); Richard Wormser, The Rise and Fall of Jim Crow (2003).

10. Robert J. Cottrol, Raymond T. Diamond, & Leland B. Ware, *Brown v. Board of Education:* Caste, Culture, and the Constitution 236–41 (2003).

11. See *supra* chapters 2–4.

12. See, e.g., Beverly Wright, *The Deep South Center for Environmental Justice: Education and Empowerment for an Engaged Citizenry,* 8 Diversity Digest 11 (2004), www.diversityweb.org/Digest/vol8no2/wright.cfm; Meyer & Boutcher, *supra* note 8.

13. For a study of the process of legal mobilization, rights declaration, and enforcement in five countries, echoing features of the struggle behind *Brown,* see Courting Social Justice: Judicial Enforcement of Social and Economic Rights in the Developing World (Varun Gauri & Daniel M. Brinks eds., 2008).

14. *See* Lester, *supra* note 4, at 460 (discussing British law permitting single-sex schooling while ensuring equal educational opportunity); Razia Ismail Abbasi, *What Has Changed for Girls in India in the Decade since Beijing and Cairo? in* A Guide to General Comment 7: "Implementing Child Rights in Early Childhood" 110 (Bernard van Leer Foundation ed., 2006), www.bernardvanleer.org/files/crc/3.C%20Razia_Ismail_Abbasi%28Womens_Coalition%29.pdf.

15. Government of the Republic of South Africa and Others v. Grootboom and Others 2000 (11) BCLR 1169 (CC) (S. Afr.); Minister of Health and Others v. Treatment Action Campaign and Others (No. 2) 2002 (5) SA 721 (CC) (S. Afr.), www.saflii.org/za/cases/ZACC/2002/15.html.

16. Aharon Barak cited *Brown* in rejecting the Lands Administration's refusal to grant Arabs the right to build homes in public areas and rejecting allocations of land in Arab communal settlement as unacceptable "separate but equal" treatment. HCJ 6698/95 Ka'adan v. The Israel Lands Administration [2000] IsrSC 54(1) 258 (Isr.).

17. Convention Against Discrimination in Education, Dec. 14, 1960, 429 U.N.T.S. 6193, www.unesco.org/education/pdf/DISCRI_E.PDF.

18. Framework Convention for the Protection of National Minorities, art. 5, Feb. 1, 1995, 34 I.L.M. 351, http://conventions.coe.int/Treaty/EN/Treaties/Html/157.htm. *See* The Rights of Minorities in Europe: A Commentary on the European Framework Convention for the Protection of National Minorities (Marc Weller ed., 2005); *See* Autonomy, Self-Governance and Conflict Resolution: Innovative Approaches to Institutional Design in Divided Societies (Marc Weller & Stefan Wolff eds., 2005).

19. European Charter for Regional or Minority Languages, May 11, 1992, Europe. T.S. No. 148, http://conventions.coe.int/Treaty/EN/Treaties/HTML/148. htm; *see* Jean Marie Woehrling, European Charter for Regional or Minority Languages: A Critical Commentary (Patricia Wheeler trans., 2005); *See* Axel Honneth, The Struggle for Recognition: The Moral Grammar of Social Conflicts (1996); Will Kymlicka, Multicultural Citizenship: A Liberal Theory of Minority Rights (1996); Richard A. Shweder, *After Just Schools: The Equality-Difference Paradox and Conflicting Varieties of Liberal Hope, in* Just Schools: Pursuing Equality in Societies of Difference 254 (Martha Minow et al. eds., 2008).

20. *See* Martha Minow, Richard A. Shweder, & Hazel Rose Markus, *Introduction* to Minow et al. *supra.*

21. *See* Missouri v. Jenkins, 515 U.S. 70, 114 (1995) (Thomas, J., concurring); Chene Blignaut, *France's First Muslim School Raises Hopes—and Concern,* Christian Sci. Monitor, Oct. 15, 2003, § 1, at 7; *Opposition Parties Welcome Afrikaans School's Concourt Victory,* Cape Times, Oct. 15, 2009, www.capetimes.co.za/

index.php?fArticleId=5203404; *see also* HERMANN GILOMEE, THE AFRIKANERS: BIOGRAPHY OF A PEOPLE 644–45 (2003).

22. Razgar Ali Hama-Jan, Chairman, Kirkuk Provincial Council in Iraq, Comments at the University of Massachusetts-Boston Forum for Cities in Transition: Divided Cities: Common and Uncommon (Apr. 14, 2009).

23. Sara Terry, *Students Mingle–Sort Of–In Postwar Bosnia's Only Integrated School,* CHRISTIAN SCI. MONITOR, Sept. 27, 2007, § 1, at 2.

24. *Id.*

25. See Carlos E. Sluzki, *The Process Toward Reconciliation, in* IMAGINE COEXISTENCE: RESTORING HUMANITY AFTER VIOLENT ETHNIC CONFLICT 21–31 (Antonia Chayes and Martha Minow, eds., 2003).

26. For a discussion of these issues as they affect the opportunities for children and grandchildren of immigrants in Europe, *see* Catherine J. Ross, *Perennial Outsiders: The Educational Experience of Turkish Youth in Germany,* 24 AM. U. INT'L L. REV. 685 (2008–9).

27. NANCY L. CLARK & WILLIAM H. WORGER, SOUTH AFRICA: THE RISE AND FALL OF APARTHEID 48–52 (2004).

28. South Africa—Education and Employment, Country Data www.country-data.com/cgi-bin/query/r-12148.html (last visited Nov. 7, 2009).

29. *See* Lester, *supra* note 4, at 459.

30. *See* Richard J. Goldstone & Brian Ray, *The International Legacy of Brown v. Board of Education,* 35 MCGEORGE L. REV. 105 (2004) (discussing efforts by Constance Baker Motley and Jack Greenberg).

31. In re Dispute Concerning the Constitutionality of Certain Provisions of the School Education Bill of 1995, 1996 (3) SA 165 (CC), at 47–52 (S. Afr.); *see* Penelope Andrews, *Perspectives on Brown: The South African Experience,* 49 N.Y.L. SCH. L. REV. 1155, 1165–67 (2005); Rassie Malherbe, *A Fresh Start I: Education Rights in South Africa,* 4 EUR. J. FOR EDUC. L. & POL'Y 1386 (2000). Courts in other countries have also referenced *Brown* for the general proposition that education is pivotal in a democratic society. *See, e.g.,* R. v. Jones, [1986] 2 S.C.R. 284 (Can.). *See also* Goldstone and Ray, *supra* note 29 (discussing a case in Trinidad and Tobago).

32. ANDREWS, *supra* note 30, at 1158–65. *See generally* MARK S. KENDE, CONSTITUTIONAL RIGHTS IN TWO WORLDS: SOUTH AFRICA AND THE UNITED STATES (2009).

33. Systems separated for whites, blacks, mixed race, and Asians had their own governance and stratified resources, with 4.6 times more resources available for white students in 1991 than for black students. Bruce Fuller & Arun Rasiah, *Schooling Citizens for Evolving Democracies, in* THE PUBLIC SCHOOLS 90 (Susan Fuhrman & Marvin Lazerson eds., 2005).

34. Celia W. Dugger, *Eager Students Fall Prey to Apartheid's Legacy,* N.Y. TIMES, Sept. 19, 2009, at A1.

35. *See* David Johnson, *Building Citizenship in Fragmented Societies: The Challenges of Deracialising and Integrating Schools in Post-apartheid South Africa,* 27 INT'L J. OF EDUC. DEV. 306, 307–10 (2007); Charlotte L. Lemanski, *Desegregation and Integration as Linked or Distinct? Evidence from a Previously "White" Suburb in Post-Apartheid Cape Town,* 30 INT'L J. OF URB. & REGIONAL RES. 564 (2006); Saloshna Vandeyar & Roy Killen, *Teacher-student Interactions in Desegregated Classrooms in South Africa,* 26, INT'L J. OF EDUC. DEV.382, 391–92 (2006). *See generally* Kholofelo Sedibe, *Dismantling Apartheid Education: An Overview*

of Change, 28 CAMBRIDGE J. EDUC. 269 (1998); Crain Soudien, *The Asymmetries of Contact: An Assessment of 30 Years of School Integration in South Africa*, 10 RACE, ETHNICITY & EDUC. 439 (2007); G. J. Van der Westhuizen, *Elusive Equity: Education Reform in Post-apartheid South Africa*, 48 AFR. STUD. REV. 184 (2005).

36. Monica Hendricks, *Brown v. Board: With All Deliberate Speed?* 105 Y.B. NAT'L SOC'Y FOR STUDY OF EDUC. 274 (2006).

37. *Id.* at 278–79, 282.

38. Head of Department: Mpumalanga Department of Education and Another v. Hoerskool Ermelo and Others (CCT 40/09) [2009] ZACC 32 (Oct. 14, 2009) (Saflii), www.saflii.org/za/cases/ZACC/ 2009/32.pdf (unpublished).

39. The case thus offers a striking contrast to *Lau v. Nichols*, in which a minority immigrant group of Chinese-speaking students successfully argued that instruction solely in English failed to provide equal educational opportunity. *See supra* chapter 2. The historic power and resources held in the Afrikaner community complicate protection for its autonomy; but for that, the case has some similarities with issues confronted by indigenous groups at risk of forced assimilation unless they can maintain their own culture. *See supra* chapter 3.

40. *The Youth Struggle: The 1976 student revolts, in* The Road to Democracy: South Africa, 1970–1980, http:www.sahistory.org/za/oages/governance-projects/june16/extract-soweto-uprising.htm; Malinda S. Smith, "Young People Are Amazing," The Soweto Uprising 30 Years On, University of Alberta, June 29, 2006, www.expressnews.ualberta.ca/article.cfm?id-7694. On the significance of language to struggles for equality in South Africa and other parts of Africa, *see* ABIODUN GOKE-PARIOLA, THE ROLE OF LANGUAGE IN THE STRUGGLE FOR POWER AND LEGITIMACY IN AFRICA (1993).

41. *Supra* note 38, at 38.

42. *Id.* at 45–47.

43. ROY GARDNER, FAITH SCHOOLS: CONSENSUS OR CONFLICT? 159 (2004).

44. *See* Northern Ireland Council for Integrated Education, IE Movement, www.nicie.org/aboutus/ default.asp?id-30 (last visited Nov. 6, 2009).

45. COLIN KNOX & PADRIAC QUIRK, PEACE BUILDING IN NORTHERN IRELAND, ISRAEL AND SOUTH AFRICA: TRANSITION, TRANSFORMATION AND RECONCILIATION 63–64 (2000).

46. Northern Ireland Council for Integrated Education, *supra* note 43.

47. *Id.*

48. See, e.g., Miles Hewstone, Ed Cairns, Alberto Voci, Stefania Paolini, Frances McLernon, Richard J. Crisp, & Ulrike Niens, *Intergroup Contact in a Divided Society: Challenging Segregation in Northern Ireland, in* THE SOCIAL PSYCHOLOGY OF INCLUSION AND EXCLUSION 265 (Dominic Abrams et al. eds., 2005); Claire McGlynn & Zvi Bekerman, The Management of Pupil Difference in Catholic-Protestant and Palestinian-Jewish Integrated Education in Northern Ireland and Israel, 37 COMPARE 689 (2007); Miles Hewstone, Ed Cairns, Alberto Voci, Juergen Hamberger, & Ulrike Niens, *Intergroup Contact, Forgiveness, and Experience of "The Troubles" in Northern Ireland*, 62 J. SOC. ISSUES 99 (2006); Jennifer C. Cornell, *Prejudice Reduction through Intergroup Contact in Northern Ireland: A Social-psychological Critique*, 14 CONFLICT Q. 30 (1994).

49. Tom Rivers, *New Wave of Violence Grips Northern Ireland*, VOANEWS, Mar. 10, 2009, www.voanews.com/english/2009–03–10-voa30.cfm; Henry McDonald & Owen Bowcott, *Ulster Violence Escalates as Policeman Is Shot Dead*, GUARDIAN, Mar. 10, 2009, at 1.

50. Johann Hari, *Northern Ireland Needs Its Own Version of "Brown vs. The Board of Education"—and Fast,* HUFFINGTON POST, Mar. 14, 2009, www.huffingtonpost.com/johann-hari/northern-ireland-needs-it_b_174939.html. Hari is a Scottish-born journalist, based in London, with the *Independent*; in 2008 he became the youngest person ever to be awarded the George Orwell Prize for political journalism.

51. *Id.*

52. *Id.* The piece explains that among those who attended integrated schools, "politics were far more amenable to peace: Some 80 percent of Protestants favour the union with Britain, but only 65 percent of those at integrated schools do. Some 51 percent of Catholics who went to a segregated school want unification with Ireland, but only 35 percent of those from integrated schools do. The middle ground—for a devolved Northern Ireland with links to both countries, within the EU—was fatter and happier." *Id.*

53. *Id.*

54. For more discussion of the descriptions offered in this paragraph, *see* ANGUS FRASER, THE GYPSIES (1992); THE GYPSIES OF EASTERN EUROPE (David Crowe & John Kolsti eds., 1992); THE FORGOTTEN MINORITIES OF EASTERN EUROPE: THE HISTORY AND TODAY OF SELECTED ETHNIC GROUPS IN FIVE COUNTRIES (Arno Tanner ed., 2004); Istvan Pogany, *Minority Rights and the Roma of Central and Eastern Europe,* 6 HUM. RTS. L. REV. 1 (2006).

55. Zoltan D. Barany, *Living on the Edge: The East European Roma in Post-communist Politics and Societies,* 53 SLAVIC REV. 321, 329 (1994), cited in Jennifer Devroye, Note, *The Case of D.H. and Others v. The Czech Republic,* 7 NW. U. J. INT'L HUM. RTS. 81 (2009).

56. *See* PETER JORNA, FORUM, PRELIMINARY REPORT ON THE HUMAN RIGHTS OF SINTI, ROMA AND TRAVELLERS IN EUROPE: ADVICE FROM THE NETHERLANDS TO THE COMMISSIONER FOR HUMAN RIGHTS, THE COUNCIL OF EUROPE 4–5 (2005), www.forum.nl/international/pdf/netherlands-advice-2005.pdf; Arno Tanner, *The Roma of Eastern Europe: Still Searching for Inclusion,* MIGRATION INFORMATION SOURCE, May 2005, www.migrationinformation.org/Feature/display.cfm?ID=308.

57. *See* Devroye, *supra* note 55, at n. 19.

58. *See* Tanner, *supra* note 54.

59. *See* Pogany, *supra* note 54, at 16.

60. *See* Devroye, *supra* note 55, at 12.

61. *The World's Billionaires: #29 George Soros,* FORBES, Mar. 11, 2009, www.forbes.com/lists/2009/   10/billionaires-2009-richest-people_George-Soros_L9II.html.

62. Application to the European Court of Human Rights, D.H. & Others v. Czech Republic, App. No. 57325/00, 47 Eur. H.R. Rep. 3 (2008) (No. 57325/00) (on file with author).

63. William New, Paper Presented at the Annual Meeting of the Law and Society Association: *D.H. and Others v. the Czech Republic:* Human Rights Law, NGOs, and Local Civil Society in the Expanded EU (2006), www.allacademic.com/meta/p95163_index.html (paper abstract).

64. Morag Goodwin, *D.H. and Others v. Czech Republic: A Major Set-back for the Development of Non-discrimination Norms in Europe,* 7 GERMAN L. J. 421 (2006).

65. European Roma Rights Centre Legal Activities, www.errc.org/Litigation_index.php (last visited Nov. 6, 2009).

66. *See* Bob Hepple, *The European Legacy of Brown v. Board of Education,* 2006 U. ILL. L. REV. 605 (2006). Sir Bob Hepple, a distinguished English law professor, was born in South Africa and is a frequent lecturer there.

67. *See* Goodwin, *supra* note 64, at 422–23.

68. *See supra* chapter 3 (discussing litigation over assignments for students labeled disabled).

69. D.H. and Others v. Czech Republic, App. No. 57325/00, 47 Eur. H.R. Rep. 3, ¶ 18 (2008), [hereinafter D.H. Grand Chamber Judgment] (citing data supplied by the applicants, based on questionnaires sent to head teachers).

70. D.H. Application, *supra* note 62, at 24–26.

71. D.H. Grand Chamber Judgment, *supra* note 69, at ¶¶ 146–60.

72. Application to the European Court of Human Rights, D.H. and Others v. Czech Republic, *supra* note 61, at 28–39.

73. D.H. Grand Chamber Judgment, *supra* note 69, at ¶ 42.

74. D.H. and Others v. Czech Republic, App. No. 57325/00, Eur. Ct. H.R., Second Section (2006). This decision, by a vote of six to one, rests on the view that the Czech Republic enjoyed a "margin of appreciation in assessing whether and to what extent differences in otherwise similar situations justify a difference in treatment" and indicated that it would not consider whether systemic discrimination existed. *Id.* at ¶¶ 44–45.

75. D.H. Grand Chamber Judgment, *supra* note 68. The decision is notable in clarifying that, at least in the context of education, the European Convention on Human Rights applies not only to cases of individual discrimination but also to systemic discrimination; that a prima facie case of discrimination can be shown through evidence of disproportionately negative effects on one racial group in the application of an apparently neutral rule; that statistical evidence can show such a prima facie case, and upon the showing of a prima facie case, the burden of proof shifts to the responding party to try to demonstrate that the rule or practice was objectively and reasonably justified. *Id.*

76. *Id.* at ¶ 207.

77. *Id.* at ¶ 50 (quoting the commissioner for human rights).

78. *Id.* at ¶ 47 (quoting the report of the European Commission against Racism and Intolerance on the Czech Republic).

79. *Id.* at ¶ 44 (citing Daniel J. Losen & Gary Orfield, *Introduction* to RACIAL INEQUITY IN SPECIAL EDUCATION (Daniel J. Losen & Gary Orfield eds., 2002).

80. *Id.* at ¶¶ 52–53.

81. *Id.* at ¶¶ 54–80 (citing recommendations adopted by the Committee of Ministers of Council of Europe, the Parliamentary Assembly of the Council of Europe, the Framework Convention for the Protection of National Minorities, and the Commissioner for Human Rights).

82. *Id.* at ¶¶ 81–91.

83. *Id.* at ¶¶ 92–102.

84. *Id.* at ¶ 107 (citing Griggs v. Duke Power Co., 401 U.S. 424 (1971)).

85. *Id.* at ¶ 124; *see also id.* at ¶¶ 175–210.

86. *Id.* at ¶ 124.

87. *Id.* at ¶ 175.

88. *Id.* at ¶¶ 157–58.

89. *Id.* at ¶¶ 195, 208–9.

90. *Id.* at ¶ 201.

91. *Id.* at ¶ 200.

92. *Id.* at ¶¶ 205–10.

93. *Id.* at ¶¶ 175–81.

94. *Id.* at ¶¶ 202–4.

95. *See id.* at 74 (Zupančič, J., dissenting).

96. *Id.* at ¶ 205. *See also* Rory O'Connell, *Substantive Equality in the European Court of Human Rights?* 107 MICH. L. REV. FIRST IMPRESSIONS 129, 132 (2009).

97. D.H., Grand Chamber Judgement, *supra* n. 69, at 75 (Jungwiert, J., dissenting). Judge Jungwiert was one of four dissenting judges.

98. *Id.*

99. Devroye, *supra* note 55, at 84–85.

100. D.H., Grand Chamber Judgement, *supra* n. 69, at 81 (Borrego Borrego, J., dissenting).

101. *See* Devroye, *supra* note 55, at 82.

102. Jack Greenberg, *A Glass Half Full,* in CHOOSING EQUALITY: ESSAYS AND NARRATIVES ON THE DESEGREGATION EXPERIENCE 109, 115 (Robert L. Hayman, Jr., & Leland Ware eds., 2009).

103. *Id.* at 115–16.

104. *See On the Anniversary of "Brown v. Board of Education," Activists Call for an End to Segregation in Schools,* ROMA RIGHTS NETWORK, May 13, 2009, www.romarights.net/content/anniversary-brown-v-board-education-activists-call-end-segregation-schools.

105. *See* AMNESTY INTERNATIONAL, STATE OF THE WORLD'S HUMAN RIGHTS: CZECH REPUBLIC (2009), http://report2009.amnesty.org/en/regions/europe-central-asia/czech-republic (European Roma Rights Centre and the Roma Education Fund).

106. Devroye, *supra* note 55, at 100.

107. D.H. Grand Chamber Judgment, *supra* note 69, at ¶ 216.

108. GOVERNMENT OF THE CZECH REPUGLIC, REPORT OF THE GOVERNMENT OF THE CZECH REPUBLIC ON GENERAL MEASURES RELATED TO THE EXECUTION OF THE JUDGMENT OF THE EUROPEAN COURT OF HUMAN RIGHTS IN CASE NO. 57325/00—*D.H. AND OTHERS V. THE CZECH REPUBLIC* 2 (Apr. 9, 2009) (on file with author) [hereinafter FIRST GOVERNMENT REPORT].

109. EUROPEAN ROMA RIGHTS CENTER, OPEN SOCIETY JUSTICE INITIATIVE, ROMA EDUCATION FUND AND OPEN SOCIETY INSTITUTE, MEMORANDUM CONCERNING THE IMPLEMENTATION AND THE STATE OF GENERAL MEASURES IN THE JUDGMENT OF *D.H. AND OTHERS V. THE CZECH REPUBLIC* (APPLICATION NO. 75325/00) 2–5 (Aug. 20, 2009) (on file with author).

110. *See* EUROPEAN ROMA RIGHTS CENTER & ROMA EDUCATION FUND, PERSISTENT SEGREGATION OF ROMA IN THE CZECH EDUCATION SYSTEM (2008) [hereinafter PERSISTENT SEGREGATION OF ROMA], www.osf.cz/konference/images/file/Czech%20Education%20Assessment%202008.ERRC.REF.pdf; GOVERNMENT OF THE CZECH REPUGLIC, REPORT OF THE GOVERNMENT OF THE CZECH REPUBLIC ON THE GENERAL MEASURES OF EXECUTION OF THE JUDGMENT OF THE EUROPEAN COURT OF HUMAN RIGHTS IN CASE NO. 57325/00—*D.H. AND OTHERS V. THE CZECH REPUBLIC:* INFORMATION ABOUT THE RESULTS OF SURVEYS AND THE INITIAL CONCLUSIONS (July 1, 2009) (on file with author) [hereinafter SECOND GOVERNMENT REPORT]; ČLOVĚK V TÍSNI, ANALÝZA INDIVIDUÁLNÍHO PŘÍSTUPU PEDAGOGŮ K ŽÁKŮM SE SPECIÁLNÍMI VZDĚLÁVACÍMI POTŘEBAMI (2009) (Czech Rep.) (on file with author); GAC, VZDĚLANOSTNÍ DRÁHY A VZDĚLANOSTNÍ ŠANCE ROMSKÝCH ŽÁKYŇ A ŽÁKŮ ZÁKLADNÍCH ŠKOL V OKOLÍ VYLOUČENÝCH ROMSKÝCH LOKALIT (2009) (Czech Rep.) (on file with author).

111. Zákon č. 561/2004 Sb., o předškolním, základním, středním, vyšším odborném a jiném vzdělávání (školský zákon) [Act No. 561/2004 on pre-school, elementary, secondary, higher vocational and other education (School Act)] art. 185.3 (Czech Rep.) [hereinafter Czech Rep. School Act].

112. *See* Persistent Segregation of Roma, *supra* note 109, at 2.

113. *See* Czech Rep. School Act, *supra* note 111, arts. 16.4–16.6.

114. *See supra* chapter 2 (discussing accommodation of language differences in the United States).

115. *See* Devroye, *supra* note 55, at 86–87.

116. *See* Ústav pro informace ve vzdělávání, Monitorink Rámcových Vzdělávácích Programů 52 (2009) (Czech Rep.) (on file with author) (study mapped the situation of Roma in the education system of the Czech Republic).

117. Člověk v Tísni, Analýza individuálního přístupu pedagogů k žákům se speciálními vzdělávacími potřebami 20–28, 88 (2009) (Czech Rep.) (on file with author) (statistical study commissioned by the Czech government to analyze the relationship of educators and pupils at specialized schools).

118. *See* Trust for Civil Society in Central and Eastern Europe, *Czech Republic Becomes Last EU State to Adopt Anti-discrimination Law* (June 25, 2009), www.ceetrust.org/article/306/; Milena Štráfeldová, *Czech Republic Adopts Anti-discrimination Act, Avoids European Commission Sanctions*, Radio Prague, June 18, 2009, http://romove.radio.cz/en/article/22523.

119. *See* Devroye, *supra* note 55, at 99 (discussing comments of advocate James Goldston).

120. *See* Amnesty International, *supra* note 104.

121. *See supra* chapter 3, text accompanying notes 11–19 (discussing *Hobson v. Hansen*).

122. *See supra* chapter 2, text accompanying notes 30–48 (discussing *Lau v. Nichols*).

123. *See* Lau v. Nichols, 414 U.S. 563 (1974); Griggs v. Duke Power Company, 401 U.S. 424 (1971). The Supreme Court has since cast doubt on the viability of an impact test under civil rights statutes. *See* Ricci v. DeStefano, 557. U.S.___ (2009); Guardians Association v. Civil Service Commission, 463 U.S. 582 (1983); Regents of the University of California v. Bakke, 438 U.S. 265 (1978).

124. *See* Jan de Graaf & Julia Choe, The Unlucky Ones: Sinti and Roma in the Netherlands 5–7 (2009), www.forum.nl/international/pdf/the-unlucky-ones-sinti-roma.pdf (citing telephone interview with Laura Punt, advisor on Roma and Sinti education for KPC Educational Consultancy (June 25, 2009)).

125. *See id.* at 6–7 (citing telephone interview with Lalla Weiss, former head of the National Sinti Organisation (June 25, 2009)).

126. Thanks to Jude Volek for raising this issue and suggesting the comparison. *See* NAACP Legal Defense Fund, *Post-racial America? Not Yet: A Voting Rights Report* (Nov. 13, 2009), http://www.naacpldf.org/content.aspx?article=1489.

127. Sherilyn Ifill, *Brown v. Board in Middle Age*, Root, May 18, 2009, www.theroot.com/blogs/ supreme-court/brown-v-board-middle-age.

128. *Compare* Michael Heise, *Equal Educational Opportunity by the Numbers: The Warren Court's Empirical Legacy*, 59 Wash. & Lee L. Rev. 1309 (2002) (asserting that *Brown* influenced uses of social science in school finance and choice litigation).

129. *See supra* chapter 6.

130. Charles Venegoni & David J. Ferrero, *A Regulated Market Model: Considering School Choice in the Netherlands as a Model for the United States*, in

EDUCATING CITIZENS: INTERNATIONAL PERSPECTIVES ON CIVIC VALUES AND SCHOOL CHOICE 368, 378 (Patrick J. Wolf & Stephen Macedo eds., 2004).

131. *See* Heather K. Gerken, *Second-order Diversity,* 118 HARV. L. REV. 1099 (2005).

132. Parents Involved in Community Schools v. Seattle School District No. 1, 552 U.S. 701 (2007).

133. *See* LISA CHAVEZ & ERICA FRANKENBERG, INTEGRATION DEFENDED: BERKELEY'S UNIFIED STRATEGY TO MAINTAIN SCHOOL DIVERSITY (2009).

134. *See* Wolf & Macedo, *supra* note 129. Richard A. Shweder, *After Just Schools: The Equality-difference Paradox and Varieties of Liberal Hope, in* Minow et al., *supra* note 19, at 254.

135. *See* AMY GUTMAN, IDENTITY IN AMERICA (2003).

136. Hecker v. Mathews, 465 U.S. 728, 740 n. 7 (1984).

137. Puerto Rico v. Branstad, 483 U.S. 219, 228–29 (1987).

138. *See* Miller v. Johnson, 515 U.S. 900, 904 (1995); H.L. v. Mathewdon, 450 U.S. 398, 436 n. 19 (1981) (Marshall, J., dissenting).

139. COTTROL ET AL., *supra* note 10, at 233.

140. George F. Will, *Taking on the Book Banners,* WASH. POST (Sept. 13, 2009), www. washingtonpost.com/wp-dyn/content/article/2009/09/11/AR2009091103320.html.

141. Jack Balkin, *Introduction* to WHAT *BROWN V. BOARD OF EDUCATION* SHOULD HAVE SAID: THE NATION'S TOP LEGAL EXPERTS REWRITE AMERICA'S LANDMARK CIVIL RIGHTS DECISION 3, 25 (Jack Balkin ed., 2002).

142. *See supra* chapter 2 (Ginsburg); *supra* chapter 3 (McConnell); *supra* chapter 5 (Bolick); and *supra* this chapter (Soros).

143. Ralph Reed, *History Shows GOP on Side of Civil Rights,* ATLANTA J.-CONST., Dec. 19, 2002, at A25.

144. Some scholars debate whether the Supreme Court's decision in *Brown* itself deserves credit for the civil rights revolution. *See* GERALD ROSENBERG, HOLLOW HOPE: CAN COURTS BRING ABOUT SOCIAL CHANGE? (2d ed. 2008); MICHAEL KLARMAN, *BROWN V. BOARD OF EDUCATION* AND THE CIVIL RIGHTS MOVEMENT (2007). In the years between 1954 and the adoption of the 1964 Civil Rights Act, southern whites practice of harassment, intimidation, and outright resistance in an effort to prevent any movement toward school desegregation. I do not here mean to resolve that debate but to recognize the confluence of social movement, court action, and legislative action surrounding *Brown* as a whole.

145. TARIQ MODOOD, MULTICULTURAL POLITICS: RACISM, ETHNICITY, AND MUSLIMS IN BRITAIN 208–9 (2005).

146. *See* Carola Suárez-Orozco, *Formulating Identity in a Globalized World, in* GLOBALIZATION: CULTURE AND EDUCATION IN THE NEW MILLENIUM 173, 185–87 (Marcelo M. Suárez-Orozco & Desiree Baolian Qin-Hilliard eds., 2004).

147. Frank Phillips & Raphael Lewis, *Two Marriage Amendments Fail, Lawmakers to Reconvene Today,* BOSTON GLOBE, Feb. 12, 2004, at A1 (quoting Wilkerson).

148. Goodridge v. Department of Public Health, 798 N.E.2d 941 (Mass. 2003).

149. *See* Michael Paulson, *Black Clergy Rejection Stirs Gay Marriage Backers,* BOSTON GLOBE, Feb. 10, 2004, at B1.

Index